The Guide to
IT Contracting

Samuel Blankson

Paperback Edition (9x6)
ISBN 10: 1-905789-04-1
ISBN 13: 978-1-905789-04-7

Hardback Edition (9x6)
ISBN 10: 1-905789-05-X
ISBN 13: 978-1-905789-05-4

E-book Edition (9x6)
ISBN 10: 1-905789-17-3
ISBN 13: 978-1-905789-17-7

Paperback Edition (11x8.5)
ISBN 10: 1-905789-20-3
ISBN 13: 978-1-905789-20-7

Hardback Edition (11x8.5)
ISBN 10: 1-905789-19-X
ISBN 13: 9781905789191

E-book Edition (11x8.5)
ISBN 10: 1-905789-18-1
ISBN 13: 9781905789184

Contents

Introduction

In today's highly competitive business world, every progressive company and organisation seeks to leverage their business using the latest technological advancements, and highly skilled professionals. This need has given birth to the IT contracting professional — a new breed of human resource.

Over the last sixty years, these professionals have added immeasurable value to the organisations who employ them and also to the burgeoning IT recruitment industry. The associated niche financial services markets, which have sprung up to service their needs, have also benefited greatly from IT professionals.

Many new recruits join the IT contracting ranks daily. These newbies, as well as many seasoned veterans, lack the guidance and knowledge of the clear path needed to establish, survive and thrive in the lucrative IT contracting industry.

This book is an endeavour to address these needs. How do you get into IT contracting? How do you set yourself up to maximize your profits? How do you keep your skills sharp and up to date? How do you avoid the many IT contracting pitfalls? These, and many more questions are addressed and resolved throughout these pages.

Because I wrote this book with the IT contractor in mind, it delves into many of the "secrets" of the trade. I will show you how to effectively operate and achieve your objectives from IT contracting. Therefore, if you are an IT contractor, or you plan to enter into this industry, this book is essential reading for you. Learn the pitfalls before you jump in and save your money, time and heartache by learning how to contract and succeed effectively in the IT industry.

How to Use This Book

The information in this book is in four main sections with an additional bonus chapter on investing for financial freedom. The chapters are as follows:

1. Installation and Set-Up.
2. Maintenance and Fine-Tuning.
3. Patching and Training.
4. Philosophy and Psychology.
5. Investing for Financial Freedom.

The "Installation and Set-Up" section covers material relevant to those new to, or considering IT contracting. It covers all the options available to those setting out on the road to IT contracting. The "Maintenance and Fine-Tuning" section covers the details and foundations establishing activities of an IT contracting business. It discusses topics such as accountants, insurance, tax planning, money management and health and pension plans. This section is for newbies and those that seek to structure their IT contracting business more effectively.

You can skip straight to this section if you only seek information on how to structure the legal, insurance and financial aspects of your business for maximum profitability, efficiency, and to avoid litigation issues.

The "Patching and Training" section covers how you can take your IT contracting business to more profitable pastures. Improving your turnover by changing contracts or negotiating an increase, changing fields within IT for higher profit and personal satisfaction, and leaving IT contracting entirely for a better life are some of the topics discussed here. This section is ideal for those frustrated or stuck in a particular field in IT. If you are considering retraining to improve the rates you command or "retiring" from IT contracting, then you could skip to this section.

The fourth section of this book is for everyone. It covers "Philosophy and Psychology," the most important consideration for a contractor. Your mindset and attitude as well as your philosophical view of IT contracting will largely determine the success you enjoy in the industry. This section covers information you will not find elsewhere; in many cases – deep secrets – that most successful contractors will never divulge. Most contractors may not even know some of the details that this section covers, however it is essential to gain that extra edge in the industry.

The final section of the book covers what to do with your money in order to build wealth and financial freedom. Here you will learn about secure investing and tax efficient investment vehicles.

There is a notes section at the back of the book, use it whilst reading this book. You should also feel free to write on the edges of the pages, underline sentences, circle paragraphs, fold back important pages or rip out pages of particular interest. After all, this is your book. Keep it as your manual to contracting and refer to it whenever you feel you have forgotten some of the subjects covered.

Anyone can enter the IT contracting field; however not everyone can build it to a level that secures their future and sets them free from ever working again. In this ideal place, you can choose to work or not to work, to concentrate on raising your children and strengthening your family, to start up other businesses, or simply to more seriously pursue your main passion or hobby. That is the power of IT contracting and the potential of this book for you. Use it wisely.

Chapter 1

Installation and Set-up

- What is IT?
- What is an IT Contractor?
- Brief History of IT Contracting
- Permies versus Contractors
- How to Break Rank with Permyism

Installation and Set-up

What is IT?

The NASA (John H. Glenn Research Centre) offers this definition for information technology (IT):

"Any equipment or interconnected system or subsystem of equipment, that is used in the automatic acquisition, storage, manipulation, management, movement, control, display, switching, interchange, transmission, or reception of data or information. The term information technology includes computers, ancillary equipment, software, firmware and similar procedures, services (including support services), and related resources. The term information technology does not include any equipment that 1) is acquired by a contractor incidental to a contract; or 2) contains imbedded information technology that is used as an integral part of the product, but the principal function of which is not the acquisition, storage, manipulation, management, movement, control, display, switching, interchange, transmission, or reception of data or information."

IT covers a broad range of products, services, hardware, software, and firmware systems. The developers, designers, sales staff, recruiters, manufacturers, wholesalers, marketers, support staff and all other ancillary industries and businesses require a staff that understands how their systems and technology work and how to support them. This invaluable human resource brings great value to organisations that have, use, or depend on IT. They help source, acquire, supply, install, integrate, maintain and support these technologies.

Companies recruit IT personnel in the following ways:

- As consultants.
- As contractors.

- As temporary workers.
- As permanent staff.

We shall look at the difference between consultants, contractors and temporary workers shortly, but for now, we can say that IT personnel fall into two main categories: permanent and non-permanent staff.

Permanent staff are normally on the payroll of the organisation, have their wages paid, pension and all benefits such as health care, company car, expense account, etc., paid directly by the organisation.

Contractors normally remove non-permanent personnel from direct financial contact with the organisation through a recruitment agency, or other third party resource supplier(s). The agency or third party company acts as a buffer between the organisation and the resource, i.e., the temporary worker, contractor or consultant.

In some rare cases, the resource may go "direct" to the organisation, however, in almost every case where this occurs, the resource acts through their own limited liability company or an Umbrella company. This is because companies like to deal with other companies through contracts and legal agreements. They also like to deal with limited liability companies, rather than sole traders or partnerships; because of the limited risks that the limited liability company structure offers.

What is an IT contractor?

Earlier we listed consultants, contractors and temporary workers as being non-permanent IT staff. We shall now juxtapose these three resource types and discuss their differences.

Consultants

An IT consultant is a person who gives professional or expert advice. Organisations call on consultants to advise them on high-level, business-critical decisions. In the IT industry, consultants are often experts in their specialist niche fields. They often have years of experience and understand IT systems implicitly. Their in-depth and advanced knowledge commands them and/or their consultancy firms a high premium. A company will pay them either a high hourly rate, or a high fixed term rate.

The companies that hire consultants greatly respect them and treat them accordingly. A company will hire them for their knowledge, and organisations are reluctant to waste costly time in getting them to work on their projects. Many consultancy firms have developed ways of lengthening the time to complete the projects they have been hired to consult for, because consultants are paid for their time. This often means that consultant costs overrun the expected time and costs initially budgeted for by the organisation.

Consultants also claim expenses, which are either paid for directly by the organisation that hired them, or indirectly through their consultation fees. These expenses include travel costs, hotel accommodations, meals and sundry expenses. Consultants and consultancy firms often use this source of income to buffer their high rates.

Consultants sit at the top of the income tree for non-permanent employees. They are often business owners themselves or hold an interest in their consultancy firm. The closer a consultant is to being a business owner or a partner in a consultancy firm, the higher paid the consultant becomes.

Consultancy firms sometimes employ the skills of contractors. A consulting contractor is well paid for their services, if a little less so than the consultant who owns or holds an interest in a consultancy firm. Consulting contractors can also be recruited directly by these firms; however, they may also operate through a recruitment agency or an outsourcing company. Probably the worst paid consultant is the permanently employed consultant.

Contractors

An IT contractor agrees to perform or provide a service for a specific rate of pay (normally an hourly, daily, or a fixed-term rate). This middle class of non-permanent IT staff is broad and at its fringes, touches on consultancy and temporary work.

Almost every industry on the planet today uses IT contractors. They offer a means of quantifying an organisation's IT human resource. They are easy to put in place and even easier to let go. Legally binding contracts control them and they come with fewer of the headaches associated with having a permanent staff. They come with their own personal liability insurance, arrange their own pensions, cost organisations nothing if they are sick or absent, and they could be likened to a photocopier or a telecoms link usage contract; rather than being a burden on the organisation's human resources payroll department.

The benefit to the contractor is freedom to decide how to manage and invest their earned money. In the UK for example, permanent staff earning £100,000 would lose the majority of it to Value Added Tax (VAT), being approximately £17,500.

IT contractors make money through five main methods. Firstly, they earn an hourly or fixed term rate for their professional work. Secondly, they can claim back on certain expenses, whether to the client (the organisation), the agency or their limited liability companies. Thirdly, in countries where a VAT is applied, they can arrange their accounts in such a way as to benefit or reduce their VAT liability.

Fourthly, they can decrease their tax liability by arranging their personal finances in a tax efficient manner.

Finally, they can outsource processes of their company, or take on staff in their limited liability companies to help reduce their corporate tax exposure – just as big corporations achieve.

Temporary workers

Temporary workers are the lowest skilled type of non-permanent employee utilized by organisations. Companies call on them for moves and installs, or general IT work such as data entry, secretarial, courtesy, security, etc. Temporary workers normally work through an agency and are the lowest paid in the IT industry. This type of role has greatly expanded since the mid 90's as more fields such as secretarial, courtesy, security and building maintenance have grown more dependent on IT.

Temporary workers use agencies to source their work; however, a few large agencies/outsourced service providers now employ their own in-house staff, who they place within organisations to fulfil lucrative contracts. These low skilled, permanent IT personnel are poorly paid, and in most cases, are poorly treated as well; giving this sector one of the highest staff turnovers in the IT industry.

Progression

Although there seems an obvious, natural progression from low skilled, non-technical to high skilled, highly knowledgeable IT careers, many do not take this path. Instead, the majority of new recruits who go into the non-permanent IT industry enters and stays within one of the three areas. Only a few move up through the ranks to a higher level, and even fewer move down to lower levels.

This is because moving out of any one area is quite difficult. It requires determination, commitment, new skills, re-education or qualifications, experience and funds. Few make it simply due to lack of commitment or funds. Similarly, you can become quite comfortable as a contractor. The field is broad enough that you can move around it your entire working life without needing to branch out as a consultant.

Add to this, the fact that you can often be paid more as a contractor in certain niche areas within IT, than you can from consulting, and the difference between consulting and contracting reduces further.

There are specialist areas within most fields however, and these specialist areas often pay higher than the prevailing market rates. Certain industries such as military, hedge funds, investment banks and other financial companies, often pay far above the prevailing market rates across the board for their IT needs. However, local governments, charities and outsource companies tend to pay the lowest in the IT industry.

In this book, we shall focus on IT contractors exclusively, how they differ from permanent staff, how to operate as one, how to run a profitable IT contracting company and how to avoid the many pitfalls that you will encounter as an IT contractor. I wrote this book specifically for all IT contractors. Non-IT contractors may find some parts of this book disturbing. If you are not an IT contractor, let me warn you beforehand; you are about to enter the wonderful world of the IT contractor.

A Brief History of IT Contracting

The military has always used IT consultants and contractors since the First World War; however, they were rare. The Second World War saw more use of IT, and thus more use of IT specialists. These specialists were at the top of their specialization, often being one of only a few people to understand a particular technology in the world. After the Second World War, more IT contractors sprang up in the scientific, financial, aerospace, intelligence and military industries.

The explosion of consumer technology – especially in the US – during the 1950's, 1960's and 1970's, saw an increase in the use of these IT specialists. At the same time, computers grew in popularity, and the number of applications they were used for, increased dramatically. Programmers, circuit board designers, computer game coders and testers sprang up leading up to the 1980's. In the office, administrative staff had to learn to use the new word processors, desktop publishing computers and applications. The temporary worker had to add IT to his/her repertoire of skills.

As more uses for computers and IT were discovered, the demand for IT support staff, programmers, managers, testers, designers, etc., also increased. By the end of the 1980's computers had moved into everyday life. Almost everything was becoming digital: from home entertainment, in-car control systems, home electronics, personal computers, musical instruments, music recording and playback equipment, telecommunication devices, and even toys, all saw improvements through IT.

Organisations found themselves needing an ever-increasing IT department and larger IT budgets to cope with the rapid growth in IT usage. Vast amounts of administrative staff were replaced with IT literate secretaries, temporary workers and clerks. Nearly every task performed within an organisation was now carried out with the assistance of either a computer, or some other IT system.

Most establishments were not ready for such a rapid growth in demand for IT. In those days, if you knew anything about IT you were almost guaranteed a job or contract in most organisations. However, companies were slowly learning what they needed from their IT staff, and those early IT contractors of the 1980's learned fast. By the time organisations had discovered what they needed from IT staff, the first wave of IT professionals were up to speed on the technical and support requirements of their companies. An industry was solidly established and in its early phase of rapid growth.

Then in the early 1990's, IT contracting exploded. It coincided with the rise in Internet usage, record numbers of new, start-up technology companies, and the subsequent dot-com stock market boom. This breakneck growth peaked leading up to 2000, driven by rising dot-com company valuations and the exaggerated fears of the "Y2K bug."

After the bubble burst on the dot-com companies in the first quarter of 2000, the IT contracting market also sagged and haemorrhaged contractors – many of whom turned towards permanent IT employment, which at the time was marginally less volatile. As rates and available contracts declined, only the highly skilled and die-hard contractors stayed loyal to the cause. Those brave few were eventually rewarded as the economy picked up again a few years later – shortly after the launch of the United States "War on Terror."

Sadly, most of the contractors who fled to go permanent, never returned. Instead, a new breed of younger, less seasoned contractors joined the ranks. Uninitiated, naive and uninformed, these contractors often treated contracting like permanent employment. This book also aims to confer upon this new generation of contractors the dos' and don'ts of contracting.

A changing world

Many countries have also adopted foreign and immigration policies which have changed the contracting landscape. The Indian and Pakistani governments have developed mature IT service industries in call centres and skilled programmers. The West gains the services at a greatly reduced cost, when compared to the same services offered by the European and

American equivalents. China, Taiwan and Korea have also developed their IT manufacturing services to lead the world; forcing western organisations to buy from them, rather than from the more expensive, and often less reliable European and American equivalents.

In Europe, the EU has also allowed many lower paid, skilled workers to enter and compete with domestic, home-grown contractors in Germany, France, the UK, Spain, Italy and Portugal. In the UK for instance, the IT contracting industry is flooded with workers from South Africa, Australia, New Zealand, West Africa, India, the West Indies and more recently, Eastern Europe and the Far East. The indigenous IT contractors in the UK must compete with these – often higher skilled and more assiduous – IT contractors. In the UK, especially in London, the locals are losing this battle.

This, compounded by an over reliance on IT certification – in addition to skills – through the early 2000's has led to textbook contractors. Many lack experience and skill, but having the required certifications – they flood the market.

Luckily, the tendency is swinging back towards skill and less so towards certification alone. Most contracts nowadays insist on some form of technical test that, although often absurdly difficult and unrelated to the associated role advertised, helps to separate the textbook contractors from the experienced and seasoned veterans.

Rate change

In the 1990's, the hourly rate was the norm; however, this has since changed towards fixed, daily rates. When the hourly rate was the norm, contractors worked differently because they were rewarded dissimilarly. Those attracted into the field held a healthy work ethic and were not shy of working long, hard hours. The clients paid well, and all involved benefited from this arrangement. Contracts paying hourly rates still exist today. However; they tend to be applied more towards the lower paid end of the IT contracting market.

The prevailing, fixed daily rate system and an over-reliance on certification, has attracted people with a different mindset than is required to be successful in IT contracting – over the long term. Because regardless of how hard they work, the daily rate will not change; many contractors have stopped working hard. This has brought lassitude and a non-committal mentality into IT contracting.

In this climate, everyone is losing. Organisations may think they are saving on their bottom line; however, the quality of work is poor and the lengths of projects are getting longer. For the IT contractor, this wide spread disease of slowing down to match the rate of pay, is destroying many good workers' work ethics and industriousness; not to mention damaging the general image held by employers of contractors.

Outsourcing

Global market trends such as outsourcing have also impacted the IT industry. IT commerce has seen a plethora of outsourcing companies spring up to monopolize many lucrative, major contracts. These companies pay their staff less handsomely (whether permanent or contractor), thus they have attracted inexperienced, lower skilled and many unprofessional people into the industry. These outsourced IT staff reflect badly on all IT professionals, and are helping to drive IT contracting professionalism into obscurity.

There is another side to outsourcing, however. When the outsourcing companies use low-skilled staff; they further highlight the value of the highly skilled IT contractor. Thus, when an organisation is looking for quality – even when it already employs the services of an outsourcing company –

they tend to turn to the skilled IT contractor, and willingly pay the extra for the quality service and advanced skills.

Tax laws

As the IT contracting market mushroomed in the 1990's, the Her Majesty's Revenue & Customs (HMRC) focused its attention towards it. In the UK, they created a new tax law called IR35. This was aimed at stopping people who where using limited companies solely for tax planning purposes, whilst working practically as a permanent employee. Initially, the HMRC was ill prepared to tackle the number of perpetrators. However, this did not stop many IT contractors either turning to permanent employment, or turning to the many schemes that sprang up to avoid the high costs of an HMRC audit.

Personal services companies, Umbrella companies and many others, sprang up, promising to be able to guarantee contractors' protection from IR35. Most of these schemes greatly reduced the benefits of being an IT contractor, and in most cases made their clients permanent employees.

The tax office – not satisfied with the numbers that turned to Pay-As-You-Earn (PAYE), and relinquished their right to claim VAT – now turned their attention towards the structure upon which most IT contractors' limited liability companies was based. They looked to stamp out the use of a spouse holding ordinary shares in a limited company – and earning dividends, but not bringing in income equivalent to their stock holding. Section 660a, as this is known, is currently being applied to IT contractors' business structures, and could spell further doom to IT contracting benefits.

Professionalism

Many contractors either have forgotten, or have never been told, that being an IT contractor binds them to an unspoken contract with the people they support. Whether you are a developer, database administrator, project manager, business analyst, tester, Web designer, helpdesk analyst, hardware engineer, trainer, floorwalker, network architect, or an IT director – professionalism, humility, courtesy, customer service and enthusiasm should precede all your actions.

As we all discovered in the bursting of the dot-com bubble, quality can never be replaced. By providing an enthusiastic, quality service with professionalism, uncommon courtesy and customer service, you will always stay far ahead of your competition. Add to this a regular and continuous new skill, and knowledge acquisition through courses, home study and on-the-job training, and you will not only earn more; but you will be headhunted for your future contracting role, rather than having to chase it.

Permies versus Contractors

In the IT contracting industry, permanent employees are referred to as "permies." Over the years, an unhealthy rivalry has grown between the two; permies and contractors. Permies think contractors are overpaid and in most cases. They wish they could benefit from the financial compensation, freedom of movement, and variety enjoyed by most contractors. However, anyone who truly understands contracting would never wish to be a permie.

The difference between permies and contractors used to be more pronounced, however, in the advent of the shortened lengths of time spent at most permanent jobs; the main difference – security – has all but vanished. Today, most permanent jobs are held for less than five years before restructuring, relocation, job elimination or some other reason causes the permie to have to move on to another job. Mergers and acquisitions, corporate takeovers, outsourcing, downsizing, modernizing, and global competition are a few of the reasons for this swing away from security in permanent jobs. This is making permanent roles seem more like contract roles.

This insecurity and unreliability in employers makes permie roles seem less secure and conversely – makes contracting roles seem more secure. Insecurity does not exist, only the feeling of insecurity is real when it comes to IT contracting. If you fear insecurity enough, even permie roles will not stem your fears. In life, there is no gain without risk, and no risk without the dual potential outcome of taking the risk. In contracting, the rewards are freedom, variety, money, self-reliance, and a more direct control of your career and earning ability.

Permie roles offer a sense of security, less money, less freedom, restricted career progression, limited career path, dependence on an employer for a limited financial gain, lack of variety, involvement in workplace politics, shallow status (often based on position and short term perks), and heavily restricted paid time off.

The benefits of permie roles are all derived from the permie's income. Therefore, the bonuses drastically reduce what the permie earns. Employee insurance, sickness, holiday and other paid time off, membership to unions, perks (e.g., health care, company car, expense account, Christmas party, office, etc.), pension plan, stock options, paid bonuses, etc., are some of the benefits that the lowered permie salary subsidizes.

In a sense, these really are not benefits – as the permie is already paying for all of them through a huge cut in their wages. In almost all cases, the loss in money does not equate to the benefits received. Paid time off for instance, is restricted to a few weeks a year, pension contribution is similarly restricted and the pension plan management is take out of the permies' hands and controlled by the organisation, and their financial services partner. These inflexible arrangements often leave pension plan investors short after a lifetime of investing.

Every time you receive a pay raise or bonus as a permie, ask yourself how much money you helped the organisation earn, and what percentage your profit share is by comparison. In most cases, permies do not receive a fair or balanced profit distribution. This is understandable, after all, the organisation is in business to make money and that means profiting on the backs of all its employees.

In IT contracting however, the control is placed squarely in the contractors hands. If you claim VAT, you are given the proper gross income. This includes VAT and claimed expenses. You then take these funds away and sort out your VAT return, tax return, VAT rebate, tax rebate, dividends, salary, personal pension, personal health care, company car (if you have one), time off subsidization, etc. You can give yourself all the benefits that a permie gets and still end up with more money than a permie, undertaking the same role.

In the case of the controller, because control is in your hands, you can make incredible savings with every benefit. For instance, you can shop around for the best deals on health insurance and offset the costs against your VAT and tax. You can also offset travel and company car costs. Knowing that you are paying for the company car yourself, you can shop around for the best deals, and take further savings in the hire-purchase deal under which you choose to acquire the vehicle.

Concerning time off; you have unlimited choice in the length of break you take. Granted, it will be unpaid through contracting, however you can subsidize this through your company savings. As an employee of your limited company, you will still be paid even whilst you are taking time off. Similarly, you will still receive all the benefits you have set in place, including dividends distribution and insurances.

I know some contractors who work during the autumn, winter and spring, taking the entire summer months off on vacation. This is something you would not be able to do easily with a permie role – and still pay your mortgage, and return to a job.

We will discuss how to find contracts when you want them and how to eliminate lost time between contracts later, but for now, rest assured that the sense of security that permies see as the main advantage of being a permie, is an illusion. You can achieve the same level of security, if not better, through contracting smartly, and applying the principles and techniques we will highlight later in this book.

By the end of this book, you will see that for as long as you are prepared to run a business professionally, contracting can reward you beyond anything that an equivalent permie role can ever give. Yes, you will be handsomely rewarded financially, and as you will learn, that will not be your only reward from contracting within IT. The examples I will use are geared towards the UK market because it has one of the broadest, most diverse and liquid IT contracting markets in the world.

How to Break Rank with Permyism

If you are currently a permie and are thinking of changing to the wonderful and rewarding world of contracting, there are a few questions you need to ask yourself first; "Can you be bothered? Is IT contracting really for you?" These may seem like basic questions, but they're important to ask, because IT contracting is not for everyone. It should only be pursued by those who are entrepreneurial, serious and prepared to commit the time and effort (and sometimes the money), necessary to establish themselves effectively, securely and sensibly for IT contacting.

First, you need to educate yourself on what is required to succeed as an IT contractor. Secondly, you need to prepare and plan for the move to your new way of working and earning. Finally, you need to take decisive action by following your plan. Once you have made the transition to being an IT contractor, you need to consistently monitor your progression, and steer yourself consciously onwards and upwards through education, qualification and discerning contract selection. We shall next look at all these points in greater detail.

Educating yourself on IT contracting

To understand how your life will change as an IT contractor, you need to meet and talk to other IT contractors. Find out how they feel about contracting, why they left permanent work, the pros and cons that they have found in the move and whether they wish to ever return to permyism. Most will tell you that they would not exchange what they have for the permie life.

The few that say they will, say so mainly because of plans to start or expand their family, or they feel a sense of insecurity because they are new to contracting and still subscribe to the old belief that contracting is insecure, and the income is erratic. In the case of the new or expanded family plans, we will see how contracting still beats going permie, even if you plan to take time off to have a child.

Planning and money management will overcome most issues you will find when comparing contracting with permanent work. Permies often grow slavishly dependent on the monthly handouts doled out to them in the form of a salary. Because they expect to receive these funds without interruption, most allocate and spend their monthly salary long before they receive it.

People who live this way either subsidize their lifestyle with credit cards and loans, or they struggle every month leading up to their next salary instalment. Sometimes permies and new contractors carry this terrible habit into IT contracting. An independent contractor's income requires a different treatment and does not flow as consistently as the permie income. New contractors often find themselves badly prepared for an unexpected tax, VAT, or delayed agency payment.

Contractors, like all business owners, plan their spending wisely and budget for the unexpected. As a contractor, if you follow this principle and build up a progressively growing buffer of income, you will comfortably ride any obstacle that comes your way. The key with contracting is not to live on what you earn, rather live on what you allocate to yourself, save the remaining and invest it to either grow, or grow your IT contracting business.

Preparing for the move to IT contracting

There are a few things to consider when making the decision whether to become a contractor or to stay and become a permie. There are many reasons why people contract in IT. Let us examine some of these reasons.

Looking at the motives of why an organisation would consider employing IT contractor's services, will explain part of the reasons why you should or should not become an IT contractor. Let us consider the pros and cons for an organisation, which chooses to employ the help of IT contractors.

From the organisations viewpoint

Firstly, the hours worked tend to be more flexible in comparison to a permie role. This is especially true if the organisation pays the contractor by an hourly rate. In this scenario, it is more prudent for the company to limit the hours worked or even reduce them, so as to control their IT budget.

For the contractor, this flexible time can be a blessing or a curse, depending on your view of time worked. For instance, if you seek to increase your turnover as an IT contractor, then limited working hours is bad news for you. However, if you are looking to reduce or limit your weekly working hours (for a better quality of life or for travel considerations, etc.), then this would be more ideal for you.

Secondly, because a contract is an agreement between companies, with one seeking the services of the other, personal consideration is often not important when the organisation decides to terminate a contract. It simply decides it no longer requires the services of the contractor, and terminates the contract according to the boundaries laid down in it.

As an IT contractor, your health situation, family or financial considerations, or any other personal situation is simply not considered in the decision; after all, you are a service provider, not an individual. Can you imagine a large organisation taking the personal and private needs of a cleaning services' staff into consideration when deciding to cancel or terminate the cleaning contract? It would be absurd, wouldn't it? Well, that is exactly how you, as an IT contactor, are viewed by most establishments. You are simply a resource or service provider whose services are contractually bound. This service can be turned on or off as is required for the benefit of the company, not you.

Permies on the other hand, cannot be so easily terminated. They are protected by powerful unions and strict employment laws. Often an organisation is obliged to pay huge sums in order to terminate a permies employment agreement. Therefore, an unfair dismissal can cost a business dramatically more than any money they may be losing through retaining the unwanted permie.

There are many schemes around this problem, however, and the human resources departments within most organisations know them. Therefore, it is not uncommon to find permies losing their jobs due to downsizing, relocations and/or reorganisations – whereby positions are simply eliminated, or opened for competition; leaving a permie to find they have to compete with other, external candidates for their old jobs.

From the IT contractors viewpoint:

The advantages

We will start by looking at some of the advantages to contracting. These are as follows:

- Tax liability.
- Flexibility in hours.
- Business ownership.
- Financial compensation.
- Variety in job and pay rate.

After discussing the advantages, we shall look at some of the major disadvantages.

Flexibility

Often, IT contractors are employed because they bring in skills that the organisation's in-house permie staff simply do not have. Other times, a business requires an IT resource to achieve targets in a project. After the project, they want the flexibility of letting the IT resource go, without the headaches associated with hiring and firing permie staff. This can also work well for the IT contractor.

As a permie, it is difficult to change your mind about an organisation after you are employed by them for some time. Leaving them may cost you bonuses, pay rises or even promotion promises. At the same time, a patchy résumé may affect your chances of getting the next permie job. Most recruiters look at irregular and short term permie roles as a sign of unreliability, something they will take into consideration when judging a candidate for permanent employment.

This is not so for the average contractor. It is not uncommon for an IT contractor to have a résumé riddled with short term roles. This simply can be sold as affording the organisation a candidate with more varied experiences. Whilst one year at an organisation is considered short term for a permie, the same time period, is considered long-term for their IT contracting counterpart.

If a contractor is unhappy with an organisation, they have a choice to terminate the contract, or allow it to run its length and then not renew. Contracts come with a termination clause, allowing for both parties to give notice prior to termination. There are also provisions for instant termination, normally afforded to the business, rather than the IT contractor. This protects the organisation from contractor incompetence or business critical damage caused by the contractor.

Because most contracts are divided into smaller lengths; e.g., three months, it is easy for the contractor to decide not to renew the contract at the next renewal date. This is a perk enjoyed by all contractors who understand the power of this freedom. You no longer have to put up with a overly-demanding boss or long, drawn-out corporate infighting and company politics. If you feel mistreated or unhappy at a particular contract position, simply give your notice of termination, work the time promised and leave.

Financial compensation

Contrary to popular belief, IT contractors actually cost an organisation less than permies do. When an company employs a permanent staff, they are obliged to take on a lot more costs than may be visible to the permie. Firstly, they have to pay or allocate funds for recruiter commissions, sick pay, holiday pay, redundancy pay and National Insurance (in the UK). They also may need to increase their insurance cover to accommodate the new permie staff. Other costs may be health benefits, maternity and paternity pay. Contractors come with none of this overhead.

Although the permie often never sees this outlay on their behalf, the employer loses revenue nonetheless. That is why an organisation can afford to pay contractors more for their services. In the case of the contractor, the organisation can afford to pay a higher rate, and still save money in comparison with hiring a permie.

This is one of the reasons most people love IT contracting so much – the financial compensation. The contractor is expected to sort out their own pension, health care, insurance, sickness pay, redundancy and pension, etc. The good news is that they are given the funds to do so, and in most cases the VAT associated, as well. This leaves the contractor more freedom and options. They can shop for the best deals in health care and other insurances, as well as decide where to invest their funds for a rainy day. An IT contractor can also use aggressive tax planning to reduce their tax overheads.

The choices available to the contractor for maximizing their returns are far greater than that afforded most permies. This makes contracting a financially prudent consideration for most IT fields. The only problem arises when a contractor is uneducated in maximizing the returns and benefits gained from the increased compensation. This is the reason this book was written; to educate IT contractors about maximizing their IT contracting business.

Business ownership

If you have ever being frustrated with being a cog in someone else's engine, felt manipulated, used, abused by the organisations you have worked for as a permie, then IT contracting may be the way out for you. Business ownership brings with it certain rewards that non-business ownership does not. One of these is the feeling of being in charge of your own life. Sure, you may contract your services to various organisations; however as an IT contractor you can be the owner and director of your own business.

If you choose to run your IT contracting concern through a limited liability company, you will have all the benefits and opportunities afforded the world's largest companies. You will have all the tax avoidance opportunities enjoyed by these companies at your fingertips. Added to that you will be able to determine your own salary, bonuses and other perks based on your turnover. You will be a company director, which opens even more doors to you. Your elevated position will – in most cases – allow you to tap into deals only available to company directors and company owners.

Every penny you bring into your company will be money that you can fully control to draw the most profit from – for your company. If you so choose, you can expand your business and recruit other staff to undertake larger, more lucrative contracts or consultations. All this is available to you when you become your own boss. You can see why a lot of people would be attracted to IT contracting – for the satisfaction and pride in building their own business and becoming their own boss.

But of course, not everyone wants the responsibilities that go with running their own company. For those who do not want to run a fully fledged business through a limited liability company; you, too, can operate as a contractor, and enjoy some of the freedoms we have just discussed: choosing when to work, where to work and for whom, as well as deciding on the lengths of your time off and vacations. No longer will you be restricted to the annual month-and-a-half of time off most permies are dependant upon.

Variety

Over time, a permie may become an expert at how to implement IT, or provide a service for their organisation. This, however, is a very narrow view of the many ways that same IT or service, may be implemented. By contrast, an IT contractor who regularly moves from organisation to organisation gains broader, more varied knowledge and skills. They are always exposed to new technology, new ways of implementing IT and providing services as well as different company cultures and people.

This variety makes a contractors life more exciting and vastly more interesting than a permies realm. Because contractors also must learn to quickly adapt, and integrate into organisations in order to provide the best service, they develop advanced interpersonal skills and learn to make friends quickly and communicate better. All this leads them to develop a vastly superior résumé – in comparison to a permie who may work at the same company for half a decade – only interacting with their limited colleagues and work associates.

Tax

In many cases, high income permies take home a smaller proportion of their income than their lower paid permie colleagues. This is simply due to their higher tax rate. As an example in the UK, currently the income tax rate is represented in Table 1:

Income Tax Rates	2007 – 08
Starting tax rate	10% £0 - £2,230
Basic tax rate	22% £2,131 - £34,600
Higher tax rate	40% Over £34,600

Table 1: Income tax rates for 2007 - 08

As an example, if a permie programmer earned £34,600 per annum and his permie boss earned £50,000 per annum, the permie programmer's income before other deductions and credits would be £27,255.60. Whilst his permie boss' income before deductions and credits would be £36,495.60. Although the permie boss' net income is higher than the permie programmer, the programmer is getting a higher proportion of his gross income due to the lowered tax rate.

Although the permie boss earns 30.8% more than the programmer, his net-to-gross ratio is dramatically less due to being a 40% tax payer. He takes home 5.78% less of his income due to his higher tax status, compared to the permie programmer.

The more this permie boss earns, the less of his money he gets to keep. If, one day he becomes the IT director and doubles his income to £100,000, his net will be £66,495.60, taking home 12.28% less of his gross income, compared to the permie programmer.

Comparatively, a contractor doing the same job as the permie programmer could earn the same gross as either the boss or the IT director. Not only that, but with simple tax planning, the same contractor could end up taking home over 85% of the gross profits[1], an improvement of 6.2% over the permie programmers ratio-net-to-gross ratio. This is because

---

[1] If your tax deductions for the year exceed 5%, you are VAT registered and on the flat rate of 13%.

for most contractors in the UK, the rate of tax on their income is similar to that for corporation tax (see Table 2):

Corporation Tax	2007 - 08
£0 - £300,000	20%
£300,001 - £1.5m	marginal relief fraction 1/40
Over £1.5m	30%

Table 2: Corporation tax rates for 2007 - 08

This incredible tax advantage only changes slightly when the contractors' distribution exceeds £300,000.99. The permie wage packet could never beat this tax advantage.

The disadvantages

We have covered some of the major advantages of contracting; now let us look at some of the disadvantages. These are as follows:

- Uncertainty.
- Lack of job security.
- Money management.
- More paperwork and rules.
- Increased personal dependence.

Security

As a contractor you will not enjoy the protection of a permie employee union. Nor will the law side with you, for some of the prejudices that permies can successfully sue their organisations. You will have to take some of these prejudices on the chin when they do occur. The best you can do in most cases is to hand in your notice, find a better contract and move away from the organisation that has offended or mistreated you.

Cost of liberty

Liberty costs money, and to increase your liberty as a contractor to the point where it equals that of a permie, will reduce most of the many financial advantages of contracting.

Another consideration is your name and reputation. If you cause an agency to lose an organisation as a client due to a lawsuit or other liberty related litigation, that client and agency may blacklist you, and avoid doing business with you in the future. Other organisations and agencies will similarly stay clear of you; fearing that you will cause them to lose business. Soon, you will be unable to secure lucrative contracts and have to return to being a permie or worse, unemployed.

Your security in contracting comes from your professionalism, skills, experience and personality, or ability to integrate seamlessly into any organisation. Your attitude, adaptability, willingness to learn and interpersonal skills will greatly improve the social aspects of your contracting experience. The reason most contractors experience problems whilst performing their jobs, is mainly due to personality clashes and incompetence. To enjoy contracting without problems, you will need to constantly improve your competence and interpersonal skills.

Uncertainty

When you start contracting, securing each new role can be daunting. There are no guarantees that you will get another secured assignment, just as there are no guarantees that an unemployed permie will ever get another job. However, this feeling is simply fear of the unknown and can be corrected through effective contract acquisition and interview techniques along with determination. We will discuss all these techniques later in this book.

One of the many obstacles for new contractors is that they continue to think as if they were still permies. Successful contractors search, apply, and secure new roles differently than permies do. These contractors also interview or bid for contracts differently, too. If you follow their example, you will have no anxiety about acquiring your next agreement.

Increased personal dependence

The life of a contractor is one of personal responsibility. You have to take charge and handle most of the things you may have taken for granted as a permie. Some of your new responsibilities may include:

- Securing and contributing into a pension.
- Saving for time off sick or holidays.
- Obtaining and keeping up the payments to various insurances, such as; professional indemnity, health, litigation and tax investigation, unemployment, and income loss insurances.
- Chasing your accountants about VAT and corporation tax payments to avoid penalties and fines.
- Undertaking training to upgrade and enhance your knowledge and skills.
- Learning about new investments so that you can grow your income and savings.
- Keeping abreast of tax and company laws.

There are also many more small and large tasks and duties that are necessary, if you are to maximise the effectiveness of your time and money.

Most people who are steeped in permie thinking will not be prepared to take on these responsibilities. Instead, they will seek Umbrella companies, personal services companies, PAYE services and other "lazy" ways out. Unfortunately, the price they pay for being indolent, or not wanting to take full responsibility is a loss of management skills and a decrease of money. Most contractors on PAYE are paying in excess of 35% of their gross earning for the privilege. This is a potential loss of up to 20% or more of their earnings, compared to if they responsibly ran a tax efficient contracting company.

Loneliness

As an IT contractor, you may feel like you are alone sometimes. Sure, you can join a new organisation and make friends; however, soon the contract will end and you have to move on, join another organisation and start all over again. This cycle can be daunting to some. To others, it is gladly welcomed.

If you are uncomfortable with change, and slow to make social and personal connections with others, then contracting may not be for you. You can still contract and keep to yourself, however, to secure regular contract renewals, your technical skills and knowledge will have to be exceptional. This is true of programmers and software developers. It is a running joke that the area of IT with the least socially skilled contractors, is in software development.

It seems this type of work attracts a lot of introverted individuals who hide themselves behind their large, multiple screens, and bury their heads in their software code. If this is how you like to work and you feel comfortable with the detachment and solitude, then that is great for you. Keep in mind though, that you will have to communicate with your managers and fellow developer colleagues at some stage – therefore, some social skills and interaction would not go amiss.

In a large organisation with many other contractors, you will feel less lonely than in a small organisation where contractors are rare. The loneliness you might feel in the latter scenario can be increased if your permie team does not like you, simply because you are a contractor. You could find yourself going to lunches alone, alienated, and kept out of social conversations, work associated activities and/or leisure situations as well.

The best way around this loneliness is to make friends in your department. Often, an IT contractor is more readily accepted by other departments of an organisation, than in the IT department. Sometimes this situation can border on the ridiculous. I recall a contractor once sharing a funny story with me about a role he accepted within a military organisation. The IT department was so jealous of contractors that the last four contractors left before a week had passed. On his first day there, he chanced to ask a permie colleague where he might find the toilets. He was told, "You're a contractor, go figure it out. Find it yourself." Strangely enough, the contractor never stayed long enough to find the toilets.

Situations such as these are where your personal tenacity to succeed and adapt will be tested. Be careful not to start off asking for favours or help. You are already viewed as being privileged in many ways.

More paperwork and rules

Taking responsibility will mean doing more paperwork, reading boring tax papers and letters from Companies House and the HMRC offices. However, you will be richly rewarded for your efforts. By keeping abreast of the laws and taxes, you can effectively steer yourself away from the tax traps and legal dangers — that could cost you vast amounts of time and money — to correct down the line.

It is important to understand what others are telling you. If you totally depend on a third-party company who is in business to make money, and part of that goal is better achieved by having complete control over your finances, then prepare and expect to be fleeced. This situation will only change through you acquiring the required knowledge about how to improve your financial situation, independently.

Ignorance is seldom free and its price is often hidden from the uninformed individual. Some say, "What you don't know can't hurt you." This statement is not true. In the IT contracting realm, what you don't know will cost you money, and what you do know will make you more money. Therefore, learn as much as you can and you will increase your dividends and financial compensation. This will mean reading, enrolling in training courses, or undertaking home study courses to improve your knowledge, qualifications and skills.

Money management

Dickens once wrote in *David Copperfield, "My other piece of advice, Copperfield," said Mr. Micawber, "you know. Annual income twenty pounds, annual expenditure nineteen nineteen six, result happiness. Annual income twenty pounds, annual expenditure twenty pounds ought and six, result misery...".* This advice is disregarded by most IT professional and permies alike; leading to misery, struggle, frustration and stress.

Like most permies, some contractors live beyond their means. This is especially true of those new to the field; they carry the bad habits from their permie work experience into contracting. The danger of this is immediately clear once you take into consideration the irregular income patterns of certain contracts.

Whilst permies can set a clock by the arrival of their next pay cheque, contractors often cannot. Some IT contract roles pay invoices weekly, bi-weekly, monthly, fortnightly, or even quarterly in some rare cases. Others have strange arrangements such as; three week delays between submitted invoices and actual payment transmission, or payment delays subject to security checks and paperwork submission (i.e., passport, indemnity insurance proof of residence, etc.).

This irregularity in income, and the insecurity associated with getting your next role, make living beyond your means a more foolish proposition for contractors than it may be for permies, who, due to the consistency of their incomes, can plan their repayments and the settling of their temporary debts – such as bills and credit card balances – more reliably.

Financial happiness has more to do with lack of stress and worry, than it has to do with earning levels. Insecurity and anxiety over your money situation comes with not having enough to settle your financial responsibilities, in a timely fashion. Most people use credit cards and loans to bridge the gap between what they make and what they spend. Some contractors carry on this disastrous habit into their lives to disastrous conclusions.

Living beyond your means accentuates and increases the insecurities associated with contracting. Living this way will cause you to run back to being a permie, abandoning contracting in disgust, blaming insecurity as the reason, whilst your bad money management habits were the real reason.

Avoid this pitfall by setting aside half to two thirds of your gross earnings for taxes, VAT (or sales taxes) and a rainy day. Doing so will allow you to live within your means whilst at the same time, building savings and financial security.

You also have to learn to apply delayed gratification. This means that if you want something, but you do not have the means within your allotted earnings to afford it, then you simply cannot buy it.

All your purchases and financial commitments such as bills, mortgage, etc., should pass the delayed gratification litmus test. Do not buy things that will cause you to exceed your allotted income.

Similarly, you should prioritise your financial expenditures. VAT and tax should always lead the list.

Payments to your various insurances should be next, followed by accountancy fees, travel for work purposes (before food), general bills, mortgage payments, clothing, leisure and luxury purchases.

Surprisingly, many contractors have this priority list reversed. They spend their earnings on luxury purchases first (flashy car, nice holidays, expensive clothing, shoes, etc.), buy food, pay their bills and mortgage, then realise they do not have enough left for anything else. Soon the HMRC comes knocking.

The successful contractor

We have covered the pros and cons of contracting; let us now summarize the traits and habits you need to become a great contractor:

- Humility.
- Adaptability.
- Interpersonal skills.
- An active networker.
- Outstanding reputation.
- Diversified experience.
- An observant self-promoter.

Adaptability

To be a great contractor you have to be adaptable. Most contracting roles require 'someone who can hit the ground running.' A contractor is paid for their skills and knowledge – therefore, most organisations will not be prepared to train you extensively to do a role that they expect you to know already. Apart from a general orientation to the organisation and a brief introduction to the location of the basic facilities and resources, you are pretty much left to adapt to the organisation's culture, working environment, technical tools and procedures.

The learning curve in a new contracting position can be sharp. It will mainly be your responsibility to fill in the gaps, ask for what you do not know and avoid making serious errors early on in the role. However, with experience you will learn to adapt almost instantly, as this cycle becomes second nature.

You will have to be observant, especially in your first week on site at a new organisation. Observe how people dress, learn to recognize the subtle boundaries in attire and grooming. Watch for the unspoken, acceptable lunch activities and duration. Listen to what most people you work with discuss, to determine the standard, unspoken boundaries of the organisation. In some IT departments, people seldom speak, whilst in others, they may have a radio on and jovial banter prevails.

Quickly learn the dos and don'ts, and acquire a list of the important people you need to be wary of as soon as you can. If possible, find a friend quickly. Someone you can trust to 'show you the ropes' and steer you out of danger.

Most importantly, do your work and do it exceptionally well, until you are told otherwise. In some organisations exceptional work may alienate you from the rest of your colleagues – therefore, try to determine the boundaries of acceptable excellence before you shoot yourself in the foot, and forego a renewal.

If you are unable to adapt, observe, learn and apply what you have learned quickly, you may find yourself losing the contract at the next renewal date.

Interpersonal skills

In most contracting roles, you have to work with other people. Learning to deal effectively with them is crucial to being great at contracting. From the first time you speak to your interviewer(s) to the contract end date – you are judged on how you fit into the department or organisation. How you interact with others, and how well other people like or dislike you, are all points taken into consideration when your renewal is being reviewed.

Every contract is different, just as every organisation is different. In some contracts, just liking a sport will get you immediately into the departmental social circle, whilst in other contracts – you have to build individual relationships with each person in the department.

A general rule will therefore never suffice for the variable conditions you will face; however, a few traits are worth developing with everyone. These are as follows:

1. Develop humility.
2. Be friendly – smile.
3. Join in social activities.
4. Develop a sense of humour.
5. Never gossip about others.
6. Show genuine interest in others.
7. Look for some good in everyone.
8. Never put down others – in front or behind their backs.
9. Participate in departmental customs (such as getting teas and coffees for everyone when it is your turn).
10. Avoid office politics (especially being used to undermine a colleague).

The list above is not always easy to follow. However, do your best to keep to the points, and you will be liked by most people and quickly accepted into future IT teams. Conversely, if you are a show-off, antagonist, unsociable, unfriendly, unhelpful, manipulative and prone to office politics and gossip, you are hardly going to be liked by many people.

Humility and helpfulness

Most contractors fall over at this hurdle. They feel that if they are helpful, they will dilute their own usefulness to the organisation. This is not true. Any manager who sees you sharing and adding to the organisations IT knowledge pool and skill base will be happy to retain your services. Similarly, if you are humble concerning your abilities, income, wealth, holidays and other material possessions, you will offend fewer people than if you boast about your advanced skills and wealth.

Bragging about being a contractor is as stupid as prematurely terminating a lucrative contract. That is because if you brag or boast about your financial position, you stand a great risk at angering your permie colleagues, some of whom may be on less than half to a quarter of your net monthly earnings, whilst performing the same or similar role.

Boasting about your experience gained through contracting and your advanced skills will cause people to constantly put you to the test or worse, cause you to make a fatal error through withholding information or using internal politics against you. Either way, you will be leaving the organisation earlier than you planned.

Be humble; let your actions tell how skilled you are rather than your tongue. Play down your income and only discuss the things that you know will not get any of your colleagues jealous of your wealth. As an example, try not to rub your situation in their faces by wearing expensive clothing, driving a flashy sports car and eating very costly lunches every day.

If you have these things, moderate how much you show and talk about them around your permie colleagues. It only takes one person to harbour bad feelings against you, and to be on good terms with your manager – and you are as good as out of the contract.

Conspicuous display of your wealth is never appealing under any circumstances. It attracts jealousy, envy and resentment. You can make others feel inadequate and undermined. The easiest reaction to you by them is to hurt you, or in some way cause you to lose some of your wealth. The easiest way for them to achieve this is to cause you to lose your job.

Be helpful to your permie colleagues and be prepared to learn from them. It is tempting to unload your vast knowledge and experience. However, try not to give unsolicited advice. Permies may feel insecure or undermined around a knowledgeable contractor. Therefore, only give advice if you are asked for it, or when you feel it will be of immediate help. If you sense a permie is talking nonsense, or trying to show their superior technical knowledge in order to belittle yours – refrain from engaging them and causing everyone to see how little they really know. You may win the battle, but you will feed the resentment growing within them. Later on, this same resentment will bear fruit elsewhere, causing you some financial inconvenience.

As always, be humble and avoid such confrontations. Your humility will save you a fortune in the long term in IT contracting. You know your "stuff" and you can do the job and do it well. Therefore, there is no need to talk about how great your knowledge is, especially when doing so will not increase your contract rate.

An observant self-promoter

This heading may seem to contradict the previous heading, however, closer examination of this topic will show otherwise. As a contractor, you are in business to attract and secure work for your business. In a sense, you have to be a working advertisement and a sales and marketing department for your business. Therefore, you have to be an observant self-promoter to spot opportunities, and once you spot an opportunity, you need to promote your services, in order to be considered for the opening.

As you contract at various organisations, you will hear of problems in which you may be able to offer solutions. This could lead to a contract extension or the start of a new contract, (either way, you stay longer in a contract). This is a great way to guarantee your contract is extended, or you are retained after your initial contract ends.

The opportunity could be in training, software development, management, hardware and/or software installation and configuration, system management, support, etc. Incidentally, this is also one of the best ways to improve your hands-on knowledge and skills.

If you have been producing excellent work for the organisation, and the decision makers and your colleagues like you; you stand a greater chance of getting the extension or new project opportunity, than if you have not.

Diversified experience

The value of a contractor to an organisation lies in the contractor knowing what to do and how to do it. This means they require no training, and can be left to carry out the required work – in most cases unsupervised. This experience and skill is mainly acquired through the hopefully diverse experience the contractor has gained.

Your employment status, after twenty-four months at any one organisation, changes to that of a permanent employee. If you are a contractor, and you are not moving around to different projects at least several times a year, or every couple of years, you could become stale and your skills may be getting outdated and stoic. You may also be putting yourself at risk with certain tax laws that are meant to catch contractors who might as well be permies – we will discuss these tax laws later and at length.

By staying at one organisation and doing the same role for years on end, you are robbing yourself of the advantages of new skills, experiences and potential higher rates. These are part of your value as a contractor – a broad and varied experience and knowledge base.

If you have not changed contracts in a long while, you may lose confidence at interviews, get out of touch with market trends and fall behind with the latest technology and procedures across different industries. You need to stay ahead of the market trends, and keep your interviewing skills and confidence high by regularly moving around to different projects. Nowadays, this has become a valid contracting tax avoidance strategy; especially with new tax laws, designed to catch contractors who carry out non-project based, long-term contracts.

An active networker

Finding contracting work is much easier if you have many contacts in the industry, than if you do not. You make these contacts by networking and building a list of sympathetic permie colleagues, agents, managers, HR personnel, IT decision makers and executives in past organisations. Even interviews you attend, but do not win the contract, can be a source of useful future contacts and sharpened interviewing skills.

If you contract through an agency, your rate will be decreased by a sizeable fraction – 10% to 30% or more (the latter, in rare cases). This decrease is the agency fees. It makes sense then, that a contract you acquire by going direct without an agency, will be that much more lucrative. It is therefore prudent to constantly be on the lookout for such contracts. You can find them through using your list of connections. Friends, managers and agencies you previously used, may be able to lead you into new opportunities that will allow you to go directly to the organisation.

Networking and building a long list of relations is only of use if you keep in touch, and update these people of your current situation and possible future requirements or availability. It is easy to get into the habit of only calling your contacts when you need them, however this can be counter-productive. It is better to stay in touch regularly, and build a social or professional friendship with them. Lunches, social meetings for drinks or celebrations, messenger chats and e-mail conversations are all good ways of keeping in touch.

You should also take every opportunity to help your contacts find resources they are looking for; even when the resource does not directly benefit you. Other contractors, agencies, managers, etc., will be more helpful to you if you are helpful to them in return. In some cases, you could earn a commission or at least earn a free drink or social lunch for your trouble. However, the long-term value of networking and helping your contacts, is that when you need help, they, too, will be more willing to help you.

It is said that people like doing business with people they like. Help others to help you by networking and maintaining contact with those who – one day – could help you secure your next lucrative contract. Once you start networking, you will find the process of securing your next contract less daunting and more profitable.

Outstanding reputation

If you want someone to help you solve a problem, would you ask someone who has a bad reputation, or someone with an impeccable record for getting the job professionally done on time? Most organisations would concur with your answer. However, some contractors are short sighted about their reputation. They leave a bloody trail of disgruntled and unhappy employers behind them – then wonder why they find it so difficult to secure their next contract.

The contracting world can be very small, and word quickly gets around among agencies, contractors and permie managers in organisations. If you do a really bad job at one organisation, and your contract is prematurely terminated, or if you manage to hold onto your contract, but infuriate your agency or other contractors whom you work, you may find that your name is passed around to their friends or agencies, and other contractors. Some of them may have a say in how successful you are at securing a future contract.

Agency staff tend to move around other agencies, taking with them knowledge and experiences gained from their previous groups. If you caused them to lose business, or acted without integrity or professionalism whilst working for them, they will remember and tell many others wherever they go. Soon your CV will be virtually blacklisted and no agent will be interested in taking you on.

Similarly, if you infuriate managers, team leaders, your permie colleagues or other contractors – when they move on to other contracts and your CV is presented to them for a role at their new organisation, they will ensure you are never called for an interview.

Produce quality work with enthusiasm and operate with integrity. Be punctual, well mannered, professional, industrious, and learn to go the extra mile whenever possible. Make yourself invaluable to the organisation and your contract will always be renewed whenever possible. Great performance coupled with developing a good rapport with the decision makers will ensure you are called back and offered future, relevant contracts.

What to do next

If you are still interested in becoming an IT contractor after reading this far, then you need to see if there is an IT contracting market for your particular IT skills. Do not worry if there is no IT contracting market for your particular skills, there are other avenues you can explore, if you really want to become an IT contractor.

Do your research

To begin your research, first talk to contractors doing similar or identical work as yourself, at your place of work. Next, look up a few IT recruitment agencies who work in your area of expertise. Get relevant information from them about the contracting market; especially what you need to more easily secure contracts in your field of expertise. Find out how much the average contract in this field – at your level of expertise – pays. Ideally, you are looking for almost double that of your permie wages.

After exhausting contractors at your workplace, recruitment agencies, and friends who may not work at your workplace but contract nonetheless, search the contracting job market for contracts requiring your skill set in your geographic area of interest.

Call the advertisers and ask if the roles are still available. If the roles are no longer available, ask how long it was available before the role was filled. Also, ask what you would need to secure similar contracts in the future.

Armed with this information, you can now proceed to acquire the relevant skills and experience, or if you already have them – highlight them in your résumé.

Be prepared to compromise

If, after your research, you find that the IT contracting market is thin and underdeveloped, (or in decline for your specialization), then you should either forget about contracting, or choose to enter the contracting market through another – more general – specialization. You can do this by choosing a well-developed and thriving IT contracting specialization, requiring most of your current skills and experience.

After selecting the IT specialization closest to your current skills and experience, you next need to acquire the missing experience, skills and knowledge. Seek first to acquire this through your permie job before venturing into a contract. Failing this, you should aim for a junior contractor position as a stepping stone to help you acquire the missing experience.

Some areas of IT contracting are easier to enter from a permie position than a contracting position. Business Analysis for instance, is easier to enter as a graduate, than it is to enter through any other means – except if you are coming from a project management background. Other IT specializations such as SAP are expensive to train for, and so it would be more prudent to use a permie training program to fund the training and certification needed for them.

Setting up your corporate foundation

As a contractor, you are a business owner in your own right. You have the option to outsource any one of the following business functions to third parties:

- Administration.
- Public relations.
- Human resources.
- Sales and marketing.
- Legal and compliance.
- Accounting and tax planning.

However, every time you outsource a function, you lose control of part of your business and possibly lose revenue as well. Whilst it is important to focus your energies on what you do best – leaving other functions that you do not specialise in to third parties, it is unwise not to understand these functions at all. Not understanding what your accountant or agency does, means that you will not know how you could improve that function. Similarly, if you do not understand your business, you will not be able to clearly identify profit haemorrhaging.

This occurs when you lose money unnecessarily due to bad planning and over-outsourcing. Contractors who can't be bothered to learn to maximise their returns, turn to companies and agencies who promise to alleviate this responsibility. An industry has grown to service these lazy contractors, offering a complete outsourcing package. For the price of their laziness, these companies literally turn contractors into permies – working for them. They strip the contractor of almost all the benefits of contracting, leaving them with less than two-thirds of their gross income.

Other outsourcing "solutions" offer a partial service, often promising to secure the contractor against tax laws, but in reality stripping their contractor clients of part of their income, for no real guaranteed security from tax office litigation.

We shall discuss the outsourcing services solutions available to UK contractors first. This section will end with how to take total control of your contracting business by running a limited liability company, with minimum outsourcing, for maximum financial benefits.

Structure choices

There are many business structures available to contractors in the UK, however, not all of them are the same. They have different characteristics and offer varying benefits and disadvantages. Each option has its own financial dynamics, costs, and maintenance requirements. The company structures available are as follows:

- Umbrella
- Composite
- Limited liability
- Other structures

These arrangements are all offered by Managed Services Companies (MSCs). An MSC is any company that offers to manage the running of your contracting affairs for you. They can be difficult to identify, but cost you dearly if you are caught using one by the HMRC. To find out if an MSC is involved with your company or contracting business, look out for the following signs:

1. They benefit financially on an ongoing basis from the provision of services to you. Often they will receive a percentage of your contracting income as their fee for providing services. This fee will be linked to your contracts, therefore you pay only whilst you earn. They will also handle invoicing of the organisation you are contracting at, and pay you with their administrative fee deducted – (in essence this is what all agencies do).

2. They will influence or control how you get or secure your contracts. An MSC will normally arrange contracts, negotiate changes to your contracts, negotiate rates, arrange when you go on site, and handle disputes between you and organisations.

3. MSCs may also influence how and when your time sheet (and their invoices) are paid by the organisation. They will normally have access to your company bank account, or control it and make payments on your behalf.

4. They often offer payroll services and calculate dividends, expenses, tax and VAT dues, and also instruct you on how much to pay yourself from the company bank account.

5. MSCs may also promote insurance schemes promising protection against tax loss due to tax investigations, or

successful HMRC legal cases brought against you. These insurances are normally related to IR53, PAYE, or VAT.

Accountants and accountancy firms can also fall into the MSC category. Therefore as a contractor, you should ensure you know your accountant and how his or her firm operates. Make sure your accountant is only acting in a professional capacity, and has no direct access or control of your company bank account. Take responsibility for your own company and be accountable for all decisions and actions taken by your company.

A word of warning about MSCs: stay away from them. Since 2006, the Chancellor has targeted them exclusively and removed all their benefits, therefore, using one will actually cost you dearly when you eventually are caught by the HMRC. Once caught, you will have to pay all benefits gained from using an MSC by having all your income treated as PAYE.

Umbrella Companies

An Umbrella company offers you the benefit of working as a contractor for someone else, namely the Umbrella company. This is because whilst you will earn the contracting fees, they will pay you a salary like a permie. It is amazing to understand why so many people choose this option, however let's look at some of the reasons.

Umbrella companies promise to remove the hassle of managing your contracting business. In return they offer you a means of contracting. Their downside is that they treat your contracting income as PAYE[2]. This means you lose the 17.5%

---

[2] Pay As You Earn – a process of taxation whereby an employer withholds taxes from your wages and/or occupational pension on behalf of the HMRC. A special tax code issued by the HMRC dictates how much tax to collect from your wages and/or occupational pension.

VAT, plus your income receives the permie tax treatment on the rest (10%, 22% and/or 40% deductions) after allowed deductions for expenses – less the Umbrella company's administration fees.

In this way, you are earning a little more than a permie without most of the permie benefits and security – all in the name of a "hassle-free" life!

A few things to beware of in Umbrella companies; make sure they do not use the services of an MSC. Similarly, you may be at risk if any of the other contractors operating under the Umbrella become involved in trouble with the HMRC.

Whilst they are currently safe this year (2007), there are no guarantees that the Chancellor will not target Umbrella companies in future budgets. Keep abreast of tax news and future announcement concerning Umbrella companies.

If you simply must join an Umbrella company, the following is a checklist of what you should look for:

- The company has never been an MSC or Composite company.
- It does not use the services of an MSC or Composite company.
- The company is not (and never has been) a subsidiary of an MSC or Composite company.
- It operates a salary only scheme and does not attempt to operate outside IR35.
- The company allows you to claim the following:

   1. VAT on expenses, if your company is VAT registered.
   2. Limited company accountancy expenses.
   3. Business insurances – professional indemnity, business contents and other related insurances.
   4. Company bank account charges and interest.
   5. HMRC approved scheme pension scheme payments.
   6. Your gross salary – usually kept to a minimum, in order to maximise shareholder dividend disbursements

and avoid paying employees and employers national insurance contributions.

7. Spouse's salary – must be a realistic, actual amount related to duties performed.
8. Travel expenses.
9. Motor expenses – mileage claims if the vehicle is personally owned and all other payments, if the vehicle is company owned.
10. Computer costs.
11. Accommodation and subsistence.
12. Telecommunications – business calls only.
13. Business related books, magazines, subscriptions and courses.

- They promptly submit invoices to agencies or organisations (if you are working directly), and pay your invoices immediately on receipt of funds.
- They pay via fast, electronic transfer methods and not by cheques through the post.
- The company offers legally binding guarantees for its services – especially relating to late payment of submitted timesheets and invoices.
- They do not withhold any of your wages for the purpose of paying you sickness, holiday or any other payment at a later date – they give you the full amount to manage yourself.
- They pay dividends weekly or at worst, monthly.
- They do not charge you a percentage of your earnings for their services.
- They charge a fixed weekly or monthly fee for their services.
- The company is run by a credible, qualified and experienced team.
- It is suitably insured to offer its services.
- The company comes highly recommended by many contractors.

Normally, the Umbrella company will provide you with a standard form requesting your name, address and banking details for wages forwarding. You will also receive a blank, standard expenses claim form to submit your claims either weekly or monthly.

Because you will be employed by the Umbrella company, you need to present them with a Form P45 from your previous employer, and inform the organisation you are going to contract directly, or – if working through an agency – inform the agency of the Umbrella company's details. They will send the contract to the Umbrella company for their Director'(s) signature and your countersignature.

The Umbrella company will provide you with an employee/shareholder contract. This will set out the contract under which they will provide their services to you, and under which you will agree to work and be paid.

From then on, you simply go to work, do your job well, get your time sheet signed and present the signed timesheet to the Umbrella company to invoice the organisation agency. Once the paid invoice arrives in the Umbrella companies' account – all going well – they will pay you your salary, withholding all related taxes on behalf of the HMRC. Along with this; the Umbrella company will also bill you periodically for their service fees (normally weekly).

There you go – congratulations, you are now a permie contractor!

Composite Companies

The Composite company is an artificial entity that enables individuals to achieve tax benefits through reductions in tax liabilities. They achieve this by paying dividends through multi-tiered, share ownership structures. According to the HMRC, 200,000 individuals in the UK – across numerous industries – use the services of Composite companies. This type of structure allows individuals to subcontract through them, by issuing shares of a unique class. These shares allow dividends to be paid to the subcontractor, based on their earnings.

Normally, the subcontractor is left to source his/her own contracts, and inform the Composite company of the terms of the contract, working hours and rate of pay. The Composite company handles all invoicing and VAT collections. In this way, the Composite company handles all accounting and company administration, charging a fee for this service to its subcontractors.

In this set-up, the subcontractor does not even need to be a director of a company. Composite companies normally only accept individuals whose annual taxable profits do not exceed £300,000. This is to avoid paying the higher rate of corporation tax applied to taxable profits larger than £300,000.

The subcontractor is paid a wage, which is equal to a personal allowance. The Composite companies management fees and any related corporation tax on the profits, are deducted from these earnings. The balance is normally distributed as a dividend on the subcontractor's shares – monthly. This set-up benefits the subcontractor greatly as it alleviates the burden of running a company, whilst endowing him/her with all the benefits of limited liability company ownership.

There are huge risks for Composite companies that take on non-limited company subcontractors. If the HMRC questions the subcontractor's status, the Composite company could face a huge – backdated – financial burden.

To reduce this risk, most Composite companies insist on limited companies only as subcontractors, and could even facilitate the setting up of a limited liabilities company for their subcontractors. This way, when trouble comes in the form of an HMRC investigation, the subcontractor will shoulder most of it. The subcontractor will have to settle tax, National Insurance Contributions, and even some VAT payments. These payments could also be backdated many years.

Composite companies are virtually useless for IT contractors now, and should be avoided. The treasury made this clear in the budget of 2007. The treasury wrote:

"5.85 Since the Pre-Budget Report, further evidence has emerged that employment income is being disguised as dividends in order to take advantage of the small companies' tax rate, often encouraged by promoters of mass-marketed managed service company schemes. There is also evidence of some agencies, contractors and employers requiring workers to use corporate structures, thereby denying them employment rights as well as avoiding paying their fair share of tax and NICs.

5.86 The Government believes that all individuals and businesses must pay their fair share of NICs and tax, irrespective of legal form. It will continue to review the tax and NICs systems to ensure that this is the case and will bring forward proposals for discussion that are consistent with simplicity for compliant businesses, support for businesses in their aspirations to grow and maintaining the attractiveness of the UK as a business location. As the first stage of this review the Government will consult on action to tackle disguised employment through managed service company schemes."

Private company limited by shares

The responsible and sensible way to operate an IT contracting business in the UK, is to use a limited liability company (Ltd). This established and trusted business structure allows contractors to take charge of their contracting business by establishing a legal entity, separate from the owners. In the UK, you are required to have at least one director and one

Samuel Blankson

secretary[3]. The Ltd. company also requires a company bank account. All company related financial transactions should be made from the company bank account. This includes the receipt of invoiced payments, dividend disbursements, tax and VAT payments, salaries, purchases and other payments.

Individuals, as well as other companies, can be shareholders in Ltd. companies. As a shareholder, you are not liable for the company's debts, however; if the company fails, you may lose funds you personally invested in the company. Shareholders are not bound to being UK citizens or companies only; they can be from any where in the world.

This makes the Ltd. company an ideal business structure for doing business with them. It is also very easy to set-up. The process for establishing a Ltd. company is as follows:

- Determine a unique name for your company.
- Check the originality of your company name by calling the Contact Centre at (0044) (0) 870 3333636, and online at www.companieshouse.gov.uk/webcheck. The Registrar gives the following guidelines to choosing a company name.

  o It is 'the same as'[4] a name already on the index.

---

[3] From 2008 UK private limited liability companies will no longer be required to have a secretary.
[4] When deciding whether a name is 'the same as' another name, the Registrar ignores punctuation, the company's status, 'the' at the start of the name, and words like 'company (or co)', 'and (or &) company (or co)'. A name that sounds the same as one already on the Company Names Index may be accepted if the two names are spelt differently.

For example, if the name 'Hands Limited' is already registered, then the following would be rejected:

  o Hands Public Limited company (or PLC)
  o H and S Limited (or Ltd.)
  o H and S Public Limited company (or PLC)

- 55 -

o It includes the words 'limited', 'unlimited', 'public limited company' or 'community interest company' anywhere except at the end of the name. This applies equally to abbreviations or the Welsh equivalent of the words.
o It ends with 'commonhold association limited' or the Welsh equivalent (unless the company is a commonhold association).
o It ends with 'community interest public limited company', 'community interest company' (or abbreviations or Welsh equivalents), unless the company is a community interest company.
o It includes anywhere in the company name, any of the following:

- 'investment company with variable capital' (or its Welsh equivalent).
- 'open-ended investment company' (or its Welsh equivalent).
- 'limited liability partnership' (or its Welsh equivalent).
- 'SE' (or the abbreviations 'SE' bracketed, or with other punctuation marks before or after the abbreviation). For more information, see our booklet *The European Company: Societas Europaea* (SE).
- it is offensive.
- its use would be a criminal offence.

Next you have to determine your company directors and your company secretary.

Fill in the following forms:

---

o H & S Limited (or Ltd).
o Any of the above, with the addition of 'Company (or Co)' or 'and (or &) Company (or Co)'.

- Form 10[5]
- Form 12[6]
- Memorandum of Association[7]
- Articles of Association[8]

You can find form numbers ten and twelve on the Companies House Web site at www.companieshouse.gov.uk/forms/formsOnline.shtml. Unfortunately, the Memorandum of Association and Articles of Association can be collected from any of the addresses below:

Cardiff	**Edinburgh**	**London**
Companies House	Companies	Companies House
Crown Way	House	Executive Agency
Maindy	37 Castle Terrace	21 Bloomsbury Street
Cardiff	Edinburgh	London
CF14 3UZ	EH1 2EB	WC1B 3XD
	DX 33050	

- Once you have determined that your chosen company name is different from others already registered or proposed, you can proceed to register your company. This process can be carried out electronically or by post. Companies House offers two methods of paying for

---

[5] This will contain the intended situation of the Registered Office, (this will be either in England and Wales, or Scotland) and the details of the consenting Secretary and Director(s).

[6] This is the declaration of Compliance with the Companies Act 1985 in respect of the registration. Once the Memorandum and Articles of Association (see below), have been completed, this must be signed in the presence of a Solicitor, Commissioner for Oaths, Notary Public or Justice of the Peace. There is often a small fee charged for this service.

[7] This states the company name, the situation of the Registered Office (to be England and Wales, Scotland or Wales), the objects of the company and its Liability.

[8] This gives the internal management affairs and running of the company. Each subscriber to the shares should sign this.

company registration: the standard way and an express, same-day service. Currently, if you are registering electronically, the standard cost is £15 and the same day service is £30. By post, the standard cost is £20, whilst the same day service is £50. However, you must get the forms and documents to Companies House before 15:00 GMT.

- Your company must have a registered office associated to it. This can be any office location within England and Wales (or Scotland if your company is registered there). However, if you do not have an office location separate of your home, it is advised you use your accountant's office address instead – as long as mail sent there will be dealt with promptly. This will also speed up communication between HMRC, Companies House and your accountants. You can always change the registration address after incorporation, using Form 287.

- Once incorporated, you will need to open a company business account. Take some time to research banks that offer low or no bank charges, check book, corporate debit card, and a high interest, business savings account for small companies.

- Use http://www.moneysupermarket.com/businessfinance or any other online business bank account comparison service, to compare business bank accounts.

- Next, if you expect to earn above £64,000 per annum, then you will need to register for VAT. If you do not expect to exceed £64,000 per annum, you can still voluntarily register for VAT. This is recommended. You can find the VAT1 form at http://customs.hmrc.gov.uk.

- To simplify your VAT payments, consider joining the Flat Rate Scheme. This allows you to pay 13%[9] instead of the standard 17.5% VAT. This is only available to companies

---

[9] Computer and IT consultancy or data processing 13%
Computer repair services 11%

with taxable turnover, (excluding VAT) in the next year of £150,000 or less, and total business income (including VAT) in the next year of £187,500 or less. You cannot join the scheme if you are associated with another business in this special sense if:

- One business is under the dominant influence of another.
- Two businesses are closely bound by financial, economic and organisational links or...
- ...Another company has the right to give directions to you.
- In practice, your company habitually complies with the directions of another. The test here is a test of the commercial reality, rather than of the legal form.

- You can apply to join the Flat Rate Scheme when you send off your VAT application, or after you become VAT registered by any of the following methods:

By post

You can download the VAT 600 FRS – Flat Rate Scheme application by post form from http://customs.hmrc.gov.uk. Fill it in and send it to the following address:

National Registration Service
HM Revenue & Customs
Deansgate
62-70 Tettenhall Road
Wolverhampton
West Midlands
WV1 4TZ.

If you are registering for VAT, you can enclose the form with your Form VAT 1 Application.

By e-mail

Download the form "VAT 600 FRS Flat Rate Scheme application by post", fill it in on your computer and send it to: frsapplications@hmrc.gov.uk.

If you want to discuss this process, call the National Advice Service on 0845 010 9000.

Other Company Structures

Some contractors, in an attempt to avoid paying UK taxes, use offshore structures to siphon money out of the UK from their contracting business. Whilst it is exceedingly difficult to find an agency that will accept a company based outside the UK – especially if it is based in an offshore tax haven, some will overlook this fact and deal with offshore companies. The HMRC rightly frowns on this type of tax evasion and will insist you pay full taxes on all UK based income sources. Their actions against those carrying out this unscrupulous activity can lead to heavy fines and even imprisonment.

As tax laws change, unscrupulous operators will adapt to the changing environment and utilise new tax loopholes. One such loophole is operated by a few companies that employ contractors as permanent employees. The contracting income earned by the contractor is then treated as income for the unscrupulous operator. The company structure of these operators is such that they manage to transfer all the income offshore, to sister or parent companies – sometimes to seemingly independent companies.

These offshore companies in turn, pay the siphoned, tax-free income back to the contractor as a foreign exchange loan, or other financial instrument loan(s). As soon as this loan is issued, the lender writes it off as a bad debt without the contractor paying a single repayment premium on the loan. Avoid this and other blatantly unscrupulous tax evasion schemes. If you are caught using them, you may face huge financial consequences from the tax office.

Other contractors use offshore limited liability companies (LLC's) to supply services to their UK based IT contracting Ltd. company. Often, these offshore companies employ nominee directors, and are established in jurisdictions that do not require reporting of company ownership or activities. Because the companies are run by nominee directors, the true owners can be masked or totally hidden from any due diligence investigators. Such a company then bills the UK Ltd. company for "services" provided; the cost of which often amounts to the total amount of profits earned by the UK based Ltd. company.

Once the funds are offshore, it is withdrawn as tax-free dividends out of the offshore LLC. This borders on money laundering and again, is frowned upon by the HMRC; however, it is a legitimate business transaction.

The issue here lies in the possibility of two companies being related through any of the UK directors, and the sole purpose of the transaction and relationship is to avoid paying UK taxes. The HMRC will overlook a situation where a legitimate and unrelated offshore company supplies a rightful service to a UK based Ltd. company, and charges a reasonable amount for this service.

Large businesses frequently utilise this method of moving company funds offshore to better tax treatment jurisdictions. Some of the worlds' largest companies manage to avoid paying billions in taxes by outsourcing many services to offshore companies and subsidiaries. These auxiliaries often overcharge for their services – further facilitating the movement of funds offshore and avoiding the payment of high onshore taxes. These practices in the United States, where world income is taxed by the Internal Revenue Service (IRS), have reached epidemic levels.

Using subsidiaries with a UK Ltd. company can bring its own headaches, for instance, you would no longer qualify for the VAT Flat Rate Scheme, and your reporting requirements in the UK will be affected. To avoid breaking the law, I advise you consult a qualified tax specialist who thoroughly understands offshore solutions. The International Tax Handbook link (www.hmrc.gov.uk/manuals), will introduce this subject in detail.

Accounting

Like any company, you need to keep good accounts. This will help you in several ways; firstly, accounts will help you track your company's performance. This will make it easier to identify where you can improve in your tax planning, reduction of your companies overheads, and reduction of running costs.

To help account for everything you buy or invoice for, you need to keep records and the original copies of all receipts and statements. An effective system for doing this can be as simple as two folders; one for receipts and copies of invoices, and the other folder for communications from your accountants, HMRC, company house, your company's meeting minutes, etc.

If you contract through a limited company, you will greatly benefit from a qualified accountant's help to balance your company books. An accountant can also help you file your accounts with the HMRC and communicate with Company House on behalf of your Ltd. company.

A good accountant will save you more in taxes than they will cost you – making their service invaluable. Normally, you have to pay a little more for a proactive accountant; however, they are worth that extra fee. It is a good idea to leave your accounts to an accountant, so that you can focus on what you do best and what brings the most money into your company. We will look at selecting an accountant in chapter 2. For now, let us see how you can organise your accounting and bookkeeping processes.

At the end of each month or every quarter, you will receive a VAT reminder from the HMRC. You normally will have over thirty days from the arrival of this reminder to file and settle your VAT bill. Depending on the type of arrangement you have with your accountant, either you can send him/her all the receipts and invoices for the period, or you can create a spreadsheet of incoming and outgoing money to the company account.

This should include all company purchases and spending, e.g., insurances, accountant fees, etc. You can use any spreadsheet software to achieve this, e.g., Microsoft Excel, or Lotus 123. The formula calculating features of these spreadsheet applications will allow you to sum and total, as well as add equations to calculate VAT and corporation tax. See Table 3 (below), for an example template of such a spreadsheet.

At the end of each quarter, translate your receipts and invoices to a spreadsheet such as that illustrated in Table 3. E-mail the spreadsheet and post all your invoices and statements, along with your signed VAT return form to your accountant. He/she will then calculate your VAT and tax as well as National Insurance and the company payroll. If your accountant files electronically, he can inform you of the sum to pay for the various taxes. You can transfer this amount electronically from your company bank account, or send a cheque to the relevant address.

Company X: Quarter 3 2007					
Source	**Date**	**Income**	**Outgoing**	**Wages**	**Notes**
Contracting Income					
Tax					
Communications					
Vehicle					
Office					
Fuel					
Travel					
Training					
Courtesy					
Lunch					
Wages					
Totals					
Income Total					
Outgoing Total					
Wages Total					
VAT					
Income Vat					
Outgoings Vat					
Corporation Tax					
Income Vat					

Table 3: Company income and outgoing template.

Develop the habit of asking for a receipt for everything you buy. You can always sort out what is claimable later. The receipt collection habit is vital for bookkeeping purposes. Similarly, using a reliable system to organise your paperwork and bookkeeping will save you countless hours and headache later on. You will be able to find receipts easily and copies of invoices, letters from HMRC, and your accountant, as well as bank statements, etc. As an example, losing a letter from HMRC that was requesting you settle some tax bill or other imperative matter, could turn out to be a very expensive mistake, especially when the late payment penalties and charges are later demanded.

Banking

IT contracting is a business and it revolves around making money. It is therefore important to make sure that this money is transparently identifiable at every stage of the transaction, and separate from your own personal finances. It is essential to open and operate with a business account. This is the simplest way to account for, and provide a high level of transparency in your business activities and transactions.

It enables the tax office, your accountant, creditors and auditors, government and corporate bodies carrying out due diligence on your company, to assess your business. A business account also gives you credibility as a business owner. It says you are worthy of being considered by a bank as a business customer.

Shopping for a business bank account is not quite as simple as finding one with the highest interest rate and lowest charges. The importance of high interest rates, or low to no transaction charges, will depend on what you plan to do with your Ltd. company. Furthermore, most banks offering low or no bank charges also offer low interest rates. Whilst banks offering high interest rates normally also have many penalties and charges for late payments, unpaid cheques, over draft and overdrawing, statement reprinting and transaction fees.

As an IT contractor your bank will require you to present your company's certificate of incorporation, VAT certificate, personal identification (passport, driving licence and household bills, etc.), of all directors, and signatures of all the directors, and witnessed by someone in the bank before an account will be opened. Some banks will also require a brief explanation of what the company will be doing and an estimate of expected profits. A deposit of cash is also a common requirement before trading can begin with business bank accounts.

The following is a simplified list of the categories of banking requirements by IT contracting companies:

1. Barebones banking requirements (mainly Internet banking with electronic fund transfers).
   These usually offer free, online banking, however, offline services can be either non-existent, poor or expensive.
2. Medium banking requirements (chequebook usage, corporate credit/debit card usage, wire transfers, overdraft and loan requirements, branch banking as well as telephone and Internet banking).
   Normally, these come with a variety of bank accounts, high interest, holding, number two account, etc. Mostly cater for offline banking; however, the banking is rarely free in the long term.
3. High use banking requirements (e-commerce, frequent small cash, cheque and credit card payments, bank loans and financing facilities, etc.).
   Normally, these offer the best offline charges due to the high number of transactions they expect. Using them for low transaction banking will decrease their value. They are best suited for companies engaged in retail or e-commerce.

Their main benefit lies in the sales processing and funding facilities they give to the companies that use them.

Barebones

If you're planning to create the basic IT contracting company structure, i.e., pay yourself a small wage out of the company, and draw the rest through dividends after paying VAT, taxes, accountant fees, insurance premiums, etc., then your cheapest option is to use an Internet based, business bank account. These accounts offer the best choice for low transaction charges and high-paying interest rates. You can settle all your bills and pay out all your payments electronically, at little to no cost – keeping your banking expenses to a minimum.

Once you have transferred your dividends to your personal bank account, you can execute your usual method of dealing with your own personal income. However, the business account should cost you almost nothing to operate online, in most cases. create

This type of banking is more secure than personally carrying funds to your local branch. You can also create transactions, or view your balance or statements, twenty-four hours a day. Be sure the one you choose offers the best choice of banking services. BACs, CHAPS, standing order set-up and maintenance, direct debit facility set-up and maintenance, debit cards and statement checking, are some of the vital services you should look for.

These accounts are great for barebones operations and transactions, as described above. If you require other services and the use of overdraft facilities, loans and other types of business funding, chequebook usage and your own personal business account manager at your local branch, then the Internet business account may not be for you. They normally have high penalties related to these other services.

Things to look out for with online business accounts:

- Is there a set-up fee?
- Is there a minimum monthly fee? How much is it?
- What is the charge for paying in cheques, transferring funds and making withdrawals?
- Is there a charge for technical or customer support?
- When is support available, and in what way is it offered (e.g., e-mail, phone, Web chat)?
- What is the banks support response time?
- Is the online banking service available 24/7?
- What is the interest rate on deposits?

You can use these questions to evaluate potential online business accounts.

Medium use

Medium use business banking requirements are better served by banks that offer branches, low costs on cheque and other transaction usages, whilst offering more avenues to business funding.

These accounts charge for the extra products and services they provide and the charges are minimised if you stay within the defined limits. Don't use or exceed your overdrafts, bounce a cheque, lose your statements and/or require reprinting of new copies, etc. All these extras will most likely come with higher charges. Some banks even charge a maintenance fee for the privilege of banking with them. Look for a bank that offers all the services you need, and charges the least for the services you will use the most.

Medium use banks are great for people who want more offline involvement with their bank. Perhaps your business makes a lot of cash or cheque deposits, or you write a lot of checks or give change in cash for your services. Others of you may like the human touch of the long queues at the bank and dealing with an account manager at your local branch. Whatever the reasons for your preferences of off-line to online banking, make sure it is a business reason and helps your business either make more money, spend less money or both.

Things to look out for with medium use business bank accounts:

- Is there a set-up fee?
- Is there a minimum required opening deposit?
- Is there a requirement for a business plan to open an IT contracting business account?
- Is there a minimum monthly fee? How much is it?
- Is there a minimum monthly balance to be maintained?
- Are telephone and Internet banking offered for free? If not, what are the charges?
- What are the transaction charges?
- Do you get a dedicated business account advisor? If so, is there a charge for the service?
- Is there a local branch near you? If so what are its opening times, and does it offer business banking support?
- What is the banks support response time?
- Is the online banking service available 24/7?
- What is the interest rate on deposits?
- Is free overdraft usage offered? If not what are the charges for its usage?
- What loan/funding facilities are available and what is the procedure and requirements for application?
- What else is offered to new account applicants?

Use these questions to evaluate your medium use, business bank accounts.

High use

If your business generates sales transactions or it receives payments regularly, you might need banking facilities to assist you to conduct business and handle the multiple transactions and trading you do. A bank account that can accommodate the receipt of payments via cheques, wire, direct debit, credit or debit cards, and e-commerce Web site payments such as Worldpay or PayPal, etc., may just be what you need.

Your business may require assistance with cash-flow and other short term loans, or perhaps you require starting capital to expand your business services. Some business owners may want to take their company public and require a bank that can accommodate that. This is the arena that a high use banking facility can assist you with.

Depending on the bank and/or account you select, you may or may not be better placed to take advantage of or to be offered the opportunity for this type of funding. However, most banks will allow you access to these funding opportunities depending on your security and credit rating, etc. Shop around for banks that offer more access to funding opportunities if you require this for your business.

In some cases you have to select a particular bank to receive a desired credit facility. In such cases the business benefit (i.e., the credit facility), will take precedence over the saving on banking charges and earning a higher interest on your companies money.

Some business bank accounts are better suited for undertaking e-commerce transactions than others. These business accounts come with facilities for accepting credit and debit card payments or the bank may partner with a major e-commerce payment clearing provider. If your business requires e-commerce merchant services, you will have to shop around for the best e-commerce banking solution.

Things to look out for with medium use business bank accounts:

- Is there a set-up fee?
- Is there a minimum required opening deposit?
- Is there a requirement for a business plan to open an IT contracting business account? If so, is there any assistance offered in its preparation?
- Is there a minimum monthly fee for the account? If so, how much is it?
- Is there a minimum monthly balance to be maintained? If so, how much is it?
- Are telephone and Internet banking offered free? If not what are the charges?
- What are the transaction fees?
- What e-commerce benefits does the bank account offer?
- What retailer benefits does the bank account offer?
- Does the bank offer weekly statements? What are the costs for them, if any?
- Do you get a dedicated business account advisor? If so, is there a charge for the service?
- Is there a local branch near you? If so, what are its opening times, and does it offer business banking support?
- What is the bank's support response time?
- Is the online banking service available 24/7?
- What is the interest rate on deposits?
- Is free overdraft usage offered? If not, what are the charges for its usage?
- Does the bank offer equity funding, factoring/invoice discounting, and other funding opportunities? If so, at what rate or cost are these funding options charged?
- What is the procedure and requirements for loan/funding facility application(s)?

- What else is offered to new account applicants?
- Does the bank offer discounted insurance to business account holders?

Use these questions to evaluate your medium use business bank accounts.

Other considerations

Selecting the right bank for your IT contracting business will play an important part in your business success. This is especially true if you plan to use your business for more than just IT contracting. For instance, if you register your business as offering computer repair services, you might need your bank for a loan, or some other funding to buy stock, outfit a shop, train staff or buy tools and equipment.

This type of business will require more overhead and more start-up capital than a computer consultancy service alone. Some banks offer specialist help to new, start-up businesses whilst other banks do not.

In some cases, if you have been a loyal customer to your local bank – especially true for smaller, non-centralised banks – your local bank manager may offer you exceptionally favourable service and rates on your new company's account. Wherever this is available, and the terms are comparable or better than is available elsewhere – take it.

If your business has a retail arm as well as your IT contracting, and you require a geographically close bank for cash deposits, etc., you may have to consider using several banks, or a single, local bank with a branch near your retail business base. In the case of two or more business accounts with several banks, you will use each for the services that benefit your business the most.

For instance, if your bank is close to your retail concern whilst the other offers free banking, you would use the local branch bank account for cash deposits, only whilst using periodic electronic transfers to move the funds to and from your other bank account.

Unless you are a very experienced accountant or bookkeeper, you need regular bank statements to plan/assess your cash flow, as well as to avoid paying high bank charges for bounced (returned unpaid) cheque(s) stopped by the drawer, or overdrawn situations.

If you are running a Ltd. company that offers many services, with a retail aspect, you need to have daily access to your bank statement, if not, then at least weekly. Make sure you have access to free bank account statement information twenty-four hours a day. Telephone banking and online banking normally offer this service for free; however, make sure you are not being charged.

New customers only

Most banks offer more to attract new business than they do to keep their old members, therefore, don't be surprised if you are offered – by a new bank – introductory offers for opening a business account, that you wouldn't qualify for at your old bank. Offers such as two years free banking, low introductory lending rates, free business advice and a broad range of other introductory benefits and services are granted to new business account applicants. Make sure you capitalise on this whenever possible.

Recent events

In the UK, high bank charges have been highlighted by the government as being a restriction on small businesses and unfair on consumers. This has led the government to force the top UK banks[10] to offer all small businesses interest accounts, at 2.5% below the Bank of England base rate, or an account that offers free transaction charges.

The banks have responded by increasing lending rates to small businesses or being more selective in who they lend to – thus reducing their risk with emerging and troubled small businesses. Some banks have also increased their transaction charges as a result.

Planning

Before you jump in and hand in your notice to your permie job, take some time to plan how you will tackle contracting, and secure yourself against potential loss of income, in the beginning of your contracting life.

Things to consider are as follows:

- Loss of income consideration.
- Terms of departure from your permie job.
- Area of expertise to focus on in contracting.
- Training or experience necessary before you begin.
- Certification(s) required or recommended before you begin.
- Travel/commuting/relocation considerations.
- Prerequisite preparation (Umbrella or Ltd. company, bank account, accountant, professional indemnity insurance, CV, suit and tie, interview techniques and practice).
- Pension planning.
- Healthcare considerations.
- Rate and length of first contract.
- IR35 and tax considerations.

---

[10] Royal Bank of Scotland, Barclays, Lloyds TSB, and HSBC currently control 86% of the UK's small business banking market.

- Financial planning.

Next, we will look closely at these considerations, one-by-one.

Loss of income consideration

The pace of the recruitment process in IT contracting is faster than in permie recruiting. Normally, contracts are inflexible in how long they will wait for you to start. One to two weeks is common. However, a one month wait or more is highly unlikely. Most permie jobs require a resignation notice period of one month or longer. Because of this, it is advisable that you hand in your notice to your permie employer before applying to contracts, and attending interviews.

This leap of faith can be scary, especially the first few times. Furthermore, there are some real dangers involved. These are related to whether you can get a contract before you run out of money searching.

Depending on your technical speciality, competence, CV, interview technique, personality and personal appearance, it could take anything from a week to over a year. Yes, over a whole year!

I have known contractors who were over-specialised. For these contractors, the chances of a contract coming on the market in their field, in the same city, country or continent was rare, to highly improbable.

We shall discuss this in greater detail later. However, bear in mind, that due to over-specialisation, it is possible to position yourself out of reach of most contract work.

Another culprit of long waiting periods between contracts – highlighted by a lack of interview requests – is overpricing your skills or applying for contracts you simply are not competent enough to carry out.

As an example: if you have previously only led a team of two engineers and you are applying for IT director positions, you will be in for a long wait before success, if successful at all. There is an old Chinese proverb that says, "Man who stands on edge of cliff waiting for roast duck to fly in mouth, has a long wait."

A bad CV is also often responsible for long waits between contracts. Review your CV regularly and update it periodically to keep it fresh and up-to-date. We shall review the entire CV process in the next chapter. For now, bear in mind that if your CV is not exciting or impressive to you, your partner or friends, then it is likely not exciting to the organisation you apply to next.

The great majority of contract applications involve a formal interview and sometimes a technical test. We have covered the need for relevant technical competence. However, the way you conduct yourself at interviews also plays a large part in how long you will wait between contracts for the next role.

We will discuss interview techniques – specifically related to IT contracting – in detail later. For now, bear in mind that if you are getting many interview requests and no success afterwards, then your interview technique or personality may be the reason.

It is important how you present yourself at interviews. The interview is the organisation's opportunity to meet you face to face. They will be looking to see if they like you and if you will bring value to their IT solution or project, and whether your CV was accurate.

Organisations spend a fortune getting the recruitment of permies right. This is because of the huge financial commitment and risk the organisation takes by recruiting a permie. It is not uncommon for permies to attend two or more interviews. Often, with panels of HR interview technique specialists and IT management, before a decision is reached whether to employ you or not.

Luckily, in IT contracting, most interviews are conducted by people who are not highly skilled at this task. Often, team leaders, IT managers and even other technical staff may sit in on or conduct the interview. These people will most likely be easier to interview with than seasoned, HR trained, interview specialists.

That said, you still have to get two things right; namely, technical tests or questions, and personality and attitude questions. Technical tests will be easier if you are competent than if you're not. However, there are a few points you should be aware of concerning this topic. This is covered in detail in the next chapter.

Your answers to personality questions are more likely going to be the reason you are offered the contract role, or not. These questions are intended to test your loyalty, commitment, motivation, amiability and attitude towards users, staff, past employees and yourself.

The interview itself also gives the organisation an insight into your professionalism through your punctuality, dress and presentation. As an example, one of the worst things you can do to give a bad impression to an interviewer, is to not value their time and turn up late for the interview. We will discuss this topic in more detail in the next chapter.

When you align, correct, and fine-tune all these points, you will find that you are never out of work for more than a couple of weeks at a time; and more importantly, you will be renewed more frequently. This will reduce your need to look for a new contract.

Terms of departure from your permie job

Before you rush to leave your permie job, make sure you leave on good terms. In IT contracting – just as in permie positions – good references are often essential. There are many ways around having good references – and we shall discuss some of these later – but the aim is to avoid putting hurdles in front of yourself.

Therefore, always try to leave every employer on a good note. With today's fear of litigation, many organisations are turning towards policies of not giving references to contractors. The most HR departments of these organisations that employ this policy are prepared to offer, is a confirmation of the duration you were in their employ.

Many managers will give you a reference privately, as long as you are on good terms with them. A word of warning is required, though. Be sure the referrer is a friend, as a bad reference can do more damage than no reference at all.

Before you leave your permie job, make sure you have at least one manager who is prepared to give you a good reference. Delay your departure if need be, if you require the time to cultivate such an associate. The effort will be worth it as you shop for your first few contracts.

Get into the habit of producing good work and conducting yourself in such a way that you deserve a great reference after you leave. This should be top of your agenda during your time at every new contract. This habit will serve you well in IT contracting.

Area of expertise to focus on in contracting

I have already mentioned how your area of specialisation could be your downfall or your lifeline. To be successful (long-term) in IT, you cannot afford to over specialise. The world of high technology moves at breakneck speed, and to avoid being left behind you need to keep an eye on two things: demand for your skill sets and the length of time you spend at each contract.

You could be in a hot niche within IT right now, but this could change very quickly if a rival technology – better, faster, more efficient and cheaper – is introduced. Suddenly, your now out-of-date skills will no longer be in high demand.

This happened to an IT contractor friend of mine who specialised in analogue telecoms. When digital technologies such as Voice over IP came along, he found himself struggling to find any analogue work. The few he came across were mainly migration projects, moving from analogue to digital.

Don't get caught in this trap. Constantly review the popularity for your skills, and if you see it waning, go with the consensus. This could mean taking a course or home studies, being a little more selective in your future contracts, so that you can steer your career in the direction of whatever is in the most demand.

Another way that contractors slowly become dinosaurs is that they stay too long at one contract, renewing perpetually without a thought to the market requirements for their skills. When the contract eventually ends, they find themselves like a person imprisoned decades previously, all of a sudden set free in a world that has passed them by.

If you only know MS DOS and Windows 3.11, and you find yourself in today's IT market competing for Windows XP, Windows 2003 and Vista, you will know exactly what I mean. Don't stay in a cushy contract if it is failing to keep your skills updated, or holding you back from advancing your skills in the direction of the market demand.

Certification, training or experience necessary before you begin

Some areas of IT require a highly recognised certification, without which, your options are seriously limited. If this is the case – as it is in IT project management with the Prince 2 certification – then acquire the certification as soon as possible. Don't delay a minute. The success of your contracting life depends on it.

There are many options you can take to get the certification. You can use books to study, Computer Based Training (CBT), courses (full-time or part-time), training boot camps, or any combination of these. Use whatever method you prefer and that is most efficient for you.

There are many resources on the Internet to assist you with this. There are user groups, forums, bulletin boards, newsgroups, guides, online tutorials and many more. You can find all these by simply searching for them using an Internet search engine. Most manufacturers such as Microsoft also offer extensive reference documentation on all their certification paths and their products.

Sometimes, you may need to lower your rate in order to change the area of IT in which you specialise. If the new skills have a higher demand and promises to continue growing in popularity longer than your previous or current specialisation, then this may be an option you should take.

Over the years, you will move across many such areas as you position yourself in higher rate brackets, so get used to it, as it's part of the magic of contracting – the ability to determine your income at will, and work to manifest it in a fraction of the time a permie job could produce.

I have personally helped many non-IT permies to become IT contractors. After starting at under £20,000 per annum gross, many of them (in less than five years), are earning in excess of £50,000 gross. One of them earns in excess of £100,000 per annum gross today, after just ten years in IT contracting.

These ex-permies came from backgrounds as diverse as bio engineering, structured cabling, hairdressing, long-term unemployment, singer/musician and accountancy. What these ex-permies have proven is that IT contracting can be very rewarding, if you use it as a tool and treat it as a business; constantly looking to improve your service and profits through retraining and the acquisition of new, highly sought-after skills.

Travel/commuting/relocation considerations

IT contracting, like most high technology industries, are more easily available in and around large industrial parks, large towns and cities. There is a simple reason for this. Most businesses want to be based at the hub of business and also where most of their customers can easily access their services. This happens to be large towns and cities. In recent decades, large businesses have attempted to cut costs of a city based office location by relocating their non-retail business to industrial parks, mostly outside these large towns and cities.

If you want the most chance of easily finding contract work, then move to, or near, a large city like London. Today, it is easier to commute via car, train, metro and buses than ever before. Because of the availability of work, and the higher rates of pay, some contractors even commute from abroad to work in large cities.

One such contractor is a friend of mine and lives in Frankfurt and commutes to London every week – staying within walking distance of his office, in a bed and breakfast, Monday through Friday. His commuting bills happen to be cheaper than if he commuted from 20 miles outside of London into the city each day. His flights to and from Frankfurt takes less than an hour each way.

Others relocate, moving from all parts of the country, and in some cases from abroad, to be near the hub of IT contracting employment. I know of many contractors from South Africa, Singapore, Australia and New Zealand who have taken this option.

Some contracts may require national or international travel to branch offices or clients' sites. This is normally associated with consultations, mobile positions such as printer or photocopier engineers and also migration projects. If you are not prepared to undertake extensive, or the occasional travel, and your skills are based in an industry which requires this, e.g., a server installation specialist or database installation consultant, then I suggest you consider acquiring skills that are more suitable to this.

In conclusion, your chances of finding contract work will be greatly affected by your geographic location. Therefore, you should consider relocating if this will greatly aid your chances of finding appropriate, highly paid contracts. If you are not able to relocate, travel or commute for work, then IT contracting may not be for you.

Prerequisite preparation

Before you jump into IT contracting, there are a few prerequisites that you should first establish. We have already discussed your CV, Umbrella or Ltd. company set-ups, bank account set-up, and acquiring the services of a good accountant (Ltd. companies only). Other things you will need to acquire are professional indemnity insurance, appropriate attire, and an effective interview technique.

In today's world, organisations need to protect themselves from all types of risk. A rogue IT contractor is one such risk. Normally, if you are working through an agency or Umbrella company, they will have sufficient, professional indemnity insurance cover for their side of the contract. However, if you are operating a Ltd. company, it may not be covered by such an insurance arrangement.

Professional indemnity insurance protects you from libel and slander, professional neglect, malicious falsehood, passing off copyrights, breach of confidentiality, and negligent statements or actions. We will examine how you can protect your company with indemnity insurance in chapter two.

Pension

Contracting is a great way to earn more money; however, if you do not put any aside for your future, you could reach retirement age with no way of maintaining your lifestyle for the rest of your life. In the UK and almost every other country around the world, governments offer tax allowances to those saving money towards their pensions.

This is normally taken care of for most permies through their company pension plans. In many cases, a permie's would automatically contribute to a pension plan, simply by joining an organisation and filling in a pension application form. Few permies stop to question where their funds are being invested, or how fast the investment is growing.

As a contractor, you can take control of the outcome of your retirement by selecting your own pension plan, and thus have more control over how fast it grows. As a company owner, an IT contractor also has many advantages relating to the type of pension plan in which he/she can invest. Similarly, the investment amount allowed, and how the funds can be used or treated, also differs slightly for company directors.

Strict rules often apply; however, pension plans are still one of the best ways to save towards your retirement. We will look at pension plans in the UK and the various rules and options you have for maximising the growth of your pension plan.

Life, health and other insurances

IT contracting roles are generally in relatively safe environments, such as offices and server rooms. Of course, you are not guaranteed to live forever. Because none of us know when our time will run out, it is best to prepare for this outcome. One of the ways you can prepare for this is by buying insurance for your loved ones who will be left behind, after you depart. Furthermore, you need to make sure you buy sufficient insurance for yourself, should you become unhealthy or permanently out of action.

There are many insurance products to choose from that will achieve this objective: Life, permanent health insurance

(PHI), private health, dental and accident, sickness and unemployment (ASU) insurances, are a few of the products we will examine in greater detail, in the next chapter.

Rate and length of your first contract

Take a look at the average figures for various, general IT skills in the UK at the following Web site address: http://www.contractoruk.com/market_stats/index.html. Click on the skill to see a breakdown of the rate profile. This site's rate tool offers a great way to gauge your average rate on the market.

A time consuming, although better way to gauge the current market worth of your IT skills, is to visit http://www.jobserve.com, and search for contracts in your area of expertise, and the region/town/country you are prepared to work in, e.g., London AND "Project Manager".

Read through the long list of jobs that will be displayed. As you read through the jobs, you will get a sense of what the going rate is for your skill set. You will also learn what the latest requirements for your area of expertise are.

From this, you can gauge how much you can ask when applying for contracts. Once you are ready to negotiate your rate with the agency or the HR department at the organisation – if you are applying direct to an organisation – you can gauge how much they are prepared to pay, before submitting your offer.

Contract negotiation is a skill you will learn to do better with time. Firstly, it requires you getting an interview. You need to guarantee that you will be interviewed – by presenting an outstanding CV along with an initial rate that falls within the organisations budget.

Secondly, at the interview, you need to show that you are worth more than the offered rate. Don't over-do this step, otherwise, you may be considered too good for the role and be eliminated from consideration. Getting this step right allows you to ask for a rate up to (and sometimes beyond), the organisations budget for the role.

Thirdly, once you start the new role, you need to continue to justify your paid rate by giving outstanding service, beyond that which you are paid. This sets you up for contract renewal in the future and a potential rate increase in the next renewal – wherever possible.

Rates of pay in IT contracting can vary widely for the same role type. For instance, helpdesk positions can pay £9 per hour at some organisations and in certain industries, whilst in various investment banks, the same role pays £35 per hour at the very high end of the market. In both cases, the jobs require a contractor to answer the phone, talk to users and extract details concerning their IT faults. However, one position certainly compensates higher than the other.

You should tailor your rate depending on the industry/sector or company within which you are applying for a contract. If you are applying to a company at the bottom end of the rate market, do not apply with top end rates. You simply will not get the contract. Similarly, do not apply to top paying contract at bottom end of the market rates. You may get the job but you will be unnecessarily losing money.

When you become an IT contractor, you are also a business owner; therefore, when looking for your next contract role, bear in mind that you are competing with many other business owners – other contractors and in some cases, large outsourcing companies – for the role. This competition will be – in most cases – technically as qualified as you, or better than you. You need to somehow stand out from the crowd. This is where your dress, grooming, personality, speech and attitude, CV, punctuality and professionalism, all come into play. It is through these attributes that you gain an edge over your competition.

We shall discuss all these subjects at length in the next chapter.

IR35 and other tax considerations

IR35

The HMRC's IR35 legislation is aimed at catching all contractors who they do not classify as 'self-employed.' If you fall out of classification and under IR35, you will pay increased income tax and National Insurance contributions. It is therefore vital to understand IR35 and how to avoid it.

IR35 is judged per contract, and so it is possible to have a mixture of IR35 and non-IR35 income flowing through your company. The non-IR35 income will not be liable to higher rate taxation and National Insurance (NI) treatment, whilst the IR35 income will. You can still claim qualifying expenses on both incomes and 5% of your turnover as intermediary expenses. The following expenses can be claimed against IR35 turnover:

- Pension payments – either personal or executive plans.
- Business travel – incurred in the course of business duties.
- Subsistence – accommodation, meals when away from home.
- Professional Indemnity insurance cover.
- Benefits in kind – e.g., private medical insurance.

Training expenses does not form part of this allowance.

The following are guideline questions to determine if you are classified as employed or self-employed by HMRC. Answer "yes" to all of the following questions and you are probably an employee according to HMRC (this list can also be accessed from http://www.hmrc.gov.uk/employment-status/index.htm):

1) Do you have to do the work yourself?

2) Can someone tell you at any time what to do, where to carry out the work or when and how to do it?
3) Can you work a set amount of hours?
4) Can someone move you from task to task?
5) Are you paid by the hour, week, or month?
6) Can you get overtime pay or a bonus payment?

Answer "yes" to all of the following questions and you are probably self-employee according to HMRC:

7) Can you hire someone to do the work or engage helpers at your own expense?
8) Do you risk your own money?
9) Do you provide the main items of equipment you need to do your job, not just the small tools that many employees provide for themselves?
10) Do you agree to do a job for a fixed price, regardless of how long the job may take?
11) Can you decide what work to do, how and when to do the work and where to provide the services?
12) Do you regularly work for a number of different people?
13) Do you have to correct unsatisfactory work in your own time and at your own expense?

Exposure to IR35 can be minimised by changing your working practices and using IR35-friendly contracts. However, due to the ambiguity of the rules, there are no guarantees. The following is a list of questions that you must also answer with "yes", in order to decrease your chances of falling within IR35:

1. What business is the organisation you are contracted to involved in?
2. Have you signed a written contract?
3. Are you exposed to any financial risk in the contract?
4. Are you working for only one organisation?

5. Do you work with your own materials on site?
6. Do you have to correct work at your own cost?
7. Do you provide a substitute contractor/employee if you are unable to personally attend the site?
8. Are you part and parcel of the organisation, or an outsider?
9. Are you restricted to deadlines and deliverables?
10. What are the intentions of both parties involved in the contract?
11. What is the length of the contract?
12. What are the terms of the contract – e.g., notice period, working hours, location and method of execution of the work?
13. What is the payment structure and method – i.e., is it based on fixed time or project time?
14. Are there permie benefits included, e.g., company car, expense account, sick or holiday pay?
15. Has a status ruling by the HMRC or Contributions Agency been previously provided?

The HMRC looks at each contract separately and treats them as individuals. The HMRC questionnaire to determine your status alone, is over eighty questions long. They do not miss much, and generally, your best option is to avoid them rather than confront them, and hope for the best.

HMRC is currently – chiefly – targeting non-limited company contractors, especially those using service companies; however, they also investigate a small number of contractors by random selection.

The chance of your limited company being selected for investigation among all the non-limited companies – including all the non-IT contractors out there – is slim. However, you would do well to take all the precautions available to you. Namely, use IR35-friendly contracts and change your working practices to align with that stated in the contract.

You could also elect to contract abroad, in a country where there are no tax hindrances to contract. If you select this option, seek a qualified tax consultant that specialises in the country you are considering. You may be surprised to discover that tax laws are generally as complex elsewhere as they may be in the UK.

If the whole dark cloud of IR35 is too much for you to handle, you could choose to return to being a permie. Normally, you can earn more money contracting, even as a PAYE than you can in the equivalent permie role, however; contracting is a way of life and may not be for everyone.

Draft contracts

The contract is your primary tool in any strategy to stay out of IR35. Firstly, you should have a contract for service between your limited company and the organisation before you undertake any contract role. Contracts are a vital tool because they set out the parameters and limitations of the business relationship you are undertaking with the organisation. When considering contracts as relates to IR35, the framework needs to be structured in such a way as to improve your chances of being outside IR35.

Therefore, the contract should include the following elements:

- A substitution clause allowing the contract work to be executed by another person provided by your limited company; this will usually include terms for veto, allowing the organisation to refuse the person you put forward, suitable presentation, qualification and experience and other points.
- A 'no mutuality of obligation' between your company and the organisation. This means you are not obligated to carry

out the work, and the organisation is not obligated to pay you.

- A 'no supervision/control/direction' clause. This states that you will not be supervised, directed or controlled as to the manner in which you choose to execute the agreed service. This allows you to work under your own initiative.

Draft contracts that include all these points are available from the Professional Contractors Group (PCG). I advise you to join PCG. You can find more information at http://www.pcg.org.uk/cms/index.php. There are currently four PCG membership options suitable to IT contractors. These are as follows:

1. PCGPlus membership – the fully comprehensive membership option.
2. Standard membership – standard membership lacking some of the PCGPlus options.
3. PCG OneStop – for new contractors. This comes in bronze, silver, gold and platinum options.
4. PCG Solo – for sole traders, partnerships and limited liability partnerships – unsuitable for IT contracting.
5. PCG Quality Umbrella (PCG (QU)) – an Umbrella company offered through Parasol.

You can read more about the membership options at http://www.pcg.org.uk. Supporting PCG is in the best interest of all IT contractors, as they represent all contractors and they lobby the government for changes that will benefit all contractors. They also actively seek to support cases that will shape the laws that affect IT contractors.

Section 660

As a limited company owner, you are free to recruit your partner and family to help run the company. This opens up a lot of room for the misuse of this right. Of primary concern to the HMRC, is the transfer of untaxed turnover from a high tax rate business owner, to a low tax rate partner of a family member. This led them to introduce the Section 660 rule.

It has already being upheld several times in court and is now a well-established legislation. Recently, this legislation was successfully applied to company dividend payments.

Essentially, Section 660 – also known as the 'married couple's business tax' – is being used to stop dividends paid to spouse/family members who do not bring an associated value to the company in relation to the dividend payment they receive. This non-fee earning family member is now being taxed by the HMRC at the same tax rate as the fee earning director. Furthermore, this legislation allows up to seven years backdated claim by the HMRC.

To avoid this legislation, simply make sure that all directors of your limited company are fee earners, and be sure you can prove this. Some contractors subcontract admin, secretarial services, job hunting, training, CV creation and CV update services to another company headed by their partner or family member. Although more complex and costly, this solution will eliminate Section 660 fears.

Consult your accountant for advice on all your tax issues. A good IT consultant will be able to help you avoid the tax burdens associated with the Section 660 legislation.

Financial planning

Before you can change careers and become an IT contractor, you need to prepare for the financial change. Many people enter the IT contracting world believing they will earn more for the use of spending more. If this is what you are hoping, please stop and read the following.

You can do more harm to yourself financially by earning more and spending more, than you can do whilst earning less and spending less. To avoid potential financial ruin, start to save towards this big change. Save enough money to sustain yourself and pay all your bills for at *least* six months. This may seem too much to you; however, keep in mind that you never know what the future holds. You could quit your permie job to start a contract role, and due to an accident, sudden failed health or the business at which you just started contracting going bust, you could find yourself in a financial crisis, if you are not prepared for the unexpected.

I remember once going to an interview on a Friday and I secured a contract to start on the following Monday. When I arrived that Monday morning, the lady who had interviewed me greeted me with teary eyes, clutching a brown box with her possessions inside. She stopped long enough to explain to that during the weekend the company had gone defunct, and her department was no longer in existence. To date, that was my shortest contract.

Similarly, I know a few contractors who had to quit their first contracts prematurely because it took too long to process their security, compliance and company registration paperwork. During the long wait, they ran out of money and literally could not afford to come to the site. Their contracts were terminated a few days later, when the client no longer could tolerate the absenteeism.

You may also need funds to purchase a travel pass, new clothing and shoes, a memory stick (flash drive), and other professional contracting tools. You simply never know, therefore, plan for the unknown and you will glide through that period or situation effortlessly.

With your nest egg in hand, you can go contracting comforted with the knowledge that no matter what happens, you can at least pay all your outgoings for six months. Once you start contracting don't dip into the savings and deplete it. Use your contracting income to fund future savings, and increase the buffer from six months to two or more years, over the next five years.

See the last chapter on investing for financial freedom for more information on some of the investments vehicles you could use to build a solid financial future.

Taxes

If you are with an Umbrella company, you need not concern yourself with this section. Your taxes will be withheld by the Umbrella company on behalf of the HMRC.

If you own a limited company, you need to be aware of the dangers of taxes, and plan to avoid tax disaster by setting aside enough funds to cover your corporation tax, VAT (if you are registered) and to settle your personal taxes arising from your salary.

Your company will be assigned a tax year cycle when you register it. This will vary for each contractor, as the period is staggered around different months by the HMRC to allow for a more evenly distributed workload for them. Your corporation tax will be due nine months and one day from the end of your tax year.

Your VAT however, will be paid quarterly unless you opt to pay monthly in fixed instalments based on the previous year's turnover. By this method, overpayments are calculated annually and are either refunded to you, or you have to pay the shortfall.

Because the VAT is due quarterly, most contractors have no problems with paying this. However, if you do not set aside money in your business bank account, you will struggle with VAT payment and incur substantial fines. Your VAT is 13% for flat rate VAT or 17.5% for non-flat rate VAT. Set this amount aside every time money comes into your company bank account.

As an example, if you receive £5,000 into your account, multiply that turnover by 0.13, and set aside £650 towards VAT if you are on flat rate. Set aside £5,000 x 0.175 = £875 if you are on non-flat rate VAT.

After you have set aside the VAT money from the turnover, multiply the remainder by the rate of corporation tax. This is currently 20% for the UK. Therefore, for flat rate VAT this will be (£5,000 - £650) x 0.20 = £870, and for non-flat rate VAT it will be (£5,000 - 875) x 0.2 = £825. Conversely, you can simply multiply your company turnover by 7/23 to get the sum total of flat rate VAT and corporation tax to set aside, or 17/50 for the non-flat rate VAT and corporation tax total, to set aside.

Ask your business banker to open a second business account or a high interest business account. Use either of these for holding VAT and tax money until due. If you follow this system you will always have sufficient funds to pay your tax and VAT whenever they are due.

In fact, you should have surplus funds after settling your taxes; due to the deductions you will make for legitimate expenses, and running costs such as accountant fees and professional indemnity insurance.

How to get into IT contracting

The IT contracting market is open to anyone who has the skills, determination and courage to break free from being an employee. If you think this lifestyle is for you, and you are prepared to sacrifice your permie comfort zone and perceived security-for-freedom that is more personal and self-reliant, then read on.

CV

The first step in getting into contracting is to have an effective CV or résumé ready and available. An effective résumé is simply a CV that gets results. If you are applying for jobs and are not getting called for interviews, it could either be your CV or the type of jobs you are applying for and your basic requirements, i.e., you are asking for too much money, or you are inadequately qualified for the roles.

Most of the time the problem will be CV based. This could be due to several reasons. One of the most common reasons is that your CV is boring, dead or lifeless. Dead CV's visually look uninteresting. The first impressions an interviewer or prospective contract employer gets when they see your CV will greatly determine if you receive a call to the interview or not.

The content of your CV is the next obstacle. Are your skills relevant to the contract role and are they current? Have you put the worst first and best last on your CV? If you apply for a role, but your CV does not mention any of the roles' key or preferred requirements, then don't be surprised when you are not called for an interview.

Finally, does your CV highlight your professionalism, punctuality, determination, hard work, loyalty and other key traits desired by almost every employer? This is where your CV begins to pave the way for your interview. I will cover these points in detail later in the "Writing an effective IT contracting CV" section, on page 109.

An effective CV will get you to the interviewing stage frequently; in fact, a truly effective CV may even bypass this stage, and get you through the door with your first attempt. To get to this stage with your CV, you need extensive experience, knowledge, abundant relevant skills and a confident, self-assured personality exuding professionalism.

Securing the first contract

Now that your CV is ready, you need to somehow get that first contract. You can do this through several routes:

- Direct – through direct application or through recommendation from a friend or acquaintance.
- Agency – through head-hunting, CV submitting and applications.

Direct

About 40% of all contract roles are secured through the direct approach. This does not necessarily mean that you submit your invoices directly to the organisation for payment. Most of the time, even though you acquired the job through personal recommendation or approaching the organisation directly, you will still be required to go through a preferred agency for invoicing.

A fraction of roles acquired without the help of an agency are executed without an agency's services. This is because the agency takes away a lot of admin and HR functionality from the organisation, further saving money for them.

Because the percentage of direct roles is so high, it is worth building into your contracting business the habits required to make the right friends and contacts, to later enable you to use this route to get your next contract.

To this end, you must keep in touch with other contacts and managers, as well as other key people such as directors and HR personnel who may come in handy later on. Constantly be on the look-out to make friends wherever you go. Contract roles often come through the strangest sources. Often a friend of a friend of a friend's girl or boyfriend may work in HR, and have a contract opening coming up which you could do. Don't ever write off any contact as not being useful. You never know who they know.

Having these connections is of no use if you don't let them know that you are available, and looking for your next contract role. Advertise this to all your friends and acquaintances, so that they will be aware and thus alerted to your need. In this way, when they hear or come to know of an appropriate role, you will be first on their mind to recommend for the job.

Always have your current, relevant CV available to e-mail or forward to prospective clients or your network of contacts. Store copies in your e-mail account online or at sites such as www.jobserve.com, where you can easily forward CVs to clients or other contacts.

Never be in a position where you cannot forward a CV because you are away from home. If possible, keep a copy online within your Web site so that you can direct people to download it immediately.

However, beware that the entire world will also be able to get hold of it. Therefore, you may want to password protect your CV or hide it from search engine indexing robots. For details of how to do this, see "META TAGS Optimising Your Website for Internet Search Engines (Google, Yahoo!, MSN, AltaVista, AOL, Alltheweb, FAST, GigaBlast, Netscape, Snap, WISEnut and Others)": ISBN-13: 978-1-905789-98-6).

Agency

The majority of IT contracting roles are acquired through the help of a recruitment agency. These are small (less than 5 staff specialising in IT), medium (single office but larger than small, often multi-industry focused), and large (multiple offices, multiple industries and contractor and permanent recruitment focused, often with offices in many cities or countries).

These recruitment agencies charge commission for placing you. This is anything from 15% to over 25% of your contract rate. The larger agencies are more likely to be inflexible about changing or reducing their commission, whilst smaller agencies are more likely to be flexible in order to place a contractor with a new or important client.

Agencies normally have their own Web site which, more often than not, contains a listing of most of their available jobs. The smaller agencies tend not to have their Web site jobs up-to-date. Therefore, you will often find old jobs or roles that are already filled still being advertised on an agency's Web site. The larger agencies can afford an IT department dedicated to maintaining the Web site and updating and deleting redundant, old jobs.

Job hunting through individual agencies' Web sites' jobs can be time consuming. Luckily, there is a solution to this. Specialist, dedicated jobsites have sprung up to act as centralised repositories for agencies and companies to post new jobs. These mega sites can hold tens of thousands of jobs. Some even offer services such as CV upload, CV storage and CV distribution.

The following are a few of these sites for the UK market:

- http://contract.monster.co.uk
- http://www.contractoruk.com/jobs/index.html
- http://www.cv-library.co.uk
- http://www.cwjobs.co.uk
- http://www.jobserve.com
- http://www.jobsite.co.uk
- http://www.reed.co.uk/it
- http://www.theitjobboard.com
- http://www.totaljobs.com

Using Jobserve.com, for instance, to hunt for contracting roles is very easy, and an efficient use of your time. Using the search facilities on the site, you can very quickly isolate and view the most current and relevant roles for yourself and apply for the positions.

You can also save your searches for future use. Jobserve.com even offers the service of immediately e-mailing you new jobs that meet your search criteria. With this feature, you will always be one of the first to know when a new, relevant contract role has been posted.

Applying for contract roles through this method is fast and easy; however, agencies who paste jobs on these job sites are often inundated with applications. Yours can easily get lost in the hundreds they receive. Therefore, to increase your chances of success with this method, I suggested you not only apply immediately to jobs that meet your requirements, but also call the agency to let them know you have applied and you are interested and available to undertake the role.

Outsourcing

Large, outsourcing IT companies have grown in popularity over the last few decades. These companies offer organisations a single source for their IT solutions. They take care of all IT staffing issues by supplying their own, and handling all the paperwork and payroll for the workers. Major outsourcers can also supply all aspects of IT resourcing, from machines movers through support staff, developers, business analysts, project mangers and IT executives, if required.

Outsourcers' main benefits to organisations is the guaranteeing of quality and the fixing of costs. Quality is guaranteed through service level agreements (SLAs) and project plans. The outsourcing company presents a proposal to the organisation for their perusal.

This includes the cost of the contract/project/or service to be provided and a service level agreement. Normally, penalties will apply when SLAs are missed. Furthermore, the outsourcing company normally absorbs any extra costs outside of their proposed bid price (unless stipulated otherwise in the contract).

After much debate and discussion, a final draft of the contract is agreed upon and signed by both parties. The outsourcing company recruits permanent staff, or hires contractors as the need arises to fulfil the contract. Because the outsourcing company's turnover from the contract is fixed, they will seek to cut costs wherever possible to increase their profits from the contract.

Normally, the first places outsourcing companies seek to cut costs are in staff wages and contractor pay. It is therefore unfortunate that working through an outsourcing company is almost never as rewarding as working through an agency or going directly to the client.

The single benefit of working through an outsourcing company is the increased security and guarantee of work. A large outsourcing company will have many clients and will be able to move you to their other clients and supported sites, should the work at your present site dry up or come to an end.

In practice, even this benefit falls short of making up the vast amounts of lost income, resulting from contracting through an agency, then to an outsourcing company or even directly with the outsourcing company.

Basic interview techniques

As we have learned, a good CV will get you to the interview; however, you will determine how far you go from the way you perform at the interview. IT contracts nowadays can arise through telephone interviews or face-to-face interviews. Occasionally the agency will insist on seeing you first, before they send you to their client.

Technical test

The trend in the UK nowadays is to test contractors with a technical test before the one-to-one interview. This test can be in an interview style, on paper or via a computer. Whenever this test is required, you have to pass it first; otherwise, your interview performance will count for very little.

Normally, interviewers are themselves IT staff or managers. Occasionally, an executive may also sit in on the interview, depending on the role that is offered. These interviewers are rarely from HR in most cases, and therefore do not have time to draft proper technical questions to test your skills. Therefore, they most likely will resort to using questions from a relevant certification exam, e.g., MCSE, CCNA, etc.

To give yourself the best chance at this technical exam, make sure you are familiar with the questions and answers for all the relevant certification exams in your field of specialization. This is important as most of the time the questions they ask will be irrelevant to the practical application and execution of your job; however, to get the role you must play the game.

Telephone interview

With the telephone interview, if you are calling the interviewer, make sure you have the job specifications, your CV, a notepad and pen, the interviewers name and the number to dial before you begin. Furthermore, make sure you will not be distracted or disturbed during the interview and if you are calling on your mobile, make sure the signal, reception and battery life are all adequate. Remove all obstructions to clear speech from your mouth, e.g., food, cigarette or chewing gum.

Call a few minutes before you are scheduled to, in case of any delays you may experience in getting through to the interviewer. Even though the interviewer will not see you, smile confidently and ask to speak to your contact. Maintain your confident smile throughout the telephone interview. If you feel nervous, imagine you are interviewing the client, rather than the other way around.

Be enthusiastic, speak clearly and sit confidently. A confident, sitting posture is with your back and spine straight, chin held high, both feet flat on the ground and arms uncrossed.

As the interview proceeds, think before answering. It is fine to pause before answering; this can give the impression that you are listening. Encourage the interviewer to speak more, by answering their questions precisely. Wherever possible, follow your answer with a question to show your interest in the clients and in the role.

Try to match the interviewer's humour. However, do not assume too much and over do this. Similarly, watch your nervous habits such as giggling, saying "errrrm" repeatedly, or rambling on. Remember, people like to hear themselves talk more than they like to hear you talk. Therefore, allow the interviewer to get his/her fair share of talking in. They will enjoy the interview more for it.

Think carefully before asking any questions. Before asking questions, ask yourself if the question will make you look more professional, competent, skilled, relevantly knowledgeable and interested in the role, or not. Never ask questions that the agency can answer such as, how far the site is from the train station, what time is lunch, how long can you take cigarette breaks and what the policy is on sickness.

Your purpose in the interview is to introduce positives about you in the role. Never introduce negatives relating to you and the role. The goal for interviews is simple: get the job. You can tackle any other problems afterward. You can ask all other questions relating to your comfort, leisure or ease of transportation, etc., after the role is yours, and before you sign the contract. Asking these questions earlier can often make you look unprofessional, uncommitted and frankly, like a complaining whiner.

Face-to-face

The face-to-face interview requires more work as the interviewer will be able to see you in person. Because of this, you have to consider your appearance and include personal hygiene in your preparation for the interview.

Make sure you are clean, your hair is presentable, your breath is pleasant smelling, your shoes are polished and if laced, your laces neatly tied. Ladies, if you are wearing a skirt, make sure it is straightened and of appropriate length (just above the knees or below is fine). Avoid mini skirts and overly seductive attire, as this may work against you in certain instances.

Normally, dark (black or grey) suits look more professional compared to brightly coloured or all white attire. This is especially true for men. Women can get away with more adventurous designs and colours, especially blouses and dresses. However, avoid garishly coloured clothes and definitely avoid distracting patterned clothing, or brightly coloured tights or stockings.

It is important to wear clothing that makes you feel confident and not self-conscious. If you wear something that is uncomfortable, you will have a tougher time during the interview. You will be distracted with thoughts of how you look and what they think of your dress, etc.

If you have a body odour problem, make sure you eliminate the odour before you set out for the interview. The most effective deodorant I know of can be found at www.pitrok.co.uk. Similarly, if your breath smells, buy some mouth freshener sweets to disguise the smell before going into the interview. It is also useful to apply some lip balm to dry lips, before setting out to meet the interviewers.

When you meet the interviewer(s), make eye contact as you greet them and smile. Offer a firm handshake. This is very important. Do not offer a limp, wet fish handshake. Conversely, do not crush the interviewer's hands with a vice-like grip. A firm, confident handshake is what is required.

When the interviewer(s) is speaking to you, look him/her in the eyes or – at least – in the face. Make small talk whilst you are being led to the interview room; ask the interviewer how their day was, comment on the weather, or inform him/her how easy your journey was. Avoid all negatives at this stage. Therefore, do not complain about the journey and/or about the difficulties you encountered finding the interview location.

If they offer a drink, always accept and ask for water (it stains the least if you accidentally spill it during the interview).

You may be introduced to several people who may or may not be involved in your interview, repeat their names and memorize them in case you have to refer to them later. People generally prefer it when you remember and use their names.

Try to smile sincerely and warmly during the interview. Sit straight, or lean slightly forward and place your hands on the table in sight of the interviewers. We will discuss the psychology behind this on page 227 under the topic "Advanced interview techniques".

Interview structure

Most IT interviews are composed roughly of three stages: introduction, questioning and closing. The introduction normally involves introduction of the interviewer(s), followed by an explanation of what the organisation does and what your role is to fulfil. This is followed by questions from the interviewers aimed at ascertaining your skill and knowledge level relevancy (relating to the role), your personality, work ethic, attitude, and relevant, past experience(s).

Introduction

The introduction section of the interview is critical. At this stage, it is very important that you listen carefully to the interviewer's meta-language. This is the hidden language behind their words, rather than just what they are saying. It is from this language that you will gain the ammunition to shine at the interview.

The way the interviewer(s) speak of the project, department, job and role can be very telling. For instance, it can tell you how they feel about their job, their role, their department and the organisation. It can also let you in on what the interviewer(s) believe they need or prefer in the successful candidate for the contract role.

They may have had someone who was not punctual, efficient, hardworking, likeable or professional enough in other ways. Listen carefully and make mental notes. You will use this information later on when the interviewer(s) question you.

Questioning

During the question phase of the interview, give succinct, precise and positive answers. Only elaborate where you think or feel you can show that you have the experience, skills and knowledge to fulfil the role. Aim to answer their questions in a way as to hint at you being hard working, conscientious, a team player, punctual, etc.

In fact, if you listened carefully enough during the introduction stage of the interview, you would have heard all that the interviewer(s) were hoping to fill with the role, and the type of person they would like to hire. Simply give them what they hinted at wanting in your answers.

Closing

The closing section is where you get to ask relevant questions about the company, department, project and role. This stage offers you the best opportunity to shine. This is where you can really sell yourself. However, you can also undo all your hard work if you are not careful.

You should only ask questions that promote your relevance for the role. Questions can also help promote your professionalism, and other positive traits such as hard working, team player, good communicator, punctual, etc. Do not over-do it. Try to gauge the interviewer(s) interest. If you see that they have had enough and want to end the interview, end your questioning. As a rule, only ask two to five role-relevant questions.

Asking no questions at all may look like you are not interested in the position or the organisation: whilst asking too many questions will bore and irritate your interviewer(s) who – likely – are anxious to get back to their busy jobs. End your questioning with a positive and upbeat comment such as, "Thank you for answering all my questions, I feel I understand the role and what you are looking for. I am confident that I can fulfil this position and add value to the project/(team)."

At the end of the interview, shake the interviewer(s) hands firmly, and thank them for their time again before departing.

Pitfalls

Never discuss or mention the following at your interview:

- Your pay rate.
- Negative experiences, people or circumstances regarding your previous employer(s).
- Any unconstructive attributes about yourself.

- Anything pessimistic about the role/project or organisation, unless specifically asked; and then an accurate and succinct answer will contribute to securing the job.

Always refer payroll queries to HR (if you are applying direct), or pose the questions to your agency. It is a major contracting faux pas to discuss your rate at the interview. It gives the impression that you care more for the money than doing a good job. It could also make you seem greedy, undeserving or overpaid in some cases.

Whilst it may be tempting to slate your previous employer – especially if you did not like them – the interview is not the place. Doing so makes you look disloyal. This could reduce your chances of securing the contract role. Always be positive about your previous employer, and if you cannot say anything positive, refrain from saying anything negative. Find a way to at least remain neutral in your comments or tone.

Similarly, refrain from talking yourself down, swearing or being vulgar. If you find the interviewer attractive in a sexual way, refrain from flirting with them and definitely do not make any comments that could be construed as a come-on/chat up, or anything else in that direction. Remain professional throughout the entire interview.

Avoid scratching, fidgeting, fussing with your hair, rocking back and forth, picking lint from your clothing or more serious antisocial habits; (e.g. winking, burping, picking your nose, wiping a runny nose with your sleeve or the back of your hand, or farting during the interview). All these actions and habits highlight weakness in your character.

Often, after you have learned what the organisation is doing, you may object to they method or process(es) being used by the organization which may be antiquated or just plain wrong. Refrain from correcting the managers or educating them at the interview. Remember your sole mission during that interview is to secure the role. Arguing, correcting, educating or lecturing the interviewer(s) is one of the quickest ways not to get the job. No one likes to be made a fool.

Negotiating a rate

Once you have been to the interview, you will have more of a feel for what the client may be prepared to pay. If, during the interview, the interviewer(s) repeatedly mentioned how expensive contractors were, and how tight the role/project budget was, you might not have much room for negotiating the rate. However, if the interviewer and client seemed oblivious to your cost, and the project budget constrictions have not been mentioned, you may be in a good position to negotiate the rate before you start the job.

If you are going direct, you will have to deal with the HR department of the organisation, or sometimes directly with the project manager. In this case, you have to be very careful not to upset the client and blow the role totally. Aim for a 10% or more increase, whenever possible.

Temper this with how much the client seemed to like you. If they really liked you and are prepared to do anything to keep you, you can negotiate for a higher rate; however, if they selected you out of several other equally good interviewees, then I suggest you do not negotiate too hard.

Going through the agency is better for this kind of negotiation. In addition, sometimes the agency will take a cut in their commission in order to place you, if the other candidates come from competing agencies. The client will also be more frank with the agency concerning what they thought of you, than you may ever find out directly from the interviewers. Therefore, the agency can give you a more accurate feedback in which to base your negotiations.

In cases where the agency put forward several contractors for the same role, you can ask for the range of tentative rates, and then negotiate for the highest – after you have safely secured the position through the interview. The aim here is to get a slight increase on your rate without losing the contract. If at any stage it looks like you could lose the role, then take what is offered. Push the limits but do not break the bank.

Writing an effective IT contracting CV

The first stop we will make on the journey to becoming an IT contractor is your CV. Agencies, lecturers and even other contractors will all be ready to advise you on how to set out your CV for maximum effectiveness. Just keep one thing in mind, a contractor CV is not the same as a permie CV.

Several things become blatantly clear when you examine what an agency and/or organisation is looking for in a contractor CV.

Firstly, the IT contractor is viewed as a resource or service provider by an organisation, whilst permies are viewed as part of the organisation. After this period, the business relation will terminate.

Secondly, the contractor is viewed as a short-term resource. They may be on the organisation's site for a few months or at most, a few years. The permie is viewed as a long-term investment by the organisation, and most organisations seek to protect and keep their investment. They also seek to get more value from this investment by training and developing their permie staff.

On the other hand, the contractor should hit the ground running, possessing all the required skills and knowledge necessary to carry out and successfully complete the contracted work.

From these two observations, you can see that emphasizing your need for further development in your permie CV may help you get a permie job, but in a contract position it will eliminate your consideration for an interview.

Whilst a permie job is offered with a long-term view in mind, most contract roles are offered with the opposite in mind. Therefore, highlighting your hobbies and other information that are not relevant to the contract is counterproductive, and a waste of space on your CV.

Details such as where you went to kindergarten, nursery school or the summer jobs you undertook between colleges or university, may not be relevant to interviewers who are primarily looking for proof of your skills, knowledge, training and ability to successfully execute and complete the contracts' objectives.

Highlight relevant current skills and knowledge

This brings us to the first point in creating an effective CV. Your IT contracting CV has to emphasize what the interviewers want to see. Stress your proficiency with the relevant skills, (and where and when you obtained the skills) and knowledge required for their roles. The more recent your skills and knowledge are, the better your chances of getting the contract – based on your skills – will be.

If you are applying for a C# contract but your most recent role was using Java, flesh out the C# experience more, and highlight the relevant skills and knowledge acquired in that position. Similarly, if you are applying for a Microsoft Vista support role, accentuate where you have previously used it, what you used it for, and how good you are with supporting it and all user groups who use it.

Do not forget to draw attention to relevant, non-technical skills, knowledge or abilities. Some of the skills, knowledge, abilities and facts to consider highlighting, to assist you in acquiring your next contract, are as follows:

- Being a team leader.
- Ability to work away from home.

- Telecommuting – (working from your home).
- Willingness or ability to perform shift work.
- Dedication to working long hours when necessary.
- Freedom to travel nationally or internationally.
- Ability to chair a meeting, or minutes taking.
- Knowledgeable at new staff interviewing.
- Skills at documentation writing.
- Experience at implementing new processes.
- Being a team player.
- Ability to work unsupervised.
- Versatility at liaising with all levels of users, from directors down.
- Verbal skills such as being bi or multilingual.
- Proximity of closeness to the contract site.
- Being a car owner with a clean driving license/record.

Remember, every contract you get will potentially earn you thousands of pounds; therefore, it is worth your while to take the time to tailor your CV to the contract role. An hour or two of effort will be more than worth it when you are selected for the position.

Eliminate potentially negative information

Some minor information on your CV can cause you to miss being selected for an interview. A piece of information such as your age, hobbies, nationality and address, could be the cause of your CV being rejected.

The CV is your ticket to the interview, whilst the interview stage is the best place to sell yourself and convince an organisation that you can do the work required, fit into their team and add instant value to their company.

Therefore, do not try to convey on your CV, what you can do better at your interview. The CV should remain what it is, a key to the interview.

Your age, nationality and address can be a consideration. Too old or too young are equally bad. Your nationality could also cause you to suffer discrimination through prejudice. Similarly, your address can seem too far from the client's site, and thus you might be overlooked for selection, based on this alone. In most cases, if you are allowed to attend an interview, you could sell yourself by eliminating any possible negative points, by explaining to the interviewers your side of the story.

For instance, at the interview you can show that you have a five-year work permit, and you are currently applying for residence and citizenship; thus nullifying the nationality issue. Similarly, you could explain how you have previously worked further from site without it affecting your punctuality or enthusiasm. You can see from these two examples how you can correct misconceptions and assumptions at the interviewing stage. In fact, if these facts were not on your CV, no judgment or prejudice would result.

Eliminate dull visual appearance

Some CVs are visually uninteresting simply because of lack of variety in font type, font sizes and colour or shading. A CV written in one font style and two font sizes can be hard on the eyes. Visually, it looks lifeless, uninteresting and even though the content might be good, when faced with hundreds of CVs to wade through; an interviewer would most likely avoid the boring ones.

An interviewer, or CV reader looks for certain information on each CV they must read. The CV selection process then, is as follows:

1. Visual presentation.
2. Immediacy of relevance.
3. Further reinforcement of relevant details.
4. Extra points that highlight your suitability for the role.

Visual presentation

What does the CV you hand to the client look like? Is it clean or dirty, properly stapled or falling apart, standard paper sized or non-standard paper size, too long or a page or two only? Is it visually exciting to read with interesting fonts, headings, colours or shadings, lines, etc., or is it monotonic in visual appearance?

Give your CV life; use at least four font sizes. Vary the presentation with italics, colour, shading or lines, bold and standard font styles. You can also use different font types, however, this is not a necessity because if executed incorrectly, it could work against you.

Use headings to break up and group related information. Headings such as 'Profile', 'Professional Experience', 'Education' and 'Professional Certification' help to direct the readers' eyes to the relevant sections faster, making your CV easier to read.

Break up the descriptions of your contract roles into several sections and use headers to highlight the sections:

- Client
- Period
- Location
- Sector
- Role
- Software
- Hardware
- Projects
- Notes

Maintain the format for all the other contract role descriptions. The uniformity of a template allows the eyes to find information quicker and follow the CV more easily. See Table 4: Sample contract role with headers. It is easy to pick out the hardware used, software used, etc., when this is the format utilized.

You could use a more minimal, and perhaps more elegant template as illustrated in Table 5: Sample simple contract CV first page. The use of the black section highlights gives the CV a sophisticated and elegant look, making it appealing at first glance.

You should always study towards the latest, relevant industry certification, and this should be highlighted on your CV with "Currently studying for MCSE" or "Currently Studying for PRINCE 2", etc.

CLIENT:	XYZ Limited
PERIOD:	Aug 2007 July 2008
LOCATION:	London
SECTOR:	Insurance
ROLE:	**Rollout Team Leader**
Software:	Windows XP Professional, MS Office 2003, SMS, Norton Antivirus, TWINS, OSCAR suite, MS IE6, Windows NT Server, Windows 2000 Server, Windows 2003 Server, Remedy, Vantive, Citrix, MS Access 97, Lotus SmartSuite, Lotus Notes 4.65, 5.x, 6.5, Windows 98, and more.
Hardware:	HP Printers, IBM Laptops, EMC, IBM Servers, IBM Desktops, Vodaphone GPRS and 3G cards, Intel Network cards, Blackberry, Palm and more.
Projects:	Deployment of Windows XP across a 780 user base in the UK for ABC Ltd. The role involved the following: **CONTRACT WAS RENEWED 4 TIMES.**
Notes:	Prior to the ABC Ltd rollout in the UK, I temporarily supervised a team of 12 support engineers for XYZ Limited with their XP deployment. This involved coordinating resources and assigning calls through the Vantive system to engineers across the UK and Europe..

Table 4: Sample contract role with headers

Jonathon A. Bloggs
☏ (044) 1234 56789 / 0123 456 789
✉ Joe_Bloggs@bloggs.com

Profile

A graduate with an upper second BSc honours degree in Technology Management, and both an MCSE 2003 & 2000. I will be bringing on board my strong analytical skills; excellent communication skills from working with clients ranging from CEOs to Traders; several years of experience working well as part of a team; and furthermore, invaluable knowledge gained from working in major Blue chip organisations. I thrive on challenges, meeting deadlines to client satisfaction, as shown with proven long term contract renewals from top major financial institutions. As a highly motivated self-starter, I am eager to prove myself invaluable in a fulfilling business career.

Professional Experience

XYZ Feb 06 – Present

Trade Floor Support (Contract – renewed 6 times)
Trade floor support for cash, derivatives, fixed income, foreign exchange, equity, energy and commodities brokers. Supported Reuters, Bloomberg, Fidessa and other market data apps (Swapswire, Trayport Global Vision, Easy Screen, Kalahari, Fenics, ICE and Eurex, etc.); and voice support of IPC Dealerboards. Applications supported were MS Office 2003, Outlook 2003, Exchange 5.5/2003, and IE 6 on Windows XP/Win 2000 to registry level. Supported Excel to macro level. Carried out Active Directory administration with AD tools. Supported BlackBerry's and undertook PC and Laptop builds. Troubleshooting network connectivity problems over the LAN/WAN. Used Citrix, Remote Desktop and VPN software. Resolved faults on bespoke Java, Oracle, Sybase, SQL, UNIX and ODBC based software. Fixed hardware faults. Users were both on site and internationally based. Supported the CEO, Brokers/Traders and Back Office staff.

Table 5: Sample simple contract CV first page

Education

MCSE (Microsoft Certified Systems Engineer) 2003

- (MCP) Managing & Maintaining a Microsoft Windows Server 2003 Environment for an MCSA. Certified on Windows 2000.
- (MCP) Planning, Implementing and Maintaining a Microsoft Windows Server 2003 environment for an MCSE. Certified on Windows 2000.

MCSE (Microsoft Certified Systems Engineer) 2000

- (MCP) Installing, Configuring & Administering Windows 2000 Professional.
- (MCP) Installing, Configuring & Administering Windows 2000 Server.
- (MCP) Installing, Configuring & Administering XP.
- (MCP) Managing a Microsoft Windows 2000 Network Environment.
- (MCP) Implementing and Administering a Microsoft Windows 2000 Directory Services Infrastructure.
- (MCP) Implementing and Administering a Microsoft Windows 2000 Network Infrastructure.
- (MCP) Designing a Microsoft Windows 2000 Directory Services Infrastructure.

BSc (Hon) Computing Degree   2:1
Sample University (The City)   1994 – 1996

Currently studying for 070-620 and 070-624 (Vista)

Table 6: Sample CV Education section

Highlight the good and mask the bad

Most of us go to great lengths to appear better than we may naturally be. Some women use make-up, hairstyles and stylish clothing to enhance their appearances. Similarly, men often use stylish attire, hairstyles, scents, watches and expensive cars to enhance their profile. You must learn to do the same on your CV.

Always emphasize your best attributes first on your CV. If you attained an inappropriate degree or college qualifications for the position in which you are applying, but have since attained excellent training and specific, relevant IT certification – stress the applicable IT certification first, at the top of the education section of your CV.

If you have a poor education and certification record, minimise the damage by drawing as little attention to it as possible on your CV. Use one-line descriptions for the education and do not include the result attained. You can explain it better at the interview if they ask questions about it. Most likely, if you are good at IT, well experienced and knowledgeable, your work experience will be sufficient to disguise your poor academic qualifications.

Never blatantly lie on your CV. This will always get you in trouble sometime in the future. Instead, use data masking techniques to hide poor sections of your CV. For instance, if you have an excellent academic performance history but a short and poor work experience, you may want to move the education section to the forefront, immediately after your profile declaration.

Flesh out all sections you wish to highlight. Therefore, in this example, you would emphasize with bullet points on the academic course(s) content, and accentuate the results attained in large, bold font. The poor work experience section can then be masked and minimised by having it follow the education section, or even further back after a skills breakdown section.

SEO considerations

SEO stands for search engine optimisation. Most agencies use search tools to crawl through their database of CVs for relevant skills matching their job requirements. By making your CV SEO friendly, you stand a better chance of being short-listed for relevant jobs.

Representatives at agencies are very busy and do not have time to look through the thousands of CVs on their database for job matches. They depend on software with search facilities to find relevant candidate CVs.

If your CV does not contain every hardware, software and relevant technology you know, you may not turn up on searches. It is for this reason why I introduced the skill matrix at the end of my CV. See Table 7: Sample CV skills matrix for more details.

In Table 7, you can see that each skill/knowledge is scored out of one hundred percent. This represents your proficiency at the particular skill or technology. The scoring is not necessary for SEO purposes, however, it will help validate the purpose of having the matrix on your CV in the first place.

This matrix is solely to help you list all the technologies and skills that you have. This greatly increases the chance of your CV being discovered among the hundreds or thousands of others held by agencies. You can also include a key to explain the scoring as illustrated in Table 7.

An industry/experience matrix is also useful (see Table 8). Contractors are often typecast based on the last roles' industry. You will find that you tend to get calls mainly for work with companies within the industry, or similar industries in which you have recently worked.

Software	%	N O/S	%	Hardware	%
MS Office 2003/2000/97/95	82	Windows 2003/200	79	PCs (HP, Compaq, Dell, IBM & others)	80
Outlook 2000/98/97, Exchange 2000/5.5/4, CC Mail, MS Mail.	89	Microsoft Virtual Server 2005	70	PC Peripherals and components (Network cards, HDDs, FDDs, CD/DVD drives, Jazz drives, Scanners, Sound cards, Modems and Memory)	80
Lotus Notes	79	NT4 Server	79	Printers (HP, Lexmark, Brother, Canon, Epson, Xerox)	75
Lotus Smartsuite	70	Windows XP	80	Laptops (HP, Sony, Compaq, Toshiba, Dell, IBM)	80
Reuters	80	Windows 2000	80	Apple Mac	58
Bloomberg	80	NT 4.0	80		
Factset	75	NT 3.51	80		
Datastream	75	Win 98/95	80		
MS Access	68	Win 3.11/3.1	80		
MS Project	65	Novell NetWare	75		
Oracle Applications	55	VAX/VMS	80		
Internet Explorer	80	DOS 6.X	70		
Rumba	75				
PDAS (BlackBerry's, Palm Pilots, Sony's, Compaq IPAQs, Psion's and HP Jornadas)	78				
Antivirus Software: McAfee, Norton and Dr Solomon's	75				
Call Logging software: Remedy, Quetzel, Altiris, Heat, Pursuit, Clarify Magic and Track-It.	40				

Key	
0-49	User
50-89	Support
90-100	Expert

Table 7: Sample CV skills matrix

Industries	Experience In Years
Finance	6
Energy	3
Bio-Tech	2 ½
Accounting	2 ¾
Media	1 ½

Table 8: Sample CV Industry experience table

Using this industry/experience matrix helps agencies whose clients prefer contractors with industry experience. However, this matrix is only worth using if you have extensive experience in many industries. Using the matrix to accentuate your experience within one or two industries, will be counterproductive.

References

Some agencies will insist that they must have references before they can put you forward for a role. Most of the time, this simply is not true. What some agencies like to do is collect key contacts at organisations and later approach them to place other clients. It is for this reason, as well as to avoid upsetting your referees, that you should never write referee details on your CV.

A simple, "References provided upon request" at the end of your CV, will suffice. Be prepared for these requests to come. Make sure you have referee details of managers or team leaders from your previous roles at hand. Normally, references from the last two roles are sufficient for this purpose, although in some cases, up to four references may be required.

Most organisations now have a HR policy of not supplying references for contractors. This is to minimise their legal obligations in cases where a contractor whom they provided a positive reference, turns out to be the opposite – causing damage to another organisation.

The most these organisations are prepared to offer is a verification of the period you worked with them. In some cases, HR departments are even reluctant to disclose these details. In these cases, they will send the reference to the agency. The agency can only provide a verification of your time in the role.

Here is where your networking and relationship with individual managers and team leaders will come into its own. Keep in touch with your colleagues and managers from previous roles. Make sure you ask their permission before you use them as references.

Furthermore, make sure you qualify and verify that they are on your side, friendly towards you and willing to provide positive references, before using them as referees. Name, role, company, contact number, contact e-mail and possibly contact address, are all that you will likely need.

Some contractors use other contractors as referees in a "scratch my back, and I will scratch yours" basis. This is dishonest and should be avoided; especially if the contractor you use as a referee was not really your manager or team leader.

Shortening your long CV

Many people will tell you that the shorter your CV is, the better. This is not necessarily true. If your CV is overly long, all that will happen is that the vast majority of it will never be read. If you have such a CV (over five pages long), then it is even more important that you place all the relevant, positive and important details at the beginning.

There are a few points to observe which might help shorten a long CV. The following are some of these tips:

- *Paper size:* Use A4 or letter sized paper only.

- ***Font size:*** Use font size 12 for the majority of the CV content. You can use larger fonts, highlighting, shading, lines, boxes or even colour throughout your CV, but the main text under each heading or section should ideally be in font size 12.
- ***Old jobs:*** Shorten all your old roles to a few lines (see Table 9). The company name, your role, the sector and the period will suffice to highlight these old roles.

OTHER CONTRACT ROLES

CLIENT:	Equitas
PERIOD:	Aug 2003 – Jun 2004 **(contract renewed 4 times)**
SECTOR:	Insurance
ROLE:	*3rd line and server support specialist role.*
CLIENT:	**EduAction**
PERIOD:	Mar 2003 – Jul 2003 **(contract renewed)**
SECTOR:	Government (Non-military)
ROLE:	*Network and desktop team leader role involving remote support of 70 plus sites in the Waltham Forrest Borough.*
CLIENT:	**Sports England**
PERIOD:	Sep 2002 – Mar 2003 **(contract renewed 2 times)**
SECTOR:	Government (Non-military)
ROLE:	*Network & desktop support role involving remote support of 10 regions in the UK.*

Table 9: Sample CV example of other roles section

- ***Short roles:*** Group your short roles together as illustrated in the following example:

SHORT ROLES   1994 – 2000

Anthony Nolan (2 months): 2nd line support for NetWare, Mac and Sun.
Westinghouse Electric (1 ½ months): 2nd and 3rd line support.
Metro New Media (1 month): Project management role for borough-wide Internet access.
The London Exchange (1 ½ months): 2nd and 3rd line support.
Bank National De Paris (1 month): Operations.
European Bank of Industry (1 ½ months): 2nd and 3rd line support.
Kingston Hospital (1 month): 2nd line dell workstation role out.
LGS Logic (3 months): Internet strategy and Business Consultant.
Morgan Stanley Dean Witter (1 week): 500 Trader floor migration and set-up.

Table 10: Sample CV short roles section

- *White spaces:* Remove excessive blank lines, spacing or double spacing, etc.
- *Eliminate non-relevant jobs:* If you have extensive contracting history (e.g., over five years), and your CV still contains summer jobs, part-time or non-IT work you did over five years ago, then eliminate them from your CV. Keep your CV relevant to the roles you are applying for. Even if your IT employment history is brief and you have to fall back on some of your non-IT roles, you can highlight and embellish the little IT you used in these roles.
- *Eliminate unnecessary past education details:* If you have a relevant degree or college qualification, you may not need to include your pre-college education details. Your high school, pre-high school and kindergarten details may not be necessary here.
- *Flatten name and address:* Decrease the number of lines you use to specify your name, address and contact details. Firstly, some agency's word processors and filing systems remove headers and footers; therefore, avoid using headers and footers on your CV. Secondly, place your name and contact details on every page of your CV (preferably at the top). This is to avoid pages becoming lost from your CV

after they are printed. Finally, avoid using your address. You only need your name on a line by itself, your number and e-mail address on a different line.

Chapter 2
Maintenance and Fine-Tuning

- How to Select an Accountant
- How to Protect Yourself from Litigation
- Handling the Tax Man Properly
- How to Secure Your Future
- Handling Your Money Effectively

*Maintenance and Fine-***Tuning**

We have covered how to prepare and enter the IT contracting industry, now we'll look at how to maintain your contracting business and build on it. We shall examine at the following areas:

1. How to select an accountant.
2. How to protect yourself from litigation.
3. Handling the tax man properly.
4. How to secure your future.
5. Handling your money effectively.

How to Select an Accountant

Like setting up your own company, you can also do your own accounts, and get it looked over and signed off by a chartered accountant once a year. However, this is not necessarily the best use of your time and energy. Moreover, a qualified specialist accountant can offer you much more than you may be able to bring to the table. Therefore, unless you were a specialist IT contracting accountant and tax specialist in your pre-contracting life, I advise you to seek the services of a chartered specialist accountant.

Specialist accountants

Unlike a general accountant, the specialist IT contracting accountant only deals with contracting issues and clients. This gives the specialist superior experience, knowledge and perspective of the pitfalls, loopholes and current and future issues related exclusively to IT contractors. Furthermore, because the specialist only deals with IT contractors, they are more likely to have specific, all inclusive packages for contactors. These packages will cost you a fixed monthly fee, and will normally include the following:

- Preparation of accounts.
- Corporation tax return.
- Payroll matters.
- Statutory affairs.
- Tax planning.
- Telephone and e-mail support.

Personal accountants

Avoid accountants that are related to you. Personal issues could get in the way of the business relationship and vice-versa. Relatives may not be the best qualified, but because they are related – and possibly dirt cheap, you may be tempted to use their services. However, this could place an unnecessary strain on your relationship further down the line when money problems arise.

MSC accountants

Avoid accountants that operate or deal with an MSC and/or come across as being open to "creative" accountancy practices. When they eventually are caught by the HMRC, you could be implicated in their accounts. This could cost you dearly in unpaid taxes – backdated.

Accountancy firms

If you select an accountancy firm, make sure you are assigned to the account of someone who is a chartered accountant. Whilst large accountancy firms offer a broad range of specialisations and services, they can also be impersonal, leaving you to always deal with the "duty" accountant or worse – a helpdesk. Not having a familiar person to deal with at the partner level, can be frustrating as you may find yourself explaining your situation and repeating your requests every time you call.

Smaller accountants

If you can find it, look for a smaller accountancy firm that does not charge to answer your questions via the telephone, or to reply to your letters and e-mail.

Fixed rate and percentage charging

Choose an accountant that charges a fixed rate for his/her services. Accountants that itemise their bills will be more interested in increasing their income though finding creative new ways to charge you, more than they would be to offer you good service.

There is a good argument for accountants that charge a percentage of the money they save you in taxes. However, these may be too motivated to go down the "creative" accountancy path in the name of boosting their profits.

Proactive or Reactive

Depending on the accountant you use, and how you pay them, your accountant will be proactive or reactive. Reactive accountants are passive. They simply do only the obligatory service paid for, whilst proactive accountants will seek out new ways to save you money – this type of accountant normally costs more. However, they are worth their weight in gold. They normally save you more than you pay them.

Selection process

Select your accountant by first asking around to other contractors for recommendations, before you follow-up on adverts and marketing propaganda. Unfortunately, most contractors do not really know how to judge a good accountant effectively. What they go by however, will weed out the terrible accountants from the rest, leaving you to ask further questions and complete your own due diligence. The following is a list of what you should look out for in an accountant:

- They are honest, open and forthright.
- They specialise in IT contracting.
- They are IT literate (spreadsheets, e-mail, FTP, Internet, e-filing, PDF files, etc.).
- They do not charge you extra for using their office as the companies registered office (if you need to);
- They do not charge you extra for answering your questions.
- They do not charge you extra for calling, faxing, mailing or e-mailing you.
- They do not charge extra for doing your personal tax return (UK Form P11D).
- They do not charge you for discontinuing their services.
- They never miss tax or VAT return deadlines.
- They answer their phones and e-mail promptly.
- They deal with mail promptly.
- They advise you of the implications of each Budget announcement by the Chancellor.
- They send you a Christmas card each year (optional).

There are IT contracting accountants that offer the entire list as part of their standard package – shop around and you will find them. Do not settle for anything less. Over time, your relationship with your accountant should grow to be your most trusted business relationship. If you find a good accountant, you will have found another source of income, after all, money you save from the taxman is extra money earned.

How to Protect Yourself from Litigation

In most cases, if you contract through a Ltd. Company, your liabilities are limited to assets owned by the company. Therefore, your main risk from litigation, will be a lawsuit aimed at your company. It is your responsibility to ensure your company can afford to defend itself or pay out if you lose the case. The most sensible way of insuring against such an outcome is through adequate, professional indemnity insurance cover.

The risks

As you contract, you will be exposed to various risks. The following are some of these hazards:

- **Libel** – False and malicious publications printed for the purpose of defaming a company.
- **Slander** – Words falsely spoken that damage a company's reputation.
- **Errors and omissions** – Neglecting to do something; leaving out, or passing over something.
- **Professional neglect** – Failure to follow a particular standard of operation.
- **Malicious falsehood** – A false and malicious lie, intentionally uttered to cause damage or harm.
- **Passing off copyrights** – A company or individual falsely presenting themselves as the owner of

copyrights (this is also known as copyright infringement).

- **Infringement of intellectual property rights** – Intellectual property rights infraction.
- **Breach of confidentiality** – A security violation where the confidentiality of data or information was lost.
- **Negligent misstatements** – A representation of fact, (carelessly made), which led to a company being disadvantaged.
- **Negligent actions** – An action which causes harm to another.
- **Loss of documents** – Loss of documents resulting in a security breach or disadvantage to another party.
- **Dishonesty of employees** – Financial loss resulting from the fraudulent activities of one or more employees.

Which types are available?

Some of the features included in professional indemnity insurance are as follows:

- Public Liability
- Employers Liability
- Legal Expenses
- Accident & Sickness

If you have been contracting without this insurance, look for policies that offer free, retroactive (backdated) cover. Most insurers charge extra for this; however, a few do not. Expect to pay less than a couple of hundred pounds sterling per year, for this cover in the UK. Caunce O'Hara provides policies with all the options mentioned above. You can find them online at www.caunceohara.co.uk.

Without this protection, you are open to all sorts of litigation and lawsuits. Therefore, secure your company from the risk by obtaining sufficient insurance cover before you undertake any IT contracting work. Normally, £500,000 to £1,000,000 professional indemnity cover is sufficient; however, please check with the agency or the organisation you are about to sign a contract with, to be sure.

Run-off cover

In most cases, even after you stop contracting, you still need cover to protect against litigation that could be brought against you for damages suffered, or that they claim resulted due to your tenure. This is called 'run off cover'.

Whilst contracting, if you suspect that you may be at risk from litigation – without breaching the clients confidentiality or taking any negligent actions – start keeping records and make copies of all communications that will assist you, if a case is brought against you. In short, cover your back.

Similarly, always operate with the highest fidelity and professionalism. This more than anything, will ensure that you avoid the vast majority of legal risks. The contracting industry is very insular and word gets around fast. If you sue and win a case against a client, it might prejudice other organisations and agencies against hiring you in the future. Some contractors will jokingly say that if the settlement is large enough, this outcome will not matter anyway, as you could retire earlier, however humorous this may be – concerning litigation – avoidance is better than involvement.

Paying your taxes

As an UK IT contractor, your company will deal with the HMRC for Pay-As-You-Earn (PAYE) income tax and National Insurance Contributions (NIC), Corporation Tax Self

Assessment (CTSA) and Value Added Tax (VAT) – if you are VAT registered.

If you are using an Umbrella company, you will only deal with HMRC for your PAYE and NIC. The Umbrella company, on behalf of the HMRC, withholds PAYE and NIC; therefore, you really have little involvement, and there is little room for getting yourself into trouble in this scenario.

However, for Ltd. company contractors, it is another story. Ltd company directors have to pay their own PAYE and NIC, CTSA and VAT. This means you have to operate your own PAYE and NIC system, and pay CTSA and VAT. Missed payments of any of these taxes, will result in heavy fines. If you default repeatedly, the severity of the fines will grow accordingly.

Furthermore, if the transgression is serious enough, you could face penalties that are more serious. It is therefore critical that you respect these tax laws and avoid the HMRC penalties, at all costs. We will next examine the various taxes a Ltd. company contractor has to pay.

National Insurance Contributions

If you employ people in your company, including yourself as a limited company director, you will need to deduct income tax and National Insurance Contributions (NIC), from their pay – before they receive their wages. All employees whose weekly income surpasses a set limit must pay NIC.

It is useful to understand how NIC is calculated; however, you can easily carry this out by using the software tools provided by the HMRC – via the Employer CD-ROM or the HMRC Web site. To calculate the correct NIC deduction, use Table 11: Rates and Allowances - National Insurance Contributions to determine the employees NIC class. The NIC class and the weekly income of the employee will determine the NIC rate to apply, (note the grey shaded rows in the table are the exception to weekly earnings – they are annual earnings and profit limits).

National Insurance - Rates and Allowances

£ per week	2006-07	2007-08
Lower earnings limit, primary Class 1	£84	£87
Upper earnings limit, primary Class 1	£645	£670
Primary threshold	£97	£100
Secondary threshold	£97	£100
Employees' primary Class 1 rate between primary threshold and upper earnings limit.	11%	11%
Employees' primary Class 1 rate above upper earnings limit.	1%	1%
Employees' contracted-out rebate.	1.6%	1.6%
Married women's reduced rate between primary threshold and upper earnings limit.	4.85%	4.85%
Married women's rate above upper earnings limit.	1%	1%
Employers' secondary Class 1 rate above secondary threshold.	12.8%	12.8%
Employers' contracted-out rebate, salary-related schemes.	3.5%	3.7%
Employers' contracted-out rebate, money-purchase schemes.	1%	1.4%
Class 2 rate	£2.10	£2.20
Class 2 small earnings exception (per year)	£4,465	£4,635
Special Class 2 rate for share fishermen	£2.75	£2.85
Special Class 2 rate for volunteer development workers	£4.20	£4.35
Class 3 rate	£7.55	£7.80
Class 4 lower profits limit (per year)	£5, 035	£5, 225
Class 4 upper profits limit (per year)	£33, 540	£34, 840
Class 4 rate between lower profits limit and upper profits limit.	8%	8%
Class 4 rate above upper profits limit.	1%	1%

Table 11: Rates and Allowances - National Insurance Contributions

NIC is a combination of the employee's contributions – deducted from the employee's pay – and contributions paid by your Ltd. company. There are many classes of NICs, however, for most contractors with a limited company class 2 and class 4 will apply. Some people may choose to pay the voluntary class 3 contributions as well. This is only necessary if your contributions in class 2 and 4 are not sufficient for you to qualify for the basic state pension. Currently the class 3 contribution is £7.80 per week.

Class	Description
Class 1	Paid by people who work as employed earners, and their employers.
Class 1A	Paid only by employers who provide certain directors and employees with benefits in kind which are available for private use, for example, cars and fuel.
Class 1B	Paid only by employers who enter into a Pay-As-You-Earn (PAYE) Settlement Agreement (PSA) with HM Revenue & Customs for tax purposes.
Class 2	Paid by people who are self-employed.
Class 3	Voluntary contributions paid by people who wish to protect their entitlement to the State Pension and who do not pay enough National Insurance contributions in another class.
Class 4	Normally paid by self-employed people in addition to Class 2. Class 4 contributions do not count towards benefits.

Table 12: Summary of the six classes of National Insurance Contributions

People under 16 years of age and women over 60, or men over 65 years, are exempt from paying NIC. A 'Certificate of Age Exception' (CA4140/CF384), is required to qualify for this exemption. You can apply for this through your accountant, or contact:

HM Revenue & Customs
National Insurance Contributions Office
Contributor Caseworker
Longbenton
Newcastle upon Tyne
NE98 1ZZ

Mileage payments

If you use your own vehicle to do business miles, you can exempt part of your wages from NIC. The following are the amounts that are deductible:

Motor cars and vans	
First 10,000 business miles	40p per mile
Over 10,000 business miles	25p per mile
Motorcycles	24p per mile
Cycles	20p per mile

Table 13: Maximum amounts deductible for own car use in doing business miles

This means that you can pay this to the employee or director without paying NIC. For NIC purposes only, use the deduction for the first 10,000 miles, irrespective of the distance travelled. The taxable value of a benefit depends on its type:

Expenses and Benefit in Kind	Exemption conditions:
Assets placed at the disposal of an employee	• For transfer of the ownership of an asset, Class 1A NIC will apply if employee earns more than £8,500 annually.
Assets transferred to an employee	• Goods and services provided by an employer to an employee are charged on the second hand value less the amount the employee paid, unless the employee is legally unable to turn the asset into cash (e.g., wines and spirits).
Beneficial loans	• Interest free loans that keep the outstanding loan within any tax year below £5,000 will be tax and NIC free. Otherwise, the excess will be charged interest on the difference between the official rate of interest (currently 5%) and the interest paid.
Car benefit	• You pay tax and Class 1A NIC if you have a car provided by an employer.
Car fuel benefit	• If your employee provides you with fuel for a car, the fuel will attract Class 1A NIC.
Homeworking	• Furniture, computer equipment (first £500), office supplies, Internet connection and telephone lines supplied by an employer for the sole purpose of an employee working from home are exempt from tax and NIC.
Living accommodation	• The value of the home or rent will be taxed and NICs will apply.
Medical treatment and insurance	• Insurance policies taken out against an employee where the employer makes the claims, and is directly reimbursed by the

	insurer without first incurring the charges, are exempt from tax and NIC.
	• All medical treatment incurred by an employer by an employee working abroad.
	• Periodic check-ups and eye tests are exempt from tax and NIC.
	• Provision of spectacles solely for VDU usage is also exempt. An employer can also save money in a trust fund which it can withdraw at will for the purpose of employee medical costs. As long as:
	  ○ Each employee does not have the right to have the cost of treatment paid from the fund.
	  ○ The annual contribution in respect of each employee is not identifiable.
	  ○ Once paid, the employer can recover its contribution.

Mileage payments	• Payments made in arrears which are calculated at pence per mile rate, where car use is for one employer only, at or below the statutory rates[11] and only for business use, are exempt from tax and NIC.
Relocation expenses and benefits	The following tax and NICs exemptions apply on the following, up to £8,000: • The relocation expenses must be incurred, or the relocation benefits provided, before the end of the tax year following the one in which the employee starts the new job.

[11] See Table 13 for the statutory rates.

- Disposal or intended disposal of an old residence.
- Acquisition or intended acquisition of a new residence, transporting belongings.
- Travelling and subsistence.
- Domestic goods for the new residence.
- Bridging loans.

Not-exempt:
- Mortgage or housing subsidies if the employee moves to a higher cost area.
- Compensation paid for any loss on sale of the employee's home.
- Interest payments for the mortgage on the employee's existing home.
- Re-direction of mail.
- Council for tax bills.
- Purchase of new school uniforms for employee's children.
- Counselling services.
- Compensation for loss in value of season tickets.
- Cost of joining new sports clubs.
- Penalties for giving insufficient notice of child's withdrawal from school – loss of school fees.
- Cost of buying new school uniforms.
- Help towards an employee's spouse finding a job; career and education counselling/job search agency.
- Home search facility.
- Financial advice.
- Nanny agency fees.
- House cleaning upon sale of employee's home.

	<ul><li>House cleaning upon purchase of employee's home.</li><li>Spouse's loss of earnings.</li><li>Help with starting a garden.</li><li>Transporting and kennelling for domestic animals (unless directly related to the actual family move, from the old to the new location).</li></ul>
Scholarships	<ul><li>Income from a scholarship is exempt from a tax charge in the scholar's hands.</li><li>The legislation only excludes from a tax charge, any scholarship provided from a trust fund or under a scheme for full time education or instruction whereas:<ul><li>In the relevant tax year, not more than 25% by value of the awards go to members of the families or households of the employees, whether or not the employee:<ul><li>Is in an excluded employment.</li><li>Is resident or ordinarily resident in the UK… or;</li><li>the duties of the individual's employment are performed outside the United Kingdom… and;</li></ul></li><li>the award was not provided by reason of the parents' employment;</li></ul></li><li>Thus, scholarships awarded to the children of all employees, whether or not the employees are in excluded employments or are working overseas, are taken into account for the purpose of</li></ul>

	the 25% test mentioned above. • Furthermore, the 25% test cannot operate to prevent a tax charge unless the connection between the award and the parents' employment is purely fortuitous.

Telephones	• Where the telephone is to be used solely for business, for example; a 2nd line for a telephone number that is only made available for business calls, there will be no liability for Class 1 NICs where you reimburse all of the costs of the telephone.
	 • You can ask for a dispensation for expense payments you make, or benefits you provide, that would attract a full tax deduction in the hands of the employee:
	  ○ expenses payments covered by the dispensation are not earnings for Class 1 NICs purposes… and;
	  ○ Benefits mentioned in it are not liable for Class 1A NICs.

	• If you provide an employee with a mobile telephone and enter into a service agreement with the telephone company, there is no liability for NICs or tax. This applies to the provision of the telephone, the service and all calls. • Where you reimburse the costs incurred by an employee in making business calls on his or her own mobile telephone, you can ask for a dispensation, as long as the tariff does not offer free time for those business calls. If you pay for the following without exceeding the cost of the service incurred by the employee:

Samuel Blankson

	• Business calls made from a payphone. • Business or private calls made from a hotel while on a business trip. • Business calls made from home where another member of the household is the subscriber.
Travelling expenses	If certain conditions are met, no taxable benefit or liability for Class 1A NICs arises for an employee from: • The provision of a bus for home to work travel, available to all employees… or; • A subsidy by the employer to a public transport undertaking, to provide transport for home to work travel, available for all employees. • You can also pay employees who are passengers in vehicles, doing business miles at a rate of 5 pence per mile. • Hotel accommodation and all other forms of transport undertaken solely for business travel, are also exempted.
Van benefit	• You only pay Class 1A NIC on the non-business usage portion of the benefit, if a van is provided by an employer.
Van fuel benefit	• If an employer provides you with fuel for a van, you will only attract Class 1A NIC on the non-business use portion of the benefit.
Vouchers and credit-tokens	• Only payments to meet the cost of business travel attract tax relief, and fall outside liability for NICs.

Table 14: Expenses and benefits in kind

- 143 -

PAYE

By the 19th day of each month – or, if you pay electronically, by the 22nd day of each month – your company should submit the most recent amounts you have deducted from all your employees' pay to HM Revenue & Customs (HMRC). If your average monthly payments are less than £1,500, you can arrange to pay them quarterly. This is another benefit of paying yourself a small salary whilst drawing the majority of your earnings via dividends.

It is critical to get this form in on time; therefore, if you are filing by post, make sure you use a delivery option that offers you a receipt. Nowadays, the safest method is to file electronically, via the HMRC Web site or a third party software product. This option also offers security and postage savings. Form P11D is available to download from the HMRC Web site.

Benefits in kind

Employees and directors are also taxed on benefits in kind. These are benefits such as a company car or medical insurance, and as an employer, you may have to pay Class 1A NICs on these benefits. If you subscribe to the PAYE system, you can delay paying this contribution until the end of the tax year.

Employers are required to pay Class 1A NICs on most benefits. Form P11D is what is in use to inform HMRC of all benefits paid to employees who earn over £8,500 per year. You must complete form P11D and submit a copy to HMRC, as well as a copy to the employee before 6 April of each year. Please note that this deadline date may fall on a weekend in some years, therefore in those years, you must arrange to submit the form by the preceding Friday.

Once you have completed form P11D for each of your employees, you may also need to complete form P11D (b) showing Class 1A NICs, on expenses and benefits. If you indicated on your employer's annual tax return (form P35) that no P11D (b) is due, then you will not need to return this form.

If you make or give expense payments to your employees, and include these payments in a PAYE Settlement Agreement, you may have to pay Class 1B NICs. Your accountant can best handle these benefit payments and the form filling on your behalf. The process can be longwinded, time consuming and if you make mistakes – costly.

For IT contracting Ltd. Companies, all benefits provided for an employee or members of their family or household, count as wages. Certain benefits such as cars and vans available for private use, loans, certain arrangements in connection with share incentive schemes, scholarships and tax not deducted from wages paid to directors, are taxed in accordance with special rules. See Table 14 for a list of expenses and facilities. To summarise, these include the following:

- The provision of living or other accommodation, including light, heat, rates and domestic or other services.
- The use of any asset provided by the employer or another person acting on the employer's behalf, for example, the use of a motorcycle, aircraft, yacht, furniture or a TV set. Cars, vans and mobile telephones have special rules.
- The provision of fuel for private, non-company cars.
- Gifts of assets to the employee, or the sale to the employee of assets, at less than their market value (this applies not only to assets such as a car or a house, but also to goods such as clothes, TV sets, wines or groceries).
- Any expenses or liabilities incurred by the employee, and paid direct by the employer, for example; hotel or

restaurant bills, whether paid directly or through a credit card company.

- Income tax not deducted from remuneration, paid to a director, but paid to HMRC by the employer and not reimbursed by the company.
- Scholarships awarded to students by reason of their parents' employment.
- Any other benefits or facilities of any kind, for example:

  o Hotel accommodation and restaurant facilities arranged by the employer, holidays, childcare (exemptions apply to some forms of childcare).
  o Shooting, fishing and other sporting facilities (exemptions apply to some sporting facilities).
  o Work carried out at the employee's residence.

Employees who earn less than £8,500 a year are only liable to pay tax on certain benefits in kind, which include:

- Provided accommodation.
- Benefits that can be converted into cash.
- Benefits provided by a voucher or credit card.
- Payment of the employee's debt.

For certain benefits provided to these employees, your company's liability for the employer to pay Class 1A NICs will not arise. However, for all employees, benefits provided by voucher, and the payment of an employee's debt are liable for employee and employer Class 1 NICs.

PAYE Thresholds

Below £100 per week or £435 per month, you do not need to pay PAYE tax. These figures coincide with thresholds for NICS. The current tax rates are as follows:

- Starting rate 10% up to £2,230.
- Basic rate 22% from £2,231 to £34,600.
- Higher rate 40% over £34,600.

In the UK, when you leave an employer, they give you a P45. This tells a new employer what your tax code is. If you do not have a tax code (i.e., no P45), you should use emergency code (522L), until you are assigned a code. Once your code is allocated, any overpayment or underpayment should be settled.

Tax codes beginning with K have a regulatory limit of 50%. This restricts the amount of tax deducted from an employee's pay, in that period. As an example, this stops deductions that could possibly exceed the employee's wages.

Statutory Sick Pay (SSP)

For employees with average weekly earnings of £87 or more, the weekly rate of SSP is £72.55. SSP is calculated daily by dividing the weekly rate of SSP by the number of qualifying days in the week. This is then multiplied by the number of qualifying days of incapacity, in the week. This figure is then rounded to the nearest penny. Weeks begin on Sunday and end on Saturday – for SSP purposes.

Unrounded Daily Rates[12]	Number of Qualifying Days in Week	Number of Qualifying Days of Incapacity for Work in the Week						
		1	2	3	4	5	6	7
Values in £ sterling								
10.3642	7	10.37	20.73	31.10	41.46	51.83	62.19	72.55
12.0916	6	12.10	24.19	36.28	48.37	60.46	72.55	
14.5100	5	14.51	29.02	43.53	58.04	72.55		
18,1375	4	18.14	36.28	54.42	72.55			
24.1833	3	24.19	48.37	72.55				
36.2750	2	36.28	72.55					
72.5500	1	72.55						

Table 15: SSP daily rates

Percentage Threshold Scheme allows you, (in certain circumstances) to recover SSP you have paid, over and above 13% of your NICs liability for the same tax month, in which you have paid SSP. Refer to the Employer Helpbook E14(2007); *What to do if your employee is sick*, for more information.

Statutory Maternity Pay (SMP)

Expectant mothers who are due on or after 15 July 2007, are entitled to SMP of £87.

---

[12] Unrounded daily rates are shown for employers with computerised Payroll Systems.
Recovery of SSP

First 6 weeks of payment	90% of employee's average weekly earnings
Remaining weeks	Pay the lesser of • 90% of average weekly earnings… or; • £112.75

Table 16: Weekly SMP, SPP and SAP payment schedule

You can see examples of SMP payments on the Internet at www.hmrc.gov.uk/employers or for more information, see the Employer Helpbook E15 (2007); *Pay and time off work for parents*.

Statutory Paternity Pay (SPP)

For employees who satisfy the qualifying conditions, SPP is paid for a maximum of 2 weeks and includes having average weekly earnings of:

- £87— if your baby is due on or after 15 July 2007, or if you are notified that you have been matched with a child, or received official notification that you are eligible to adopt a child from abroad, on or after 2 April 2007.
- See Table 16 for the SPP payment rules.

Further details can be found in the Employer Helpbook E15 (2007); *Pay and time off work for parents, if your employee is entitled to SPP because a baby was born*. Also, see the Employer Helpbook E16 (2007); *Pay and time off work for adoptive parents*, for more specific information (if your employee is entitled to SPP because a child was being adopted in the UK or, from abroad).

Statutory Adoption Pay (SAP)

Employees who are adopting a child and are notified that they have been matched with a child, or received official notification that they are eligible to adopt a child from abroad, on or after 1 April 2007, and who satisfy the qualifying conditions, are entitled to a maximum of 39 weeks of SAP. These include having average weekly earnings of:

- £87—if they are notified that they have been matched with a child, or received official notification that they are eligible to adopt a child from abroad, on or after 1 April 2007.
- See Table 16 for the SAP payment rules.

For further details refer to the Employer Helpbook E16 (2007); *Pay and time off work for adoptive parents*.

Funding of SMP/SPP/SAP

As an employer, if you qualify for Small Employer's Relief[13], you are entitled to recover 100% of the SMP/SPP/SAP you pay, plus 4.5% for payments made on or after 6 April 2007. Otherwise, if you do not qualify for Small Employer's Relief, you are only entitled to 92%.

For further information, refer to Employer Helpbook E15 (2007); *Pay and time off work for parents when baby is born*, and Employer Helpbook E16 (2007); *Pay and time off work for adoptive parents where a child has been adopted in the UK or from abroad*. The learning packages on your Employer CD-ROM also contain this information.

---

[13] Small Employer's Relief Threshold is £45,000 for payments made on or after 6 April 2007.

National Minimum Wage

From 1 October 2007, the legal rate of pay for non-executive employees is as follows:

- Main rate: £5.52 per hour (22 years and over).
- Development rate: £4.60 per hour (18 to 21 year olds).
- Young workers rate: £3.40 per hour (for workers under 18 who are above compulsory school leaving age).

For the latest information, call the National Minimum Wage Helpline on 0845 6000 678 – Monday thru Friday, 09.00 to 17.00. Or visit the Department of Trade and Industry's (DTI's) interactive Web site, at www.dti.gov.uk.

Collection of Student Loans

Student loan repayments are not due if the employee earns less than £15,000 per year. Employers can use the calculator on the CD-ROM or the SL3, Student Loan Deduction Tables, to calculate deductions. For more information on how to calculate and withhold the repayments from employee's wages, see the Employer Helpbook, E17, *Collection of Student Loans*.

Corporation tax

Your company's taxable profits are subject to corporation tax in the UK. This tax is due 8 months and 1 day after your company's year-end annually – for 12 month-long accounting periods. Large companies with profits exceeding £1,500,000 or companies that voluntarily opt out of annual filing, can file quarterly.

Companies have to self-assess their corporation tax liabilities, each reporting period. This return should include:

- A self-assessment of the company's tax liabilities for the accounting period. This includes tax on shareholder loans and tax arising from anti-avoidance rules.
- Statutory accounts and corporation tax computations.

Rates, limits and fractions for financial years starting 1 April	2006	2007
Main rate of corporation tax	30%	30%
Small companies' rate (SCR)[14]	19%	20%
SCR can be claimed by qualifying companies with profits at an annual rate not exceeding	£300,000	£300,000
Marginal, small companies' relief (MSCR) lower limit	£300,000	£300,000
MSCR upper limit	£1,500,000	£1,500,000
MSCR fraction	11/400	1/40
Special rate for unit trusts and open-ended investment companies	20%	20%

Table 17: Corporation Tax on profits – figures

HMRC reserves the right to make enquiries into any filing. These enquiries are subject to similar rules as applies to income tax. Your company's tax assessment is usually regarded as finalised, 12 months after the returns filing date. For most contracting companies which are smaller (with less than £1,500,000 profits), you have to pay your tax 9 months and 1 day after the end of your accounting period.

Companies with profits over £1.5 million must file quarterly in the 7th, 10th, 13th and 16th month following the

---

[14] For companies with ring fence profits, the small companies' rate of tax on those profits is 19%, and the MSCR fraction is 11/400 for the financial year starting 1 April 2007. Ring fence profits refer to the income and gains from oil extraction activities, or oil rights in the UK and UK Continental Shelf.

start of the accounting period. In the first period in which a company's profits exceed £1.5 million, it does not have to file quarterly, if its turnover does not exceed £10 million.

For the current tax rates for corporation tax, see Table 17.

Rates of Interest for Corporation Tax

Interest rate on late payments (from 6/08/2007)

Income Tax, NIC & Capital Gains Tax Stamp Duty and Stamp Duty Reserve Tax.	8.5%
Corporation Tax Pay & File.	6.75%
Corporation Tax Pre-Pay & File Stamp Duty Reserve Tax	6.5%
CTSA, from normal due date.	8.5%
Inheritance Tax, CTT & Estate Duty.	5.0%
Income Tax-CP and other duties attracting S87 interest.	8.5%

Interest rate on repayments (from 6/08/2007)

Income Tax, NIC & CGT Stamp Duty and Stamp Duty Reserve Tax.	4.0%
Corporation Tax Pay & File.	3.5%
Corporation Tax Pre-Pay & File Stamp Duty Reserve Tax	6.5%
CTSA, Repayment Interest.	5.0%
Inheritance Tax, CTT & Estate Duty.	5.0%

Other CTSA Interest Rates applying up to the normal due date:
Interest charged on underpaid quarterly instalment payments:

From	To	%
16/07/2007		6.75
21/05/2007	15/07/2007	6.50
22/01/2007	20/05/2007	6.25

Interest paid on overpaid quarterly instalment payments, and on early payments of Corporation Tax not due by instalments.

From	To	%
16/07/2007		5.50
21/05/2007	15/07/2007	5.25
22/01/2007	20/05/2007	5.00

Beneficial loan arrangements – Official rates

Use the table below to find the average official rate of interest for years when:

- The loan was outstanding throughout the Income Tax year… and;
- You are using the normal averaging method of calculation.

Table of average official rates

Year	Average official rate
2002-03	5.00%
2003-04	5.00%
2004-05	5.00%
2005-06	5.00%
2006-07	5.00%

Table 18: Average official rates

Use the table below in cases not within one above:

Table of actual official rates

From	To	Rate
6.01.02	5.04.03	5.00%
6.04.03	5.04.04	5.00%
6.04.04	5.04.05	5.00%
6.04.05	5.04.06	5.00%
6.04.06	5.04.07	5.00%
06.04.07		6.25%

Table 19: Actual official rates

Indexation Allowance

Concerning indexation allowance for corporation tax on chargeable gains, the rate to be used for calculations changes every month with the retail price index. Therefore, you have to calculate these according to the figures for the month the disposal was made. Find the latest rate at http://www.hmrc.gov.uk/rates/c_gains_subject_c_tax.htm.

How to Secure Your Future

When you become an IT contractor, there are many things you need to take care of yourself. You will no longer depend on an employer to look out for your future; instead, you will be your own boss and employee. Along with the responsibilities this entails also come some new rewards.

Being your own boss means you can dictate pretty much almost every aspect of your working life. This includes when you choose to retire and the income level you will enjoy after you retire. To achieve this, you need to establish some form of a savings plan. By putting aside a small amount each time you receive an income, you will be able to build the critical mass required to make your retirement goals a reality.

Pension planning

In essence, a pension is a legal tax avoidance scheme. This plan is approved by the government and the tax offices of most countries, although the rules that govern its usage may differ slightly from country to country. That said, a pension plan is perhaps the best investment vehicle for growing your retirement savings.

Pension plans allow you to contribute a proportion of your gross income towards a saving and/or an investment vehicle. Not all pension plans are approved, however; those that are not approved offer no tax benefits, whilst the vast majority that are approved, do provide for the benefits.

In the approved plans, the tax office adds the associated tax to the sum invested in the pension plan. This total sum then grows tax-free until the plan matures. Pension plan maturity is determined either by the type of pension plan, or by a nationally recognized retirement age. In the UK, this mandatory, government-set age is 65 years[15].

Upon maturity, you have several options. Depending on the type of pension you contributed to, you can draw a regular income from the lump sum through an annuity plan, or take a fraction (normally up to a quarter) in cash – tax free – and draw the rest as income.

You can also arrange for a fraction of your pension to be paid to your heirs upon your death, and in the UK and other countries, you can index link the income drawn from the annuity in an attempt to make it inflation proof (note this tends to considerably reduce the sum you can draw).

Today, the pension plan has evolved to be quite a sophisticated retirement planning tool, allowing you to include real estate, fine wine, company shares, funds, bonds (or gilts) and much more within the plans portfolio. Above this, the pension plan rules afford company directors special treatment and allowances that are not available to non-directors. This special treatment allows directors to contribute more into their pensions as well as retire earlier than the mandatory ages.

There are three main sources of pension plans available: government, company and personal.

Government pensions

Government pensions in most western countries are of the unfunded kind. This means the payouts are made by

---

[15] This was changed in 2006. Workers can request to continue working past this age.

contributors or tax payer's current contributions. Their benefits are often defined by some obscure calculation; few people, short of actuaries and experts, are able to roughly calculate.

Unfunded government pensions resemble the illegal investment structure known as a Ponzi. In a Ponzi scheme there is no real investment; payouts are funded solely by current contributions. The scheme collapses when more people attempt to withdraw, than are paying in.

In many ways, the majority of Western countries' national pensions are structured this way. As the amount of people living longer increases, the average family size decreases and the concept of marriage and the family itself is eroded, and replaced with a more temporary arrangement – as is the current trend – these national pension plans are doomed to collapse.

To combat this, governments can either increase taxes and/or raise the national retirement age. Their other option is to replace these hopeless, national pensions with funded pensions – the other type of pension plan. However, few governments are prepared to take on this mammoth change.

Although company pensions can also be of the unfunded kind, this is rare. If you are in an unfunded company pension scheme, I suggest you make other arrangements for your retirement.

Company pensions

Company pension plans are normally of the funded kind. The funded retirement benefits are based on the contributions made. This means that their payouts are mainly based on the amount that has been contributed. Therefore, the more funds contributed, the higher the retirement income payments will be. Conversely, the fewer funds are contributed, the less the pension payouts will be.

Company pension's plans are optional arrangements offered by employers to their employees. When opted for, a variable fraction of the employee's wages is paid into a retirement fund. The plan benefits can be pre-set with the contribution payments being variable – due to economic and other changes – or purely based on the contributions made.

In the case of the former, an option offered by most civil services and utilities, pays current retirees with the contributions being made by the current workers. This is similar to the government plans discussed previously. In this type of situation, the employer often tops up the contributions by matching a fraction of the employees contributions into the fund.

In the case of the latter type of plan, the contributions paid in, determine the benefits. The maximum contributions are capped to a fixed percentage, based on income. Once this ceiling is reached, the employee cannot make any further increases to their retirement plan.

Contribution-based benefit plans are normally transferable from employer to employer; however, this may not always be the case. Fixed benefit arrangements on the other hand, because of their structure, are rarely transferable.

When you run your own business, you can determine the type of benefit you want from your pension and make contributions directly into the plan from your company bank account, thus avoiding the payment of income tax and national insurance contributions. Now we shall look at these important factors.

Personal pensions

There are two types of retirement plan options that make the most sense for IT contractors. These are:

1. Personal/Stakeholder Pensions.

2. Executive Pensions.

The pension you decide on will depend on your personal circumstances.

Personal/Stakeholder Pensions

Personal/Stakeholder Pension plans have grown in popularity to be the most utilised investment vehicles in the UK. They are very flexible and can be used by virtually anyone, including children and non-working spouses. The only exception as to who may use them are contractors running a limited company (and are already contributing into an Executive Pension).

Currently, anyone can invest up to £300 per month into this vehicle. Above this figure rules apply based on salary, age and taxable benefits in kind received.

These plans should be funded directly from your limited company business bank account. New contractors who were non-pensioned permies within the last 5 years have the option of nominating a base year from the last 5 years. The income earned in this base year will be used to determine how much you can contribute into your Personal/Stakeholder Pension Plan. Therefore, it is prudent to select the best permie year in which you earned the most income as the base year. This allows you to contribute the most into your pension plan when you start contracting.

The key benefit to stake holder pensions over personal pensions is a 1% cap on pension plan provider charges. Personal retirement funds do not offer this cap, although most have reduced their charges to compete with the stakeholder pensions. The main disadvantages to the stakeholder pension over the personal pension are the limited funds available to invest in, as opposed to the broad range offered by personal pensions.

Executive Pensions

At the price of higher administration fees by its providers, Executive Pension Plans (EPP) offer more scope for tax savings than all the previously discussed pension plan options. They offer confidentiality to a company's executives and senior staff by separating their pension arrangements from the general company pension scheme.

EPPs were created to help entrepreneurs running their own limited companies, general business people, and executives; who in the course of their business, inevitably neglect pension planning. EPPs allow executives and directors to fund a pension as well as have their company contribute to that plan. Currently, pension contributions greater than £3,600 per annum (2007/2008) or 100% of your income – whichever is greater – are allowed to grow in an EPP, tax-free. Contributions above this figure will attract 40% tax.

There is also a maximum amount (Annual Allowance) allowed to be contributed to EPPs. However, this can often be higher than is allowed for any other pension type. Your company can top up this contribution up to the Annual Allowance. This Annual Allowance is set for the tax years 2007-2008 to 2010-2011 as follows:

Annual Allowance

2007-2008	£225,000
2008-2009	£235,000
2009-2010	£245,000
2010-2011	£255,000

The total sum allowed to be invested in the EPP must not exceed the Lifetime Allowance, currently set at £1.6 million. There is a possibility of protecting contributions prior to April 5th 2006. Seek financial advice on this matter. It might be a beneficial decision, based upon your personal circumstances.

You can transfer payments (transfer-in) from EPPs. However, be warned! Charges may be applied by the provider.

Each provider sets the minimum they are willing to receive through this method (roughly around £2500). There is no maximum. The same minimum normally applies for any single payments made into the EPP. Single payments can be made whenever you want. Furthermore, you can select to make regular payments. These regular payments must normally exceed £90 per month or £1,080 per year. Non-regular payments can be for any amount.

In the Individual Executive Pension Plans these additional, voluntary payments can be started and stopped in alignment with your contracting income, and often without any additional charge by the provider.

Life insurance cover can be added to the EPP to include your dependents, in case you die before you begin drawing on your annuity.

Some providers allow you to withdraw the entire contributions made as a refund, if you leave your employer within two years of taking out the plan. In this scenario, the Trustees or your employer or company will also receive their contribution(s) back.

Transfers are also possible, however; depending on the duration the plan was held, you may lose some of your contributions through administration fees. Remember that whilst you are in such a scheme, you have a lot of flexibility; however, once you leave, you may not be able to return to it. Make sure you seek advice before making this decision.

It is important to select the right pension provider for your circumstances. Aim for flexibility and low charges. Of greatest importance is flexibility in the selection of the funds or securities in which the plan invests. Make sure these products agree with your ethics and investment return expectations. Don't discover too late that the growth of your plan has been greatly slowed, due to a poor investment choice.

Seek independent, financial advice before getting into any plan. Avoid non-independent advisers, as they are only allowed to advise you on a limited range of products. Also to be avoided, are financial advisers who council you based on the commissions they stand to receive from the plan you select. These plans normally have high charges to pay for the high commissions. If possible, do as much research yourself before talking to anyone. This will help you identify the good from the bad, independent financial advisers.

Look for the following in your plan:

- Low set-up costs.
- Plan flexibility (in case your career moves back and forth from permie to contracting in the future).
- Contribution flexibility which allows you to stop, start or cease contributions with little prior notice (e.g., a month or less).
- It is provided by a strong institution that will be around for at least the next ten years.
- Provider stability; (good fund managers will often leave if a provider's future is uncertain, i.e., in the case of a merger, acquisition or takeover).
- Provider liquidity; (the provider has large reserves of capital to allow the investment freedom needed to grow your contributions).

A pension is perhaps the best investment and tax saving vehicle available to IT contractors. You can best maximise your pension by using your limited company to contribute towards it through an EPP. Through clever tax planning, you should be able to lower your tax liabilities even further with the use of a private pension. Seek independent, financial advice to suit your particular circumstances.

Like everything worth doing, your pension will require a little effort to maximise its benefits. Don't just sign up to one, and blindly contribute to whatever fund or security the provider invests in.

Your pension provider will supply annual or bi-annual fund performance reports. You can use these to compare your current funds' with the all the available funds' performances. Check on the performance – twice to four times a year – to make sure it is growing in the desired direction. If it is not, review your pension funds and the securities in your portfolio and make appropriate changes. You can also research your pension funds at http://www.trustnet.com/pen.

Healthcare considerations

As a self-employed individual, it is easy to forget to set aside funds for your future and emergencies. Permies are protected by strong employment laws allowing them to take time off for medical reasons or during a difficult period in their lives. Contractors on the other hand, do not get maternity, paternity or sick pay unless they arrange these themselves through some kind of insurance or savings plan.

There are several such insurances that an IT contractor can utilise to protect him/herself from medical, personal or employment emergencies or disasters. We shall look at the options available to you as a self-employed IT contractor.

The following are the various insurances available to the self-employed business owner:

1. Life insurance;
     a. Pension term assurance (PTA).
2. Permanent health insurance.
3. Private health insurance.
4. Dental insurance.
5. Income Protection Cover (IPC).
6. Accident, Sickness and Unemployment (ASU) Cover.

Securing your financial future is important. However, what if you should become deceased, or your health fails before you can retire? You will need to protect yourself and your family against such outcomes. One of the best ways to do this is through insurance policies. We shall examine the various types offered for the IT contractor in this section.

Life insurance

Life insurance protects your family from the loss of your earnings. Obviously, it won't bring you back from the dead, but it could pay out a lump sum to your loved ones. When you become a contractor, it becomes even more important to take out this type of insurance for the benefit of your loved ones and your own peace of mind.

There are different types of life insurance. Understanding them will serve you well and save you and your loved ones a fortune in the tragic event of your untimely demise. There are two main types of life insurance cover; Term and Whole-of-Life.

Term

Term insurance is a life insurance policy that covers you for a fixed term. It is a temporary form of insurance offered by most insurance companies, a number of friendly societies and other financial products providers.

With term life insurance, you specify the term of cover. During this period, the insurer agrees to pay out if you die. The term can be from 24 months to several decades long. Term tends to be the cheapest way to buy life insurance. Because the term is limited and known before hand, the insurer can more accurately calculate their risk.

Normally, males will cost more than females to insure, as they tend to die earlier than women. Similarly, premiums are higher for smokers and other high risk people.

Types of term insurance

There are many types of term insurance policies. The following is a list of those available in the UK:

1. Level term.
2. Decreasing term.
3. Convertible term.
4. Renewable term.
5. Increasing term.
6. Family income benefit.

Level Term

This type of policy is often used to cover the repayment of a loan or an interest-only mortgage. The mortgage benefits from a level term policy; because the benefit remains constant during the term of the policy, and is paid upon the death of the policy holder. Therefore, it is ideal for repaying the outstanding sum of a loan.

Decreasing Term

The benefit due on a decreasing term policy is reduced each year until it reaches zero, at the end of the term. It is best used for insuring a repayment mortgage. As the repayment mortgages capital value reduces over the term, the decreasing term insurance policy is often bought in conjunction with this type of mortgage. Normally, the premiums on this type of insurance cover are lower than that for the level term policy.

Convertible Term

Term policies can be a bad idea, especially if your health degrades near the end of the term. It may be difficult to extend the cover or buy a policy that covers the whole of your life. To get around this problem, you can buy a convertible term policy. This type of policy allows you to convert to a permanent cover by buying a whole-of-life policy, or an endowment policy when the term policy expires.

The convertible term policy guarantees that you cannot be refused the right to extend life cover, even if your health greatly degrades. However, the following rules govern this right to policy conversion:

- The sum assured it is restricted to the amount on the original policy.
- You must convert before the term insurance ends.
- The new premiums will be determined by your age and sex (not the state of your health).
- Conversion tends to be 10% higher than basic term.

Renewable term policies are often an option on convertible term policies.

Renewable term

If you do not want a conversion, but you wish to exchange policies at the end of your term policy, you can purchase a renewable term policy. Like the convertible term policy, it offers you guaranteed insurability, irrespective of the state of your health, age or sex. It can be offered as an option on convertible term policies.

Increasing term

As time passes, inflation tends to eat into your insurance benefits. You can avoid this by taking a term policy that increases its payout annually by a fixed percentage (typically 5% to 10%). The added protection will cost you more; however, your benefits will keep up with inflation or increase above it. With this policy type, you normally lose the right to increase the sum assured, when you reach age sixty-five.

Family income benefit

With all the life insurance policies available, it is possible to include a family income benefit. This benefit is paid to your partner and/or child after you die. The premiums switch immediately – on confirmation of the policy holders death – to the joint policy holder or a named beneficiary.

The policy is written to coincide with the expected period of dependency of the youngest child in the family; in the case of a dependent child or children. This income can also be written to increase over the term of the policy.

Pension term assurance (PTA)

PTAs offer the same benefits as the term insurance; however, it offers tax benefits that help to lower its premiums. PTAs offer up to a 22% tax break on premiums. It does this by allowing you to pay premiums with non-taxed income (gross income). High rate tax payers need to file a return to the HMRC to receive relief at the higher rate of 40%.

In reality, the true saving is around 15% for 22% tax payers. This is because the PTA has higher maintenance costs than the other life insurance types. 40% taxpayers may receive over 30% savings by using a PTA.

Previously, some insurers offered this product with a pension plan; however, PTAs are being sold nowadays without the need to take out a pension plan with the insurer. PTAs can be used to cover repayment or interest only mortgages and allow index linking.

PTAs come with some restrictions. The following is a list of these restrictions:

- Non-combinable with other life insurance policies.
- Cannot be included within critical illness cover, income protection or family income benefit. (Before you swap your existing life cover with a PTA, seriously consider the cost of maintenance and how your life insurance benefits will be affected. In some cases, all the savings may be swallowed up in the move, as you may need to replace other insurance policies).
- The lump sum from a PTA policy will count towards your lifetime allowance for tax-free pension contributions.[16]
- If your pension pot added to the lump sum in the PTA exceeds £1.5 million, you will have to pay 55% tax on the excess. You can avert this by buying a PTA that pays out the death benefit to your beneficiaries as an income, instead of a lump sum.
- Those that already exceed £1.5 million, and who have already applied for 'enhanced protection' for the excess, will nullify the protection by using a PTA – leaving themselves open to the 55% tax charge.
- Currently, only Liverpool Victoria insurance provider offers a joint cover PTA.
- Standard Life, Friends Provident, Royal Liver and Scottish Equitable allow customers to switch back to

---

[16] The current limit is £1.5 million.

their old policies whilst keeping the same premiums. Other insurers will apply their current premiums.

The last point should be taken seriously, as the status of the PTA is currently uncertain. If their tax benefits change it will be beneficial to have selected a policy that froze premiums in cases of a switch.

PTAs can be purchased without financial advisers; however, you need to fully understand how they work and what you stand to gain or lose by using one. Check that you are nowhere near the £1.5 million pension pot limit, before taking out a PTA. Keep in mind also, that savings made may be swallowed up if your health changes to make it more expensive to insure.

Whole-of-life cover

Another type of policy on offer by most insurance companies is the whole-of-life policy. This insurance policy, unlike the term is unlimited to time. Because this policy eventually pays out when you die, its premiums cost more than the term policy premiums.

There are several types of whole-of-life policies. They are as follows:

- Unit-linked
- With profits
- Universal

Unit-linked

In unit-linked whole-of-life policies, the premiums you pay are used to buy units in life funds. These funds generally grow with time. Part of the units purchased is encashed to maintain the payments of the insurance policy cover.

The amount encashed is determined by the level of cover you want. The rest remain in the life fund and grows with the funds. This growth should provide sufficient funds to maintain any premium increases after the first ten years, and should normally grow to completely sustain the monthly premiums so that at the age of 70 or 80, the fund pays your monthly premiums.

However, because whole-of-life policies are investment-based, if your fund investment growth has not achieved self-sufficiency by age 70 - 80, you will need to maintain the monthly premium payments. Similarly, if the funds invested perform badly, you may see increases in your monthly premium after the first ten years.

Your insurance company will normally offer a range of cover options. These will range in insurance cover. By opting for less cover, you allow less money to be encashed towards the monthly premium to pay for insurance cover. This leaves more money in your funds, allowing them to grow faster.

If you opt for more insurance coverage, more of your fund units will need to be encashed to buy the life cover. This leaves little in your funds for rapid growth. Choosing this option will mean that after five or ten years, you may need to increase your premiums to maintain the level of cover.

With profits

This policy guarantees to pay a minimum amount of life cover upon your death; however, this sum increases each year if you do not die. This occurs through the addition of annual reversionary bonuses – permanently increasing the sum insured.

Upon your death, a terminal bonus is paid, further increasing your life insurance payout. This type of whole-of-life policy has an investment value which tends to be low in the early years, but will grow rapidly in later years.

Universal

Universal whole-of-life policies work in the same way as unit-linked policies; however, they offer more benefits than the latter. These benefits can include the following:

- Waiver of premium – ensures that your policy payments are made if you are unable to work.
- Disability benefit – allows for the sum assured to be paid if you become permanently disabled.
- Critical illness cover – covers your medical costs if you become critically ill with a lethal illness, e.g., an incurable cancer.
- Fatal accident benefit – pays an amount over and above the sum assured, if you die an accidental death.

By offering all these added benefits, the universal whole-of-life policy falls short as a savings vehicle, and premiums are normally higher for this product.

In summary, we have looked at term insurance and whole-of-life insurance. Whole-of-life insurance mixes savings with insurance, and in doing so raises the cost of the insurances and reduces the growth potential of the savings. Salesmen get higher commissions for selling whole-of-life insurance; as a result, you may be enticed and encouraged to take out the most heavily laden, whole-of-life insurance offered by a provider. Seek independent financial advice before you select a product.

Generally, it is best to save separately in a pension, ISA and/or other tax exempt vehicles, separate from your life insurance. Term insurance is your best bet for getting life insurance for your specific needs. By adding the two – savings and insurance – you may be making a rod for your own back.

In short, always go for the simple options so that you can clearly determine where you are getting the best value. The term insurance product offers this in a competitively priced, simple to understand and manageable package. As always, in all personal financial matters, seek independent financial advice from a qualified professional before making your final decision.

Permanent health insurance (PHI)

As a contractor, your time is literally money. Therefore, you must protect yourself from unplanned time off. A serious accident or long-term illness can deal a huge blow to your company profits. The time off could cost you a contract as well as the associated income. You can protect your income with a permanent health insurance policy designed to replace your income, should you become ill for a long term.

PHI pays you a replacement income if you are unable to work through an illness or accident. This income, although it will never match your income whilst you were working, will go some way to cover your important outgoings during the injury or illness.

Normally, you can only claim the government's incapacity benefit after 28 weeks of illness. Before the funds are released, you must undergo a rigorous examination and work related tests to verify that your condition is genuine and eligible. The tests check your ability to walk, sit and use stairs.

The benefit you eventually receive upon qualifying is meagre and taxable. To get around this problem, you can take out PHI. This is also referred to as income replacement, personal disability, income protection, long-term disability, or disability income – insurance. It is offered by most insurance companies.

PHI cover pays you a regular income to maintain your standard of living, if you suffer a long-term sickness or injury. The maximum monthly benefit for an Income Protection Plan is currently £14,583, although, if you receive full sick pay from your employer, you will not be able to claim on the policy until all of your sick pay has been used. Proportional amounts may be paid if you receive half or quarter sick pay. The benefit of PHI can be arranged to kick in after an initial waiting period of 4, 13, 26 or 52 weeks (the sooner the benefits are activated, the costlier the insurance). It continues until you return to work, become deceased, or the term of the policy runs out – whichever occurs first.

PHI gets its name from the fact that the insurer may not cancel the policy, no matter how often you claim for benefit. Normally, policies usually expire when the policyholder reaches age 60 (for women) or 65 (for men), and most insurers will never write a policy for applicants within five years of these age limits.

There are a few insurers who offer policies best suited to IT contractors, except that the list of insurers changes, and no two policies are the same. Due to these factors, you should seek the advice of a qualified, independent financial advisor (IFA), before taking out a PHI.

You can use your limited company to buy PHI coverage for all of your staff, including yourself. This group, corporate policy is normally cheaper than buying a private, individual policy.

Read the small print before buying a PHI. Some insurers insist that you be unable to undertake any type of employment before they payout the benefits, whilst others pay benefits, if you are unable to undertake your usual occupation, due to an accident or illness.

Some policies also allow partial recovery. Making a partial recovery and returning to part-time work, or taking a lower paid job – for instance – would reduce your benefit accordingly, in this case. Note that this payment is structured, so that you would be slightly better off to return to partial work, rather than staying full time at home. Though the payout will not make you better off, than if you were to return to full time employment.

The exclusions list for most PHI policies can be extensive. Most PHI policies do not normally cover stress-related illness(es), aid(s), self-inflicted injury(s), illness(es) caused by drug or alcohol abuse, an act of war, criminal activity, pregnancy, childbirth (or associated complications), or exposure to radiation as a result of nuclear war.

It is vital that you read and fully familiarise yourself with the full list of exclusions before buying PHI.

PHI premiums are calculated with your occupation, gender, whether you smoke or not, the waiting and payment periods in mind. You can increase or decrease your premiums, simply by changing the payment and waiting periods. Luckily, IT contracting is not classed as a high risk occupation. If you change jobs, remember to inform your insurer. Failure to do so can be used to invalidate a future claim for benefit.

Selecting a long waiting period will decrease your premium. Although, you will have to wait a long time before PHI benefit payments kicked in. If you select a distant waiting period, make sure you have sufficient savings to tide you over, should you need to file a claim.

The payment period decides how long you want the payments to continue, after you make a claim. The longer the period of claims, the more expensive the premium will be.

Although women generally live longer than men, they tend to suffer ill health more often during their working lives. Because of this statistic, premiums are higher for women than for men.

You can select an insurer that guarantees that the premium of your policy will never change unless you change the cover it provides. Other insurers also offer a term guarantee. During this period – normally five years – the premiums will not increase. However, after this period, the insurer may increase your premium or reduce your cover – keeping your premium the same – if they decide that their claims position requires it.

With the conventional PHI, if you do not make a claim when the policy expires, you will get nothing. There is no investment value, and you cannot surrender the policy for a cash sum. Some insurers offer unit-linked PHI's with an investment element. They use a portion of the premium paid to purchase units in a fund. Avoid this type of PHI. As before, try to keep your investments separate to your insurances. You compromise both insurance cover and investment growth potential, when you use a PHI as an investment tool.

In the case of the unit-linked PHI, you can surrender it for a cash sum; as the units purchased have value. Keep in mind also, that early surrender will leave you with far less than you would have put in.

If you need to make a claim on your PHI policy, do not delay. Fill the claim form as soon as possible after the injury or illness occurs. The insurer will process the form, and determine how many payments (and at what value), you will receive. They may also ask for proof of income, prior to the claim and also a medical examination. Premiums are waived during the period in which benefits are being paid. The premium resumes when your benefit payment stops, and/or you return to work.

PHI benefits are tax free and are calculated at 50% to 60% of your gross income from the year preceding the incident that led to the claim. You can index link or set a predefined annual increase on your benefit, or you can leave it level. The former options cost more than the level rate income option.

You must contact your insurer when you are ready to return to work. They will stop the benefit payments, and resume premium collection. You may continue to receive a reduced benefit if you return to work on a part-time basis, or take a lower paid job. The benefit received in case of the latter is called a proportionate benefit.

Watch out for the hassle-free moratoria format of buying a PHI. By this format, you do not have to take a medical examination, although, any illness that you have within two years of getting the policy, will not be covered. This is the easiest type of cover to arrange, but can cause the most problems when you file a claim, and are turned down based on past health issues.

You can opt instead for the medical history examination. This format requires you to have a thorough medical prior to the arrangement of the cover. You must declare all known conditions you have (or have had), at this stage. The insurer will then decide to not cover certain conditions, cover conditions at an increased premium cost, or refuse you cover based on the medical examination. This is perhaps the best option, if you want to avoid problems down the line.

Private health insurance

The National Health Service (NHS), in the UK is the world's largest centralized health service. As an employer, the NHS is third in size – behind the Chinese army and the Indian railways. However, the magnitude of the organisation has caused funding and administration problems. This has consequently affected the speed of service provided for some of the treatment offered by the NHS.

As a contractor who earns money only when he/she works, you cannot afford to have to wait six weeks or longer in an NHS queue for medical treatment. To bypass the queues, you can take out private health insurance.

This type of policy allows you to shortcut NHS queues, and enjoy attentive and more pleasant hospital environment with better facilities, as you receive treatment for minor, non-life-threatening conditions.

Private health insurance policies do not cover the following: long-term or incurable health conditions, medical treatments such as dental work, (see the next section for details on dental cover), alcoholism/drug abuse, infertility, normal pregnancy, HIV/AIDS, or cosmetic surgery. PHI does provide cover for the costs of private medical treatment for curable, short-term medical conditions.

Normally, private hospitals do not offer accident and emergency facilities, or more serious treatment facilities; therefore, they are not a complete alternative to the NHS hospitals. They do offer faster treatment when you prefer more pleasant surroundings. For instance, it is typical – in most private hospitals – to get a private room with a phone, flowers and your own television set.

There are private wards and rooms in most top NHS hospitals. These afford you the same treatment you can expect from the best NHS hospitals, but in more private surroundings.

Generally, private health policies cover the cost of accommodation and nursing bills in a private hospital, or in a private ward in an NHS hospital, along with surgery, specialists, drugs and x-rays.

The time to buy private health insurance is now. You cannot buy a policy after it becomes apparent you will need it for a current medical treatment or an operation. Similarly, this type of insurance does not cover pre-existing medical conditions or treatment of long-term illnesses that cannot be cured.

The list of exempt conditions is often extensive and detailed, therefore, read the small print carefully. It is important to note that normal pregnancy or complications from pregnancy is not usually covered. New customers below a certain age are accepted by all insurers, except for those with certain terminal conditions. Some insurers refuse applications from new applicants, beyond a certain age, regardless of their health.

Typically, the older you are, the more expensive your premiums will be. Also smokers and women pay more than non-smokers and men. You can also elect to cover your partner with a joint policy, or your family with a family plan. Corporate plans also exist and will generally offer lower premiums than individual cover.

Comprehensive cover allowing treatment at the best private hospitals, or the top NHS teaching hospitals in the country, will cost more than less comprehensive cover with a restricted list of less expensive hospitals.

There are three classes, depending on hospital choice. The budget option is the cheapest, and covers you for treatment not available on the NHS (within a set period). The standard and comprehensive options offer more hospitals, and may cover more treatments, but they also cost more.

Lowering premiums

To further reduce premiums, select a policy that rewards you with lowered rates for not making minor claims, and consider opting to pay a larger portion of claims, or select a more restricted choice of hospitals.

Business policies

Buying health insurance through your company is another way of reducing the cost. You can get a better deal by arranging cover for all company employees, and offer the insurance as a benefit to employees. Keep in mind that as an employee, if your earnings exceed a certain limit, you will have to pay a tax on this perk. Similarly, people over 60 years of age, no longer get tax relief on private medical insurance.

If your private health insurance policy is included in your employment contract and the contract is terminated, you will need to renegotiate a new private health insurance policy. However, you may qualify for discounts.

Health history declaration options

The rules for private and permanent health insurance are similar. Just like the permanent health policies, some insurers offer the fast track application via a moratoria style method, where you do not need a medical examination.

Selecting this route however, may cause you problems later when you claim benefits for a condition that the insurer can claim as being present up to five years before your application for insurance coverage. In this case, they will refuse claims for benefits. If you remain free of treatment, symptoms, tests or medication for these conditions for over five years, coverage will normally resume for the conditions. Incurable and recurring diseases will therefore never be covered, in this case.

Opting for the examination route will eliminate most of these problems. However, if the examination reveals a condition you were unaware of, the insurer could refuse to insure you, increase your premiums to cover the new condition, or offer you coverage exempt of the new condition.

Choosing the examination route may be wise in most cases although, you should be sure you do not omit any conditions you have (or have had), when you fill in the application form. Failure to declare accurate information on an application may nullify future claims.

Filling in the form will suffice for some insurers, whilst others will insist on writing to your doctor directly for your medical history.

Claims process

Normally, your doctor will inform you when you need medical care. He/she will refer you to a private consultant. At this stage, get a quote for the treatment and then contact your insurer. Make sure the insurer will pay all of the costs before you start treatment through the private consultant. If the insurer will not pay all the costs, and it is not a serious condition – unlikely to cost you IT contracting days for the treatment – then you may opt to receive the medical care via the NHS.

If the healing will cost you lost working days, then you may want to select the normally faster, private route and bridge the expenses yourself.

In cases where the insurer will cover all costs, always select the private option, after-all, you have paid already for the cover. Some policies may require you to settle the bills yourself first, before claiming back funds from the insurer.

Buying private health cover

Shop around for the best cover possible for your situation. Use an agent wherever possible. They may know of insurers offering lower premiums for cover or conditions that relate to you, and that are generally not covered by other mainstream insurers.

Similarly, there are some IT contractor-specific insurance policies and providers who offer more specialised policies for IT contractors; and the agent may be aware of them. Do your research before consulting the agent, so that you can opt to not use their advice, if you have already found a cheaper and more appropriate insurer, during your research.

Dental insurance

As an IT contractor, time is of the essence. Therefore, long waiting periods between treatments for dental issues will be unacceptable. Depending on the NHS for all your dental work could cost you more than you save, if it requires you to lose time at your contract. In light of this, you may wish to take out dental insurance along with your private health plan.

Dental insurance allows you more flexibility on the choice of dentist, and you can select a time and place that's right for you. It also allows you to get more complex treatment faster, as opposed to going on the NHS waiting lists.

Normally, under dental insurance, you attend a qualifying dentist to get your treatment and pay for it yourself, claiming back the payment from your insurer, at a later date. You either use a qualifying NHS dentist or go to a private dentist under most standard dental policies. Furthermore, you do not need to go for a check-up before taking out a premium; however, your age and the extent of dental cover do affect your dental policy premium.

The following are types of dental policies available in the UK:

1. Cash Plans – this type of plan can include health insurance cover and is offered with part-cover by some large providers. Part-cover pays between 50% and 75% of the cost of treatment with an annual cap. It can include other benefits such as optical treatment and health screening.
2. Capitation Schemes – this allows you to spread the cost of cover by paying a regular (normally monthly) premium. This is determined after a consultation with a dentist. Check-ups, regular treatment and fillings, x-rays and extractions are usually covered under capitation schemes.

Capitation schemes are a good idea if you are healthy and just need to maintain your good dental health. Denplan Care, the largest capitation scheme provider in the UK, offers plans with premiums that are based on the dental centres you use, and the state of your dental health. You can therefore further reduce the premiums you pay, by electing to use cheaper dentists and maintaining good dental health.

With capitation schemes, you are also limited to the centres you can attend for treatment. Therefore, you may find that your local dentist may not be part of the list. If you have a strong preference to your local dentist, you may need to change providers or opt for the cash plan option.

Dental insurance plan allow emergency treatments for general treatment such as crowns, root canals, bridges, dentures and other laboratory work–up, to the maximum annual limits. However, they normally exclude more serious dental work such as treatment of serious dental abscesses, oral cancer, treatments on salivary glands, surgical removal of roots, cosmetic work and orthodontic treatment, such as braces and implants. Some providers offer extended cover for these treatments at the cost of higher premiums.

Most providers require you to have enrolled for a period of three to six months before making a claim, and may not cover you for serious dental work arising from conditions prior to cover being taken.

The NHS has a free search facility for finding NHS dentists. Call 044 (0845) 4647.

Accident, Sickness and Unemployment (ASU) Cover

Accident, Sickness and Unemployment (ASU) policies provide for a shorter term of cover than Permanent Health Protection cover or Income Protection insurance cover. ASU therefore, can only be claimed for a maximum of 1-2 years, depending upon the provider. ASU policies normally do not cover you for redundancy; however, some insurers do provide the extra cover for a higher premium. In most cases, business owners will not qualify for this as it is only useful to permies.

ASU is usually offered when you take out loans, credit cards, hired purchase (as in the case for car purchases), or a mortgage policy. The current maximum benefit for ASU is £1,500 per month; however, this benefit can be claimed alongside sick pay from your employer, in the event of an accident or sickness.

ASU is normally not worth the paper it is printed on when it comes to covering IT contractors. It is exceedingly difficult to successfully claim any benefits from this type of policy, as the conditions and exemptions generally disqualify any IT contractor from making a claim. In a sense, for IT contractors, this is a rip-off. Avoid it like the plague.

The following is an example of a typical ASU exemptions list.

What is not covered

You will not receive incapacity benefit for any claim which is caused by, or resulting from:

- A pre-existing medical condition; but you will be entitled to benefit if you have not suffered from that condition for two years before the first date you became unable to work. You have not suffered from a condition, if throughout that two year period you:

  o Have not consulted a doctor for that condition.
  o Have not received treatment for that condition.
  o Have been free of symptoms of that condition.

- Any physical or mental condition which you knew of or should reasonably have known about at the start date, or which you asked or received treatment or counselling for, from any doctor before the start date.
- Suicide, attempted suicide or self-inflicted injuries.
- Any chronic condition.
- Alcohol or drugs, unless they are prescribed for treatment (other than for addiction) by a doctor.
- Human Immunodeficiency Virus (HIV) and/or HIV related illness including Acquired Immune Deficiency Syndrome (AIDS) and/or mutant derivatives or variations thereof, regardless of cause.
- Backache and related conditions howsoever caused, unless you have medical documents (for example, a MRI scan or x-rays), as evidence of a diagnosed medical condition.
- Psychiatric illness or mental disorders including depression, bereavement, stress, or stress related conditions, unless diagnosed by a consultant who is a member of the Royal College of Psychiatrists and is recognised by that Royal College as being a consultant.

- Geriatric care, medical operations or treatments which are not medically necessary, including cosmetic or beauty treatment, unless this is the result of an accident where your doctor recommends you have cosmetic treatment.
- Pregnancy, childbirth, miscarriage, abortion or any related conditions, unless this is a result from complications which are diagnosed as such by a doctor, or consultant, who specialises in obstetrics.
- In addition you will not receive incapacity benefit for:

  o Any period when your incapacity is not confirmed by a doctor; unless you are in receipt of statutory sick pay from your employer, or short term incapacity benefit from the Job Centre Plus…
  o …for any period where you are in receipt of your salary,
  o if you are receiving unemployment benefit.

You will not receive unemployment benefits under the following circumstances:

- If you were not in continuous work for 6 months immediately before your employment ended (if you were not in work for 2 weeks or less, they will not count this as a break in your employment).
- Unemployment was caused or resulted from your employment ending within the exclusion periods.
- Being told, or made aware, either before the start date or within the exclusion period, that your employment will end. This is irrespective of when employment actually ends.
- Unemployment which is normal or seasonal in your line of work.
- Unemployment which you knew of, or should reasonably have known of, on the start date.

- Misconduct which contributes or leads to your dismissal.
- Any wilful act by you.
- Dismissal due to the inability to pass a probationary period or inability to perform any elements of your job.
- Resignation, voluntary unemployment or voluntary redundancy.
- If you are employed on a specific project, including any temporary assignment and the project finishes.
- If your employment ends as a result of the expiry of an apprenticeship or training contract.
- If you are self-employed and your business temporarily stops trading.
- If you are a contract worker, your contract would have expired.
- If you are self-employed and you cannot give them evidence that your business:

  o has permanently stopped trading and/or being in the process of being wound up; or…
  o …has been put into the hands of a company dealing with insolvency; or…
  o …is a partnership which has been dissolved or is in the process of being dissolved.

- For any period in which you have received, or are entitled to receive, payment in lieu of notice.
- If you are receiving incapacity benefit.

In addition to the above, you will not receive any benefits for unemployment or incapacity which is caused by, or resulting from:

- Taking part in, attempting, or acting as an accessory to, any crime.

- Taking part in a strike, labour dispute, industrial action or lock-out.
- Radioactive contamination, war, invasion, act of foreign enemy hostilities (whether war be declared or not), civil war, rebellion, revolution, insurrection, riots, civil commotion, military or usurped power.
- If you are working outside the UK, unless you are:
- Working for the British Armed Forces or as a civil servant in a British Embassy or consulate; or...
- ...working for an employer that is a UK registered company who assigns you to work in the European Union on the same terms and conditions; or...
- ...working on a specific project for less than 30 days outside the UK, and were actually outside the UK for less than 30 days.

How to Claim

If you need to make a claim, you must contact the insurers as soon as reasonably possible and at least within 30 days of the event that leads to your claim.

Please fill in the claim form and return it to them, and they will process your claim. They should receive the claim form within 120 days. If you do not do this, your benefit may be affected.

General Conditions

You can be covered under ASU if, on the start date you:

- Are a permanent resident and working within the UK, Channel Islands or Isle of Man; and...
- ...are at least 18 and under 65 years of age; and...
- ...you are actively working (i.e., not off sick), when you apply, and have been for at least 6 months immediately prior to this time.

As you can see from the list above, the policy is worded in such a way as to avoid paying out for any claim made by an IT contractor, especially those who are self-employed, company owners. In fact, in most cases, even permies would have great challenges claiming ASU. For general information and comparison of policies, visit Money Supermarket's pages www.moneysupermarket.com/insurance, or a similar comparison Web site.

Handling Your Money Effectively

A very successful man once told me to handle my money using the four-basket system. In the first basket, I was to place the majority of my money and assets. This was to be my security basket. In there, my assets were able to grow tax-free and my insurance policies remained untouched.

The second basket was to hold all my buy and hold assets and investments. This basket is where I placed my properties, funds, stocks and shares, bonds and other long term and medium risk investments.

Into the third basket, I was to place the least amount of money. This is because this basket was my high-risk momentum basket. This is where I was to put my derivatives, risky foreign investments and other high-risk investments. This left the fourth basket – my lifestyle basket. It had a hole in the bottom, causing anything placed within to fall out.

My mentor then told me to fill the first basket until it was full, then allow the excess to overflow into the second basket until it was full, flowing into the third basket. When I asked about the fourth basket, the mentor told me to put it away until a time when the funds in the first three baskets became self-funding.

This is the same advice I would offer anyone starting out in IT contracting. Unfortunately, most contractors come into contracting in the hope of filling this fourth basket with their increased earnings. Extravagant homes, sports cars, luxury holidays, fashionable gadgets and overpriced designer clothing are some of the "bling" that attracts these short-sighted people.

The fourth basket brings very short-term pleasure; however, it has the unfortunate side effect of leaving you feeling empty. Most people attempt to fill this emptiness by more shopping, buying and fast living. Restaurants, clubs and bars can all seem like a lot of fun at the time. Be aware if you are spending more than you are saving. If so, you are heading for disaster.

Contracting, like any industry, has slow-growth years and fast-growth years. Your thrifty saving during the good years will see you through the lean years. Furthermore, the long term effect of saving regularly, investing wisely and planning for you future, will allow you to retire comfortably and with financial dignity.

In many cases, frugal living will also help you avoid other dangers you will encounter whilst contracting.

I once undertook a contract with a colleague who drove a Porsche, and wore the best and most expensive designer clothing, shoes and watches – to work. Within a very short period, his manager called him into his office and terminated his contract.

The reason given was that he had made a few mistakes with a task he had been assigned. In truth, he was innocent; however, his extravagance and outward display of the benefits of his contracting rate, led to envy and jealousy from the permies on the team.

I did not see him for several years after that. When we met up again, he told me the rest of the story. The truth of the matter was that he was actually spending his contracting income as a permie would their wages. He had more days left in each month than he had money.

He was working to keep up interest payments on the extravagant purchases, and worst of all, he had ignored to pay his taxes. Losing the contract coincided with the arrival of a five-digit tax bill. This forced him into bankruptcy and in the end; he lost all the luxury purchases, including his home and company.

Delayed gratification

Your contracting income is not guaranteed to continue indefinitely. Contracts can be terminated abruptly; departments can be closed, moved to another town or country and industries can suffer great financial difficulties. After 9/11, the airline industry suffered a terrible blow and recently, the mortgage industry in America and the UK staggered under two such downward spirals with Countrywide and Northern Rock.

You never know what can happen in your industry or market. You could find yourself – as many contractors did after the uneventful Y2K bug, struggling to earn half the rate you commanded a few months previously. To this end, you must be thrifty, and learn to live well within your means.

You have to learn to practice delayed gratification with all your expenses – from your lunches to buying a new home. Ignoring this advice could lead you to financial disaster.

Delayed gratification is not an easy habit to cultivate; after-all, it is human nature to always want more, and whenever possible, to gratify your wishes. This is easily done when the funds are at your fingertips, or a loan can be easily extended to allow you to afford more.

An old friend once told me, "If you can't afford it, you can't afford it." I have found this to be so true. Do not buy a car simply because you want it; instead, earn it first. Better yet, let the interest on your investments buy it, rather than your contracting income.

Delay your gratification long enough to save up for the purchase. In the process of earning the money to buy the desired item, you probably will discover it is either not worth it, or you may have found a better way of using the money. This is true of most big goals. Similarly, waiting to earn the money to buy a luxury item with cash or the interest from your investments, will cause you to learn the value of money and your time. You will also learn determination, and the exhilarating, natural rush you get from achieving a worthwhile achievement.

With smaller, extravagant purchases, you have to use a different approach. There are three categories of purchases:

- Necessities – economically priced, basic food, drink, clothing and shelter.
- Extras – higher quality food, drink, clothing and a comfortable home.
- Luxuries – spendthrift and extravagant dining, drinking, dressing and opulent homes.

These categories are subjective. The meaning assigned to them and the items you will place within each category will differ from what others will identify with these categories. What may be an economical meal to one contractor, may be a rare treat for another. Similarly, what may be a comfortable home to you may not be a comfortable home to others.

Ideally, you should adjust or learn to live only on a third of your income. The remaining two-thirds of you income should be saved and invested, preferably in secure, tax efficient investment vehicles. See Chapter 5 for further details of these investments types.

Living within the 'necessities' and 'extras' categories with occasional purchases, or spending carefully within the 'luxuries' category is a prudent way to live. This will do one of several things. It will motivate you to increase your income in an effort to raise your living standards. It will secure you against the contracting market down trends, and finally, it will help you to quickly build a savings nest egg and increase your net worth – through your growing investments.

Living only on a third of your income will entail you cutting back on certain frivolous purchases. You should buy only what you need and save part of the one-third of your income for rewards, treats or the occasional pampering, that we all enjoy from time to time. These rare treats or rewards will have more significance, and you will find you enjoy them better after you reduce their regularity. As an example, imagine if Christmas, Chinese New Year or Dewali occurred every weekend. Would they be as special as they are now?

Living well within your means will also humble you, reduce your stress level and increase your available funds for those inevitable emergencies that we all experience through our lives.

The collector mentality

Avoid the collector mentality and 'competing with the Joneses' at all costs. Whether it stems from a non-profitable hobby or interest, or simply a spendthrift habit, the collector mentality wastes your money on non-investment purchases.

The habit of regularly buying shoes, hats, jewellery, perfume, clothing, handbags, sunglasses and other items, is in many cases, a neurotic condition.

Highlighting this type of waste, are also unnecessary purchases of collecting objects of desire such as cars, home entertainment systems, electronic gadgets, watches and other non-essential, luxury objects of desire.

Excessive spending habit

Excessive spending habits can also manifest in many other ways. Some of the manifestations are as follows:

- Regular beauty treatments such as frequent hairdos, manicures and pedicures, artificial tanning and regular spa visits.
- Unused gym memberships.
- High entertainment subscriptions.
- Regular trips to nightclubs, restaurants, bars or pubs.
- Costly daily lunch expenditures.
- Excessively high mortgage or rental costs – to maintain a home that you are struggling to keep.
- High rental or hired purchase costs for an expensive motorbike or motorcar.
- Expensive luxury holidays.
- Memberships to societies and clubs to gain a higher sense of status.
- Expensive newspaper and magazine subscriptions.
- Non-essential, domestic staff.
- Gambling debts.
- Fines due to negligence to settle bills on time.
- Anything you do not need, but do or have, because of peer group pressure.
- Addiction to paid sex, smoking, drinking or drugs.

To realize financial success and security, avoid all the above. My brother once told me – in a rare moment of inspired wisdom – "Too much of anything is bad for you." To this end, avoid surpluses of any kind – especially expensive ones.

The justification for these unrestrained behaviours will often be irrational and nonsensical. However, because they are based on the gratification of your desires, very few sensible arguments will convince you otherwise. It is up to you to practice self-control and reasonable thinking. Evaluate yourself fairly, and determine where you are over spending, then reduce your squandering accordingly.

We will now look in more detail at a few points that were highlighted in the excessive spending list.

Lunches

This is perhaps one of the most deceptive of all the listed points on the excessive spending list. We all need to eat between breakfast and dinner. Lunch is the time most of us elect to satisfy this need, and often to socialise with colleagues as well. The satisfaction of these needs can cost you two to three times the amount you spend on your groceries bill, if you are unaware of the cost of city lunches.

In London for instance, a sandwich, drink and a piece of sweet pudding or cake can set you back by £5 to over £10. If you spend this amount daily, Monday thru Friday, and work (on average) ten and a half months each year, you will spend between £1,020 and £2,040, just on work lunches.

On the other hand, if you spend £80 to £150 per month on your home grocery shopping, you will only total £960 to £1,800 each year. In most cases, your lunch expenditures are the same (or more), than your entire personal groceries spending. Most people go out with their associates from the office to a pub or bar after work each week. The added costs of this greatly increases the money spent for food and entertainment, whilst "at work".

You have three options for cutting back on this spending. All three require a change of your habits. The first option is to stop eating lunches and instead have only breakfast and dinner. This may be too austere for most. Your second option is to bring in a packed lunch. Making your own lunch for work can save you a fortune. The raw materials for a sandwich for instance may cost a tiny fraction of what the city shops charge.

In a very short time, you will see your savings mounting to a significant level. You could be saving upwards of £100 a month and in some cases, almost double that.

The downside is that you have to plan and make this lunch prior to coming to work. This could mean getting up a little earlier, remembering to buy the ingredients that go into your sandwiches or lunch meal. Some people are fortunate and have the lunches made for them. If you are such a person then that is even better. You not only save money on your lunch but you also save on your time in the preparation.

If your workplace offers heating facilities, i.e., a microwave oven, then you could even bring in a proper meal and enjoy a warm lunch, instead of cold sandwiches, salads and fruits. You also save time in queuing to buy your lunch when you bring in a homemade lunch.

Your third choice for saving on lunches is to visit a grocery store each lunch time and purchase a cheaper meal. Avoid the restaurants and take away, pubs and bars where food costs more, and temptation to have the odd, expensive drink from the bar is too much to resist. Choose the less expensive option. Supermarkets and grocery stores sell soups, sandwiches and salads among many other delicious, nutritious and tasty lunch choices. Whilst not cheaper than the home-made lunch, the grocery store or supermarket option is a good second. The only downside to buying lunch, is that the long lunch queues can often steal your limited lunch time.

Travelling to work

You may be restricted in the method by which you get to work. The site could be located in a remote, rural area hardly serviced by public transport, or in the middle of a city where car parking is restricted, and congestion charges and high parking fees apply. However you travel to where you contract, make sure you are using the most cost effective mode of transportation.

Walking or jogging

If you live within walking distance to your work site, you could elect to walk to work. This reduces your personal, carbon footprint, assists your health by strengthening your heart, and allows you to get a free aerobic workout twice a day. When you opt to walk to work, you save on public transportation costs and/or wear and tear (and fuel) costs on your motorbike or motorcar. You also greatly reduce the chances of being involved in a transport accident. If your contract site offers showers and changing rooms, you could also consider jogging to work. This option is not for everyone, however, jogging to work is a great way to keep fit, lose weight, improve your health and save a lot of money.

Cycling

Similar benefits can be gained through cycling to your work. Again, you can improve your health, lose weight and build stamina and strength. Furthermore, the upkeep of a peddle bike is almost negligible compared to that of a motorbike or a motorcar. You will reduce your carbon footprint and help to reduce the damage to our environment at the same time. You will also save money by not paying for the extra fuel for your own motor vehicle, or travel tickets for public transportation.

Public transport

Although public transportation is overcrowded in most large cities, it is the next best method for getting to work. Because many people will be sharing the bus, train, metro or riverboat, there is a greatly reduced, group carbon footprint than there will be if each person on the public transport was to drive a motor vehicle to work. In most cases, if you leave early or late enough, you can avoid the rush hour crowds. Most public transport services offer extra savings through a weekly, monthly or annual travel passes. Normally, the longer the period, the more discounted the pass will be per trip.

You will also save on the high costs of car ownership if you use public transport, cycle or walk. You could also cut down your travel costs by only owning one car – if you are a multi-car family. You could reserve the use of the car for longer journeys, where your destination would be otherwise impossible or very difficult to reach, with public transportation.

Personal vehicle

Finally, if you must drive, at least elect to drive an economical car. This is not necessarily one that only saves on fuel, but you should also seek a vehicle that economises on the regularity of repairs and cost of maintenance. A reliable car which will last you for many years before it starts to show signs of its age, is a better buy than an inferior, but fuel economical car, that requires constant maintenance.

If you must use your car to travel to work, explore all the avenues of sharing the costs of the ride with a neighbour, friend or colleague. You could either drive or be driven to work, or you could take turns with other driver(s) to ride to work. In the case of the former, you could share the cost of the fuel and/or maintenance of the vehicle with the other passenger(s)/driver(s). If you take it in turns to drive your own cars (as in the case of the latter example), you would naturally decrease the cost of fuel and wear and tear on your vehicle through the division of the usage.

Whichever way you select, if you must drive to a contract/work site, make sure you are driving an economical car, and wherever possible share the running costs of that car with others.

Subscriptions

Many of us subscribe to magazines, newspapers, books, CD/DVD clubs, financial services, mobile telecommunication and/or phone services, shopping services and many other packaged deals, only to forget that we are still paying for these services, months – sometimes years – later. Many businesses depend upon your negligence to help increase their profits each year. Through direct debits, standing orders, credit cards, your phone or mobile bill, you may still be paying for these services. You will continue to pay for services that you subscribed to, but later forget to cancel or unsubscribe, when you no longer needed them.

Request a statement from your bank and look for regular payments you should no longer be making. If indeed, you no longer use a service that you are paying for, then cancel them *immediately*. Unsubscribing from these services, cancelling direct debits and ceasing standing orders for unwanted services and/or subscriptions, can save you a small fortune. Wherever possible, try to get a rebate on some (if not all) of your overpaid funds.

Manage your bank account better in the future. Regularly review it for outdated subscriptions, unwanted memberships and regular, outgoing payments. Avoid subscribing to services that you do not really need. If you must subscribe to a service for a short period, make a note to cancel the subscription at a definite date. Mark this on a calendar, in your diary or stick a note on your fridge – whatever reminder technique works best for you.

Limited period offers and credit cards

Credit card companies and other service providers sometimes offer zero percent offers for a limited period. These deals are tempting and can be great if you remember to return the borrowed funds, and cancel the card or service, before the offer period expires. Forgetting to do so could leave you paying high interests on loans and borrowing for many months before you realize it.

Mobile phone companies and utility companies (as well as many other service providers), use this method of marketing to lure new customers to their company. Most of these new customers soon forget about the limited-time offer and never cancel the service after the expiration date. Normally, after the expiry period, the service ceases to be attractive, and in many cases, is designed to get you "hooked" on something that you will pay for, far into the future. A perfect rule-of-thumb to remember, whenever considering sales offers is this: The big print gives it to you, whilst the small print takes it away. Therefore, it is always prudent to read *all* the fine print of an offer, before accepting or signing anything.

Again, if you must take advantage of these deals, make sure to terminate the service before "the deal" expires. Review all your services and utilities every quarter. Use comparison Web sites such as http://www.uswitch.com or http://www.switchwithwhich.co.uk to find the best deals. Whenever you discover your current service provider no longer supplies you with the best deal, switch to a different company with better prices.

Chapter 3

Patching and Training

- Effectively Improve Your IT Market Value
- How to Consistently Develop Your IT Skills
- How to Change Fields

Patching and Training

Like all new undertakings (and even in established businesses), continuous competition, market changes, tax laws, company operation rules (as well as many other factors), will require you to make constant changes, in order to stay competitive, compliant and profitable. IT contracting is no different; however, the changes required mostly in IT contracting is in maintaining or increasing your market value, and staying ahead of tax changes. Whilst a good accountant can help you achieve the latter, the former will rest squarely on your shoulders.

We will now examine how you can tackle this responsibility effectively. Your market value, reputation, professionalism and survival in the IT contracting field will depend greatly on getting these factors right and constantly working to improve on them.

You will effectively improve your IT contracting market value, in this section which covers the following points:

- Your CV.
- Your interview technique.
- Your professionalism.
- Your marketing and promotion.
- Your learning program.
- Changing your specialization.

Effectively Improve Your IT Market Value

There is no guarantee that the market value of your skills will increase, or even keep up with the times or inflation. Many trends and factors will influence how much your skills command. The following list emphasizes some of these factors:

- Skills demand – are your abilities greatly desired?
- Area of expertise – are you in a 'hot' area of the IT industry?
- Certification and accreditation – do you have the latest accreditation required in your area of work?
- Industry/sector – are you in a 'hot' industry/sector (e.g., finance, banking, investment banking, and hedge funds)?
- Geographic location – is the area you work in offering the highest paid and abundant IT contracts?
- CV/interview and professionalism – is your CV, interview techniques, and professionalism selling you short, or nicely honed?
- Psychological factor – do you believe you are worth more?

Skills demand

If your skills are no longer in demand, you will command less money than if your expertise is in keeping with the times. IT talents can either be:

- Redundant – obsolete, or superseded by a newer skill.
- Saturated – the supply has surpassed the need, i.e., over-supplied.
- Commanding – in great demand, i.e., the supply does not meet the current needs of the industry.

Normally, the more greatly desired a skill is, the higher paying that skill will be. Therefore, it pays to be in areas of expertise that are in large demand. This usually requires specialisation. You may need special training and/or certification to qualify to compete with your new skills. You may also be required to stay ahead of changing technologies by regularly updating your abilities. This is especially true of Web development and programming in general; however, other areas such as databases, storage, network security, network design and system migration may also require continuing education.

The IT industry runs on new technology, where everything changes rapidly. It is easy for expertises to become superseded from over-specialization. Therefore, be careful not to specialize so much that your skills are susceptible to becoming obsolete.

Possibly the safest area to specialize in, is IT management. Although you have to keep up with new initiatives and compliances, the risk of becoming outmoded is smaller, as your core abilities are based on managing resources at a higher level of abstraction. Although IT technology changes rapidly, the system classes do not change as fast.

Help desk, PC support, network support, application support, mail, database, development, security, and storage are some of the major system classes. These will rarely become obsolete. An IT manager supervises these resources and the people who install, maintain, and support them. Therefore, if you want an area of high demand and high rates, manoeuvre yourself into IT management.

Area of expertise

Certain systems classes naturally pay more than others do. For instance, developers generally earn more than support staff. Therefore, if you were a developer with skills that are in high demand, you would earn far more than a contractor who is in the first, second or 3rd line of support. There are exceptions to this, but they are rare.

You can often double the rate you command simply by changing fields of expertise. The change will require you to acquire new skills and/or accreditation. However, this will be very worthwhile in the medium to long term. You can quickly recoup the cost of the change in no time.

Visit http://www.contractoruk.com/market_stats or http://www.itjobswatch.co.uk/contract.aspx for statistics on areas of expertise ranking and current, average contractor rates. The 7th October 2007 statistics courtesy of ITJobsWatch.co.uk is as follows:

Rank	IT Skill	IT Jobs Proportion	Average Hourly Rates	Average Daily Rates
1	Developer	23.86 %	£33.02	£421
2	Analyst	20.43 %	£20.82	£404
3	Consultant	8.37 %	£32.09	£442
4	Business Analyst	7.83 %	£31.54	£453
5	Project Manager	7.45 %	£36.75	£432
6	Java Developer	4.13 %	£38.96	£440
7	.NET Developer	3.64 %	£33.28	£342
8	Administrator	3.53 %	£21.45	£323
9	C# Developer	3.49 %	£34.79	£444
10	Support Analyst	3.01 %	£19.47	£357

Table 20: Top Ten Contracting Skills – 'Source: ITJobsWatch.co.uk'

Rank	IT Skill	IT Jobs Proportion	Average Hourly Rates	Average Daily Rates
1	Internet	2.41 %	£27.86	£353
2	TCP/IP	2.12 %	£25.38	£348
3	Firewall	1.98 %	£26.09	£377
4	LAN	1.90 %	£22.84	£341
5	WAN	1.76 %	£23.89	£345
6	SAN	1.75 %	£30.70	£392
7	DNS	1.15 %	£25.33	£361
8	Intranet	1.01 %	£23.31	£340
9	VPN	0.97 %	£23.14	£354
10	VoIP	0.80 %	£28.73	£377

Table 21: Top Ten Communication and Networking Skills for Contracting – 'Source: ITJobsWatch.co.uk'

Rank	IT Skill	IT Jobs Proportion	Average Hourly Rates	Average Daily Rates
1	SQL	10.97 %	£30.33	£412
2	Java	9.62 %	£34.07	£448
3	C#	8.15 %	£33.99	£441
4	C++	4.31 %	£36.71	£531
5	JavaScript	3.64 %	£30.42	£340
6	C	2.74 %	£34.19	£397
7	Perl	2.53 %	£33.53	£430
8	VB	2.42 %	£27.60	£428
9	PL/SQL	2.34 %	£38.30	£384
10	VBA	2.26 %	£26.12	£502

Table 22: Top Ten Programming Languages for Contracting - 'Source: ITJobsWatch.co.uk'

Rank	IT Skill	IT Jobs Proportion	Average Hourly Rates	Average Daily Rates
1	Windows	11.42 %	£20.59	£357
2	Unix	9.25 %	£31.26	£431
3	Linux	4.27 %	£32.27	£412
4	Solaris	3.11 %	£31.91	£420
5	Windows 2000	2.63 %	£19.79	£327
6	Windows XP	2.38 %	£18.15	£273
7	Windows NT	2.04 %	£19.87	£390
8	Windows Server 2003	1.51 %	£22.48	£342
9	AIX	1.21 %	£33.49	£415
10	HPUX	0.76 %	£32.43	£394

Table 23: Top Ten Operating Systems for Contracting - 'Source: ITJobsWatch.co.uk'

IT contracting is a business, so if you find that your skills are never in the top ten lists, then you may want to consider acquiring new skills, that are in the top paying categories.

Doing so will put you in the top earning area of expertise, and earn you more money than you may have previously brought home.

Certification and accreditation

The difference between the bottom end of a skill area and the top end, could be accreditation. In IT contracting, skill is king, where accreditation runs a close second in importance. Two contractors with the same skill set will command a very different rate, if one is accredited and the other is not.

Accreditation often gives you that extra professionalism, where lack of certification does not. Most corporate organisations feel more secure hiring accredited contractors. The accreditation confirms what your experience and training emphasizes. It reassures the organisation, without requiring proof that you know what you are doing.

A few points about accreditation: It may open doors wider, but that is where it stops. Once you are hired, you no longer can rely on your accreditation to sway the organisation. The practical application of your skills – learned through experience – will be the only thing highlighting and confirming your excellence and competence, in performing your role.

Industry/sector

Industrial growth is cyclical, and no industry or sector will reign supreme forever. During the rapid growth of the car industry; manufacturers, transportation, car sales, road construction, as well as car insurance and car maintenance companies, all led the way. They demanded more staff, and with greater skills. Wherever the supply was short of the demand, people made money.

In the same way, in the rapid growth stages of the personal computer, related organisations topped the earnings and wages charts. Again, those whose skills were in great demand, such as microchip designers, computer programmers and software developers, made money.

During the heady dotcom years of the late nineties, dotcomers and Internet companies peaked the growth and income charts. Banking and finance also has its turn, every time the economic cycle comes around in their favour. Property developers also enjoy an industry rotation in the limelight, during low interest rate periods in the economy.

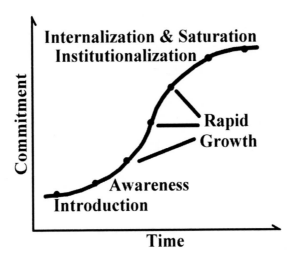

Figure 1: S-curve

Whilst certain sectors come in and out of the public interest during various times of economic cycles, some sectors only have one cycle of fame, after–which, they reach the internalization and saturation phase of the commitment over time S curve (see Figure 1).

During the introduction through awareness phases of a new technology or industry, there is hardly any money to be made by IT contractors. This is because the time period requires more investment than it yields, making this stage generally a loss, leading the development phase. However, as soon as the technology or industry is adopted and starts to develop, it goes through rapid growth, as more and more people embrace it. Soon, the big money realises there is money to be made here, and the institutions and large corporations get involved. Once it is institutionalised, it is not long before it is saturated and becomes well established.

Normally, for IT contractors, this is the time to make money from any economic phenomena, technology, emerging market, industry or sector, which is during the rapid growth phase, (as illustrated in Figure 1). After this phase, it becomes more competitive and the profit margins become thinner.

You can find the industries or sectors going through rapid growth by reading the financial papers, or through http://www.iii.co.uk/markets/?type=sectors&period=year&ord erby=change, http://www.investor.reuters.com/Industries.aspx or, http://biz.yahoo.com/ic/l/g5r.html. Many other Web sites and IT periodicals offer news and performance information on industries in the UK, Europe, U.S. and other markets.

Geographic location

As mentioned before, the best advice is to contract in or near, the financial and business centre of a large city or town. Remote, rural areas rarely offer the variety and choice for contracting that a city does. This is because there are more businesses located within cities and business parks, than there are elsewhere; therefore, the geographic areas you restrict yourself to, will directly affect your ability for finding your next role.

Similarly, the ease in which you can attend interviews, without taking time off from your current contract role, is also important to consider. If you are working in Poole, but you have an interview in the centre of London, you will definitely have to take time off, to attend the meeting. This will increase the cost of your hunt for the next role, and thus lower your earnings.

In this example, you will also lose money through travelling into London for the interview, and you might upset your current organisation, due to this. It is therefore more cost effective and less hassle, to live near where you contract and contract in an area – where there is an abundance of contracting opportunities – so that you lose no money in searching for your next role, and you can attend interviews within your lunch break, or after work.

CV/Interview and professionalism

We have already covered basic CV creation and interview techniques. In this section, we will expand this information to cover more advanced CV design, and interview techniques. Your résumé or CV and interview technique, will determine whether you get a contract or not.

The CV will open the door to the interview, whilst the interview will allow you to sell yourself to the organisation, and convince them of your competence, professionalism, skills, work ethics and usefulness to the requirements. Once you get the contract, your professionalism will determine whether you last for the duration of the contract and are renewed, or if your contract is terminated prematurely.

Introduction to professionalism

Concerning professionalism: there are a few points you should always keep in mind when contracting:

1. Technical incompetence – inability to perform the tasks and duties required by the role.
2. Punctuality – constant lateness and bad time keeping.

3. Work ethic and attitude – laziness, bad workmanship and poor quality of work, mixed with an unhelpful and non-proactive attitude.

4. Profane language usage – involuntary and uncontrollable swearing in your natural speech.

5. Anti-social behaviour – aggressive and antagonistic actions, sexism, racism, ageism, spitting and extreme unhelpfulness.

6. Dress – unprofessional dressing, excessively casual attire, unclean or careless appearance, overtly sexy and/or, clothing displaying unseemly images or slogans.

7. Personal hygiene – bad breath, body odour, dandruff, flatulence, nose picking, spitting and other unclean or unacceptable, personal traits or habits.

8. Integrity and compliance – disloyalty, dishonesty, unreliability and breach of compliance rules and/or abuse of e-mail, telephone, and Internet usage.

9. Flexibility – unwillingness to perform certain tasks, e.g., overtime, shift work, working through lunches, necessary manual work and/or weekend work.

10. Professional confidence – acute shyness, lack of confidence in your ability to perform tasks with your skills, lack of confidence in your professional conduct, fear of certain users (i.e., traders and executives).

This list is in order of importance. I have tried to list them by priority of their ability to get your contract terminated. You will notice Integrity is listed at number 8. Personally, I believe it should be first for all companies; however, my experience from working at more than thirty-five organisations has taught me otherwise.

Integrity is only a problem if your lack of it costs the company money. Unfortunately, most of the time, integrity is low on the priority list of organisations, especially when they are making money by condoning or ignoring their staffs' lack of integrity.

The first three points, technical incompetence, lateness, poor work ethic and bad attitude, are most likely to get your contract terminated earlier than the remaining topics. Although, excessive and regular abuse of the other points is also likely to get you marched off the premises.

In financial organisations, compliance issues will be moved to the first or second position, immediately after technical incompetence. As, the Financial Services Authority (FSA) and other governing bodies can shut down a bank or financial organisation's operations, if they find that organisation (or a member of their staff), has (or is) breaking compliance rules.

For most IT contractors, the most common compliance risks are password secrecy, software piracy and software licensing. Avoid losing your contract over these issues by never asking for passwords, borrowing software or worse, stealing software from your contracts, and never installing software without the correct licenses.

We will look at advanced professionalism issues after looking at advanced CV writing and advanced interview techniques.

Advanced CV writing

We have already looked at how to layout your CV. Next, we will look more closely at what to say, and how to say it in your CV. Your CV will stand out, due to its layout and readability. However, the reader will soon discard it if – once he/she picks up the CV from the stack of applicants – the content is weak, boring, unprofessional, has grammatical errors and/or avoidable spelling errors. These factors alone tells the organisation a lot about you.

Tone

The tone of your CV sets the mood of everything that is reflective of yourself, and is important to develop appropriately. It can be used to give a professional impression all on its own. You have to be careful what characteristics you select. There are three basic qualities:

1. **Casual/social:** "Joe is an amiable C, C++ and C# developer, who loves nothing better than to solve complex programming problems. Since he was young, Joe has found programming his main love and nothing brings him more pleasure than to code. He has enjoyed many years with some of the top fortune 500 companies. And enjoyed working on...".

2. **Formal/Business:** "Joe Bloggs is a qualified C, C++ and C# developer with over ten years commercial experience. Having worked with five of the top ten Fortune 500 companies in the last four years alone, he brings his honed skills and knowledge from working on major international projects such as...".

3. **Academic/Scientific:** "Joe Bloggs is a C, C++ and C# programmer. He has worked in the field for over ten years. In that time, he has undertaken projects for more than five, top fortune 500 companies. He is proficient with CASE tools, OOD, SSDM, and other industry standard, programming design standards and tools. Joe Bloggs has worked on...".

Each tone has its place in document writing. Although, when it comes to IT contracting CVs, it is unwise to use a casual approach. This can come across as being overly familiar with the reader, unprofessional and not serious enough for the business environment.

Similarly, the academic overtone, normally used for journals, technical papers and white papers, is too formal and can be boring at times. It is therefore not ideal to use this characteristic for your IT contracting CV.

This leaves the formal or business approach, which is the ideal tone to use for your contracting CV. It will make you look like a professional business person. It also adds professionalism to everything you present in your CV. As long as your CV set-up is professional, the use of the formal business tone will enhance your professional image in the eyes of the reader.

To get this quality right, simply imagine you were giving a presentation to the board of directors of a large, multinational organisation. This presentation is about you. How would you present yourself? These are the attributes you seek to harness in your CV: punchy, snappy, smart, concise, relevant, to the point, slick, professional and dynamic.

Verb Tense

You should write your CV in the present or past tense, and avoid writing in the future tense or using a blend of all three. The verb tone in which you elect to write your CV will affect how you are perceived by the reader. Therefore, your CV should only include present and/or past tense, whenever possible. Future tense should either never be used, or only used in the parts of your CV that describe future events.

Wherever you find a future tense sentence in your CV, rewrite it in the present tense. For example:

"Joe Bloggs will graduate from St. Martins College in mid 2012."

Should be rewritten as;

"Joe Bloggs started his four year degree studies at St. Martins College in 2008."

Or

"Joe Bloggs is currently studying a four year degree in Computer Engineering at St. Martins College."

Normally, the present tense reads and sounds better than the past or future tense. It brings the reader closer to you – through your CV. Past tense tends to distance the CV reader from you. Future tense – the worst CV tense of them all – tends to plant doubt in the CV reader's mind concerning the subject being covered.

Why is this? Because few can argue with an event that is history. Similarly, who can argue with something currently happening? However, ask the same questions of a future event, and everyone will have an opinion or belief. Those who are cynical, sceptical, suspicious, distrusting, biased, jealous or simply antagonistic or unfriendly, will all have negative opinions of your future tense statement or comment.

Remove this negativity magnet from your CV by never using future tense. Always use present or past tense in cases where future tense could be replaced.

Personal Pronouns

In what person is your CV written? You can select one of three. The basics of the three persons are as follows:

1. First person is the person speaking:
   I, we, me, us, my, mine, our, ours.
2. Second person is the person spoken to:

You, your, yours.
3. Third person is the person or thing spoken about:
    He, she, it, his, her, hers, its, him, her, it, they, them, their, theirs.

In other literary works, each person personal pronoun has a lot to offer, however, in IT contracting CVs, some of them are inappropriate.

The first person – for instance – reads as you speaking directly to the reader. It is difficult to promote yourself effectively when using the personal pronouns assigned to this person. "I have a first class degree from …," sounds boastful and somehow repellent. "He received a first class degree from …," sounds much more humble. This is because praise about yourself comes better from third parties, rather than from yourself directly. It is also more believable from others, than from yourself.

The second person is rarely used in literature because it sounds weird (and generally reads incorrectly) for the reader to read about you, from the reader's point of view. "You have a first class degree from …," just doesn't work. Writing in second person makes you sound like you are the reader. This is likely to create a lot of confusion and a highly inefficient CV.

The third person personal pronouns are the best personal pronouns to use for your IT contracting CV. "He has a first class degree from …," has a comfortable, natural and believable sound to it.

Pacing

When using the third person personal pronoun, pace the writing by switching between your name and the personal pronouns. The following example illustrates what I mean by this:

"Joe Bloggs is fully MCSE 2003 qualified and he is currently studying for an MCP in Vista installation and configuration. He has a first class degree from ...".

Two poor examples of phrasing are as follows:

"Joe Bloggs is fully MCSE 2003 qualified and Joe Bloggs is currently studying for an MCP in Vista installation and configuration. Joe Bloggs has a first class degree from ...".

Or

"He is fully MCSE 2003 qualified and he is currently studying for an MCP in Vista installation and configuration. He has a first class degree from ...".

Similarly, pace the reading by keeping the speed slow enough to be comfortably read. Make it too fast and your CV will no longer seem professional. An example of a fast paced sentence is as follows:

"Joe Bloggs is fully MCSE 2003 qualified, is currently studying for an MCP in Vista installation and configuration and has a first class degree from ...".

The above reads as if it were written on the run. You can slow your CVs pace by using shorter sentences and commas.

"Joe Bloggs is fully MCSE 2003 qualified. He is currently studying for an MCP in Vista installation and configuration, and he has a first class degree from ...".

Or

"Joe Bloggs is fully MCSE 2003 qualified. He is currently studying for his MCP in installation and configuration of Microsoft Vista. He also has a first class degree from ...".

Phrasing

The last sentence, "He also has a first class degree from ...," uses the "also" to soften the repetitiveness of the last sentence. You can also use, *"Furthermore, Joe Bloggs also has a first class degree from ..."* or *"Furthermore, he also has a first class degree from ...".*

Familiarity and Formality

Avoid making your CVs third person sound overly familiar with yourself. Do not use first name references such as; *"Furthermore, Joe also has a first class degree from ..."* You can also go overboard and make your CV overly formal by using formal references such as; *"Furthermore, Mr. Bloggs also has a first class degree from ...".* This tends to make your CV not relatable to the reader.

It is important not to come across on your CV as being overly hyped. Title usage within sentences is one sure way of doing this. You may have a Ph.D. or other qualification which certifies you to be referred to as Dr., Master, Lord, Dame, Sir, etc.; however, where appropriate, avoid using these titles for the purpose of establishing your status within sentences.

When used on your CV, they can make you seem pompous, bigheaded or 'stuck-up'. Similarly, avoid titles such as Mr., Mrs., Miss, Ms., etc., in the sentences of your IT contracting CV. These formal titles generally detract from your CV more than they add. Use pronouns and full names instead, e.g., *Joe Bloggs, he or she.*

Wordiness

Always aim for direct, concise and reasonable sentences or points in your CV. Avoid using elaborate or flowery language. Do not be fooled; using large words will not always make you seem intelligent. This is especially true if the words are used in the wrong context, or if a simpler word choice would have sufficed. See the following for an example of a direct, concise and reasonable sentence:

"Joe Bloggs is MCSE 2003 qualified, and is currently studying for his Microsoft Vista MCP. He holds a first class degree in computer engineering from ... ".

Here is an example of an excessively wordy and pretentious sentence. The long and unnecessary words in this sentence give it a exaggerated feel which distracts the reader from the facts and information. Sentences like the one that follows will cause the reader not to take you seriously.

"Joe Bloggs is unreservedly Microsoft Certified Systems Engineer 2003 qualified. At the moment, he is excogitating for his Microsoft Certified Practitioner examination in Microsoft Vista. He is also endowed with the highest distinction in an honours degree from ... ".

The CV reader may be unable to understand some of your words. This may cause them to reject your CV out of hand, or you may intimidate them enough to make them avoid facing you. There are few managers who will hire someone who they feel is intellectually far superior to them.

Similarly, you could cause the CV reader to prejudge you as being someone who thinks he/she is 'all that'. Your CV could be rejected simply because of the presumption. Therefore, avoid attracting negative prejudgement through your CV – stick to direct, concise and reasonable sentences, and avoid being perceived as wordy, long-winded, braggadocios or obscure.

Spelling

Regardless of how professionally worded your CV is, just one bad spelling or grammatical error could undo a lot of the good your CV – up to that point – had done. People tend to focus on the negative, especially when they are in a position of a judge or critic.

Most CV readers do not start by looking for the good candidates; they start by weeding out the unqualified, disliked and/or unsuitable candidates. Once they eliminate the easily identified, unsuitable candidates, the CV reader becomes even more critical in order to eliminate more people from the remaining suitable pile of CVs.

To increase your CV's chances of being in the final CV selection for interviewing, you have to eliminate all possible negative visual errors. These include spelling and grammar errors.

It is easy to miss spelling and grammatical errors in any writing. I have even discovered errors in certain versions of the Holy Bible, a book which is supposedly edited and proofread by thousands of reviewers before publishing.

It is understandable that some error may miss reviewers and editors of large publications; however, your CV is not one of these documents. At most, your CV will contain a handful of pages. Spelling and grammar checking your CV should therefore be simple.

Many people use word processors for spellchecking and grammar checking. Whilst these tools are great for preliminary editing, they are not adequate for final proofing. To do this, you need to resort to manually reading your CV word by word and line by line.

Whilst reading, have a dictionary and thesaurus at hand. Be careful not to skip over any part of your CV. All that is required to tarnish your good work is a single, bad error.

When spell checking, watch out for words that are spelled differently from the word you initially intended to use. Some prime examples are: 'lose' and 'loose', 'cite' and 'site', 'home' and 'hone', 'computer' and 'compute', etc. Your word processor will not flag these words as spelling errors. This is why it is vital that you read and re-read your CV, to identify and eliminate these types of spelling error.

Grammar

Similarly, when grammar checking, watch out for long sentences, comma splices and run-on sentences. Run-on sentences join two or more complete sentences with no punctuation, whilst the comma splice is a sentence in which two independent clauses are joined by a comma with no conjunction. They make your CV unprofessional and potentially confusing. An example of a comma splice is, *"It is nearly seven o'clock, we cannot reach our destination before dark."* One way to fix the comma splice is to use a semi-colon thusly, *"It is nearly seven o'clock; we cannot reach our destination before dark."*

Also to be avoided are sentence fragments. These are incomplete sentences. Normally, any sentence which you cannot apply 'the yes/no test' to, is a fragment. The test simply uses the sentence to ask a question, which should only be answered with a 'yes' or a 'no'.

As an example, let's examine the following sentence: *"He is currently studying for his MCP in installation and configuration of Microsoft Vista"*.

The yes/no question would be:

"Is he currently studying for his MCP in installation and configuration of Microsoft Vista?"

The answer would be 'yes'. If the sentence was a fragment; such as:

"He is currently studying for his MCP in installation and configuration".

Then the 'yes/no' question would be;

"Is he currently studying for his MCP in installation and configuration of a specific program?".

The answer here can only be 'no'. The sentence does not make sense because it is a fragmented sentence. Apply the 'yes/no' question to each sentence in your CV to eliminate sentence fragments.

Parallelism

When you make lists or bullet points in your CV, watch out for parallelisms. Parallelisms occur if you make comparisons or lists, and one or more item in the list or comparison does not match the majority of the format. As an example:

"Joe Bloggs undertook support of:

- *Hardware*
- *Software*
- *The operating systems supported in-house."*

The third does not belong in this list. Its format is different from the others. To make them all parallel, you have to change the format of the non-conforming point, to match the others.

"Joe Bloggs undertook support of:

- *Hardware*
- *Software*
- *In-house operating systems"*

Watch out for parallelisms. There are five cases where you might find them. These are as follows:

1. Coordinating conjunctions (and, or, but, for, so, yet, or nor). Example*: "Joe Bloggs loves tennis and to program."* This should be changed to, *"Joe Bloggs loves tennis and programming,"* or *"Joe Bloggs likes to play tennis and to program."*
2. Correlative Conjunctions (either A or B, neither A nor B, both A and B, not only A but also B, or whether A or B). Example: *"Joe Bloggs not only has a Ph.D., but also is studying CCIE."* This should be changed to, *"Joe Bloggs not only has a Ph.D., but has also been studying for CCIE,"* or *"Joe Bloggs is not only a Ph.D., but is also studying CCIE."*
3. Words in a series. Example: *"Joe Bloggs programs in C, C++, and some C#."* This should be changed to, *"Joe Bloggs programs in C, C++, and C#."*
4. Comparisons and contrasts using 'than' or 'as' (i.e., more than, as much as). Example: *"Joe Bloggs knows C#, more than VB."* This should be changed to, *"Joe Bloggs knows C#, more than he knows VB."*
5. Function words: prepositions e.g., (to, by, in, for), articles (a, an, the), the infinitive (to), introductory words (that, who, which, because, when). *"Joe Bloggs often codes for*

W3 organisation." This should be changed to, *"Joe Bloggs often codes for the W3 organisation."*

Misplaced Modifiers

You can have phrases that make no logical sense if you misplace sentence modifiers. An example of a misplaced modifier is as follows:

"Joe Bloggs joined HP after the stock market crash".

This should be changed to

"After the stock market crash, Joe Bloggs joined HP".

Similarly –ing modifiers can be left dangling when they are not logically connected to the main part of the sentence. As an example:

"Working on HP Blades, Joe Bloggs learned to write Perl scripts".

This is a dangling modifier. It makes no sense. It could be corrected as follows:

"Joe Bloggs learned to write Perl scripts whilst working on HP Blades".

Passive voice

Watch out for the passive voice when you write your CV. This occurs when the subject and the acting agent are not the same. Here is an example:

"Coding has taught Joe Bloggs many things".

In this case, the subject is coding, the action is teaching, and the agent is Joe Bloggs. Because the subject and the acting agent are not the same, this sentence is in passive voice. The sentence can be corrected as follows:

"Joe Bloggs has learned many things from coding".

Not all passive voice sentences can be corrected to non-passive voice. Some active voice sentences do not have easily identifiable, acting agents. Wherever possible, totally rewrite these sentences or eliminate them.

Subject-verb disagreements

When verbs disagree with a subject, you will have a subject verb agreement problem. You can spot these quite easily. Use the following samples to identify subject-verb disagreement:

1. Separated subject and verb — Example: *"Joe Bloggs' experience in IT have taught him all he knows today,"* should be rewritten as, *"Joe Bloggs' experience in IT has taught him all he knows today".*
2. Compound subjects: When two subjects are joined, the verb normally changes. There are a few exceptions to this rule; such as, when the joined subjects are preceded by "every", "no", or "nothing". Furthermore, if the subjects are joined by "nor" or "or", the verb agrees with the last subject. Example: *"Joe Bloggs and Intercorp has worked together for many years",* should be rewritten as, *"Joe Bloggs and Intercorp have worked together for many years".*
3. Indefinite pronoun: There are two types of indefinite pronouns; single and plural. Examples of single indefinite

pronouns are: anyone, anybody, each, either, none. These all use singular verbs. Examples of plural indefinite pronouns are: few, both, many and several. These all use plural verbs. Example: *"Each of Joe Bloggs' contracts uses UNIX"*, or *"Both of Joe Bloggs' contracts trust UNIX"*.

4. Collective nouns (band, minority, majority, class, community, dozen, family, public, team). These are nouns that are singular in form, but plural in meaning. Example: *"The majority of Joe Bloggs' contracts have been in a team"*. Should be rewritten as, *"The majority of Joe Bloggs' contracts have been in teams"*.

5. Plural nouns which are singular in meaning (athletics, economics, politics, news, mumps, and measles), E.G., *"The contracting economics have delayed Joe Bloggs' SAP skills development"*. Should be rewritten as, *"The contracting economics has delayed Joe Bloggs' SAP skills development"*.

6. Titles: When used in sentences, your titles should be singular, never plural. Example: *"Joe Bloggs' 3D VB modules are standard reading in many colleges"*. Should be rewritten as, *"Joe Bloggs' 3D VB modules is standard reading in many colleges"*.

Indicating possession

It is often difficult to know the correct way to indicate possession. You should use *'s* or *s'* As an example, *"Joe Bloggs certificates are on file"*. Should be written as, *"Joe Bloggs' certificates are on file"*.

The following are the possession rules:

Singular nouns

Always add an *'s*. For example, *"Joe Bloggs will need to drive fifty miles to reach Microsoft's testing centre"*.

Plural nouns

If the word does not end with an *s* (or end with an *s* or *z* sound), then add *'s* otherwise, add an apostrophe after the *s* thusly: *s'*. For example, Joe Bloggs last name ends with an *s*. Therefore, to indicate plurality (and ownership, in this case), the following example would apply: *"Joe Bloggs' documents are in good order"*.

Compound nouns

An example of a compound noun is the word "firewall". Compound nouns are words treated jointly as a noun. These words can be separated as in *"server room"*, bunched together as in *"helpdesk"*, or separated with hyphens as in *"check-in"*. There can also be combinations, such as *"transistor-transistor logic"*.

Whenever you want to show possession with compound nouns, place the *'s* on the end.

"It was my helpdesk's role to help the trader".

Joint ownership

When two or more nouns possess something, place the *'s* on the end of the last noun. If, on the other hand, all nouns possess something individually, place the *'s* after each noun.

"It was Fred and Ann's laptop".
"It was Fred's desk, but Ann's laptop".

Possessive pronouns

Possessive pronouns do not use apostrophes. They are not to be confused with the contractions such as, *it's (it is)*, *you're (you are)*, *they're (they are)*, and so on. Remember, the apostrophe in this case replaces something that is missing. The following is the proper use of possessive pronouns:

I	my	mine
you	your	yours
she	her	hers
he	his	his
us	our	ours
they	their	theirs
it	its	its

Example: *"Lets go to yours, I prefer it to mine", or "Lets see how ours does in the test", or "We abandoned its test", or "She offered me hers, but I preferred his to ours"* and, *"They renewed the contract at theirs".*

Indefinite pronouns (e.g., one, somebody, else).
All infinite pronouns use an apostrophe to show ownership. Example: *"Every day, somebody's PC blue screened"* and, *"It was someone else's computer, that crashed".*

Advanced interview techniques

We previously covered simple interview techniques, now we will look at more advanced interview topics. Some of the points discussed in this section will be alien to you, and some may even challenge you. Do not dismiss them out-of-hand without first trying them. You will be pleasantly surprised at the change they will make to your interviewing success.

Mind Polarization

Your mind can either be focused on negative thoughts, images, ideas, worries and imagined fears (until proven real, everything feared, is imagined), or it can be focused on positive thoughts, images, ideas, memories and dreams. It is not possible for your mind to focus on both poles of thought at the same time.

When you focus on negative images, thoughts, memories, and fears, your mind becomes polarized towards similar thoughts, images, memories, and fears that support and manifest more of the same. Similarly, when you focus on positive images, thoughts, memories, and dreams; your mind becomes polarized towards similar positive thoughts, scenarios and events.

The conscious/subconscious mind relationship

It is beyond the scope of this book to delve any deeper into explaining this phenomena. For a better explanation and a visual delight, watch "The Secret" DVD (www.thesecret.tv). You can also read more about this phenomenon in the self-help classic, "Think and Grow Rich" by Napoleon Hill. This information is also available in audio format through Earl Nightingale's "The Strangest Secret".

Your mind is divided into two very different sections – much like an iceberg. And, like an iceberg, you are only conscious of the small part which lies above the icy waters, separating consciousness and unconsciousness. The smaller, younger mind is the seat of conscious awareness and we can control it and direct it at will – in most cases.

The larger, older and more powerful subconscious mind controls all the subconscious processes of the body and mind; activities such as breathing, hair growth, food digestion and blinking, to name but a few. Without the subconscious realm our conscious mind would not be able to manage the millions of small processes and sub-processes imperative to the maintenance of our bodies.

The subconscious mind is so powerful and mysterious that we have yet to learn a fraction of its powers, even in our modern society and scientific advancements of today. Deep within the subconscious mind lies abilities that we do not know we have. The subconscious mind runs mainly automatically, unless guided by the conscious mind.

Unfortunately, most of the time, the conscious mind – unaware of its ability to use and guide the subconscious mind – allows the subconscious mind to operate on autopilot. Furthermore, most people allow their thoughts to wander and dwell on the negative (baseless worries and fears), as well as deriding self-thoughts.

The subconscious mind gives you whatever you ask it for. In fact, even if you don't know you are asking it for something, your lack of direction will be an input for it. Because the subconscious mind is operating on autopilot, and it receives and processes all inputs to the body and mind; it picks up these negative inputs and uses them to program itself.

And, like a good servant, it will mobilise immeasurable powers and literally move heaven and earth to get you what you vividly imagine, fear, dream, believe and desire.

This is true whether what you ask for is good for you or not, positive or negative; happiness or sorrow, success or failure.

Mental preparation for interviews

I have taken some time to explain the relationship between the two parts of your mind to help illustrate the importance of mind polarization. If your mind is full of fears, worries, self-doubt and thoughts of failure in the interview, you will swing your mental polarity from positive to negative. You will start to visualise how you will fail in the upcoming interview. By dwelling on your worries or anxieties, you will help your conscious mind to instruct your obedient subconscious mind to 'fetch' more of what you are imagining.

Your subconscious mind is very efficient and effective at manifesting results from given instructions. Visions, thoughts and verbalised failure will aid it to manifest more failure. Your self-consciousness, fear and worry will be magnified and fed back to you amplified. In fact, your subconscious mind will do better than that. Through a process not yet understood by neurological scientists, the subconscious mind is able to contact and attract events, people and situations to you, that will help manifest the state you so vividly imagine, worry about, fear and think about, the majority of the time.

Bearing these facts in mind, consider the following questions: What do you think about the night before an interview? What are your thoughts, on the way to the meeting? And, what do you think the most about, during the interview?

Are your thoughts of absolute confidence? Do you have a relaxed, self assured belief that you have got the job? Do you know beyond a shadow of any doubt that you will impress the interviewers to the point of being offered the role?

Your subconscious mind will help manifest whatever is in your thoughts. Whatever you believe, think, and know deep down, so shall it be.

Winning before the fight

To prepare for your interview, first get your mind straight and positive. Then, prepare by learning about the organisation, the role, answers to potential technical tests, and route planning. Finally, familiarize yourself with the rest of the topics we covered in basic interview techniques.

If you have a deep enough, (positive) belief about your performance in the interview, you could fail at many things, (and even arrive late) and still be offered the role, before the end of the interview. I know this to be true from personal experience.

One IT contractor who I know, uses the belief system to such great effects, that she has never lost a job which she was interviewed for in nearly ten years. In fact, in most cases, she turns down roles because of multiple offers.

To get to this level, you will need to first start by building belief in yourself and in your interviewing skills. You can do this in three ways. Firstly, tell yourself regularly that you are exceptionally good at interviewing, and you always get every role you go for. Secondly, visualise by closing your eyes and creating mental images of yourself, successfully interviewing. Thirdly, build your confidence on successes. Only go for roles that you are qualified for, and are able to comfortably perform.

The final point is important for those starting out in using this system. Belief is a fragile creation. Don't grow it among weeds. When building belief in your interview success, regular failure at interviews will undermine all your positive self-talk and visualisation.

This is because in the beginning, the belief is weak. I liken belief building to building legs under a table. In the beginning, when you only have a board on the floor with no legs underneath it, the task will seem daunting. It is at this stage that you have to stack the odds in your favour. You do this by going for jobs that you can easily secure. This will quickly build the base foundation of three or four legs under your "belief table".

With three legs under the table, it is still fairly unstable and can be knocked down easily. Therefore, you still have to continue helping the belief grow strong, by obtaining many early successes. Once you have four or more legs under the table, it can stand up by itself and also withstand some shoving and prodding. You can then start to slowly increase your job applications with more ambitious interviews. Again, do not rush this process or instead, you might lose a leg from under the table.

Continuing this belief building process over many years – with many interviews – will create an ironclad self-belief in your interviewing skills and ability to secure roles at any interview you attend.

If you want to turn these years into months, then you will need to use self-talk (auto self-suggestion) and visualisation. Next, we will examine these two incredible tools for building belief and creating new realities in your life.

Self-Talk

You spend more hours talking to yourself than you do talking to anyone else. The silent mental commands, reassurances, and putdowns you give yourself each moment of your waking day, affect you more than you will ever know. Sometimes you may actually verbalise your comments. Are you verbalising positive comments about yourself and your actions?

Most people's self-talk is heavy on the negative, deriding and critical side. They spend all day repeating how stupid, clumsy, dumb, unattractive, fat, ugly, slow, unintelligent or unpopular they are – to themselves. This constant barrage of negative self-talk is absorbed and acted upon by the subconscious mind. If you believe you are no good, not loved, not smart and broke, then it's no wonder your subconscious mind has helped you physically manifest these factors into your life.

Whilst the scope of this book will not allow a more thorough exposure of this subject, you can read more about self-talk from, "What to Say When You Talk to Your Self" by Shad Helmstetter, Ph.D. or the classic book, "Self-Mastery Through Conscious Auto-Suggestion" by Emile Coue.

What you believe and say to yourself and others, about your IT contracting, abilities, income and skills (especially winning contracts through interviews), will greatly affect your contracting business. If you believe you are not worth more than you are currently earning then you are right, you are not. However, if you believe that you are worth more than you are earning, then likewise, you are also correct.

Whatever you believe and say regularly to yourself and others – how you really see yourself – will always be your reality. To this extent, no matter where you are right now, you truly deserve it, because you believe you belong there. Change your belief and you change your life. Change your beliefs about your contracting worth and your rates will also change to match.

This is a powerful tool, once you learn to use it correctly. I know of a contractor who had very few skills or technical knowledge. The only thing going for her within the IT world, was her fiancée who was a fanatical contractor.

Before she became a contractor, she was a hairdresser. Her fiancée isolated her from all others, and instilled in her a solid belief about her earning potential in IT contracting. He personally trained her in interview techniques and some basic technical IT skills.

Armed only with his teachings, he sent her off contracting. She so believed in her fiancée that she never questioned what he had told her about her earning potential. Sure enough, her first few contracts were incredible opportunities; which further reinforced in her how truthful his instructional beliefs had been. She landed some very high paying helpdesk support roles and very quickly increased her rates to the mid-£20s per hour mark, in less than a year.

In her mind contracting was easy, interviews were simply an informal chat prior to starting the role. She also simply believed that large, international blue chip companies were easy to contractually land. She knew no difference, and had no negative anchors or references to make her believe otherwise. Her beliefs concerning contracting were all positive, and so she seemed to only experience positive results in her contracting roles.

Others who knew her, thought she was just lucky at first. But when she repeated her success again and again over many years, they started to see her in a different light. As the years passed, she improved in her technical skills and knowledge;

however, her self-belief, self-talk and positive expectations, had paved the way for her years, before her skills and knowledge caught up.

Before you go to the interview, prepare for it by telling yourself over and over again that you have got the role. Whenever a negative thought about the forthcoming interview starts to creep into your mind, quickly replace it with a verbal declaration of your desired result. Tell yourself, "I am working as a contractor at "XYZ company, earning £......... per day." Fill in the rate and replace XYZ with the company you are actually interviewing with.

Make sure the last thing you do the night before the interview, is to repeat the statement in the mirror at least fifty times before you fall asleep. You need not shout it, however, speak it with confidence and feel the emotions you will feel when you acquire the job. Feel them now, as you tell yourself you have the contract.

During the interview day, repeat the affirmation with every opportunity you get. It is said that repetition is the mother of skill; this is also true of belief. If you hear anything repeated long enough, you will believe it. That is how the news media and advertisers manage to convince the nation to buy a product, or believe a story.

Although this technique is great to use leading up to an interview, positive self-talk can be used for improving your beliefs, and therefore your reality, on any subject. You should incorporate it into your waking up and going to bed routine – even when you are in a contract. Don't wait until you need it to build the belief. Build the belief now and when you need it, it will be even stronger and more effective.

Build belief whilst you sleep

Because the subconscious mind – unlike the conscious mind – does not sleep, you can continue to program and change your subconscious beliefs, even as you sleep. You can do this using a recorded affirmation.

You can create the recording, using the sound recorder on your computer. Once you have the digital version of the recording, you can either use an MP3 player, or create a CD of the recording and play it at a very low volume in the room in which you sleep.

The positive messages will be absorbed by your subconscious mind as you sleep. Your powerful subconscious mind – which cannot tell reality from fantasy – will set out to make your most dominant thoughts come true.

Components of a good self-talk

For your self-talk to be effective, you need to arrange and format it in the way that works best. The affirmation must be stated in the present and in first person tense. The following are some examples:

"I get every contract role I want."
"I am exceptionally effective at interviews."
"My contracting rate is top in its class."
"My rate increases with every new contract role."

Avoid stating ambiguities or mentioning any negative points in your affirmations. The following statements should be avoided:

"I am not scared at interviews anymore."
"I pass all difficult, technical tests and questions given in interviews."
"My voice will not shake at interviews."
"I am not afraid or intimidated by interviewers."

By mentioning negative remarks, you add it to what the subconscious mind absorbs. Your mind works in the input formats in which it is accustomed. These are sight, taste, smell, touch and hearing. Therefore, when you input any message into your subconscious mind, this message is converted or interpreted first, into an input format.

Because of this, the subconscious mind does not recognise negations such as "not" or "nor." Because it cannot convert negations into images or any of the other formats it recognises, your subconscious mind ignores negations, preferring instead to render inputs without them. Therefore, *"My voice will not shake at interviews"* becomes, *"My voice will shake at interviews."*

You are the most important person in your life. Your mind trusts you more than almost any other power. Therefore, affirmations spoken by yourself are more potent than affirmations spoken by others.

Furthermore, affirmations spoken aloud are best spoken in front of a mirror. The feedback from seeing yourself say the affirmation, drives the statement deeper than a recording, or speaking without a mirror, can achieve.

If you want to add music to your self-talk recording, make sure it is purely instrumental music – preferably soft classical or easy listening.

Conflicts

Sometimes, you may be saying one thing concerning your contracting abilities, whilst still maintaining negative self-talk in other areas of your life. This can cause conflicts and confusion for your subconscious mind. The conflicting beliefs could cancel each other out, if both are of the exact same intensity of belief.

Eliminate belief conflicts by eliminating negative beliefs from your life. A negative belief is any belief that limits you. Beliefs about yourself as a person, your family, your habits, your abilities, your intelligence, your ethics or any other personal topics, in which you hold a negative self-belief.

Don't just stop saying or thinking the negative thoughts. Replace the negative thoughts and negative self-talk with positive replacements. If your previous negative self-talk and belief was that you were clumsy, replace it with, "I am careful, (steady or graceful), in all I do."

The average person is pretty negative at best, and therefore trying to replace all your negative beliefs at one time may be unreasonable. Tackle negative self-talk by breaking them it into groups of similar negative self-talk, or tackle each thing individually. This way, negative thoughts will be easier to deal with.

The process for eliminating any negative self-talk is as follows:

1. Identify the negative self-talk.
2. Replace it with a positive equivalent.
3. Reinforce by regularly repeating the positive.

In the identification section for eliminating your negative self-talk, you need to be vigilant in the lookout for any occurrence or recurrence of the negative self-talk. If you catch yourself saying negative statements, thinking negative thoughts or doing negative acts, then immediately replace them with their positive equivalent, and repeat the positive statement five times.

Whilst eliminating your negative beliefs will improve your IT contracting interviewing results, and thus improve your earnings, it will also make you a more confident and happier person.

Visualization

Because your mind thinks in pictures, smells, tastes and feelings through touch, imagining yourself performing successfully at the interview will quickly instil the belief more so, than by using self-talk alone.

The steps involved in using visualisation are as follows:

1. Find somewhere you wont be disturbed for a few minutes.
2. Close your eyes and vividly imagine yourself successfully going through the entire interview, from beginning through to the end.
3. Visualise yourself comfortably answering the interviewer's questions, and asking them insightful and relevant questions of your own.
4. Finally, visualise the end of the interview with the interviewer complimenting you on an outstanding interview. Visualize yourself leaving the interview feeling and knowing, the role is yours.
5. Open your eyes and maintain the feelings from the visualization interview. State your positive self-talk concerning your interview abilities.

Once you have played the images and felt the feelings a couple of times, you can repeat them anywhere at anytime. The more your repeat the visualisation, the more effective it will be for you

Visualisation can be used in conjunction with self-talk. The two compliment each other well. You can use one to reinforce the other; however, self-talk generally takes effect over a longer period than visualisation does. Visualisation often has a more immediate effect. Furthermore, like self-talk, you can use visualisation to materialise any goal you desire.

Confidence

A confident applicant will get better results at interviews than a hesitant or shy applicant. Furthermore, if you are confident, you project assurance and cause people to relax, and feel more comfortable around you. You are trusted more, and generally given more responsibilities. Even if you are normally confident, it doesn't guarantee that you will always feel and be that way – especially at the interview when it counts the most.

If you are not naturally confident, do not despair. You can do something to remedy the problem. Like all personality traits, you can assume confidence simply by assuming the posture, mannerisms and thought patterns of a confident person.

So what makes one person more confident than another? There are three main reasons why some people are more self-assured. These reasons are as follows:

- Self-belief – a strong belief that you are confident.
- Familiarity – familiar people and surroundings, i.e., your home and family.
- Environment – a relaxing, calm environment like a park, spa, or when you are on vacation.

When you believe you are a confident person, you will act and feel confident in most environments; however, with some people and in certain familiar situations, you will also feel confident. Furthermore, some environments evoke this feeling in you automatically. In fact, most of us tend to feel this way when on vacation, or at home with friends and our family.

We have already covered how you can build your belief in yourself, of being more confident through self-talk and visualisation. Now we will look at a quicker method of feeling and acting confident in an interview scenario.

Posture

Confident people stand, walk, talk, hold their heads, breathe and act differently from shy, unsure people. Their posture is different; it is a posture of confidence. By assuming a posture of confidence, you will instantly feel more confident.

But what is a posture of confidence? The following is a list of some of the major features of a confident posture:

- Smiling.
- A firm handshake.
- Giving eye contact.
- Calm, deep breathing.
- Sitting back in a chair.
- Walking with long strides.
- Crossing legs when sitting.
- Standing tall with chin up and head held high.
- Talking *slightly* louder, and more thoughtfully.
- Speaking fluently without stuttering, "umming" and "ahhing".
- Leaving hands on the table when sitting, and/or simply keeping hands relaxed (and not fidgety).

Observe confident people. Note their posture and mirror it for when you need it the most – at your interviews. You will notice they stand taller without slouching or rounding their shoulders. When you stand, straighten your back, square your shoulders and hold your head high with your chin parallel to the ground.

Smile where appropriate. A ready smile is a very confident sign. Be first to introduce yourself. Extend your hand and give a firm handshake. Imagine the people in the room as your peers. Confident people are not easily intimidated by managers or directors. This is because they hold themselves in high esteem, equal or higher than they may hold a manager or director.

Assertiveness

A mentor once told me, "The will that weakens, strengthens the other." If you are apologetic and quick to back down in confrontations at an interview, the interviewers will grow stronger in their assertiveness, and likely walk all over you. This is why you need to go in strong, confident, assertive and smiling.

In all interviews where you feel intimidated, it will be due to one of two things: Yourself, or them.

When it is due to yourself, you can resolve the problem quickly by assuming the posture of a confident, assertive individual. However, when it is due to them, you will need to use posture and assertiveness to let them see that you are not easily intimidated.

Some interviewers set out to intimidate you, to catch you off guard and put you under pressure, in order to better determine how you handle yourself in stressful situations. You will need to be assertive in these instances.

Some interviewers use caffeine to get you on edge before the interview begins. If you are offered a drink, always opt for water rather than coffee or soda. Similarly, avoid eating any biscuits or other sweets, as the sugar could also throw you off your peak performance.

If the interviewers seem to be giving you a hard time by asking you non-technical, tough interview questions such as, "Why should we hire you?", "What are your weakest characteristics?", "What would you change about yourself if you could?", or "What do you hate about your current contract?", etc., avoid getting involved in their game. Lean back in your chair, slow down your breathing and take deeper breaths (without sighing), smile, *think*, take your time, and then reply.

Never rush to answer difficult questions. Appear relaxed whilst you take your time, and smile before answering. This process will give you time to think of an answer, and the interviewers will think you are very relaxed. This will likely make them pursue another line of questioning.

When you are asked a tough question such as, "If you are as good as your CV claims, why did you only score 56% in the technical test?" It will normally be followed with an intimidating stare. Do not avoid the eye contact, meet it, and give a short, thoughtful response, without being rude. I was asked that question once. I returned the interviewers stare, stopped smiling and replied, "That is because I did not revise for it."

Play on weakness

In some interviews, you will identify a weakness in the interviewers, or the scenario. Always capitalise on this and play it in your favour. Some interviewers are not very technical, others are not very confident, and still others may even find you attractive. Whatever the weakness is, capitalise on it to secure the role.

A friend once attended an interview where he faced a panel of four IT executives. In the course of the interview, he noticed that they purposefully steered away for discussing one aspect of the project. This was their weakness and my friend's golden key. When it came to him asking the interviewers a few questions, he aimed straight for their weak spot, and asked them about the 'weak' phase of the project.

After "umming" and "ahhing", fidgeting and looking at each other for support, he pointed out at his vast experience in their area of weakness. He sold them on himself being able to make that weak phase, stronger. After the interview, he had barely left the building when the agency called to inform him that he got the job.

Technical intimidation

The last story was an example of technical intimidation. You should only use this technique if you are very strong in the technical aspects you wish to exploit. Furthermore, only exploit this if the interviewer is weaker than you, on the subject. If you misjudge this, and the interviewer is stronger in that area than yourself, the interview might turn into a technical match between yourself and the in-house guru (whom you thought was weak on the subject).

The technical intimidation technique works like this: Whenever you are asked a non-technical, difficult question, try and turn it into a technical answer. If the interviewers are weak on the technical side of things, they will keep these questions shorter, if you use the technical intimidation.

Amiability

Which do you prefer: a friendly, sociable, positive, helpful, hardworking, result orientated member of your team, or an unhelpful, miserable, negative, hardworking member of your team? Most employers would select the former.

Your ability to be amiable will help you get along with more people – including interviewers – than having no affable qualities at all. Therefore, smiling, being upbeat and generally looking like you are happy to be at the interview, and looking forward to working with the organisation, will also help your interview results.

If you hear anything that may be a problem during the interview, do not let it show in your reactions. Later, you can always decline the role if it turns out to be unsuitable; however, reacting negatively at the interview may be unprofessional, and is to be avoided at all costs.

You want to appear good-natured before, during and after the interview. The interviewer(s) will most likely be working with you after you join the organisation. They would not like to work with a sad, miserable, unfriendly and disagreeable complainer. Be assertive, but also be friendly, upbeat and helpful.

If you are not interested in the role you are interviewing for, or can not show enthusiasm and excitement about it, cancel the interview. Your enthusiasm and excitement about the role and the interviewers, will be picked up through your body language, voice, and your mental projection.

Thought projection

Your mind can be likened to a radio antenna. It constantly broadcasts your true feelings and beliefs to neighbouring minds. These signals give others 'a feeling' about you. You probably have had this 'feeling' about someone before. It is that eerie sense you get about people before you get to know their true intentions towards you. Later on, you find out that first impression or sensation was unexplainably accurate.

Again, it is beyond the scope of this book to give this topic the treatment it truly deserves. However, there are many self-help and spiritual books that cover ESP (extra sensory perception), telepathy and the mind's supernatural abilities.

Concerning IT contracting interviews – you can utilise your mind's fantastic ability to project your thoughts and feelings into neighbouring minds, to give you that extra edge at interviews. The process is quite simple. First, think a thought and associate a feeling to the thought. Second, associate this thought and feeling towards the interviewer(s). Third, project the thought and feelings, whilst giving the interviewers your full attention. Maintain these thoughts and feelings whilst looking at the interviewers.

Love is the most potent feeling to project, and the most effective thought is, "I love you." This thought generates the primary feeling of love, whilst the sensation of love leads to the thought, "I love you." They compliment each other, and are self promoting.

The effect of this technique is subtle. Firstly, it leads to the interviewer(s) reciprocating the feeling. They will attribute their feelings to having 'a good hunch' or 'a gut feeling' about you. The feeling of love does not dissipate as quickly as the feelings of 'like' or 'prefer'. Similarly, a logical decision based on the facts, stands no chance against a feeling based on 'love'. People will go to great lengths to create logical reasons justifying their 'feelings-based' decisions.

Use this to your advantage; project love towards your interviewer(s) at IT contracting interviews.

Warning against thought projection usage

There are a few aspects of warning, to consider. In certain cases, it is not advisable that you use this technique. These are as follows:

1. When you find an interviewer sexually attractive – "I love you as a human being" and "I love you sexually", are two subtly different thoughts and they generate two distinct feelings. The sexual kind may offend the interviewer, especially if they find you sexually objectionable.

2. If you actually find the interviewer attractive – you may have involuntary reactions such as; blushing, sweating, staring, drooling, or similar behaviour, which will detract from your professionalism.

It is an entirely different case if the interviewer(s) finds you attractive. First, maintain your professionalism at all times. Second, project your feeling and thoughts of love, as normal.

If the interviewer already finds you attractive, the results will be even more effective and immediate. In fact, they will be the one blushing and acting irrationally; however, your chances of securing the contract due to the interviewer(s) recommendation, will be very high.

Association

Thought projection works for all thoughts; therefore, not only project positive thoughts, but suppress your negative thoughts as well. The interviewers are also projecting their own thoughts about you. These thoughts might be negative. Therefore, if you get 'bad vibes' from interviewer(s), or if you do not like the interviewer(s), do not reflect the feelings back to them, as this will start an avalanche of bad feelings flying between the two camps.

Nothing good can come out of negative thought reflection or mirroring, try instead to intercede or replace your involuntary negative feelings concerning the interviewer(s) with positive feelings and thoughts instead.

Use the technique of association to change your feelings about people you find yourself not liking, or people who you think do not like you. The process is as follows:

1. In your mind, get an image of your most happy memory. Any memory where you felt a high degree of love will do for this exercise. Play the feeling and thoughts through your mind.
2. Whilst the happy memory is playing, superimpose an image of the interviewer(s) on the happy image. Imagine the happy-memory feelings being absorbed into the image of the interviewer(s). You will start to feel the same about the interviewer(s), as you do about the memory.
3. Next, imagine all the negative feelings associated to the interviewer(s) as a black smoke or mist. Imagine this dispersing, and drifting away from the blended image of the interviewer and your happy memory.

4. When all the smoke has drifted away and disappeared, imagine the blended image glowing with a bright white light.
5. Now, step into the blended image and see it fully absorbed by you. Feel the feelings, and think the loving thoughts whenever you look at the interviewer(s).

You can do this exercise in less than a minute. It is best to do this exercise as soon as you meet the interviewer(s), and discover the 'bad vibes' issue. Whilst you are walking to the interview room, waiting for your drink of water or during the introductory part of the interview, and before the interviewing really starts, is the best time for this exercise.

If you cannot find any time to do this exercise before the interview starts, or if the problem interviewer(s) joins the interview after it gets underway, then simply suppress your reciprocal bad feelings and bad thoughts, and only project your "I love you" thoughts and feelings.

Personality traits

One of the reasons conflicts are created at interviews, may be related to the personality trait of the interviewer(s) clashing with your personality. Not all personalities are complimentary. Some are diametrically opposite. When these two personality traits meet, tensions can mound.

Apart from avoiding people of opposing personalities to your own, there are a few methods you can employ to minimise the conflict, and in some cases, eliminate antagonism during the interview. Whilst the scope of this book does not allow a more thorough discussion of personality traits, you will find more information in, "Personality Plus: How to Understand Others by Understanding Yourself" by Florence Littauer, and "Positive Personality Profiles: "D-I-S-

C-OVER" PERSONALITY INSIGHTS to understand yourself... and others!" by Robert A. Rohm, Ph.D.

We will examine the four, main personalities and discuss how they interact with each other. The personality traits are:

- **Doer** – extrovert, task oriented, confrontational, dictatorial, domineering, always right, competitive, go-getter, etc.
- **Socialite** – extrovert, people orientated, optimistic, hopeful, upbeat, easily excitable, flighty, bright, overly positive, etc.
- **Follower** – introvert, people oriented, low energy, apathetic, indifferent, placid, unconcerned, tranquil, etc.
- **Thinker** – introvert, task oriented, moody, particular, thoughtful, quite, habitual, unsociable, etc.

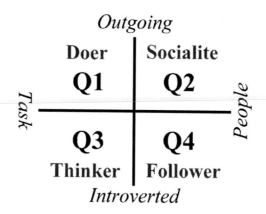

Table 24: Personality quadrant chart

Table 24 illustrates how the personalities relate to each other. The chart is divided into Introverted (bottom), Outgoing (top), Task oriented (left) and People oriented (right). The four personalities each sit in its own quadrant of the universe. The Doer (Q1), is in the top left hand corner, exactly opposite to the Follower (Q4). These two share nothing in common. They are exact opposites. Very few people have an equal share of these personalities.

Similarly, the Socialite (Q2), lies diagonally opposed to the Thinker (Q3). These two are also opposites of each other, and again very few people will have both of these personalities, in equal amounts.

What is common, is a blend of two or more personalities. Normally, one personality is more present than the others. This is the pivotal personality, and is often supported by its two immediate neighbours. For instance, a pivotal Doer would have supporting Socialite and Thinker personality traits.

Doer

The Doer is task-orientated and outgoing therefore, this personality prefers direct talk and immediate action. People possessing this trait prefer working with things, and working on activities, more than with people.

They often are autocratic, insensitive, highly motivated to achieve their goals and prepared to do anything necessary to achieve success. They prefer to act (do), rather than to talk about things, or indeed, to plan.

Socialite

The Socialite on the other hand, is an outgoing people-oriented personality; therefore, this type prefers dealing with people, talking and discussing, especially if it is fun.

People who possess this personality, like to be the centre of attention; they are extroverts who like having fun, more than they do achieving any worthwhile goals. They tend to not be able to focus for long periods, and are easily distracted. They will only join activities that are fun, involve dealing with people, and/or that are centred on themselves.

Follower

Luckily for employers, there are more people with the Follower personality than the Doer personality. Around 10% of people are Doers, whilst over 40% are Followers. This is just as well, because the Doers are very competitive and aggressive. The Followers are in the majority and it's a good thing too, because it would be a very hostile world without them.

People possessing the Follower personality are the peacemakers of this world. They are introverted and people-orientated. They secretly seek social attention, however, they are too introverted to directly go after it, as the Socialite does. They are also very good followers and consistent workers.

Unlike the Socialite, they are dependable to the point of boredom compared to the Socialite. They are prepared to be part of activities, even if they are not the centre of attention. In fact, they do not actually want to be the centre of attention. They just want to be part of the group. They seek acceptance in organisations and will often be walkovers.

Unlike their opposite (the Doer), Followers prefer to let others take the lead. They detest confrontations and would rather give in, than fight.

Thinker

Finally, we come to the Thinker. This personality is introverted and task-oriented. People with this personality will seem moody and anti-social, or unfriendly. They prefer their own company and can lose themselves in their work.

The great scientists, engineers and inventors of our history, all had great amounts of Thinker personality in their traits. In IT, the stereotypical geek is the personification of this personality type.

Personality conflicts

Conflicts arise when people with opposing personalities meet. Each tries to communicate and work the way they know and prefer; however, this grates on the nerves of those with an opposing personality.

As an example, people with Follower or Socialite personalities tend to take longer to explain things, than people with the task-oriented, Doer or Thinker personalities. Add to this, the fact that people with the Doer and Thinker personalities are generally more impatient, direct and generally less tactful than people with the Socialite and Follower personalities, and you can see how sparks begin to fly.

Similarly, the harsh, insensitive and direct approach of people with the Doer and Thinker personalities, can lead people with the Socialite and Follower personalities easily feeling insulted, mistreated, disrespected and/or hurt.

Identifying personalities

Know your own personality well. You can identify this by asking two simple questions: Are you a task oriented or people oriented person, and are you an introvert or more of an outgoing person? Your answers to these two questions will place you within your pivotal quadrant. Sometimes, you will feel that you are both task and people oriented. However, you will rarely be confused about your answer to both questions.

If you answer "both" for any of the two questions, this means you straddle both halves and thus you may have your pivotal personality in one quadrant and supporting personalities firmly placed in either half (Task or Outgoing, Outgoing or People, People or Introverted, and Introverted or Task).

We all have some of all the personalities within us, although some are more pronounced and stronger than others.

Because you have all the personalities present within you, you can choose to raise or lower any one of them at will.

It is useful to develop the ability to quickly identify other people's personalities. Normally, you can determine when someone is either outgoing or introverted, or task or people oriented. However, people with a mixture of two or more personality quadrant memberships, can be confusing.

Some people also have dependent behaviour. By this I mean their personality traits seem to change depending on what they are doing. As an example, do you know someone who is timid and meek but in the club, pub or on holiday they take on a totally different personality matrix?

Some people go through this type of metamorphosis when it comes to interviews. They may have seemed like they were mainly a 'socialite' in the reception when they came to collect you for the interview, however, as the interview was underway, they switched to a 'doer' or worse, the opposite personality to their precious 'socialite' – the 'thinker'.

Generally in communication, it is always best to mirror people's personalities. If you are speaking to a 'doer', keep your answers succinct and relevant. 'Doers' will generally respect you more for your attention to detail and for your respect of their time.

Similarly, 'thinkers' also prefer this, although they like a more factually oriented and/or thoughtful speech, than the 'doer' requires. The 'thinker' generally likes facts, figures, charts and supporting data to your answers. Therefore, do your best to supply as much factual backing details as you can.

Concerning the 'socialite' and 'follower'; you will have to adopt a different style to please either of them. With the 'socialite', it is best to keep your answers positive and interesting, always bringing him or her into your answer, whenever possible. It is also good to give the 'socialite' as many opportunities to speak as you possibly can. They love to talk and be the centre of attention – feed their need.

The 'follower' likes agreeable people and non-threatening situations. They do not like to be put on the spot; therefore, try not to reply in a way that seems confrontational, contradictory, or that will call attention specifically to them. If you must be pointed, ask them easy questions that will not embarrass or antagonise them in any way.

Preferring the human touch, the 'follower' doesn't identify easily with facts and figures. You are more likely to please them by telling them how wonderful your last employer was, and how you really enjoyed working with your previous team, than by reeling out the impressive statistics that led to your last successful project.

The following are some examples of answers to the question, "Tell us a bit about yourself":

Answer to 'Doer'; *"I have been contracting for 4 years, in which time I have successfully completed 3 major system migrations, two of which were similar to your requirements here. I am qualified, highly motivated and ready to start this role and help you achieve your 22 April deadline ahead of schedule."*

Answer to 'Socialite'; *"I am a good team player and like to get involved in team or company activities. In fact, in my last job, I organised a paintball day-out for the team to help everyone get to know each other better, everyone had a great time and it really helped create a better environment at work."*

Answer to 'Follower'; *"I get on well with everyone I work with, and like to help in every way that I can. I like sharing what I know with my team members and I am always available whenever anyone in the team needs help. I don't mind doing inconvenient hours if the role requires it. I have worked 24 hour rotating shifts before in my previous two roles. I think it is better to be flexible, especially when it will help the team."*

Answer to 'Thinker'; *"I have been supporting XP and MS Office apps since XP was in Beta. In fact, I was a beta tester for XP and currently for Vista. I have also supported Reuters 3000 Xtra, Kobra and Bloomberg in my last two roles."*

By gearing your answers towards the interviewer's personality, you stand a better chance at avoiding conflicts, and making your interviewer feel very comfortable with you. However, watch out for another type of personality-type conflict – 'same personality' clashes.

Sometimes, two people of the same personality cannot be in the same room without conflicts arising. A 'doer' can try to outdo your 'doer'; a 'socialite' may feel threatened if you seem more popular than they are; you may make a 'follower' feel insecure and threatened; and a 'thinker' may feel threatened because you seem more technical than they are.

So, how can you tell if that 'same personality' conflict is occurring? Watch the interviewer's body language. Their body language will give away what the they are thinking. As soon as you identify the body language signals which we will cover next, change your tack and tone down the conflicting personality.

Body Language

Interviewers are only human; therefore, they have feelings and thoughts too. Some of these thoughts and feelings manifest through their posture and body language – much like yours will, if unchecked.

They will lean forward and listen intently when they are interested in what they are hearing. Conversely, they will sit back and slouch in their seats, if they are bored with whatever is going on, or being said. Some will rub their eyes if they 'can't see' what you mean, others will rub and pull at their ear lobes if they have 'heard enough', picking lint off their clothing signifies a lack of interest, still others will stroke their chins if they think you are lying, and many will rub their noses if they 'smell something fishy'.

Other body signals are involuntarily crossed arms, signalling a defensive action. People do this when they feel threatened. They place a barrier between themselves and the threat. In this case, the barrier can be a notepad, their crossed arms, crossed legs, a table, etc.

Also, avoid hiding your hands, eyes or any part of your body. Unless you need dark glasses for medical reasons, do not wear them to the interview. Similarly, avoid hiding your hands under the table. It implies or suggests that you are hiding something.

Some of the signals that may be made by those who find you attractive are; prolonged eye contact, playing with their hair, reaching across the table towards your hands, touching your knee, thigh, or arm. The last point is not to be confused with the pat on the back or the squeezing of the shoulder, this is a sign of affection, but not sexual attraction.

The full education on body language is beyond the scope of this book. For a more thorough review of this topic; see, "The Definitive Book of Body Language" by Barbara Pease and Allan Pease.

Other interview points

Avoid inappropriate laughing, staring or otherwise mistreating and/or disrespecting interviewer(s) with any of the following characteristics:

- Baldness.
- Facial defect.
- Large breasts.
- Funny walk.

- Abnormal fashion sense.
- Speech impediment.
- Artificial hair (wigs, toupees, etc.).
- Dwarfism, gigantism, being underweight or obese.
- Medical cast, crutches, prosthetics, wheelchair, or any physical handicap or disability.
- Obvious sexuality discrepancies (sex change, gayness, etc.).

People may be sensitive and feel insecure; therefore, when you feed this insecurity by treating them with anything but respect, you cannot blame them for not liking you. If you make them feel uncomfortable, they will do their best to ensure you do not secure the contract.

How to Consistently Develop Your IT Skills

Training and certification are important in almost every field of work. IT contracting is no different. Often, a qualification or certification will be the difference between you securing a contract, or its going to another contractor, who has the certification and experience the company requires for the role.

In this section, we will look at how you can acquire certification efficiently and effectively. We will cover the following topics:

- Certification – see Appendix 3 for a comprehensive list of certification exams.
- Training – home study, computer based training (CBT), online, classroom, boot camps.
- Examination – costs, booking, identification, etiquette, re-take rules.
- Updating – requirements.

Certification

Appendix 3 lists the majority of all IT certification options. Most of these exams are computer based multiple-choice exams; however, a few are offline and essay type exams. You need to select the appropriate certification and the track in which you wish to be certified. As an example, if you are a 2nd line support engineer, you may want to take the ITIL exams, Microsoft MCSE, and CISCO CCNA.

There is a broad range of certification tracks you could pursue. However, I advise only pursuing the qualifications that are the most in demand, in the market. You do not need to be certified in a subject that is loosing its appeal. To find out what examinations are currently highly sought after for your area of expertise, I suggest you search on www.jobserve.com for similar roles and read the requirements. You will very quickly find out what exams are in great demand in your area of expertise.

Once you learn which certification(s) could help you increase your rate in the IT contracting market, you need to research the certification provider's Web site for more details of your options.

Visit the learning centre at Microsoft's Web site for details on their certification options and exam tracks at http://www.microsoft.com/learning/mcp/certifications.mspx.

You can investigate Cisco exams at their site at http://cisco.com/web/learning/le3/learning_career_certificatio ns_and_learning_paths_home.html.

You can find other certification providers by searching for the manufacturer or exam board and certification – e.g., Microsoft Certification – in an Internet search engine.

Some qualifications will require you to take more than one test. For instance, to become an MCSE requires seven exams.

Once you know what certification you are after, and which exams will be required to obtain it, you are ready to start investigating how you will get training to prepare for the tests.

Training

When it comes to training for your certification exams, you have many choices. You can select to read textbooks, use CBTs, use classroom based courses, DVD and online courses or even use book camps nationally, or as far away as India and Pakistan.

There are two main reasons people seek training, these reasons are either for certification or for experience and knowledge.

Although at first glance, this may seem like the same objective, they are quite different in several ways. Firstly, if you only seek certification from training, you need to learn less than you would if your objective was to gain new skills, and to acquire hands-on experience and knowledge.

In the market today, there are many contractors with an MCSE. However, some of these people do not know how to undertake the simplest network design task. If that is what you want, then you only need the Five Read-Through System for passing most multiple-choice exams. I will cover the system later in this chapter.

Boot Camps

You could also book yourself into a boot camp course. These courses only teach you what you need to know to pass the exams (and not much else). They have an extremely high success rate for getting students to pass their tests on their first try. The "camps" normally last no more than a week, and often include the taking of exams in that same period.

Some entrepreneurial business people have incorporated boot camps with trips to exotic locations such as Goa – in India. Due to the lower price of certification in India, the trip, accommodation, food, excursions, water sports and other activities, IT training and certification exams, are all included in a single packaged deal. This arrangement is often lower in expense than boot camp or classroom training courses in the UK. See http://www.koenig-solutions.com for an example of these types of offers.

Other destinations offered are Florida, Hawaii, Cornwall and many major cities around the world. These packages are generally more expensive than the ones offered in the Far East and India.

Textbooks and home study

Textbook learning is perhaps the slowest and least effective form of training. This is especially true if you do not set a definite deadline for taking your exams. You can waste a lot of time dragging out your studies over many months – sometimes years. If you do not have strong willpower, determination and are highly motivated, you will fail using this method alone.

However, if you still want to use this avenue, make sure you use the textbooks recommended by the certification provider. You can search for these books under Certification Central on Amazon.com, or 'books/computer & Internet certification' on Amazon.co.uk.

You can purchase all other certification provider textbooks directly from their Web site or through a third-party supplier; the details of which will most likely be available from the certification provider's Web site.

If you are using textbook-based training alone, you might want to supplement your learning with brain dumps or sample test questions. These tools are explained later in this chapter.

Courses

This method is more immersion based. You will be in a room full of other students. A lecturer, teacher or trainer imparts his knowledge and wisdom to the class to help you pass the exams. You can ask questions and interact with the teacher as needed.

Most of the time – as long as the class is small enough to get personal attention – the classroom course is the best way to quickly learn new skills and acquire the knowledge to obtain your certification.

Whenever possible, always choose courses that offer some hands-on tutorial, or practical application of what you learn. Always make your own notes no matter how good the provided course notes are. You will retain more of what you learn when you put it in your own notes.

Most certification providers offer their own training courses. In most cases, these courses are excellent; however, they tend to be expensive compared to competitor courses.

Furthermore, few of these courses offer the flexibility a contractor demands; namely, weekend and evening courses only. Other courses on the market cater more for the small business owner and contractors. They offer courses that suit IT contractors better.

Shop around for good deals. Ask other contractors about their experience with a course before booking yours. Whenever possible, aim for a course that offers guarantees. Today, many such courses exist. They promise to help you obtain your exams or your money back, or future attempts at the same exams will be paid for by them, and so on.

Offers like these are great, but always read the contract and small print. Some offers have time limits or exceptions that render them useless.

Computer or Internet Based Training

There are many suppliers of online-based and computer-based training courses. You only need to search for "computer-based training" and the certification you seek on an Internet search engine, to see what I mean.

Unless you have used a particular CBT or Internet based training in the past, or a reliable source has recommended one, I suggest you only buy or subscribe to those that offer a free trial period, and offer guarantees.

Up to a point, CBTs, whether offline or online via the Internet or Intranet, are a hit or miss proposition. It is all down to personal preference. Whilst I might like one supplier's GUI, you might not. Similarly, I might like a certain supplier's system, but I may fall asleep using it, whilst I might not like another supplier but I learn, retain and pass more exams using them.

Almost every contractor I know has tried and abandoned CBTs as a reliable source for acquiring certification. Saying that, CBT companies are doing great business; therefore, someone must like their tools, and they must be working for someone – but for whom, I don't know.

CBTs are popular with corporate entities. They are a great way of training staff at their desk. They are also used for compliance training purposes, as they offer a way of monitoring exactly how far along the course, a student has achieved.

For IT contractors, this tool is only slightly useful. The time required going through the courses and the retention levels attainable, tend to be lower than that for classroom based training. However, CBTs are a convenient and flexible way of learning. You can use them literally from anywhere as long as you have a computer with the CBT software installed. Internet versions are less flexible as they require an Internet connection.

If you are thinking of using CBTs to train and acquire your certification, I suggest you also supplement this with other forms of training. I find that they require a lot of patience and motivation, as well as self-control and will-power, to use for certification purposes.

Brain dumps and cheat sheets

In the 1980s and early nineties, brain dump sites appeared on the Internet; offering members and the general public free access to exam questions. These questions were posted by other members and everyone was free to post ideas and comments on what they thought was the correct answer.

In those days, using brain dumps was highly inefficient, as the information was distributed across many Web sites and forums. It did not stay that way for long. In a few years, the likes of Test King and many others organised the collection of exam questions and collated them into regular updates, which they sold online.

Over the years that followed, these test resources became more accurate, timely and effective. Today, hundreds of Web sites offer this service. The sample exam papers have become so accurate, that in many cases, you can pass the certification exams simply by memorising the sample test papers.

By far the best deal I have found online is ActualTest's $99 offer for a lifetime membership and unlimited downloads. Find out more about this at http://actualtests.com. Armed with the adobe .PDF file of sample questions, all that you need to do is to memorize the questions and go take your exams.

Five Read-Through System

An effective system for using ActualTest's questions is as follows:

1. Book your exam five days in advance.
2. Print your downloaded exam file. If possible, use double sided printing to save on paper.
3. Have two different coloured pens or highlighters at hand.
4. Start from the first question, and whilst covering the correct answer provided, read and attempt to guess the correct answer.

5. Uncover the answer and check if you were correct. Whether you were correct or not, *only* read the correct answer and explanation for why it is correct. *Do not* read the incorrect answers and their explanations.
6. For all answers you guess correctly, mark them with your pen or highlighter. If you guessed correctly but you really did not know the answer, do not highlight or mark the question.
7. Continue until you have read and answered all the questions.
8. Allow one night to pass.
9. Return to the beginning, repeat the read-through and answer exercise a second time. This time, only answer the questions you did not guess correctly during the previous read-through (the un-highlighted or unmarked questions).
10. Repeat the read-through and marking or highlighting process, four times in a row.
11. The night before your exam – just before going to bed – read the entire paper again. Cover all the answers and try to answer them all correctly. If you get any questions wrong, mark them with the other pen or highlighter and only read the correct answer and explanation.
12. The next day, do not look over the questions again, before taking the exam.

Examination

IT certification exams are held at approved test centres. There are many such test centres dotted across the world. The majority of IT exams can be booked through Thomson Prometric, found at http://securereg3.prometric.com or, Pearson Vue at http://www.vue.com. The main difference between them is that Thomson Prometric does not charge VAT, hosts more exams and has more locations in prestigious venues, whilst Pearson Vue charges VAT and has sites located in places where Thomson Prometric does not cover. I have to say that Pearson Vue sites are hosted by smaller businesses than Thomson Prometric sites.

A few other certification providers such as SAP, host their own test sites – independent of Thomson Prometric and Pearson Vue. You can book tests online through the test provider. During the booking process, you will get a chance to select a venue, time and date of the test.

The routine at these test centres is simple. They all require that you bring a picture proof of identification such as a password, national identity card or a driver's license. Some will also require you to bring a printout of the online receipt for your booking.

You will be taken to the test room. At this stage, it is a good idea to switch off your mobile phone or pager, and disable the alarm on your watch, if it has one. Unless the exam is an open book exam, you will not be allowed to take any books or bags into the exam room.

Almost all test sites have cameras monitoring the candidates in the room. You are not allowed to confer, talk or disrupt the other candidates in the room.

The examination will be loaded and made ready for you to proceed. From then on, all further instructions will normally be on-screen. Read the instructions carefully, as they will give you the rules and guidelines for the test you are about to take.

Some exams allow you to use a calculator and to refer to a book. However, for the majority of IT examinations, you cannot use any of these aids. Additionally, multiple choice, computer-based exams such as the Microsoft Exams, allow you to revisit answered or unanswered questions during the exam.

Many other certification providers do not allow you to return to previous questions. CISCO exams are notorious for this – only allowing you to move forward to the next question without ever returning to previous questions.

All exams will have a timer clearly indicating your remaining time to complete the exam.

Your results will usually be calculated and displayed as soon as you complete the test. However, for other exams such as Prince 2, you will have to wait some weeks (or even months) before you receive the results.

Retake rules

Every certification provider has their own rules concerning failed examination retakes. Some allow you to have your first retake immediately upon failing your first attempt. Subsequent retakes (i.e., all other attempts after your second, must be undertaken after a two week waiting period).

As an example, Microsoft professional exams observe the following rules:

1. Candidates may retake the same exam one time without restriction. However, candidates who wish to retake the assessment a second or subsequent time, must wait a minimum of seven days before retaking the test.

2. Candidates participating in exam beta testing, may take each beta exam only one time.
The rules for Cisco are slightly different. The following is the current Cisco retake policy:

3. Candidates who sit for a beta exam may take the exam only once (no retakes).

4. Candidates who fail an exam must wait a period of five calendar days, beginning the day after the failed attempt, before retaking the test. For example, if a candidate tests

on Tuesday, he or she may test again no sooner than the following Monday.

5. Once passed, you cannot retake an exam, with the exception of CCIE written tests. Candidates who do not pass a CCIE written exam must wait a minimum of six months to retake it. This policy applies to CCIE certification exams, with identical exam numbers.

Novell on the other hand, offers different rules for the first exam retake. The following is an illustration of Novell's retake policy and the punishment for violating the policy:

1. In the event a candidate fails a Novell exam on his or her first attempt, Novell will not require any waiting period between the first and second attempt to pass the same exam. However, before any candidates' third or subsequent attempt to pass a Novell exam, the candidate shall be required to wait for a period of no less than thirty calendar days from the date of the candidate's last attempt to pass the same exam.

2. In the event a candidate fails a Novell exam, the candidate shall be required to wait a period of twelve months before retaking the same Novell exam, unless Novell has changed the test objectives by revising the course related to that specific exam.

3. In the event it has been determined a candidate has violated Novell's exam retake policy, the candidate may not be eligible to register or schedule a Novell exam for a minimum period of twelve months from the date of such determination.

Any candidate determined to have violated Novell's exam retake policy may be subject to the following:

a. Denial of Novell certification for a period of twelve months from the date of such determination, or...

b. Revocation of Novell certification, if such certification had been previously granted to the candidate, or...

c. Revocation of all Novell certifications previously granted to candidate, or...

d. Ineligibility to receive any Novell certification for a minimum of twelve months from the date of such determination, or...

e. Any other appropriate actions, including legal remedies, that Novell deems necessary or appropriate to enforce Novell's exam retake policy.

Finally, SAP offers still different retake rules. They are as follows:

1. Unsuccessful candidates may retake the same examination.

2. No candidate may take the same examination for the same release more than three times. A candidate who has failed at an examination three times for a release, may not attempt that examination again until the next release.

3. A candidate may not retake an examination before 30 days following the failure.

4. Before admission to the same examination a third time, the candidate must produce evidence of training suitable to

rectify the gaps identified in the candidate's competence at previous examinations.

5. SAP does not undertake that candidates can retake an examination for a particular release. Retake candidates may have to attempt the examination for a later release.

6. Candidates pay a fee for all retakes.

You can see from the retake policies that each provider has different rules. Make sure you read the rules for your certification provider, before taking their examination. Whatever you do, do not violate their rules.

Updating

Most certification providers update their software, systems and examination rules every few years. If you are certified in the providers' previous version of a particular certificate, you may not need to redo the full set of examinations that was required for the certificate you currently hold. In many cases, only a small subset of examinations will be required to qualify for the update.

As an example: if you are MCSE 2000 certified, you only need to redo two core exams to update to MCSE 2003. Other providers also offer this option. Normally, it is only available if updating to the immediate next version. If you skip versions, i.e., if you were MCSE NT, you would have to redo the full seven exams to qualify for MCSE 2003.

Therefore, before updating your certification, make sure you read the provider's rules on this point. It pays to keep your certification up to date. Allowing them to lapse could cost you over two times more in exam registration fees.

Depending on your area of specialization, the latest certification will be in demand earlier or later by employers.

Check www.jobserve.com for patterns in certification requirements. You should aim to have acquired yours, as more and more jobs request applicants to have the latest certification.

If you are using brain dumps, it is wise to allow at least twelve to eighteen months to pass, for the full question sets to be available. Being the first to take an exam using brain dumps can be an expensive undertaking. In the early release of these brain dumps, the question sets are incomplete and most of the suggested answers are incorrect as well.

This is not the case if you are using training courses or CBT and home study materials. However, you will be alone in this undertaking. Few people will be able to offer you advice in forums, and so on.

How to Change Fields

If you are new to IT, you most probably entered the field through one of the following routes:

1 Moves and Changes
2 Support
3 Training
4 Development
5 Testing
6 Packaging
7 Webbing
8 Project Management
9 Business Analysis
10 Executive Roles

Moves and Changes

This low skilled area requires few (or no) skills or experience to enter. It is little more than manual labour. In most cases, moves and changes involve either physically moving machines and/or other peripherals or equipment (desks, fax machines, pointers, chairs, plants, etc.), from one location to another, and/or connecting them and testing to make sure that there is power to them. This might also involve a slightly higher skill requirement of moving telecom lines, network connection patching, etc. Doing this kind of work may give you some exposure to IT and telecoms; however, you will very quickly reach a dead end down this avenue, after you reach team leader or a moves and changes managerial role.

Support

The support route offers opportunities in the following:

- Helpdesk, telephone, call centre, 1st line support.
- 2nd line, desktop, desk side, trade floor, handhelds, PC, hardware support, virtual desktop.
- 3rd line, 4th line mail, server, networking, application, data warehouse, disaster recovery, infrastructure, executive, comms, telephony, security, database, storage, printing, wireless, terminal services, virtual server, data feeds, anti-viruses.
- Specialization (or 4th line support) – mail, database, antivirus, storage, telecoms, disaster recovery, networking, security, virtualization, data feeds and trading applications, infrastructure design.

If you are a helpdesk support engineer and want to move up in rates, the natural and easiest route would be along the support hierarchy, through 2nd line, then 3rd line support. After 3rd line support you can only move sideways or towards a specialization.

Within your specialization, you can only move back to 3rd line or lower, to 2nd or 1st line support, or sideways to another specialization. This is a dead end. To move forward, you need to move out of support and into another entry area of IT.

Training

IT trainers are educators who teach candidates and students how to use IT systems. There are software, hardware, as well as systems and processes trainers. One of the most basic training roles is a floorwalker. This role is employed leading to, or following, some form of systems migration.

The floorwalker literally walks around helping and training users on the newly deployed systems. They ask questions and show users how to perform business tasks with the new systems.

Classroom trainers can be freelance trainers, permanent or contract staff working for a third party training supplier. They normally specialize in a handful of subjects and become very proficient at teaching these.

If you are a freelance trainer working directly with a client, you stand to make more money than if you work through an agency or third-party training company. The career path in the training field is flat. You can command higher rates if you work with financial institutions or legal firms. Financial institutions pay a premium to trainers who offer courses for their traders, fund managers and executives.

Normally, trainers understand the user's side of the systems, applications or processes. This means that in most cases, to re-enter IT through another way, will require the trainer starting from the lower areas of another entry point.

Trainers however, can develop advanced people and communication skills, making them ideal for managerial and business analysis roles.

Testing

A tester is someone who uses scripts, software and/or hardware, and processes to test computer systems, applications and software. This is another easy-to-enter field of IT contracting. The lower end of testing requires little skill; however, there is a wide range of abilities and skill levels within testing.

At the high end, testers require scripting and programming skills. In some cases, testers may even have Ph.D.s in mathematics, geology or other related fields of study.

For instance, in the finance industry, software testers may be required to know complex mathematical algorithms and/or to develop them. Similarly, in the oil and natural gas research fields, software testers may be required to understand geology, risk management, oil rig design tolerances, etc., and/or help to refine complex graphical imaging and modelling tools.

Often, testers aspire to be developers. It is therefore understandable why they naturally gravitate there, when they seek to change course in their IT careers.

Development

Developers create software or firmware systems. These systems could be entire applications, or portions of code. This entry point is very broad. There is a wide variety of technologies to choose from programming languages and systems. This avenue also accommodates combinations of skills and knowledge more than most of the other IT entry areas.

Furthermore, a programmer is required to carry out most of the following:

- Requirements Analysis
- Specification Writing

- Software Architecture Design
- Code Authoring
- Compilation
- Software Testing
- Documentation
- Integration
- Maintenance
- Supporting

Because there are many tasks involved in the software lifecycle, many IT roles have developed to undertake some of these roles. For instance, business analysts carry out the 'requirements analysis' and 'specification writing' portions of the software development lifecycle. Support staff undertake the 'integration and maintenance' supporting positions of the software development lifecycle.

This leaves most programmers to do the 'documentation', 'software testing', 'compilation', 'code authoring' and 'software architecture design', portions of the software development lifecycle. In large projects, software testers may be separately employed to undertake the testing role, instead of the programmers.

For a list of programming languages, visit the following Web sites:

- http://home.nvg.org/~sk/lang
- http://home.nvg.org/~sk/lang/lang.html
- http://oop.rosweb.ru/Other
- http://www.scriptol.org/encyclopedia.html
- www.people.ku.edu/~nkinners/LangList/Extras/search.htm

Some of these languages are no longer in great demand. At the time of writing this, the following programming languages ranked as the thirty most sought after programming language skills to have for IT contactors:

Source: ITJobsWatch.co.uk.

1. SQL
2. Java
3. C#
4. C++
5. JavaScript
6. C
7. Perl
8. VB
9. PL/SQL
10. VBA
11. VB.NET
12. Shell Script
13. PHP
14. Transact-SQL
15. VB6
16. VBScript
17. Embedded C
18. VC++
19. ActionScript
20. DHTML
21. ABAP
22. Embedded C++
23. COBOL
24. Python
25. Korn
26. RPG
27. Ada
28. Delphi
29. JCL
30. Assembly Language

Currently, SQL, Java, C#, C++ and JavaScript are in highest demand. However, over time, this will change. Keep a close watch on this list through www.ITJobsWatch.co.uk for emerging technologies.

To earn the most money in computer programming; either have a skill in high demand, or be involved in a field that (although it may not lead the list of high demand programming languages), has few competitors and/or offers jobs which command high rates. Advanced Business Application Programming (ABAP), by the German software company SAP, is one such language skill.

Some programming languages such as C, C++, C#, Embedded C, Embedded C++, and VC++ are similar. Therefore, if you are proficient in one, you can more easily learn and master the others. To guarantee that you always have skills that are in great demand, and to move sideways and take up a new skill, you might want to enter the programming field through a language that is in high demand, and broad enough to accommodate easier sideways movement.

Packaging

A packager uses software tools to create installable applications that install in a directed manner. Most of the time, a packager will remove all pop-ups and prompts during the installation process, thereby automating the installation of the application. At other times, packagers do more to the application. In the case of using an unsupported application, or that naturally does not work on a particular operating system or platform, a packager can make it work by repackaging the code.

Normally, the more programming skills a packager requires to do their work, the higher their contracting rate will be. In a way, packaging is reverse engineering and resembles hacking; however, this is the legal form.

The field is divided into two clear sections: application packagers and application developers. The latter is closer to programming, whilst the former uses tools such as WinINSTALL, Wise Package Studio, MSI Package Builder, etc., to package installable applications for automatic deployment, or manual installation. Most packagers branch either into application development, or into software support.

Entry through this route is as easy as gaining experience and/or qualifying in the use of one of the major packaging software applications. Alternatively, developers can gain easy access via this way, due to their experience in application development. This is especially true for non-Microsoft operating system application developers.

Webbing

The Web designer entry point is a relatively new avenue, compared to some of the other more established trades. It involves Web site design (graphical), Web site designer (programming), search engine optimization (SEO), Web site database manager (database support) and Web server management (hardware and software support). A Web master might be involved in all the above duties.

Generally, in a large, corporate environment, your role is defined clearly. For instance, the DBAs would not normally know much about anything, other than managing the databases, adding queries, fine-tuning databases, etc. On the other hand, the graphical Web designers are situated in the design area using Photoshop, Dreamweaver and/or SharePoint.

The Web developers would be using JavaScript, CSS, PHP, DHTML, and/or Visual Studio, and so on. At the same time, the databases team will be primarily involved in My SQL or SQL database management.

The Web server team would be involved in backing-up the Web servers, updating service packs, adding and removing hardware, retiring and adding servers to server farms, installing applications, running monitoring tools and managing clustered servers.

The SEO team is more marketing than IT. They create Web pages that attract higher hits from search engines. They use news releases, back-linking, Web pages, META tags, and social marketing (blogs, forums, YouTube, MySpace, etc.).

Because Web masters can get involved in so many areas, this route is one that you can move around in for a long time, dabbling in many areas of expertise. The Web is also an area that is more future-proof than most of the other avenues into IT that we have covered.

Depending on what they were previously involved in, within the Web arena, most IT contractors looking to leave the Web area of expertise, normally go into other fields, such as development or packaging, support, business analysis or management.

Business Analysis

A business analyst lives with one foot firmly planted in the technical IT world, whilst the other firmly rests within the client's business world. They understand the business enough to model its processes. By clearly understanding the processes the client uses to do their business, the business analyst can test and refine business procedural changes.
These business changes normally save the client time and money, whilst improving services to customers.

Business analysis can be broken down into the following sets of activities:

Strategic Analysis – This is the highest paid area of expertise in business analysis. It involves the business analyst advising senior management on business policy and strategy. In this role, the business analyst examines the organisation, its competition and the business environment, and the market(s) that the organisation operates within. This role is heavily orientated towards the business, and uses little IT.

Organisational Analysis – This is also a business focused analysis area of expertise. It involves converting strategic analysis into newly re-designed or improved business practices. These changes can often require organisational restructuring as well. The role utilises a business analysts' knowledge of the business, and may involve requirements engineering, and stakeholder analysis. Jobs in this area often use business process modeling and related software, such as those offered by the following manufacturers:

- BEA Systems: AquaLogic Business Process Management System (BPMS).
- IDS-Scheer: Business Process Excellence.
- Intec Systems: BPR Consulting and Process Modeling Software.
- Interfacing Technology: FirstStep BPR Tool.
- KBSI: Process Modeling Software.
- Meta Software: BPR Software.
- Micrografx: ABC Flowcharter (now part of Corel Corporation).
- Microsoft Corporation: Visio Modeling Software.
- Oracle Corporation: Designer/2000 BPR Software.
- Popkin: System Architect – BPR.
- Proforma Corporation: Business Process Modeling Software.
- Silverrun BPM: Business Process Modeler.

At this level, core business processes re-design, how to apply enabling technologies to support the new core processes, and the management of the resultant organisational changes, will be the experiences and knowledge most required.

Systems analyst – Generally, after a case for change has been identified by the organisation, a systems analyst is brought in to understand the business IT systems, identify areas in need of improvement, and make suggestions for systems and procedural changes. The systems analyst role overlaps in places with the developer and testing roles. Unlike the strategic analyst and organisational analyst, the systems analyst is primarily focused on IT.

Becoming a BA

Getting into business analysis is slightly different from most of the other entry points we have discussed so far. The first way in is through a graduate recruitment program, straight out of university.

If you missed that opportunity, then the next easiest entry point is via project management. Project managers wanting to move to business analysis will find it easier than non-project managers.

However, since project managers earn comparable rates to BAs, the only reason you would want to make this move is possibly to reduce your stress level, and/or to find another route to an executive position or strategic consulting.

The last option left open, (if you do not fall into the two options previously discussed), is by training and experience. The first of this; training, starts with certification. Table 25 illustrates the contents of a BA certification course. In less than two weeks, and for less than £5,000 in most cases, you can become trained and certified in the various aspects of business analysis.

The course prepares you for the ISEB examination. You have to pass the three core units, and one specialist unit to be able to attempt acquiring the diploma. The diploma examination involves a face to face interview with two examiners, who will test your knowledge of the various BA subject areas, as well as your professionalism and presentation skills.

Module	Course	Duration	Fee
Core	Organisational Context (formerly Business Organisation)	2 days	£885
Core	Business Analysis Essentials	3 days	£1195
Core	Requirements Engineering	3 days	£1195
Specialist	Modelling Business Processes	2 days	£885
Specialist	Systems Development Essentials (formerly Business Systems Investigation)	3 days	£1195
Specialist	Systems Modeling Techniques (formerly Analysis & Design Techniques)	3 days	£1195
Specialist	Benefits Management and Business Acceptance	3 days	£1195

Table 25: Sample BA course structure and fees (as of October 2007)

After acquiring your training and ISEB diploma in business analysis, you can update your CV, and start marketing yourself for junior BA roles (at first), until you acquire enough experience to apply for higher BA roles.

Most enthusiasts reach the lofty heights of strategic business analysis. However, you will find it easier and more useful to move into project management. This will give you invaluable experience and exposure to climb the BA career pole towards strategic business analysis.

Project Management

Most ambitious IT contractors will eventually end up in management. Normally, permies occupy management roles within IT, as they represent a more long-term investment than an IT contractor does. However, IT contractor managers fill the project management roles abundantly, due to the role's short term premise.

Managers from other fields (other than IT) who become IT contractors, can walk straight into a project management role; although it is more likely to obtain one of these positions, if you were previously in IT management.

The role has developed due to the regularity of change within the IT industry. Software updates and versions are constantly releasing, new industry compliance regulations, hardware redundancy, Web integration requirements, and a whole load of other migration requirements, has helped to create the IT project management position.

Today, most large companies are constantly undertaking systems migration projects. Desktop, mail, application, database, server, hardware and firmware migrations and rollouts, are some of the many projects constantly underway.

These projects all need experienced project managers. Often, the permie IT manager is not equipped, skilled or experienced enough in managing these types of projects. To avoid paying for the permie managers' education as he/she goes through the learning curve, a project manager is hired.

Contractor project managers are nomadic. Because they move from one project to the next, often back to back, they quickly amass a broad and wide range of migration and rollout project management experience. There is little or no learning curve required when they join a project. They can hit the ground running.

The current rates these contractors command are some of the highest in the industry. It is common for a senior IT manager to command over £1,000 per day. Less senior project managers normally command half of this amount.

The key requirement for this role is an understanding of the processes involved, in successfully managing an IT project. The Prince 2 Practitioner certification is one of the more respected and acknowledged indicators that a project manager is fully conversant with all the processes involved in managing an IT project. See http://www.prince2.org.uk for more information about Prince 2.

With your Prince 2 certificate and experience of Microsoft Project and MS Outlook or Lotus Notes under your belt, your next step is to secure a team leader or junior project manager role. After undertaking a few junior project manager and assistant project manager roles, you may be ready to manage a small project of your own. Within a few short years, you could be well on your way as a contracting project manager.

The good thing about project management is that no matter which specialisation you previously contracted in, you can upgrade to a related project management role, and continue to grow in project managing.

Most project managers aspire to be executives. They do this by climbing up the experience ladder in project management, until they are experienced enough to recruit for a fixed term IT executive position. This would normally be a transitional position, that may eventually lead to a permie executive role.

Executive Roles

Because of the Internet, strategic e-commerce decisions have moved to the boardroom level. No longer can an organisation trust these decisions to the IT director alone. He/she may be knowledgeable on the organisations current IT set-up, however, going forward, an increasing number of organisations are trusting e-commerce decisions to outside specialists, executives and executive consultants.

A sizeable proportion of organisations' sales revenues now comes from the Internet. Therefore, misplaced, strategic decisions regarding any electronic commercial business, could be fatal. It is becoming more commonplace to see blue chip companies calling in e-commerce consultants to advise the board of directors (and other executives within their companies) on these vital decisions.

This prospect only opens to you, if you have already acquired extensive business and IT knowledge through project management and business analysis. You may also have successfully implemented e-commerce solutions for your own company, or/and many others. With your success and record of accomplishment, you can start consulting to organisations.

Unless you are so successful that organisations seek you out for your services, you will have to pitch for consulting contracts, and produce proposals for board level members. You may also have to set-up a consultancy with several partners to ensure your mutual success.

One source of international executive roles can be found at http://www.executivesontheweb.com; however, you can also approach organisations directly with a proposal to improve their current services.

Executive consulting is currently experiencing a lot of success in the area of e-commerce, however, trends change, and around the world, different problems and opportunities exist.

This role is not a 9 to 5 job, and do not expect to come home each night to your bed, either. Most likely, it will take you all over the world. This is especially true if you are consulting for large, blue chip corporations. From this point, the only choice left to you is to grow your own company into an international institution.

Chapter 4

Philosophy and Psychology

- Professionalism, Industriousness and Conscientiousness
- Self-Belief, Self-Confidence and Self-Worth
- Procrastinating
- Office Etiquette
- Profits
- Contracting Ethics and Practices
- Personal Considerations
- Offshore and Foreign Contracts
- Agencies
- Technical Considerations

Philosophy and Psychology

The mindset of a professional and highly paid contractor differs greatly from that of an unprofessional and erratically employed contractor. Whilst skills and experience help to define a good contractor, professionalism, excellence in communication, having a good work ethic, a positive mental attitude, and a strong self-belief, all go a long way to create the perfect contractor.

Professionalism, Industriousness and Conscientiousness

Your philosophical view of IT contracting will greatly dictate how you treat your employers, your agency, yourself, your work and every other aspect of your IT contracting life.

Are you proud of what you do in IT? What do you think your relationship with users, team leaders and managers, or third party suppliers should be like? Are you being paid what your skills are worth? Are you worth what you are paid? Do you enjoy what you do? Do others appreciate what you do? Are you constantly striving to improve?

The answers you give to these questions will clearly answer if you are professional in your conduct and work. It will also give an indication as to whether you are meticulous, conscientious and hardworking, or lazy, careless and shoddy in your work.

Laziness has no place in any business; however, it is easy to avoid being sacked for it, in permie roles. This is not so for contracting. If you are lazy, careless and slapdash, you will not last long in IT contracting. You will very quickly get to understand what fair dismissal means.

The only way to last in any contract is to produce. Contractors do not tolerate excuses, such as repetition of mistakes, whilst carrying out your duties. Your incompetence will be rightfully rewarded with the prompt termination of your contract.

To survive in most permie roles, you simply have to show up at work. To survive in most IT contracting roles, you have to be self-driven, professional, hardworking and conscientious.

Pervasive Permie Syndrome (PPS)

When most permies turn to contracting, they bring with them many beliefs that applied to permyism, but that no longer support them in contracting. The pervasive thoughts can creep around your mind until you find yourself either returning to being a permie, or until you greatly handicap your contracting business through mismanagement.

The cure

To rid yourself of (PPS), you need to change the way you view contracting. IT contracting is not a job; it is a business and a way of life. Like all businesses, to succeed in IT contracting you need to dedicate yourself to acquiring the right skills and knowledge, learn to conduct yourself with professionalism, and have a positive attitude towards yourself, your business and your client.

You are in competition with your peers and your previous year's performance. Always seek to improve your income, professionalism, skills and knowledge.

This is achieved by providing a service or product that exceeds the client's expectations in every way. The litmus test for how good a contractor you are, lies in how often you are renewed and how much you command within the rate range of your area of expertise.

Wholly submitting to a corporate master

You will work at different organisations in your contracting career, however, this does not make any organisation your boss. Working at different sites as a contractor does not change who you are really working for. That always defaults to you. When permies first join the contracting ranks, they often come with years of conditioning in seeing an organisation as their "master". It is often difficult to shed this belief in the early days as a contractor. This old mind-set can lead you to mismanage yourself and thus fail at being an independent contractor.

Sadly, many contactors soon learn the hard way, that most organisations only care about themselves. They will never forget that you are a hired hand. When they need to reduce overhead, cut spending or 'pull' a project, they will not bat an eye when terminating your contract.

The first time this happens, you may be hurt, shocked and disappointed, to say the least. You may even experience feelings of rejection. Your self-esteem could suffer and your confidence may feel badly bruised. Eventually the depression will end and you will pull yourself up, dust yourself off, and return to the fray a little wiser and certainly better informed. Never take being let go from a contract on a personal level. There is nothing personal about it – everything you do for an organisation is strictly business.

The fact that you are expendable to the client will become clear. You would have learned that your services were needed only because the organisation saw a way of making a profit from them. When they no longer need you, or when you start costing them more than they can earn from your services, the contract will have to end.

Normally, you will only need to be disappointed three to five times before the lesson becomes ingrained. At some point, you will learn the hard way that you should never "sell your soul" to any organisation, except the one that you head.

Mismanaging 'the perfect contract'

You will occasionally come across 'the perfect contract'. I have had a few of these in my time of contracting. These contracts empower you. They give you more than they take, but are often few and far in between. Your definition of 'the perfect contract' will be different from mine. In fact, it will be different from your own varying definitions of 'the perfect contract' at assorted stages of your life.

For instance, if you become a parent, 'the perfect contract' may be one that allows you to take time off and return to the same contract many months later, or work two or three days a week from home, or start work later after taking the child or children to a child minder or kindergarten.

Similarly, if you are planning to buy a home, 'the perfect contract' could be one that pays you top market rates and allows you unlimited overtime. The extra money could enable you to purchase a better home and save enough to facilitate the relocation, purchase of furnishing and decorating of the new home.

If you are new to an area of expertise within IT contracting, 'the perfect contract' could be one that allows you to greatly increase your skills, acquire vast amounts of knowledge or perhaps acquire expensive-to-get certification, for free.

Finally, 'the perfect contract' could simply mean your managers, colleagues and users respect you. It could mean that you have sufficient responsibility to be effective in your role, and you get to build deep and lasting friendships that last far beyond the contract's duration.

Whatever definition you have for your 'perfect contract', you can be sure of one thing; the contract will eventually end. Just make sure it does not end due to early termination. When everything is great, it is easy to lower your guard and start taking advantage or taking the situation for granted.

Do not fall into this common trap. Stay humble and professional at all times. Remember that you are in a service business. Whether you are a programmer, support engineer, migration project manager, application specialist, hardware engineer or Web developer, your continued efforts of professional operation will be required to succeed.

Office e-mail usage

Most companies also have an e-mail usage policy. The result of many litigation cases have hinged on the contents of a careless e-mail. An organisation's e-mail usage policy normally contains the following points (courtesy of www.businesslink.gov.uk):

- What shouldn't be circulated on the company e-mail system, including any offensive, indecent or obscene material, or anything likely to cause offence on grounds of sex, sexual orientation, race, disability, age, religion or belief.
- What can be construed as inappropriate, discriminatory or libellous content.
- Rules for sending confidential business information via e-mail, – e.g., using encryption software to prevent unauthorised persons accessing it.
- What you consider to be appropriate e-mail etiquette, such as terms of address and sign-off, and the need to be formal and businesslike in all communications.
- How attachments should be handled, such as checking for viruses – you may also want to set a maximum file size for attachments.
- How much personal e-mail use is generally acceptable.
- How the laws governing data protection, e-commerce and e-mail marketing affect the business.

- Guidance on saving, filing and photocopying e-mails for company records.

Familiarize yourself with organisations' e-mail usage policies and stay in compliance of them. Do not use your work e-mail to buy or subscribe to any personal products or services. Similarly, avoid using your Web e-mail address to subscribe to technical forums or other work related services. E-mail harvesting robots could get hold of your e-mail address. These robots harvest e-mails for bulk sellers who sell the address to anyone, including unscrupulous Web masters.

When this occurs, you will then become bombarded with junk e-mail, viruses, spy-ware, porn and other content and attachments that could see you falling out of compliance of an e-mail usage policy.

Furthermore, do not give your e-mail address to friends or family members that are likely to include you in joke e-mail chains. These e-mails may cause you to accept content and attachments that fall out of compliance of policy(s).

Lastly, be careful in what you include in your e-mails. Avoid making offensive or prejudiced comments, promises or legal commitments via e-mail. This could act as evidence in a litigation case. Similarly, always archive your correspondences for the same reasons – to cover your back.

Theft, withholding assets and other foolish notions

Not all contracts end amicably, and some terminate without fully compensating you for your services. This could be due to a disagreement or some contractual discrepancy. Whatever the reason, do not take the foolish action of withholding the organisation's assets for any part of payments which may be due for your services.. If the organisation takes legal action against you, you may have to face fines or a prison sentence.

I know of a few contractors who acquired laptops, pagers, Blackberry's and other electronic equipment from previous organisations they had worked for. Whilst these contractors may have gained a few electronic gadgets, they have risked a lot more and acted without integrity. They were fortunate that their clients never took legal action, but you may not be so lucky.

Stealing from your client is unprofessional, reckless and foolish. In most cases, the items stolen are worth less than your daily rate; however, you risk the profits of the entire role, as well as your good name and standing in society as a law-abiding citizen without a criminal record.

Follow the correct procedure to reclaim owed money. Try to end all your contracts on good terms. Going back for another term at a previous organisation is more profitable than any 'kit' you may appropriate.

Software theft and software piracy

As you work in the industry, it is very easy to get ahold of software – licensed to the organisations at whose sites you work – and use them privately. However, this is illegal, unethical and dishonest; saying that, I have never met a contractor who does not flout software license rules.

Stealing software and software licenses from a client's site and using them for your own personal use, passing them on to friends and family or worse, selling them for profit is a criminal offence. You risk severe fines and a jail sentence – possibly – if caught.

Against the small price of doing the right thing, you are willing to stake your reputation, loss of income, the stigma of being branded a criminal as well as the stress and shame you will put yourself and your family through. Is it worth it? I do not think so.

A more pervasive software licensing issue is software piracy. Nowadays, it is easy to download almost any software you want free of charge from any peer- to-peer (P2P) Web site such as, www.edonkey.com, www.limewire.com, www.emule.com, or www.overnet.com, or P2P programs such as, uTorrent, BitComet, ABC, BitLord, TurboBT, Azureus, or The Original BitTorrent Client.

What these Web sites and programs are doing is robbing money from software companies. Over time, this theft will affect us all. As the software company's profits dwindle, the quality of software may also decline.

When software companies no longer can afford the huge research and development funding required for constantly improving their products, we the users, will be ones affected. At the same time, software piracy threatens to drive the price of software ownership – for the people that purchase legal copies – up.

Furthermore, software companies will focus more on corporate clients where their licensing policies can be enforced more effectively. This is likely to drive up corporate software spending and increase the cost of IT in general. In a roundabout way, this could see contractor's rates reduced to compensate for part of the increase in IT costs.

Self-Belief, Self-Confidence and Self-Worth

The secret to being able to command double what the average rate per day is – for the same contracting role – lies in your self-belief, self-confidence and self-worth. Without self-confidence and self-belief, you will have a low pay; as you will not even attempt to apply for the top end roles.

In most cases, the divide exists because of differing skill sets and unrelated industries. In the majority of cases, it is traced to a lack of self-belief, laziness or a lack of professionalism.

A lack of self-confidence and self-belief are both psychological states that arise from a poor self-image. Your self-image is fragile and easily damaged by self-doubt, constant deriding, insults and disrespect from yourself or others. This negative habit will rob you of thousands of pounds in the course of a single contract.

Whilst disrespectful treatment from others will eventually erode your self-image, constant self-ridicule will destroy it even quicker. If you are a pessimist, sceptical cynic, and regularly doubt your own abilities and self-worth, you need to take immediate action to reverse the damage you have done (and are still doing), to your self-image and thus, your confidence.

Use the immediate reversal technique to change your self-belief. It involves identifying the self-disdaining thoughts, comments, behaviour and actions. First, identify your negative patterns; second, consciously stop yourself in mid-act, mid-thought or mid-statement. Third, replace the negative thought, speech, or action with a positive, complimentary equivalent. As an example, if you are prone to saying of yourself, "What a clumsy fool." Stop when you catch yourself about to say this, and instead replace the statement with, "Day by day in every way, I am more careful."

Do this for all negative thoughts. If you cannot see yourself succeeding at something, replace the thought with an image of yourself successfully executing that same action. Similarly, change your patterns of negative actions. For example, if you are physically afraid of traders, CEOs, or even users, and you avoid dealing with them by passing support calls to your colleagues; you can reverse this by taking on the job yourself and fulfilling the support requirement.

This will take courage and will require you to face your fears – head on. However, be assured that you are not alone in this undertaking. Around the world, many people are facing similar fears and winning their battles. Therefore, you can change your habits and improve your life as well as anyone else. "Feel the Fear and Do It Anyway", by Susan Jeffers, is a book that has helped many people find freedom from fear; by using *action* to conquer fear. Get a copy and put your fears behind you, once and for all.

Handling career progression fears

If you are planning to change your IT contracting specialization, many fears and anxieties may rear their ugly head. Do not be frozen by this fear, take action and stop thinking about all that could go wrong. Procrastination and over analysis enforce fear, whilst action cures fear.

In order to change your area of IT contracting specialization, you will need to take a specific set of actions. These are as follows:

- Obtain training – take courses to attain the relevant certification(s) you will need.
- Get experience – carefully select your next few contracts to help you gain exposure to the desired area of specialization.
- Use your current contract – discuss with your current client, about the subject of expanding your skill set into the desired area of expertise. You never know; there may be an opportunity to move into that area, where you currently work.
- Amend your CV – change the CV to cater more for the desired area of expertise.
- Apply – start job hunting.

When you clearly define a set of things you need to do, you will remove most of the anxiety related issues with the move. Then, all you need to do, is to take the identified actions – *now*.

Posture

We have already covered how you can use posture to your best advantage at interviews (see page 239). Now we shall look closer at posture in the workplace.

Your body reacts to how you feel and what you think. If you do not consciously check it, it will betray your true feelings and thoughts. There are a myriad of body postures and gestures representing each thought or feeling you have about yourself; however, we will deal with a few of the major ones.

In the journey to professionalism, posture (and breathing) is the external protection you need to appear confident, knowledgeable, enthusiastic, patient, understanding, and industrious. Let us look at each one of these elements:

1. **Confidence:** The way you stand or walk, talk, shake hands, maintain eye contact, and approach a problem (in attitude), define your sense of confidence and thus, your professionalism.

The first thing to maintain is a cool, calm demeanour. "Never let them see you sweat" is a good rule of thumb, to remember. You can do this by never rushing, and through taking deeper, more purposeful breaths. By avoiding rushing, I do not mean that you should be late in arriving everywhere you go. By taking your time in all endeavours, you should remain in control, in everything you do.

When you rush, you can make mistakes, forget steps in a process, leave vital parts out of a design, and/or plan badly. By not rushing through your work, you will make fewer mistakes, remember more things and appear more professional.

Take the time to truly think through what you are doing. By planning ahead and being prepared, you will have the answers you need, when required by your job. Slow down in preparation, so that you can speed up in execution of your plans.

Similarly, the way you walk and speak will also determine your level of confidence. Taking short, quick steps gives the impression of being rushed, flustered or even panicked. Stand tall and take long, purposeful strides. A confidant gait will also help give the impression that you are someone of authority.

How your eyes move will also determine how confident you feel. If they dart around and never maintain a gaze, you will come across as being shy, nervous, or untrustworthy. Avoid this by giving good eye contact and holding it whilst talking or looking at someone. Move your eyes slower as you look around yourself, or at the people with whom you are conversing.

Move your head in conjunction with your eyes. Moving only your eyes (without your head) – in the direction you are looking – will make you appear shifty, devious or even distrustful of others.

When standing, a posture with your legs, shoulder width apart, gives more of a confident image than standing slouched, or with your legs and feet closely together. Of course, this is only true for men.

For men's sitting positions, crossing one ankle over the knee of the other leg, or simply keeping both feet on the floor in front of you, with your feet and knees shoulder width apart, will make you appear more confident. Sitting with your knees further apart than your shoulder width, makes you appear arrogant and, when in close proximity to other people, will also make you appear thoughtless and disrespectful of other people's personal space.

For women, it is always appropriate to keep the close knees together, or cross one knee over the other whilst sitting.

When standing still, women's ankles should be close together. The most important thing to remember, whether you are wearing a dress or slacks, is to never have your legs too far apart. This position will give others the impression that (at the very least), you are unrefined or unprofessional.

For both men and women, it is important not to cross your legs 'away' from an interviewer or boss. Doing so will make them subconsciously feel "cut off" from you. Therefore, when crossing your legs, the foot you lift should go in the direction of the boss or interviewer, if they are sitting on the same side of the table, as you are. If the important person is sitting across from you, then it doesn't matter which way you cross your legs.

Similarly, be mindful of not crossing your arms in front of you. Again, this makes people feel "cut off" from you, and it is also a body language indicating stress.

2. **Breathing:** Your level of stress is closely related to the depth and frequency of your breathing. Coincidentally, your confidence level also correlates to your breathing. Quick, shallow breaths relate to a lack of confidence and higher stress. Whilst deep, slow breaths convey more self-confidence, lower stress and aid in more thoughtful responses during conversations.

Confident people take deeper and slower breaths, than do stressed and nervous people. Therefore, to appear and feel more confident, learn to control the way you breathe. Observe calm, relaxed and confident looking individuals. You will notice their breathing pattern is smooth, deep and slower.

3. **Knowledge:** To appear well informed, you either have to know what you are talking about, or at least appear to know the answers to questions which may be posed in any given situation. If you do know the answers, you should not simply blurt them out; otherwise, you may seem like a show off or know-it-all.

A better way to share your knowledge is to allow others to fully express their ideas, partial truths and half solutions, (whichever the case may be), before you interject your thoughts. Even then, do not outwardly make other people seem like they are wrong. Instead, use a humble approach. Start by saying something like, "That's a good idea, what about ...?", "Have we tried ...?" or "That could be one way of achieving the objective, but what do you think about ...?"... and so on. Notice the similarities in the statements which "include" the thoughts, actions or ideas of others, rather than discount them.

You have two options as to how you can tackle cases where you do not know an answer, or where you do not have all the information. Firstly, you can listen to others and form a possible hypothesis from what they say or secondly, you can be honest and admit that you do not know.

The former requires you asking leading questions that will guide them to resolving the problem themselves, or give you a notion of how you can resolve a situation. Often, knowing what to ask is more useful than offering a partial solution.

Admitting you do not know is best followed with a suggestion as to how you think the information could be acquired. Never admit you do not know an answer without offering a partial solution or advice on how the knowledge may be acquired. This allows you to maintain your informed status and still retain your professionalism. In this case, you could simply reply something to the affect of, "I'm sorry, I do not know, but I can get the answers very quickly, and I'll get back to you immediately with the solution."

Always make sure you find out if the solution you offered was any good, or in the case where you did not know the answer, find out what the correct response should have been. This helps build up your understanding for the future. Don't be too busy to add value to your knowledge-base. Always seek to learn something new daily. Above all however, *never* simply make something up and blurt it out, as this can easily reveal your limited knowledge on a subject, or worse, make you look ridiculously ill-informed.

4. Enthusiasm: If you had a choice, which would you employ- someone who was enthusiastic about their work or someone who was seemingly apathetic? Indifferent people look bored, lazy and appear uncaring. They give an unprofessional impression by their attitude and posture, alone. Normally, the quality of their work also suffers because of this general demeanour. Furthermore, they are usually the first to be let go and the decision to do so, is unanimously agreed upon.

Whenever you are around an apathetic person, you too, start feeling listless, bored and lethargic. They are an energy sponge. They soak up all the energy around them, and unless you are highly motivated, they will begin to affect your performance. Avoid languid people wherever you can.

Opt to be enthusiastic, keen, excited, eager and passionate. We all have ups and downs; however, you should treat your contracting business like a theatrical performance. The show must go on, and part of the show is your zeal. There is one particular contractor that I have had the good fortune of working with, several times. Every time I see him, I am amazed that he is always energetically engaged in his work. He has been selected for renewal several times, against all the odds.

This contractor is not highly skilled, nor is he very knowledgeable. In fact, he can seem a little mentally slow at times, however, he is always enthusiastic, happy, excited and willing to do anything he is instructed, without a fuss or complaint.

His eagerness is infectious. Just thinking of him makes me feel happy and upbeat. That's how he affects others. People just love to be around him. Are you like that, or do people leave the room shortly after you enter? If so, you need to acquire more fervour.

There are four main steps you can take to be more enthusiastic. These are as follows:

4a. Smile! It is an instant sign of being jovial, relaxed, excited and keen. Smiling is also a universal sign of warmth and friendliness.

4b. If you are naturally a slow talker, speak a little faster to avoid sounding lethargic or boring. Do not speak so fast that people cannot understand you; however, increase your speaking speed to add some excitement and energy to your conversations.

4c. Move faster when asked to do something. Start immediately, walk faster and with real purpose.

4d. Develop a positive mental attitude. Look on the bright side of everything. Develop global metaphors which assist you in being more positive. A global metaphor is a belief that affects your entire life. Some examples are, "I always find a way", or "I succeed at all that I do", or "I am lucky" or "I can overcome any obstacle", etc.

Following these four steps will instantly make you more enthusiastic. The last step is the most important of the four. Work on becoming more positive, your entire life. Eliminate all negatives from your belief system and replace them all with positive beliefs. You can effortlessly achieve amazing things when you are not sabotaging your efforts through negative thoughts.

5. **Patience:** Everyone makes mistakes sometimes and each of us have our own idiosyncrasies. Do not think you are the only person having to tolerate others. Each day, many people are tolerating the things you do – often without your knowledge. Learn to be more tolerant, understanding and empathetic to others.

Impatience leads to anger, disrespect and even accidents. As a contractor working onsite for an organisation, you cannot afford to show your anger, or be aggressive or impatient towards anyone.

Furthermore, you should not be disrespectful towards any other employee, especially permies. This is true if you act physically or through memos, e-mails or letters. Your mistakes, due to impatience, will be worsened if they can be proven with recorded evidence, such as e-mail or CCTV footage.

A colleague once taught me this saying, "If you don't have anything good to say, say nothing at all." If your comment is not going to help the situation, or worse, if it is going to aggravate the circumstances, then do not offer it. You could easily regret your words or actions, later.

Practicing patience is even more important for contractors who are involved in building servers, writing scripts, coding applications, maintaining databases or data backup services, or Web mastering an organisation's Web site. This is because lack of patience often leads to mistakes, and making a mistake on a client's live data, or when dealing with other important assets of the organisation such as their customers, could be costly to you – or your professional indemnity insurance underwriter.

You could lose your contract – instantly – if your lack of patience is the cause of an accident. Therefore, avoid making potentially fatal mistakes by being patient in all endeavours. Learn to always think before you speak or act.

If necessary, try counting down from ten, before you react impatiently. This is often enough to curb impatience; however, it requires discipline and self-control. A more effective method is to walk away from a situation, whenever you can, before you act on your intolerance.

6. **Industriousness:** A good work ethic is hard to find nowadays. In our modern world of instant gratification, where few people have planted a seed, watered and cared for it for months, sometimes years until harvest time, we tend to want

everything *right now*. This has led to the decline of good work ethics. People spend more time looking for shortcuts than actually getting on with the task.

Do the work, put in the hours and most importantly, enjoy doing so. Hard work is its own reward. As a contractor, you will be paid for your hard work and possibly renewed due to your diligence, as well. Furthermore, you will reinforce your knowledge, skills and experience by working hard, and most importantly, you will feel self-pride, and a deep satisfaction of accomplishment, that no shortcut can inspire.

Procrastinating

Running a close second place to a low self-image, or lack of self-belief, and/or having an unprofessional or lazy attitude, contractors, or would-be contractors who never take action, will similarly never get far in IT contracting. Opportunities come around frequently in the IT contracting market. However, if you postpone taking action until a later date, another contractor will step in your place and secure that golden contract.

If you are prone to vacillation, waiting for the perfect time, beating around the bush, or putting things off until another day, you will miss many opportunities. They will slip through your fingers each time, and you will never get to enjoy the benefits from them. Higher rates, fantastic learning opportunities and career boosting roles will go to those who prepared and acted promptly and decisively upon finding out about the opportunities.

Procrastination is a terrible habit. It is half laziness and half fear – fear of success or fear of failure. In almost all cases, your fears of handiwork, being more responsible, rejection, ridicule or embarrassment is unfounded. Unfortunate and unrelated past events can cause you to avoid any chance of a repetition of a similar scenario, in the future. Unfortunately, in most cases, the fear is not life threatening; however, you may be treating it and acting as if it is.

Far too often, people neglect to see the real value in their failures, which, although may have caused them some embarrassment at the time, also provided them with extremely valuable information. If you learn anything from any failure, it simply becomes a stepping stone toward your success, *if* you use what you learned to advance, in any endeavour.

You have to break away from living in fear and take the risk of winning, or failing. Without taking this risk regularly in IT contracting, your career progression will never experience rapid growth.

These fears and anxieties will be strongest when you are either entering into contracting for the first time, or changing paths of entry into a different field, or when moving up within a particular area of expertise.

Change is inevitable. You cannot permit yourself to stand still. Inflation, the economy, contracting rates and market forces are in constant flux. Therefore, when you think you are standing still, you will actually be sliding backwards. You must move forward in order to stay at the same relative financial level. Therefore, never put off change and always stay keen for new opportunities.

I once offered to help a bank worker with the training and advice he needed, in order for him to enter and succeed at IT contracting. He deliberated, hesitated and procrastinated for two years, after–which, he came to me and asked if the opportunity was still available. Unfortunately, I no longer had the time to help him and the market had vastly changed, making it harder for him to enter IT contracting, than prior to Y2K.

If you are miserable at your permie role, or fed up with your low paying contracts, do something different. Stop complaining and talking about what you will one day do, and start by taking a small, positive action *today*. Create an IT contracting CV, sign up to the automatic e-mail job updates from Jobserve.com, or sign up for an appropriate training course that will award you the skills you need to compete in the IT contracting marketplace. After-all, as the old saying goes, "the definition of insanity is the act of doing the same thing over and over, whilst expecting a different result."

How to appear completely committed to a client

Every organisation likes to hire staff that is committed, and always prioritises the organisation. In any case, whether you are truly committed or not, it will serve you better to at least appear that you are, even if you are not. As a contractor and business owner, you must prioritise your own business concerns before all other matters. However, you must not make your true priorities obvious to the businesses with whom you are contracting. Doing so will cause you to seem disloyal to them.   In order to appear completely committed to an organisation, adhere to the following practices:

- Consistent punctuality.
- Gladly accepting paid overtime.
- Showing daily enthusiasm.
- Willingness to accept challenges.
- Performing industriously.
- Happily sharing knowledge.

Being a team player summarizes these points. You must be willing to enthusiastically accept all challenges that will support, help and benefit the organisation and your team, as long as it also benefits your business. For example, if overtime is not included in your contract, do not do it. Only undertake unpaid overtime, if not doing so, will cause you to lose the contract. However, whenever it is optional, avoid it entirely.

Similarly, always accept the challenge of performing a difficult task or project. Accepting a technical project, presenting ideas through public speaking, training staff, or creating a system to help the business, are examples of potential challenges. These also have the added benefit of enhancing your skills which can be added to your CV. Tackling them successfully will give you more knowledge and experience to support your roles.

Most employers see you being busy (or even looking busy), as sufficient justification for the rate they pay you. Therefore, find ways to keep yourself busy. Ask for more work whenever you are without anything to do, and your day will pass faster, and you will avoid boredom. Looking bored is one of the worst states you can be in, within any organisation.

Keep yourself busy and enthusiastic, and you will grow to be an invaluable asset to the organisation. When your contract renewal date is up, you will be the last person they will think of cutting. In fact, the more of an asset you are to the organisation, the more bargaining power you will yield when it comes to asking for a rate increase.

Punctuality is vital to your professional image as a contractor. It also highlights your dependability to the client. Failing at this first hurdle will cut your contracts short. Always aim to be early rather than on time. It is 'sods law' that whenever you think you will be on time, the public transport system or road traffic will cause you to be otherwise.

Therefore, leave half an hour early whenever possible and aim to be in early, relaxed, prepared and ready to start your day on time, each day.

Be willing to add value to the organisation by passing on your knowledge to others in the team. Whilst this may seem like you will be making yourself redundant, it is not so. No one should be as industrious, punctual, hardworking, enthusiastic and helpful, as you are. Therefore, in light of these other assets, your knowledge alone should not be the only value the client would consider, when deciding on your renewal. In fact, if you are generous with your knowledge, it will only serve to get your tenure with the client lengthened.

Office Etiquette

Most IT contracting roles are in an IT department within an office or a set of offices, within an organisation. These offices come with their own rules of conduct and acceptable behaviours. To maintain your professionalism, you will need to understand these rules and operate within their boundaries. We shall look closely at some of these rules and etiquettes in this section.

Avoid office politics

Within each organisation, there is a struggle by management and staff to rise above others. Sometimes those above wish to keep those beneath them from catching up and overtaking them, and other times people below seek to undermine their superiors or peers for their own personal gain. Normally, the root of these political agendas is with permies; however, ever-so-often, you will come across a misguided contractor also engaging in these political games.

To play these games requires you to either take sides – gaining an enemy and an ally instantly – or to work alone, secretly undermining others, or manipulating your colleagues or bosses to achieve your secret agenda(s).

Playing office politics is unwise, especially if you are a contractor. This is because, as a contractor, you can never afford to make any enemies. You never know when you will meet (or need) that "enemy" either in the same contract, or later in another organisation.

Furthermore, people in the IT market tend to know other people at other organisations, that you may work at in the future. The enemy you made a year ago in a precious contract, could turn out to be best friends with your current IT manager, or one of your new colleagues. Not long into your new role you may find out that the enemy you thought you had left behind, is somehow influencing your enjoyment, renewal and thus, your contracting profits.

Another result that could manifest from playing the office politics game, is that when trouble comes, and someone needs to take the fall, your permie enemies and so-called allies will unite and oust you. In such games, there are no real allies or friends, only strategic supporters. When your allies are seriously threatened, they will channel their support for you elsewhere.

For contractors, the best way to behave is impartially and professionally, at all times. Avoid office politics, and other permie corporate infighting games, else you risk prematurely having your contract ended or not renewed.

Each, to their own

Each of us has our own way of reasoning, our own quirky ways of doing things, and our own way of being. It is unwise to try to get everyone to be like you, think like you, reason like you, or see life the way you see it.

I once did a contract with a fascinating contractor who had an insightful mantra, "Each, to their own." Whenever he encountered an unhelpful colleague or a difficult user, he would say this mantra quietly to himself. I also noticed that he never argued with permies concerning ways of carrying out tasks or achieving a technical outcome. He listened silently to their views first and later, when we were away from the situation, he would again say "Each, to their own."

The remarkable thing about this contractor was that he learned more from not trying to enforce his will, knowledge or skills on others, than other contractors, who bluntly pointed out faults in the way other people undertook tasks. He also avoided prejudging others in difficult situations, by accepting what they wanted to do, and how they wanted to do it.

You will greatly reduce your stress level, frustration and avoid angering your colleagues, managers and users when you learn to listen and accept people for what they are, rather than being judgmental and trying to force your ways on them.

Save your energies; remember, "Each, to their own," or you may prefer, "To each their own." Allow others to be different and give them enough time and space to do it their way. You never know, you could learn something new or find a way of doing the same thing more efficiently. Doing this will also aid your professionalism and help you avoid annoying people you work for and with.

Clean desk policy

As a professional IT contractor, you should always operate a clean desk policy, even if this is not formally practiced by your client. A clean desk promotes efficiency, and effective working practices and hygiene. It also aids client security.

Leaving pieces of paper, notes, passwords, and other information all over your desk or work area is not prudent, secure or professional. Some items can be potentially dangerous to the client if it were to land in the wrong hands.

Avoid also leaving money, food, coffee cups, sweet wrappers, toys, etc., on your desk. Your money could be stolen, your food could cause a hygiene problem, and your coffee cups can spill onto your keyboard, clothes or the carpet. An untidy desk implies you are a slob, untidy, disorganised and unprofessional. Psychologically, an untidy desk also causes you stress and anxiety.

Massaging the real boss

Every business treats their big-ticket customers extra special; if not to avoid losing their business, they do it to guarantee and encourage the customer's future patronage.

However, to do this you need to know who your real boss is. Do not be fooled by the supposed power of your colleagues, team leaders or managers. The real boss is the person or persons who will decide on (and sign) your contract renewal.

Sometimes your team leader, HR, or a manager may be responsible for signing your timesheet; however, many times these people are not responsible for deciding who stays and who goes. The person(s) who decides this, should be to whom you give extra special treatment. You should aim to impress the people who are involved in your contract renewal.

Make sure that whenever the real boss is around or observing you, that you behave professionally, with enthusiasm and a positive attitude emphasizing your technical competence. Similarly, if you know that word about your work and conduct will get back to the real boss; make sure you perform professionally and proficiently. Give the real boss no reason for not renewing your contract.

Beware of people who attempt to boss you around, but have no say in whether you are renewed or not. These people would like to be the real boss, but they do not have sign-off authority for the budget. They should get your special treatment; however, reserve your 'extra special treatment' for the real boss.

Handling company social events

You should always be wary of situations where you can lose your professionalism. Getting drunk and dancing on the table at parties will be remembered, and will also greatly tarnish your professionalism. It can also make you more relatable, if the work environment is less formal, (than are most companies in the city). With this in mind, company social events and Christmas parties present two challenges for the professional contractor.

The first is monetary and the second is in evaluating your business' benefit from attending the event. If there is no benefit to your contracting business, then do not go, especially if it will cost you money. However, if there is a business value there or it is free, then attend at will.

Sexual considerations

Mixing business with sexual pleasure in IT contracting can be a very bad idea. This is especially true if one of the parties involved is a permie and the other is an IT contractor. There are many reasons to advise against this type of relationship. Firstly, the employer may frown upon your conduct.

Secondly, your colleagues, manager, or other permies could be jealous of your relationship, and secretly use their influence with your real boss to shorten your tenure.

Thirdly, your (sexual) partner could relay personal information about you to his/her colleagues. When this information is circulated around the office, it could lead to your real boss changing his mind about your professionalism and suitability for an extension.

Fourthly, if an argument arises between you and your new partner, it could negatively affect your office image, professionalism and good name.

Finally, your advances could lead to an accusation of sexual harassment. As a contractor, you would hardly stand a chance against such a charge.

The final point may seem funny or silly, but it is perhaps the best argument against making advances towards any permie in the office. I recall a contractor I once worked with who – in an attempt to comfort a permie female suffering from a cold – placed his arm around her shoulders. At the time, she did not say anything to him, however, thirty minutes later, the contractor's agency called him and asked him to leave the site and to never return. Apparently, the woman in question had called HR and complained about the 'hug'. The contractor was marched off the premises, and his contract was promptly terminated.

Save your personal relationship building for outside your contract role. During your time on the client's site, never forget that you are always at risk from misinterpretation of your behaviour and speech. Do not overstep the professional boundaries, as the risks are seldom worth any potential reward.

Similarly, outside the office, on business trips, over the phone, via e-mail and on chat tools, always maintain a professional distance. If a permie makes advances towards you in the office, quickly steer the conversion towards more appropriate topics, and avoid getting into an emotional entanglement with them in future. Do not make them feel bad for trying; however, never lead them on.

Gossip and blabbermouths

Nobody likes a gossip, especially when the gossip is at his or her expense. When you break the trust people give you through 'running your mouth', people will stop coming to you with personal and/or important information. Losing trust can cut you out of the loop and make you miss many advantages and opportunities.

Often, management sees people who gossip as being a disruptive force in the organisation. Whenever possible, managers will try to weed gossips out. Furthermore, someone who gossips will be excluded from social groups, over time. A crowd dispersing around the coffee machine, when the gossiper approaches, highlights this point.

If you have gossiped in the past and find yourself alienated and excluded in the office, there is hope yet for repairing your tarnished reputation. However, because lost trust requires so much effort and time to regain, it is perhaps easier to rebuild your trust starting from your next contract.

Avoid gossip; this requires that you do not gossip about others to anyone, you do not allow others to gossip about anyone to you, and you defend anyone not present who is the subject of gossip, (simply on the fact that they are not there to defend themselves).

Stay impartial. State something like, "I don't think it is fair to talk about him like this when he is not here." You will find few gossips that will have the courage to repeat the gossip in front of the victim.

Permie jealousy

Most contractors earn considerably more than their permie counterparts. In many cases, they can earn more than their managers. This can pose a problem to permies who are prone to jealousy. It is therefore wise to avoid allowing such staff to find out how much you earn.

Whilst this is relatively easy to do for the majority of permie staff, this is not so for those in payroll and HR as they can get to see your wages. I once had a long and lucrative contract role terminated, because of someone in HR who felt I was far too young to be earning a six-figure income.

The jealous HR member took it upon themselves to replace me with a permie. They first suggested to my manager that I worked too many hours and that I should take some time off. Whilst I was away, they eliminated my position and replaced me with a permie.

You can do little about jealous permies, especially those in HR and payroll. However, there is a lot you can do to avoid provoking all permies. Observe the following points and you will greatly reduce the envy you may attract from a permie:

1. Do not discuss your contract rates with anyone.

2. Do not portray yourself as being rich, privileged or having a lot of money. This includes not discussing your purchases, cars, homes or vacations. If they are beyond the means of the permies you work with:
    a. Do not brag about the benefits of contracting.
    b. Do not drive a 'flash' car to the client's site.
    c. Do not wear ostentatious and outwardly expensive clothes.
3. Do not act as if you are above your colleagues.

To summarize, be humble and try to remain a little low-key. You would do better to play down your wealth than to show it off. Similarly, if you do have a flashy car, either; buy a 'cheap runner' for contracting, or park the expensive car well away from where your workplace personnel will see it.

This may seem a tad extreme, but I know of two contractors in particular, one of which drove a Porsche 911 and the other who sported around in a Lotus Elise – both exquisite cars. However, they were not good to drive to work, as they did nothing to minimize jealousy or hatred. The owners of these beautiful cars were shocked to find their cars badly scratched. Furthermore, in both cases, the jealous permies persuaded their managers not to renew the contractor's positions.

Power-mad permies

You will come across permies (and occasionally some misguided contractors) in positions of limited authority or importance. However, this little taste of power can sometimes go to a person's head. This is especially common with traders, and personal assistants (PAs). With traders, it is understandable. They may be making a lot of money for the organisation, and therefore may feel that they are indispensable.

Furthermore, many traders are highly stressed. Because of this, they can easily 'fly off the handle', especially if they are having IT problems.

To deal with this group, you should maintain a high level of professionalism and speak with confidence and authority. They may behave like infants throwing a tantrum, and sometimes they will aim their outbursts directly at you; however, do not allow their behaviour to get you emotionally involved in their problem or issue. Stay objective and focus only on solving the problem. Maintaining a professional "distance" should keep their venom at bay.

You should lower your voice whilst talking to them, to help calm them down (or avoid getting them riled-up in the first place); however, finding them a solution to their problem quickly, and reassuring them with a definite answer or estimated time of completion, is your best course of action for dealing with them, in most situations.

If they become verbally abusive or worse, physically abusive, calmly and gently warn them that if they persist with the abuse, you will need to walk away, or hang up the phone. If they persist with their aggression, remain very calm, take a long, slow, deep breath, and exhale slowly. Then, if you must, either walk away or hang up the phone.

However, validating their concerns can often diffuse the situation, and allow you to continue with your work. One such example of validation is calmly stating something like, "I understand exactly what your concern is, and I will begin rectifying the problem as immediately as possible." Most often, people simply want to *feel* that they are being *heard*. However, if you only deal with them when they are being civil, they will quickly learn that you are a professional, and that they obtain the best results from you, when you are treated civilly.

In some organisations, you will likely have your contract terminated for not tolerating abusive traders and fund managers; therefore, the final judgment is for you to decide how far you will allow someone to abuse you, before you take professional action to end the abuse.

The other user group most prone to power-madness, is the executive personal assistant. It is interesting that in most cases, the executive is a lovely person. However, the PAs that fall under this category forget that they work for the person with the real power. Being so close to someone at the top can make you feel like you, too, are at the top.

Power-mad, executive PAs act as if they are the executive. They expect everyone – especially IT personnel – to be at their disposal and beck and call. To flex their power-hungry muscle, they will often escalate even the most trivial of requirements.

Because of their relationship with the executive, they manage to get away with this behaviour. They can also use their power to influence your managers; therefore, it is vital that you do not get on their wrong side.

Dealing with power-mad, executive PAs requires you – again – to act professionally. Act promptly and give them regular feedback on the status of the solution to their problem. Do not become overly casual with PAs, and never give them any information that they do not specifically request, or that is unrelated to their problem. In most cases, these PAs will use any information against you, if the problem is not satisfactorily resolved.

Dealing with spies, informants, jealous permies and insurgents

Sometimes, to assess the effectiveness of a segregated, isolated or independent team or departmental unit, the team will have a mole placed within it. The mole will report everything that he or she hears and sees, to whomever planted him or her. It is often difficult to determine who the mole is; in fact, it could be you.

A mole is used within organisations for several reasons: firstly, to aid corporate infighting and office politics. In this case, one manager will try to weaken the support of another manager by finding reasons to break up his strong and supportive team; another way a mole is used is to assess the effectiveness of a group of people within a team or organisational group.

Moles do not have to be within a team. They can also be situated strategically within earshot and/or line of sight of the team, who is being spied on. This method of infiltration is most popular, in open floor-plan offices.

To the industrious, conscientious, hardworking, punctual, meticulous and professional contractor, moles pose no threat. As, they will find nothing negative to report against you. However, your team members' behaviour and conduct could lead to your entire team suffering.

Therefore, to guard against this eventuality, keep your eyes and ears primed for the following signs of an insurgent, informant, spy, mole or jealous permie:

- All new arrivals to your department.
- Any new arrivals who sit near your team.
- Anyone who seems interested in your team members' punctuality.
- Anyone who takes a sudden interest in your teams' activities.
- Anyone who suddenly seems interested in getting to know you, or begins asking questions about other employees or team members.

This may seem strange, but I have seen many contracts end, due to several managers playing office politics at the expense of their individual team members. In one instance, my voraciously ambitious manager – who had set his sights on being the head of another team – approached me one morning to ask me to spy on the rival team.

I found nothing to report, and later discovered I was not the only person he had engaged to spy. Some of the other people he asked were very productive informants. The information they supplied to my ambitious manager, enabled him to have the manager of the rival team dismissed, and the two teams merged. My insatiably determined manager then headed the new, larger team.

The first action he took was to purposely fail renewing the contracts of all the contractors in his new team. He also delegated the permies from that team into inferior roles, causing most of them to leave the organisation within a year of the change. New people he recruited eventually replaced them all.

Do not entangle yourself in the game by feeding the spy false information. When the dust settles, this could be your undoing. Stay professional at all times; however, carefully warn your team members of the dangerous activities of the informant.

Avoiding after-work drinks

You are running a business. The main purpose of any business is to provide an outstanding service to its customers and collect compensation for providing the service. To then turn around each day or week, and squander the net profits on alcohol should never be on the agenda of any business owner, let alone a contractor.

In some organisations, staff congregate at the local bar or pub after work to socialize. I have even seen this habit extended to lunch hours in some departments. It usually involves taking turns buying rounds of drinks for your colleagues.

Whilst this is acceptable to do on rare occasions, especially if it will help maintain or increase your rate, it should never become the norm. A round of drinks in a London pub for 5 people could set you back at least £15. If you do this once each day, it equates to £75 at the end of each week and £300 at the end of the month. £300 could be the equivalent of a large proportion of your daily rate – squandered on drinks for no business benefit.

In fact, in most cases this habit could be losing you your professional edge in the eyes of your drinking friends. You may also be damaging your health through the abuse of your liver and other organs with this daily alcohol abuse.

Avoid regular and/or habitual after hours drinking, it will cost you a fortune over time and damage your health and professionalism.

Smoking breaks

Smoking is no longer a tolerated habit in most private and public buildings. Those who still smoke are progressively being alienated, isolated, and forced to congregate in open spaces around their place of work, or in specially designated smoking areas, provided by their employers. Although many people still smoke, almost every non-smoker will tell you that the habit reduces your professionalism. Your breath, clothes, hair and hands smell badly after each cigarette.

Furthermore, the average smoker takes several smoke breaks before lunch and several more after lunch — with each smoking break lasting around five minutes. It is easy to see how employees are losing nearly a full day of work every fortnight, from staff who are smokers.

If you smoke, consider quitting – simply for the betterment of your health. Furthermore, unless the person who signs your timesheets, and/or who is responsible for signing off your contract renewal also smokes, your habit of smoking could be hampering your contracting profitability and continuity of work.

To eliminate any chance of this, consider doing the following:

1. Mask the cigarette smell from your clothes and body with a perfumed spray and wash your hands with soap after smoking.
2. Eliminate the cigarette smell from your breath with mints, sweets, lozenges or a mouth spray.
3. Condition yourself not to smoke during your working hours – save your smoking for before you start work, lunchtime and after work.
4. Smoke inconspicuously – avoid the regular smokers area where you are likely to be spotted by colleagues, managers or even users.

It is rare for smokers to be prejudiced against non-smokers for not smoking; however, it is common for a non-smoker to be prejudiced against a smoker. When the non-smoker is your manager, interviewer or the person who signs off your renewal, you will feel the effects of your smoking habit economically, as well as through the long-term health effects. Maintain your professionalism, improve your health and reduce the negative effects of non-smoker prejudice by either quitting smoking entirely, or confining your smoking habit to non-work time.

Restroom breaks

Unlike smoking breaks, management finds toilet breaks harder to detect and even more difficult to control. We all need to relieve ourselves during the working day, however, depending on what your role is, you may need to be a little more discreet and considerate, in the breaks you take away from your desk.

For instance, contractors who work on a helpdesk, call centre, telephone hotline, emergency systems monitoring desk, or those whose job involves being constantly accessible to the client or user, must take extra care in when (and how), they take leave of their post or desk.

Leaving your desk without following the correct procedure could jeopardize your contract. Therefore, if you are in this type of role, you may be required to log off the system, place your phone on divert and/or inform a colleague or manger, before you leave your desk or post. Whatever the procedure is, make sure you always follow it.

Female considerations – the female manager

Most female contractors will agree that the female interviewer or manager is the most difficult person they have worked with. This is because IT tends to be a male-dominated industry. It can be difficult for females to settle in, and work in such an environment. However, most females eventually succeed and make their place in the industry.

However, it is not surprising that these females can occasionally feel a little threatened when another female joins the IT team. They can see it as another female encroaching on 'their turf'. This is especially true if the new female is more physically attractive, or has some other attribute that is more likeable or valuable to the organisation.

When you join an organisation with few females, and one of them happens to be a manager, you may encounter a silently (or openly) antagonistic atmosphere, especially in the beginning of your term. Sometimes, this mood will never improve between you and your female manager. However, the less "threatening" you can be to her, the better. Remember, she probably worked just as hard (or harder), to obtain the position she now holds within the company, as you did to get where you are today, in the IT industry.

The Guide to IT Contracting

The best you can do to diffuse a negative vibe between yourself and territorially protective female managers, is to be professional in all of your conduct. Consistent politeness, courteousness, respectfulness, and warmth towards the female manager will serve you well.

Similarly, being hardworking and never "putting her on the spot" will help her relax, and not feel threatened by you. There is little more you can do about the situation if she chooses not to reciprocate your civilities. But often, the smallest gestures of sincere courtesy or thoughtfulness, can go a long way with a professional woman in a position of power.

Office politics

Another sign of a contracting, having contracted, or displaying signs of PPS, is through the involvement in office politics. PPS sufferers forget they are only at the organisation for the duration of their contract, and any extensions that may come from it. These contractors will not be there for the long haul; therefore, plotting and scheming to outdo others is futile.

Due to the short term of most contracts (in comparison with typical permie tenures), you are ill advised to jeopardize your short-term role by making enemies, or through being on the wrong side of the office politics. Remember, an enemy you make today, may be someone you need to impress tomorrow.

Trusting the wrong people

The PPS suffering contractor will forget that permies can quickly become resentful and spiteful after they discover how much more you are paid, compared to them. The PPS sufferer makes the grave mistake of trusting a permie with details of his/her contracting rate. Keep your private business exactly that — *private*. Therefore, if a nosey permie or mole is so bold as to ask you pointedly what you earn, simply reply, "Oh, I'm sorry, I'm not at liberty to discuss my contracts," turn and walk away, or immediately change the subject. Use the statement as your standard answer, regardless of the number of times you may be asked.

Status

In some cases, this situation is worsened by chronic PPS symptoms of boasting, bragging and 'rubbing it in the faces of the permies'. This is mainly due to the permie reliance on status. Because the differences in permie salaries is often small, permies use status to further express how much more important they are, compared to their peers or subordinates.

They may have two phones on their desk, a personal bin, and three screens as opposed to everyone else's single or dual screen. They may even have their own office, a window seat with a nice view, a PA, a reserved parking spot, a special mouse and keyboard, a better chair, etc.

All these things do not actually add any monetary value to the permie they are assigned to; however, it makes them feel above others in the organisation, and somehow compensates for their poor salary.

When a permie becomes a contractor, they are suddenly in status heaven. They earn more than every other permie doing their job. To help display this fact and – in their mind – to gain status, the PPS suffering contractor buys and displays material things, spends money inconspicuously, and in many cases verbally tells other permies how good they have it.

Note that status is not confined to the office. The PPS sufferer will inflict it on their neighbours, family members, friends and anyone who will listen to them brag about what they have. But almost nothing could be more dangerous, and boasting could cost you everything.

Avoiding the debate and strong values discussion trap

People go to war over disagreements relating to strongly held beliefs. There is no worse way to insult someone than to deride his or her religion, political choices, family or sports team.

All of us have subjects that we feel strongly about. When we discuss these subjects with others, we can easily feel insulted if they disagree with us. This could lead to an argument and possibly a parting of ways in any relationship.

As one of your primary aims as a contractor is to not attract any negative feelings toward yourself, it is not wise to allow yourself to fall into the trap of discussing strongly held values. Remember, "Each to their own." Respect other people's opinions, even if you do not believe in these views yourself.

Avoid entering into arguments and debates where someone holds a strong opinion. Whenever you find yourself in a discussion that is starting to get heated, repair the situation by first lowering your voice and listening to the other person, more than you speak. Try to find something you can agree on, or simply acknowledge that you respect their opinion, even though you do not agree with it entirely.

How much should you take lying down?

There are times when permie colleagues and permie managers feel they can treat you badly because the money paid to you more than compensates for the mistreatment. This exploitation may be in the form of an unequal distribution of work.

Contractors may be given the jobs that the permies do not want to do, or they could be given all the complex and difficult tasks. Whichever way around it is, the treatment is meant to punish you for being a contractor.

Similarly, you could have to endure constant comments about tight-fisted contractors and other snide comments aimed at making the permies feel a little better about your advantage as a contractor.

In rare situations, this maltreatment is in the form of physical intimidation or even violence. This type normally only happens in very small organisations where HR and human rights laws are flouted.

Wherever you encounter these types of abuse, you have the choice to grin, bear it and take the money, or to complain and/or to hand in your notice of resignation. What you decide to do should be a personal decision based on your personal preferences, principles, tolerance levels and financial situation.

I suggest that you draw the line at physical violence, duress and any self-image deteriorating treatment, unless you're very thick-skinned. If the actions do not encroach on any of these limits, you can turn the behaviour against the perpetrators by 'milking the cow' until it becomes anorexic. The oldest trick in the book can often work the best; kill them with kindness, and hope for the best.

Internet usage abuse

The Internet helps many people to communicate faster than ever in human history. Today, it is shaping our generation and has changed many of our habits. We use it to shop, socialize, find news and sports results, conduct research, entertain us and we it extensively for conducting business.

It is so vast and contains so much information that it is easy to 'surf' all day and never tire of it. However, Web surfing should be minimized or avoided at your place of work, unless your role requires it of you and the client condones it.

There are a few places you should definitely avoid when using the Internet in the course of a contracting job. These sites are as follows:

- Sexually explicit material of any kind.
- Violence, profanity, racist or prejudice promoting sites.
- Sites and content that break the organisations Web policies (this includes using anonymous proxy sites such as http://proxify.com).
- Web mail sites such as http://mail.yahoo.com and www.hotmail.com. (Most organisations now block the ports used by these mail services, and also block the sites to stop foreign e-mail coming into the company unchecked.
- Movie and music download sites.
- Gaming and gambling sites.
- Any site not conforming to an organisation's Web usage policy(s).

Most organisations now use security software running on their gateway servers and firewalls to monitor Web usage. This software not only allows the organisation to monitor all Internet usage, but also to run regular reports on Internet usage abusers.

Contractors or permies browsing unsavoury Web content at work can often be dismissed immediately, and escorted offsite. Those who abuse or disregard the Web usage policy(s) may also be cautioned, receive a written warning, or have their Web access revoked.

Contractors who disregard an organisations Web usage policy could also face legal action against your agency or your company, if your actions resulted in the organisation's exposure to a security risk.

Therefore, avoid any Internet usage abuse in any of your contracts. If you are allowed to, use the Internet conservatively for accessing your personal Web services such as online banking, sports results and news, and/or for personal researching during your lunch break. Do not use the Internet for personal browsing outside of your lunch break, unless the company policy clearly specifies that it is allowed.

Profits

One of the main benefits to IT contracting is the compensation. If your job did not pay you, would you still go there daily? Most people will answer "no" to that question, proving that money is important and a major driver for most people. Contractors are no different. In many ways, they may be even more so inclined.

Because contractors earn based on their time, they tend to value their time more than a permie might. Time for a contactor truly is money. Therefore, we shall next look at some important topics relating to making money, keeping more of your earnings and spending your money wisely.

How to always stay in work

We have covered how to raise your value through your CV, training and professional conduct. Getting these factors right will help you keep in work most of the time, however, to fill the small gaps between major contracts, you may need to take short-term filler roles. Either these roles can pay a lot, or they only pay a little.

The reason for the discrepancy in pay is due to the type of roles. Some highly skilled technical roles like building, installing, testing, fine-tuning and deployment of servers, SEO, Web site design, and script writing, can take less than a week. Other IT work such as application installation and desktop deployment or moves can take as little as a few days, but pay less.

To stay in work continuously, you may need to take some low paid roles between contracts for a few days or weeks. This allows you to earn an income whilst you are lining up the next role. There are a few third party suppliers such as Hays IT (http://www.hays.com/it) and recruitment agencies such as Reed (http://www.reed.co.uk) that specialize in this type of short-term work.

Keep moving up

Always set goals to improve your professionalism, income, skills, knowledge and your business effectiveness. Review your progress at the end of each quarter, each contract and at the end of each year.

In each review, identify where you have moved forward, and in what areas you still need to work on; ways in which you can improve, training requirements that you still need, and so on. Write your findings down, and take immediate steps toward the improvements you need to make.

Tight-fistism and how to avoid it

The money you earn from contracting can lead you into becoming a workaholic. If you never take a break from contracting, and always work long hours, you never actually get to spend your hard-earned income. When this occurs you are vulnerable to falling victim to tight-fistism.

This state of mind is a disease that stems from greed and the belief and feeling that if you do not take all you can get from the world, you will somehow lose out. Nothing could be further from the truth, however, and you only need to visit Dubai or Las Vegas to see that even when things seem impossibly bleak, as both areas once were, something amazing can come out of even a desert.

Once you start earning well from contracting, it is tempting to try to pile up as much as possible. This is the wrong away to work. You could burn yourself out and require a prolonged break from contracting to recover, eliminating most of the surplus funds you gathered in the process.

The 'race' to earning money is not a sprint; it is more of a marathon. You have to learn to pace yourself and take regular breaks and holidays. Money is nothing if it cannot be enjoyed with the people you love; therefore, do not risk alienating your family through overwork and a greedy attitude with your money. Learn the value of sharing and giving.

You will not wish you spent more time at the office, on your deathbed. You most likely will wish you spent more time appreciating life and the many wonders it presented you, like your children, wife, family, friends, nature or even art. Learn to value these gifts more by creating memories with your loved ones and truly enjoying your time on our magnificent plant. Avoid tight-fistism by sharing your wealth and time with the people you care about the most.

Money management

The most popular of these pervasive permie behaviours occurs in the area of money management. Illustrated by how a contractor spends his/her money, PPS suffering contractors live payday to payday, just as they use to do as permies.

Unfortunately, unlike when they were permies, PPS sufferers have to pay tax and possibly VAT, insurances, accountant's fees, and other sundry costs relating to the running of an IT contracting business. Furthermore, there is no guaranteed income between contracts. Budgeting in advance, and according to your new earnings schedule, will serve you well in the contracting business.

Milking the cow

When you are in a lucrative "fat cow" contract, you should not rest on your laurels and only accept your standard income as the only way of milking this cow. Within the heart of each contract is an opportunity to increase your income. Either through overtime, expenses claims, rate increases or simply by cutting down on your spending.

The opportunities will not chase you home and knock down your door though; you will actively need to seek them out. Constantly look for ways to improve your earnings in every contract you do. Believe me, there is more "milk" to be found in contracts, than may be initially apparent.

Here is an example of an effective contractor who was on the look-out for ways to earn more money through his contracting role.

A friend of mine told me of an inventive contractor who undertook a lucrative contract that required long distance driving to the client's site. A colleague of hers lived relatively close to her, and so she offered to give him a ride to the office. To make the most out of the situation, she billed him at premium rates for the chauffeur services of her contracting company's car.

The colleague claimed this cost against his expenses. He also saved wear and tear on his own car and was still paid travel time for the daily journey. At the same time, the client also reimbursed the driver for travel time and car fuel.

Claiming expenses effectively

Every year, literally millions, if not more, are lost to the HMRC because small business owners do not claim all the expenses they are entitled. One of the ways you can and should improve your bottom line turnover, is to claim all allowed expenses. You should condition yourself to collect a receipt for every purchase you make. Getting into this habit will help you capture all your business related expense receipts.

We have covered many of these expenses in the previous chapter, however, knowing what to claim and claiming it are two separate things. Most people fall over at the first hurdle – collecting receipts and accounting for all expenses.

You need not be an accounting genius to account for your expenses. You simply need a receipt collection system such as Microsoft Excel or some other spreadsheet package, and access to a computer once every month.

Deposit all collected receipts from your pockets or wallet into a receipts folder at the end of each day or week – whichever is most convenient, but do it on a schedule as part of conducting your business.

Once a month, update your expenses spreadsheets with all the expense receipts collected that month. Do not forget expenses such as Internet access, mobile telephone usage, hotel accommodation and public transport fares, etc.

On your spreadsheet, list the date you received the receipt (it should be on the receipt in most cases), the company who gave you the receipt, what you purchased and how much you paid for it. Do this for each receipt. After noting a receipt, you should place it in a separate folder for updated receipts.

Different companies and agencies operate different methods of expense claiming. Some are paper-based whilst others are online. Some add expenses to your normal invoice of work undertaken, whilst others pay expenses separately. Some pay expenses monthly whilst others pay expenses weekly or quarterly.

Regardless of what the client or agency's system is, make sure you follow their rules and claim everything you are entitled to, as well as claiming all expenses through your own company.

Money for nothing

It is a sad fact that many permies see contractors as shoddy workers, people with no pride in the results they produce, greedy and looking only to make easy money. The next cause of PPS is responsible for this.

Unfortunately, a lot of permies enter contracting thinking it is a way of making easy money. Their intention is not to attain a high level of professionalism and be paid for it; they simply want to be paid for doing next to nothing.

As they inflict their poor work and unprofessional conduct on more and more organisations, they feed the belief even further. Misguided permies see these PPS sufferers ploughing their way through short contracts, and think to themselves, "if that idiot can make a fortune by being so poor at his job and so unprofessional, so can I," and the cycle continues.

Managing travel costs

In today's busy cities, it is important to analyze your travel options carefully. This is not always black and white. Reliability, cost, duration and impact on the environment are some of the key points you should consider. Of prime importance is reliability, however we shall briefly cover each important topic, as follows:

1. **Reliability:** Of all the travel considerations, the one you are most likely to have your contract terminated for is reliability. It affects your punctuality and dependability to the client.

No client will tolerate continual tardiness due to cancelled trains, road traffic, personal car troubles or any other commuting issues. Therefore, whatever form of transportation you elect, make sure it is reliable. If you travel by public transport, make sure you take the earlier train, tube or metro, bus or boat to avoid unforeseen delays. It is better to be half an hour to fifteen minutes early each day, (or on time), when there are unforeseen delays, than to be on time each day and late when there is an impediment to your arrival.

2. **Cost:** Normally, buying individual tickets for your journey works out to be considerably more expensive than buying a season ticket. Therefore, get organized and arrange your travel costs in such a way as to maximize savings. If you use public transport, buy a season ticket. In most cases, you can get a travel pass for the exact duration of the contract.

Purchase your ticket in the most cost-effective way. For instance, if you receive discounts for purchasing online or over the phone, then use this method to buy your travel pass.

Devise a system that ensures that you never forget your travel pass; keep it in your work bag, or coat pocket by the front door, in the car you drive to the station, or where ever you will guarantee never to forget it. Forgetting your pass is one of the unavoidable reasons for lateness and avoidable increases in your travel bill.

Avoid taking cabs and taxis unless the cost is absorbed by someone else and doesn't decrease your income in any way. Normally, these forms of transportation always work out to be more expensive than other means.

In cases where you have to use your car to get to work, make sure you have the car properly serviced and fuelled before you set out in it. Car problems will guarantee that you are avoidably delayed in reaching work on time. Check your fuel, oil, tyres, and tyre pressures, radiator water, brake fluid, etc., regularly.

Wherever you are unsure about travel cost comparisons, run a test to compare. Never assume that one form of transport is cheaper than the other just because it may appear so. There are hidden costs involved when you travel by motor vehicle, bicycle or boat. Compare and make an informed decision.

3. **Duration:** The time needed to commute or travel to the client's site is also of prime importance. Your true contract rate you are paid should be divided by the total time taken each day from when you leave your home, to when you return to it.

If you take over an hour each way to reach the client's site, this adds two more hours to your day. Does the true rate reflect how you can get maximum profit from contracts that are nearer to your home?

Make the most of your time by using less of it to travel to and from work, whenever possible. The time you save can be poured into another venture, or simply allocated to your family and friends – or even your health through getting more sleep.

Sometimes you may have the option to fly to a client's site. Depending on the expenses paid for driving or taking a train, always select a travel method that is most profitable for your company. For instance, if you are paid travel time as well as fuel allowance and subsistence costs, it may be more profitable to drive than to fly.

If long journeys are inevitable, find a way to make the best use of your travel time. Make some extra money for the journey by giving someone who works near your workplace a lift for contribution to the running costs of your car, or simply use the time to learn and improve your knowledge and skills.

You can learn a new language, read about new technology or learn more about investing and growing your wealth in the duration of time taken to get to work. Don't just stare out of the window bored. Find ways to extract value from your time.

4. **Impact on the environment:** Damage to the environment through each of our combined carbon footprints has come to be of paramount importance to our generation and future generations. It is vital that we each contribute by reducing how much dirty fuels we use. With that in mind, analyse your transport scenario and evaluate changes you could make to help the environment. Perhaps instead of driving to the station, you could cycle, or walk.

Similarly, you could take public transport rather than driving, whenever feasible. If you must drive, try and join a car pool or share the journey in your or another person's car.

You could also consider swapping your high emissions car for a more efficient and cleaner option.

We can all make a difference in our own little way. Do not downplay your importance in this matter. Travel responsibly and be a part of the carbon emissions solution, rather than being part of the problem.

Travelling for the client

If you have to travel for the client, make sure you prearrange your compensation package either before you accept the contract (so that it is part of the contract), or if the travel was unexpected, before you undertake the travel. There are several things to ask for in advance. These are as follows:

1. Travel time (paid at same rate as your normal contracting rate, including overtime considerations).
2. Travel costs:

   a. Fuel costs.
   b. Car hire costs.
   c. Parking costs.
   d. Travel ticket costs.
   e. Toll gate charges.
   f. Taxi or transfer expenses.
   g. Cost of taxi for travel back and forth from the hotel to a remote site.

3. Fax usage.
4. Internet usage.
5. Accommodation costs.
6. Baggage storage and handling fees.
7. Breakfast, lunch and dinner expenses.
8. Normal contract and overtime rate.
9. Travel and medical insurance costs for the trip.

10. Overnight allowance (phone calls, newspapers, etc.).

You will not need to claim all the above in most cases, however, you should be able to claim at least eight of them in most travel situations. Do not allow an organisation to cheat you when you travel within a contract. Insist on the appropriate compensation and insurance every time you travel within a contract.

Avoiding the rate/period trap

If you earn a fixed daily rate, or if your contact is a fixed term contract, i.e., it has a fixed length and pays a predetermined amount for that term, then you may be heading for, or already in the rate/period trap.

The best rate/period is a variable hourly rate. This type of compensation allows you to make extra money for overtime and weekend work. The direct compensation encourages you to work longer and harder.

Interpersonal skills

Your ability to deal effectively with other people will progress your business further than almost any other factor. Life is mostly about selling. From selling our abilities and our dreams to ourselves; selling ourselves to our future partners, selling our ideals and right of authority to our children, selling our suitability for contract work to interviewers, to selling others we meet and deal with in our daily lives, and on a myriad of other things.

If you are no good at selling, convincing, inspiring, motivating, or making others understand what you mean and how it could benefit them, you will have a harder time achieving what you want especially when working with others. If you choose to get ahead in contracting, you will have to learn to sell better, and that will require that you transact effectively with others. Dealing with others will require three things: communication skills, sales skills and a pleasing personality.

Effective communication

You can equate the delivery of a message to sticking a small pin into someone. Whilst they will feel a small prick and be aware of what has just happened, the effects of the message will not last for long. However, the same message delivered with effective interpersonal skills is like putting the pin at the head of a jackhammer and using its full force to deliver the message. This message will drive deeper, and its effects will be longer lasting.

This is one of the main reasons to learn to be an effective communicator and to develop successful interpersonal skills. It will help you sell yourself and your ideas better. It will also help others to understand what you mean.

Keys to better communication

To be a better communicator requires you to understand the fact that people are primarily obsessed with themselves. Their ultimate concerns are what they think, what they desire and they others to love them. Ask yourself, what do you primarily desire from others?

We all think we are the most important person alive, and that is healthy. It also helps you to know how to get people to like you, listen to you, value what you say and buy into what you have to offer. The following factors are important skills to develop in becoming a better communicator:

1. **Listening:** To be more effective with others, listen more and talk less. Allow them to talk more by asking open-ended

questions that require them to share their views, ideas and thoughts. Once you know what they desire, their concerns and constraints, you can tailor your requests, explanations, sales pitch and argument to satisfy their needs.

Listening not only requires you to close your mouth, it also requires you to open your mind and heart. Empathy and understanding are desirable traits that no listener is over-endowed with. We could all improve in the art of hearing on several levels when others speak.

When listening, show that you understand or at least seek to understand better by asking questions for the speaker to clarify certain points. Nod, agree and react positively to what he or she is saying. Do not simply act; truly seek to understand and make the speaker feel they have been heard.

2. **Disagreeing:** If you disagree, do not make it personal. Reply objectively. Comment on the subject, not the person. As an example, "Tom, that is a dumb idea," is a personalized disagreement whilst, "I don't think it is a good idea to switch the live server off during office hours," is more objective and deals with the subject being discussed.

Never make anyone feel inferior, stupid, dumb or totally wrong. Focus on the topic and be objective. A person's suggestion can be wrong, impractical, ignorant and even ineffective; however, that person should never be made to feel these things, simply for making statement or suggestion.

3. **Sales skills:** Convincing people to buy into your views, plans and ideas, can be trying without effective sales techniques. Perhaps the simplest method of getting by is to make the buyer feel the decision to buy is theirs. To do this, you first have to find out what the buyer desires, their objectives and their limitations.

This is the same, whether you are selling your ideas, services or products. You first listen to gather information to allow you to personalise your sales pitch. Once you know what the person really wants and under what circumstances, they will buy into your idea or product, you can give them a sales pitch packaged just for their needs.

If they have several objections, you can use the 'peeling the onion technique' as described next.

4. **Peeling the onion:** Sometimes, when people have an objection they are not comfortable discussing, they will present you with many layers of secondary objections which are not really important to them. You need to remove these layers and get to the root of the problem. Peeling the onion gets it name from the removal of many layers – like an onion – to get to the true objection.

"If we could get around that, would there be another reason why you cannot work this weekend?" is an example of a peeling the onion question. Keep phrasing your questions in the same manner, until the recipient of your questions has no more objections. Once you get to the heart of their objections, you will have a better understanding of what is really bothering them about your idea, service or product, and/or what is preventing them from agreeing with you.

5. **Practical application of effective sales skills:** One contractor who was asking for a dramatic rate increase used the following technique. He first asked his manager to tell him if the organisation had benefited from his work. The manager answered positively.

"Yes, we are very happy with what you have done here and what you are doing. We have no complaints," said the manager.

The contractor then asked where he could improve. Once more, the manager answered positively.

"Nope, you have more than exceeded our expectations, we couldn't ask for more from you than you are already giving," said the manager.

Armed with this positive information, the contractor delivered his sales pitch, highlighting the discrepancy in his rate as compared to his true market value, the offers made by others and his preference to stay with the organisation for the right package. He stated his desired rate and it was instantly accepted.

Furthermore, to secure his services for longer under the new rate, the manager changed the three-month contract extension to a twelve-month contract.

To sell more effectively, do the following:

- Determine needs.
- Personalize your pitch or package.
- Deliver the personalised package effectively.

There is little anyone can object to when your pitch satisfies all their requirements and allays all their concerns. They have only one option – buy.

6. **A pleasing personality:** We have already covered how having an amiable and professional disposition and attitude will help you get on with those who secure your services. Having a pleasing personality will also help you to deal more effectively with people.

Friendly people are easy to like, confide in and trust. You feel better being around them and you leave their presence feeling happier than before you met or spoke with them. When they speak, you listen with a more naturally open mind and heart than when you speak to disagreeable and antagonistic people.

Developing an effective wardrobe for contracting

Contractors are business people; therefore, they should think and act as such. If your business requires expensive suits, dresses and shoes in order to make money, then by all means, invest in them.

Unfortunately, most contractors are back office workers. This means they never see customers face to face. In some IT roles such as those involving data centres and server farms, you will hardly see anyone, apart from your colleagues and other engineers.

Any money spent on clothing for working in this type of environment will never realize a return on the expense, back to your company. It is a total waste of business profits and you should avoid it. Even in roles where you are required to look smart and professional, do not overspend on fashion items, especially if your purpose is simply to show off to others.

Save your money. Invest it where you will see a better return. If shoes, a shirt, a tie and a suit are all that is required to appear professional, get exactly that. Shop around, look for bargains, and save wherever possible. Find a retailer and negotiate a deal whenever possible. That is what a smart businessperson should do.

Similarly, you can simplify your office clothing to create a contracting uniform. For men, this is simpler than for women. However, if you keep the colours and cuts as classic as possible, you will not look out of date in your clothes a year from now. Match suit jackets and trousers with a broad selection of blouses and tops. Men can literally wear the same suits for years without anyone batting an eye.

Asda's George range (www.george.com), Matalan (www.matalan.co.uk) and Primark (www.primark.co.uk), are a few of the low priced clothing stores available to you. You can also shop at the more expensive shops during sales. This is a great way of picking up quality clothing at bargain prices.

Avoid expensive designer labels. When you spend under £50 for a jacket and trousers, you can afford to buy four jackets instead of only one, for over £200, from an expensive designer label.

Choose materials that are easy and cost effective to maintain. Avoid delicate materials that require dry-cleaning and opt for more easy care fabrics. Do not pay for dry cleaning bills when you unnecessary.

Buy easily repaired and maintainable shoes. Avoid shoes with heels, which after worn down, you have to replace the entire shoe. Buy shoes with heels that are replaceable. It is wiser to spend £2.50 for a replacement heel or sole and get another a year of use out of a pair of shoes than have to throw them away and spend another £60 for a new pair – which, no doubt will only last a year.

I know of some contractors who spend over £60 each on Pink shirts to do the same job as a contractor wearing a £3 Asda's George brand shirt. Similarly, I also know of females who spend £120 on Karen Miller blouses, to work alongside of contractors or permies wearing Marks and Spencer's blouses and skirts, for less than half the price. Who is a better steward of their profits? Furthermore, because the George shirt is £3, you can afford to buy twenty of them for the same price as one £60 Pink shirt.

The Pink shopper cannot afford to wear a different shirt for every workday in the month as the Asda shopper can. Furthermore, the Pink shopper probably has to dry-clean his shirts, further raising the price of ownership.

In the end, if you do not need it, save your money and be frugal. Invest the money where it will bear more fruit. Avoid chasing fashion and view your business as a businessperson should – lower operating costs and increase profits.

Rapidly increase your contract rate

To increase your contracting income, you either ask for a rate increase (normally at each renewal offering), or change contracts for a higher paying one. Generally, the latter is the easier and most effective option; however, I have known contractors who raised their pay from £18 per hour to £35 per hour – within eighteen months – through expert re-newal negotiation.

Remember, your desired rate increase should never exceed the highest levels offered on the market, otherwise you will find yourself waiting a long time for your next role. To surpass these high compensation levels, your best chances of success will be to change your area of expertise (or relocate to a major city, if you currently contract in a small town or rural area).

Each field of expertise has a rate range within which you must operate. This usually follows a bell shaped, normal distribution curve. Extremely low and high rates are rare, whilst average ones are more popular.

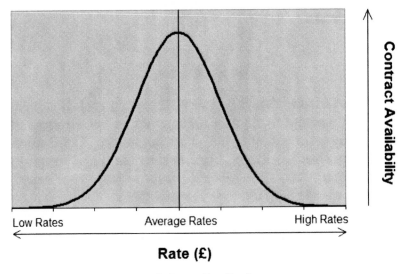

Rate (£)

Figure 2: Rate distribution curve

Figure 2 illustrates the bell curve for an example IT contracting area of specialization. You will notice that the jobs thin-out near either pay extremes. The easiest areas to find a contract is always somewhere near the mid or average range.

If your current rate is in the lower end of the curve for your area of specialization, you can rapidly increase it by moving from contract to contract within the same area of specialization.

However, if your current pay lies within the high end of the market, you will be restricted in how you can improve your income within the same area of specialization. Increases will be less dramatic and waiting periods will tend to lengthen between each contract. To bypass this problem, you need to avoid the area of specialization. You have to leave the area entirely, and enter a new area where your current rate will be among the low end of the market.

This will sometimes require further training, certification or even a reduction in pay. However, the new rate range will have more room for you to grow your future incomes.

Tax avoidance

Tax avoidance should be every taxpayer's goal. It is legal and every taxpayer's right to arrange his or her business in such a way as to minimize his or her tax burden. Tax evasion on the other hand, is illegal. Evasion aims use illegal means to avoid paying tax. You should never evade your taxes; however, always look for ways to avoid them.

There are many ways to avoid your Ltd. Company paying VAT, NI and Corporation tax. We have discussed many of these already; however, let us look at some of these tax avoidance techniques in detail.

VAT

The easiest way to avoid paying 17.5% VAT is to subscribe to the flat rate VAT scheme. If your business only provides computer services, you can reduce your VAT rate from 17.5% to 13%.

Some entrepreneurial contractors who offer computer repair services register their Ltd. company as a computer repairs service company, when they join the flat rate VAT scheme. This further reduces their VAT rate another 2%, from 13% to 11%.

As a part of their business, they undertake computer repair contracts as an extension of their companies' offered services. They charge 17.5% VAT for computer equipment they source, supply or repair for their clients; however, they only need to pay 11% VAT, thus saving 6.5% in VAT alone.

Corporation tax

You only pay corporation tax when you draw dividends on income. Leaving the funds in the company account attracts no tax. Therefore, you should leave profits in your company bank account for as long as possible.

All company related spending can then be taken out of this amount and written off against your company's tax liability. The following are some examples of company related costs:

1. Training.
2. Stationary.
3. Insurance.
4. Fuel costs.
5. Premises hiring.
6. Company business related travel costs.
7. Office maintenance and repairs.
8. Company car maintenance.
9. Computer equipment.
10. Company parties and Christmas parties.
11. Company phone and mobile phone rental costs.
12. Company related Internet access costs.

13. Company business related parking charges.
14. Accounting services.
15. Legal services.
16. Subcontractors and consultancy expenses.
17. Company pension contributions.
18. VAT charges.
19. NI contributions.
20. Corporation tax charges.
21. Insurance policy premiums (indemnity, health, critical illness, dentistry, etc.).
22. Low or no interest directors loans below £5,000 per annum and more.

Whatever remains after these company-related expenditures, should be withdrawn as dividends. Dividends are taxed at 20% rather than the higher 22% or 40% (for high rate tax) rates applied to an individual's income tax.

Income tax

To avoid paying high income taxes, you should reduce your director's salary to as low as possible. Luckily, minimum wage restrictions do not affect executives; therefore, you can reduce your income further than a non-executive's income.

There are several things you need to be aware of. Firstly, NI contribution thresholds (£4,635), and secondly Income Tax thresholds (starting rate for 2007/2008 is 10% up to £2,230 and basic rate 22% from £2,231 to £34,600).

If your income is below £185.83 per month (2007/2008), you will avoid having to pay NI and 22% income tax. You will only have to pay 10% income tax and no NI. The rest you will draw as dividends at 20% (2007/2008).

Charges

Avoid paying any further taxes by never attracting tax fines. Always file your taxes on time. Normally, you have a month for VAT, NI and PAYE and nine months and a day for corporation tax. This is sufficient time to get all your tax returns and payments in on time.

Overtime

Undertake overtime only if it is paid, or if it pays you indirectly, i.e., if you gain a valuable skill, knowledge or experience that will help dramatically increase your rates in the next contract. You are in a business, not a charity; therefore leave unpaid overtime to permies.

Wherever possible, try to negotiate for time and a half or double time for overtime. You will not always get this; however, do not miss out on it, simply because you did not ask. Check this detail and negotiate it before signing and stating each contract.

Evaluating business value

Determining whether or not an event is of business value, can often be tricky. Important considerations are as follows:

1. Will the real boss be there?
2. Do you have a bad habit? Is it likely you will highlight it at the event? An example would be if you cannot control your drink, or if you have a history of acting unprofessionally, e.g., vomiting, being violent, or extremely loud, crass, antisocial, or making a fool of yourself in other ways.

3. Would the event allow you to create a more positive bond with your colleagues and managers?
4. Do you have another meeting scheduled that is of more business value?
5. Will attending the affair affect your punctuality record the following day?

Contracting Ethics and Practices

If you have read each point up until here, you will have a good idea of the mindset a professional contractor ought to have. At the forefront of contracting ethics is integrity. Your employer has to be able to trust you in all ways. Firstly, they have to trust that you can provide the service they require; secondly, they have to know that you will not cause them professional damage, whether maliciously or unintentionally.

As you start each contract, the client will be wary of you. You have to prove yourself worthy of their trust by performing your role exceptionally well and abiding by all their security and compliance policies. It is critical that you do not flout any policies early-on in the relationship – if ever.

Furthermore, your integrity is also judged on smaller issues such as time keeping and attendance, e-mail and Internet usage, actual time spent working, pride in your work and quality of your work, as well as how you interact with other team members.

Second on the ethics list of required characteristics for contractors, is professionalism. This will determine how you react or behave under any situation or work condition. Do you dress appropriately? Do you communicate effectively? Are you objective? Are you proactive or reactive? In stressful situations, do you reduce the pressure or add to it? How are your telephone manners? How is your attitude towards your work, your colleagues and the organisation?

Your professionalism will also determine if you are given the opportunity to represent the team, department or organisation in high profile situations. It will also determine how much responsibility you will be entrusted with, and what type of work you will be given to do. Your goal is to become indispensable to the organization.

During your contracts, you may be contacted by agencies or other employers about other contracts. Some will be very tempting, however, remember that your good name and reputation is on the line. If you jump ship and leave your current contract for another because of more money, a better role or any other reason, you will have broken the contractual agreement, and the current organisation's trust.

If you are lucky, they won't take legal action against you; however, they will be even more wary, if not totally negative, towards ever recruiting your services in future.

The best time to leave a contract is at the end of a role and only if you are not being renewed, or if you have secured another role to start after your current role ends. Leaving at this stage is not unethical; you have fulfilled your contractual duty and are now free from the bond. Leaving earlier, whether you do so illegally, or through other unethical means (such as taking your notice period off ill), is wrong.

Cheating, lying and stealing

You should never cheat the organisation employing your services by giving them less than they are paying for. Similarly, you should never steal or lie from them. If you have undertaken six hours of work in a day, and you are paid hourly, do not lie by submitting a timesheet with eight hours on it.

Lastly, never steal from a client. We have covered this already in part; however, stealing stationary, time, quantity and quality of work, equipment, software and copyright protected materials as well as other intellectual material should be avoided at all costs.

You are not a thief, you are a professional IT contractor and you should be proud of your business. Even if you are not caught, your own personal, integrity barometer should warn you against unethical behaviour. Operate your business and conduct yourself with professionalism and the highest integrity.

Workspace Security

Make sure your computer is secured; (locked or logged out) whenever you leave your desk. If the organisation provides a lock, use it to lock your desk drawers and filing cabinets at the end of each day. Take the key with you. Do not leave them lying around or hidden under a flower pot. The cleaners find these sooner or later and it defeats the security.

Telephone security

Agencies and other data collectors, and even people involved in industrial espionage may contact you via e-mail or the phone. If you do not know the caller, or what the call is about, do not give any details of your client's set-up, staff names or business operations. If the caller does not have a specific name or if they cannot tell you how they got your number, do not divulge any information to them, no matter how trivial that information may seem to you.

Terminating your contract prematurely

This section covers premature termination of your contract. You should avoid prematurely terminating your contract whenever possible; however, situations will arise where you may need to leave some contracts quickly. When these situations arise, you must judge whether it is wiser to inform the client of the full issue, or if doing so would be unwise for your business.

Similarly, informing your agency of the true nature of your early departure may be unwise, especially when the reason relates to you securing another contract through one of their competitors. Reasons for early termination falls into four major categories:

1. Death – a family member or close friend has suddenly died.
2. Health – you are unable to continue performing the role due to health issues.
3. Conflict – you do not like the environment, a certain situation, or a person you have to work with.
4. Wealth – you have found a better role or suddenly have a windfall.

Bereavement and health

In some cases, the client will allow you the time off to deal with health and bereavement issues. In these situations, normally, your role will be kept open until you return. The more common occurrence is to allow you to amicably terminate your contract after working the mandatory notice period. Some organisations will kindly waive the notice period if your reason is related to health or bereavement due to death.

Conflicts

In the case of conflicts, the client may not be the best person to trust with the full story. This is especially true if the environment is hostile to contractors, or the conflict involves a senior manager or the person who decides if you are to be renewed or not. Complaining may be futile, in this situation.

Your best option may be to quietly secure another contract, hand in your notice and work your notice period and then leave to start the new contract. Some contractors who secure new contracts requiring immediate starts, unwisely take the option of calling in sick through the entire notice period. This is unethical and should be avoided. If the previous client takes legal action, you would be found guilty of claiming to be sick whilst working at another contract.

When the conflict is with a colleague, you could first try to report the situation to your manager or HR. If they do not react proactively and the situation persists, you can take the departure option and hand in your notice.

Racism, anti-contractorism and other prejudices

Contractors encounter all the prejudices that everyone, including permies, have to put up with. However, it always comes mixed with anti-contractorism. If you are obese and a contractor, you will not only be teased about being obese but you will have the added insult of being an obese contractor. Similarly, if you are of an ethnic minority and attract racist comments concerning your race, you will have to deal with the added insults for being an ethnic minority contractor.

To some extent, this is life. You can either do something about it (if possible), or learn to deal with it. If you opt to do something about it, you have three choices:

1. Report it to your manager or HR (if your manager is involved).
2. Avoid it as best you can.
3. Leave the role to get away from it.

Luckily, in today's multinational environment, you will rarely encounter racism; however, you will encounter other types of prejudices. Ageism, sexism, lookism, and general bullying still occur in many organisations.

Some organisations have processes in place to deal effectively with this kind of abuse, however, many do not. Furthermore, the department or site where this abuse takes place could be out of reach of the HR influence, allowing their reprimands and warnings to the abusers to go unheeded.

Sometimes, simply reporting the abuse can worsen it. If the abuse is causing you undue stress, anxiety and/or eroding your self-esteem, I advise you to terminate the contract and find another contract where you do not have to deal with abuse. However, never underestimate the power of completely ignoring abusers' comments. The less of a reaction they receive from you, the less fun it will be for them to dish it out. Another affective treatment for rude people is simply to smile at them, turn and walk away.

Wealth (or career building and greed)

When the reason you want to quickly depart involves seeking more money, pursuing a more challenging or interesting role, or is due to an advantageous career progression, you have to be extra careful how you handle ending your term. Firstly, these situations are the most likely to cause a client or agency to take legal action against your company for breach of contract.

This is because it involves them losing money. The agency loses the income for the remainder of your contract, whilst the client loses your services and gains the added costs and hassle of recruiting and training someone new to replace you.

Whilst it is very rare for an agency or client to take legal action against a contractor, this does not mean it cannot or will not happen to you. Make sure you protect yourself against this outcome by either never breaching your contracts, or taking adequate professional indemnity insurance. Read the small print of your policy to ensure that it covers you for contract breaching liabilities.

If you find a better role and the new client cannot or will not wait for you to work out your termination period, you should not default on your current contract. As a contractor, your reputation, professionalism, experience and qualifications are all you have. Try never to lose any of these assets. Never lose a good reputation by reneging on a contract agreement.

If you are on good terms with your manager, you can talk to them about your predicament. They may allow you to leave earlier without working out the full notice period. You can even come to an out-of-court settlement where you pay some penalty fee to your current client, in order for them to release you from the legal bind of the contract.

There are dangers with leaving any contract prematurely, however, if you handle it professionally and with integrity, you will avoid these dangers.

Avoiding skill loss through consecutive short contracts

Before getting yourself carried away with increasing your rate through taking many short-term contracts, let us look at the major risks.

When you move from one unrelated, consecutive short contract to another, you can start to lose some of your skills. This may be due to not having enough time (during any one contract), to hone your skills and build on your knowledge.

Avoid this by aiming to undertake at least one contract that lasts six months or longer, within every year. The contract you select to renew and prolong your stay at, should offer new knowledge, skills and experience. Avoid over-staying in contracts that teach you nothing new. Such contracts will dull your skills and erode your knowledge.

If a contract is paying top money but teaches you nothing new, stay there for the money, however, undertake a course or training in your spare time to learn something new with the extra money you are earning there.

Advanced contract renewal techniques

At the end of your contract, you will be either terminated or renewed. There is not much you can do if your contract is terminated; except leave amicably and professionally.

If the contract is renewed, you should always attempt to renegotiate a new and higher rate. The way you go about doing this will determine how successful (or unsuccessful) your rate renegotiation will be. The following is a breakdown of these imperative techniques:

1. **The threat:** One of the best ways to negotiate is to go in with the upper hand. You can do this in one of two ways: threatening or invited. When using the threatening technique, you will need first to secure a better contract. You then use the new contract to secure a better offer from your current client.

The process goes something like this: Either the agency will call you to ask if you want to accept the renewal, or the client approaches you with the renewal offer. Whichever the case, make sure you tell them that you already have another offer and state how the offer benefits you.

Furthermore, let them know that you have not accepted the other offer yet, and that you will let it lapse and accept the current one, if the current client is prepared to meet or exceed the competitor's offer.

This technique is great, because either way, you win. If the client matches the offer you gain because you get the rate you want, and if the client refuses, you still have a better paying roll with the new contract.

2. **The half–threat:** Some contactors use the half-threat. This is an unethical technique requiring you to lie about having

another role. You then cause your current client to match your imaginary contract rate. This can backfire when they refuse to match the new rate, leaving you to either come clean and lose face, or leave and be without a contract.

3. **The invite:** This method is more subtle compared to the threat. It involves you having a meeting with the client. In this meeting, you ask them several questions concerning your performance, value for money, effectiveness, professionalism and efficiency. You also ask them to tell you where you can improve. You should also ask about their plans concerning your renewal.

Providing all their answers – especially concerning your renewal – are positive, you explain that you are willing to accept the renewal; however, you would like a rate change to reflect your current market value. Make sure you have a realistic value clearly in mind before you call this meeting. I have found this technique to be highly effective in producing rate increases during renewals.

If you are unprofessional, lazy and a terrible worker, please do not even call this meeting, as the negative answers to these questions will likely make them decide to definitely not renew you.

Contracting in the stealth mode

You should aim to increase your income by a set percentage each year. Set yourself a goal to increase your turnover by twenty-five percent each year. As an example, if you start contracting on £30,000 in your first year, the following could be your projected increase for subsequent years:

Year 1: £30,000
Year 2: £37,500

Year 3: £46,875
Year 4: £58,594
Year 5: £73,242
Year 6: £91,553
Year 7: £114,441
Year 8: £143,051
Year 9: £178,814
Year 10: £223,517

The above example is easy enough to achieve given a ten-year period; however, along the way, you will need to learn new skills, acquire new knowledge and change areas of specialization. We shall now look at an example of a helpdesk analyst on £15 per hour:

- In the first year, she earns £30,000. By the end of that year, she should have acquired a couple of Microsoft Certified Practitioner (MCP) certificates and should slowly start to gain 2nd line skills. In her second year, she would start at the bottom rung of 2nd line support.
- She should now be earning roughly £18.75 per hour. As her second year progresses, she should complete her MCSE certification and start earning better rates. She should also undertake more server related roles involving backups and restores, troubleshooting with server logs, adding print queues to print servers, stopping and starting print spoolers and perhaps running some morning checks and status reports.
- In her third year, she should see her earnings around £23.50 for 2nd line support roles. She should also be involved in improving her server support skills and should now be able to build a server. By this time, she could also undertake more 3rd line support functions, alongside her 2nd line support tasks. Backup restore, antivirus updates, unblocking e-mails and undertaking simple firewall tasks, should all be part of her daily tasks.

- As year four comes along, she should now be at nearly £30.00 an hour; undertaking mainly 3rd line server support roles with some minor 2nd line tasks. At this point, she would spend most of her time on the server team and may assist with some migration projects. Part of her role should be to build application servers and test new applications that the application packages develop.
- Year five: she should now be learning how to package applications herself and should have attained her VMWare certification. She would now be on £36.50 per hour. She should now consider getting into application packaging, and should enrol in a VB programming course.
- Year six would see her becoming more involved in application packaging. She could get a job in an investment bank and learn to package banking and trading applications. She could now earn over £46.00 per hour.
- At year seven, she should finish her VB course and take a C# course. She would now be a trading applications developer. She should be able to write components that interface with Microsoft .net, and is now commanding £57.00 per hour. She is now ready to be put in charge of a small team to lead.
- Her team leading skills should mature and develop over time. She would mainly be in meetings and programming less and less. It would now be her eighth year and now involved with developmental projects. She should now be responsible for a small development team and control a small budget. She should be earning over £570.00 a day.
- During year nine, she should be able to bring her projects in on time and within budget, and she should study a Prince 2 course. She should now be a project manager with a larger team and bigger budget. Some of her projects could involve travel to Europe, U.S.A. and Singapore. Her team could be spread across three continents, but her earnings could now command £720.00 per day.

- In her tenth year of contracting; she would now be a fully-fledged project manager. She should have other project managers reporting to her on her latest project. Now, her projects could involve integrating the systems of two conglomerates that have merged. A lot of ad-hoc coding would be required to port the two companies' systems. Her career would now require even more travel and she should have her own personal assistant. She should be approaching nearly £900.00 per day.

In this example, an ambitious 1st line support engineer ploughed her way through 1st line, 2nd line, 3rd line, application packaging, testing, development, team leading, all the way to project management, in ten years. Each year she improved her income by 25%. This is not impossible; you too can do something similar to this. All you need is the dedication, motivation, education and ambition. It begins with setting the goal and being prepared to work towards the wonderful rewards IT contracting has to offer.

Goal tagging with contracting

You can achieve incredible things when you make them a burning desire. See my other books, *Taking Action* and *Planning and Goal Setting for Personal Success* for a more thorough coverage of this subject. If you have no goal and simply work to pay the bills, you will just pay the bills. However, when you aim to purchase a house, buy a new car, start another business or even write a book, you will be pleasantly surprised that in the same time that it would have taken to pay the bills alone, you could also have achieved a major undertaking.

After purchasing my first property with the proceeds from a contract, I learned the power of goal tagging. Prior to setting the objective, my rate was unexciting. However, once I set the target, suddenly, opportunities appeared from all around me. Within seven months, my rate doubled and in the same time, I saved up the money to pay for the property, cash down.

Since then, I have always set goals and assigned them to my contracts. This book is one such achievement. I wrote this entire book whilst undertaking one contract.

The contract gave me access to thousands of contractors I could talk to, ask questions of, run ideas by, and get their opinions on various topics that are discussed herein. I wanted to complete the book before the contract ended. However, when I needed more time, I negotiated an extension.

Having a purpose aligns and focuses your thinking and your actions. You stop wasting time and start taking actions that lead to successful achievement of your goals. Moreover, because you are constantly thinking about your objective, your mind acts like a mental transmitter, telling all other minds that you are interested in achieving this aim. These attract opportunities your way, through luck, serendipity and sheer coincidences – or are they?

Setting a goal is like driving to work. Each day you set out and get to work. You have a plan, a route, a destination and a deadline time by which to arrive. Even though sometimes you are early and sometimes late, you get there each day, nevertheless. This is because you had a definite destination, planned route and a time limit.

Imagine if you did not have a destination, planned route or time limit to get to work. Imagine if you did not even have a reason to go to work. Do you think you would ever get there? I do not think so either. That is why, without a goal, plan, and deadline, you wander aimlessly through life, buffeted by the waves of events without direction or purpose.

Similarly, if you contract without a purpose, you will progress very slowly, pummelled against the tides of events, trends and market forces. With a target in mind, you will steer yourself through all the obstructions and influences with your sails filled with the knowledge of what you need to do to succeed. You'll head towards a fixed destination according to your plan, before a predetermined deadline.

When setting goals, make sure they are meaningful to you and truly what you passionately want. A burning desire will pull you, as well as have you running to it. An unimportant wish will not motivate you when the going is tough and the outcome looks bleak.

Be sure to make your goals achievable. Do not make them too easily achieved or impossible to reach. Set challenging objectives but make them attainable. If they prove to be easier to accomplish than you originally thought, re-set the objective with a different deadline, to make it slightly more challenging.

Make sure you date your goals with deadlines. Without a deadline, your ambitions become wishes. Your dreams will never come to be, because you will not be motivated to get started or finished. You may not even begin, because you do not have a deadline specified. Give yourself the motivation to start by setting a finishing date and time.

Normally, the completion of an aspiration is in itself the reward; however, you may want to assign a reward to the achievement. This reward should be proportionate to the achieved target. Do not set a goal to learn VB, and reward yourself with a new home. This is not proportionate. Instead, value the worth of the objective and assign a reward worth around 10% or less of the acquired goal. In the case of learning VB, you may want to reward yourself with a new peripheral for your computer (as an example).

Handling termination professionally

As a contractor, at the end of each contract, you may not always be renewed. Get used to this. How you handle contract termination will determine how often you are called back, and who is prepared to give you a good reference.

Your work should not degrade near the end of your contracts. You should maintain the same high standards of work, motivation and professionalism, even if you are not going to be renewed. People have memories that recall the most recent events, better than less recent ones. Similarly, people recall odd events better than normal ones. Therefore, do not suddenly change overnight from being a professional, responsible, conscientious, and hardworking contractor to a shiftless, indolent, selfish contractor.

Leave the organisation in a manner in which you would want others to remember you. You should leave as a hardworking, professional contractor. You will be remembered and increase your chances of being called back in the future.

How to professionally terminate your contract

If you need to terminate a contract, the correct protocol is to write a note, memo or e-mail to your manager. The note should contain your name and contact details. It should also contain the date you wish to start your notice period. Your reasons for leaning are optional; however, there should never be any negative reasons within the letter concerning the manager, department, or organisation (remember you may one day need a reference).

Nowadays, e-mail is perhaps the better of the three methods of informing your manager of your contract termination. This gives you a copy of the correspondence. You can also send a copy to your personal e-mail address and your agency's e-mail address.

The resignation letter should also include a thank you to the employer for giving you the contract opportunity. If it is true, you can also mention how you have enjoyed your time there.

Never give a verbal resignation without immediately following it with a written one – that same day. Check your contract wording before writing the resignation letter. Remember to include the agency in the recipients of the e-mail, as your contract involves them, too.

Always try to leave on an amicable note. Do not use your last few weeks or days to be destructive, disagreeable or vengeful. In fact, you might want to do the opposite during these last few days. Strive to be remembered for your professionalism and hard work.

Personal Considerations

This section covers personal issues related to IT contracting. We will look at maternity leave and pregnancy, avoiding geekism and other anti-social behaviour, developing amiability, holidaying within your contract, racism, anti-contractorism and other considerations.

Maternity leave

Many women turn back to permanent employment leading up to their pregnancy because they wish to either work part-time, or take the financial compensation offered by their employer in the form of a maternity leave. A permie maternity leave however, does not always offer a better option than a contracting maternity leave.

Firstly, the permie maternity leave does not pay a full salary for the whole duration of the maternity leave. Most employment contract's offer 'stepped' or 'decrementing' maternity leave payments. Starting with a few months at 100% of the permie salary, then dropping progressively until it vanishes within twelve months of the maternity leave. Therefore, if you took a year's maternity leave, you could end up earning less than 65% of your normal permie salary in the twelve months of maternity leave.

This money could be saved in less than eight months prior to the start of the maternity leave through contracting – if you lived on the same salary as your permie equivalent, whilst saving the rest. That is the key; live below your means and save for a rainy day, emergencies or purely for investing for further income growth.

If you do not master living within or even better, below your means, you will always be a slave to your income source, be it a permie boss or your own inability to take time off between contracts to recuperate and enjoy your hard-earned money and freedom.

Planning your pregnancy while contracting

Take time to plan your pregnancy and maternity leave. Save for it, then take the time off and enjoy your pregnancy or paternity leave. Because you are the boss, you can take as much time off as you want. All you need to do prior to this is to earn the money and save up first.

By reducing your spending to match that of a permie in your area of expertise, you, too, can save a permie salary within eight months. In sixteen months, you will have saved two years worth of permie income. From this savings, you can then take the time out to have your child or help rear your baby.

When you are nearing the end of your maternity leave, you can either return to contracting full time, or to contract intermittently, simply to earn the money to spend more time with your newborn child.

Child care and IT contracting

Just like permies, contractors with children still need someone to take care of them during working hours. However, because of the higher contractor incomes, contractors have better options as to which childcare centre they can afford for their child.

The private and more expensive childcare centres need no longer be out of reach. As a contractor, you can have more choices and better options where you send your child. From private childcare to a live in Au Pair to help with the daily pick-ups and drop-offs of the child.

Furthermore, your Ltd. company can pay your child minder and/or childcare costs, as long as the service is available to the entire staff of your company. See Table 14 (page 143), for details on this topic. You could attract National Insurance (NI) for this type of benefit. Investigate these things with your accountant or tax advisor to plan accordingly.

Avoiding geekism and other antisocial behaviour

The biggest part of IT deals with technology, mainly computer software and hardware. It is easy to get so absorbed in the technology that you start to live in your own world. When this occurs, you can slowly lose your social skills or under-develop your social skills, because you stop interacting directly with other human beings.

Bankers do not go home and play with money, neither do doctors go home to play with their instruments; however, IT contractors can often be found working, using, playing with, or on their own computers, almost all the time outside of the work place.

Continued exposure to this type of lifestyle and leisure time will make you antisocial. It will cause you to become out of touch with socially accepted behaviour and inter-personal skills. You can easily become a geek. Prolonged exposure to the Internet, computers and information technology can cause you to start preferring computer and software systems, to human contact and interaction.

Soon, you will estrange yourself from your non-computer, geek friends and attract new friends who are also overly dependent and attached to computers, the Internet and software.

Beware of this spiralling descent into the world of computer geeks. Once you are deeply entrenched in it, you will find it extremely difficult to get back out. What will be even stranger, is how you will cease to see what the problem is, with being a computer geek.

Avoid computer geekism by separating your work from your home life. Spend time without technology several hours each day and enjoy good, old fashioned, human company, (and I do not mean through online chat, face booking or blogging, either).

Holidaying within your contract

It is far easier to find a new contract whilst you are already in another contract. This is due to your lack of desperation, neediness and nervousness in interviews when you are in between contracts. When you are in a contract, you naturally radiate a sense of confidence at interviews because you do not *need* to get that job. You are already working.

Similarly, it may take you a couple of weeks to get back into the swing of contract hunting when you return from vacation. It normally takes a couple of weeks for your CV to penetrate the market deep enough to give you a broad exposure to enough recruitment agents and clients. Therefore, it makes sense to start looking for your next job two to four weeks in advance, before the end of your contract.

Similarly, it makes sense to take a holiday within a contract, whenever you can. This allows you to come back from holiday straight into a contract. This saves you a lot of wasted time in job hunting straight after you return from vacation.

It is best to arrange vacations after your first or subsequent renewals. This is because during the interview for the first term of a contract, any mention of a pre-booked vacation will often greatly disadvantage your application for the role. It is far easier to get away with taking a holiday in your second term, than your first.

If you have proven yourself conscientious, hardworking and professional during your first term, the client should be willing to hold the role for a week or two until your return.

However, do not take more than two weeks off on vacation. Long periods will require another person – possibly another contractor – to be recruited to replace you for the vacation period. By the time you return, the client may prefer the new contractor over you.

Finally, before you leave for your vacation, and when you return, be modest and conservative with the details of your holiday. Do not divulge details that could make the permies jealous – especially your managers. I recall one contractor who took a two-week vacation to Sandals, the ultra all-inclusive resort in Jamaica. He bragged about it so often that, as soon as he left, his manager terminated his role to spite him.

Offshore and Foreign Contracts

Contracting abroad can be refreshingly lucrative, especially in tax havens such as Jersey, Guernsey, Isle of Man, Dubai and the Caribbean, among others. Other jurisdictions such as Australia, South Africa, Canada, Netherlands, Luxembourg, America, Belgium, Germany, Singapore, and Switzerland as well as many other countries around the world, offer contract opportunities that pay well. Furthermore, in most cases, your flights and accommodation may also be provided for you.

There are many factors to consider before making the move to contracting abroad. In most cases, a company has to first 'sponsor' you before you can acquire the proper paperwork to work in a foreign country. Once you acquire a sponsor, you have to determine how you will financially structure your business. There are many options from which to choose. Each choice comes with its own set of pros and cons. For instance, you could:

- Use a Ltd. company based in your original country.
- Set-up a Ltd. company in the new jurisdiction.
- Use an offshore LLC, based in a third party jurisdiction.
- Use a managed services provider based in your original country that operates in the new jurisdiction.
- Use a managed services company based entirely in the new jurisdiction.
- Become a permie with the sponsor.
- Become a permie with a foreign recruitment agency.

Depending on which option you elect to use, the jurisdiction you are looking to contract in, the relationship with the sponsor or employer, your permanent residency status, and the length of the contract, you will have to consider your legal rights, your tax status and tax liability. Furthermore, your security and the continuity of the role, after the relationship with the sponsor ends, will also be an important factor to consider.

You should also seriously consider how you would commute or relocate for the contract role. Some jurisdictions, European destinations for example, such as Paris and Frankfurt are less than an hour's flight from the UK. If based in the UK, you could consider countries such as, Ireland, Jersey and Guernsey, Isle of Man, Switzerland, Germany, Luxembourg, Belgium or The Netherlands. Some, like Jersey and Guernsey, Isle of Man, Ireland and Switzerland, have more favourable tax laws compared to the UK.

Another consideration is social security. As a foreigner, you may not be entitled to free medical care in most foreign jurisdictions. Normally, the sponsor will offer this, however, be prepared to arrange your own private medical care and insurances.

Those prepared to travel further abroad, could consider, the U.A.E., Canada, America, Australia, South Africa or Singapore. Beware however; some jurisdictions such as America, Canada and Australia have tax stings in their tails. Unlike the UK which only taxes residents on income generated in the UK or its territories, America, Canada and Australia, (as well as other countries such as India) tax residents on their worldwide incomes.

Residency status is normally automatic, if you are resident in the country for more than 90 to 93 days. Other rules may apply. For instance, your average stay over a three to four year period, even if it never exceeded 90 days, could amount to a figure that changes your status from non-resident alien to a resident alien.

Normally, in the jurisdictions that have worldwide tax laws for residents, non-residents are taxed 30% (or more) on any incomes generated within the jurisdiction.

Other jurisdictions such as Dubai, have no taxes to IT contractors and offer rates and benefits that often match UK London rates.

Visit Work Permits site at www.workpermit.com and Contractor UK at www.contractoruk.com/overseas_guides for more information on working abroad as a contractor.

The following is a list of the important points on some of the jurisdictions where contracting can be lucrative:

1. **Ireland:**
- To work in Ireland you need a PPS number, which is a tax and social security reference number. You can obtain one

by visiting your local Social, Community and Family Affairs Office with your passport, an additional form of photographic ID and proof of your Irish address.

- Employees in Ireland are required to operate under local PAYE rules. Doing this will greatly increase your income taxes. Use a management company or a European accountant to help you arrange the most advantageous financial set-up.
- Corporate taxes are low in Ireland. This offers a few loopholes to the contractor. Remittance taxation does not apply to investments and dividends.
- If you can obtain an E101[17], you can get a European Health Insurance Card (EHIC), entitling you to Irish health care. Most high income earners will not be entitled to this.
- You are entitled to tax credits based on your marital status, number of children, etc. This helps reduce your monthly tax liabilities.
- The Irish tax year runs from January to December, and tax return filing is available online.

2. **Switzerland:**
- Rates are generally better than in the UK.
- No tax returns are required, however; you need to be on a local payroll for PAYE.
- You will need a resident permit. This entitles you to work for a certain sponsor within a particular canton for a specified period. A management services company will be able to apply for the permit on your behalf, if your sponsor is not willing to.

---

[17] Form E101 is used to confirm to the authorities in participating host countries that Social Security payments are being maintained. This prevents the host country from demanding payments and also allows you to receive social benefit in the host country if you require it. Your host employer should obtain an E101 on your behalf from the host countries Social Security office, before you travel to take up the new post. Form E101 is valid for up to 12 months.

- A standard CHF 1500 expatriate allowance is offered across all the regions. Other expenses allowed, vary from area to area; therefore, you need to either use a tax specialist, or be astute at calculating and including them.
- The Swiss employer of a contractor needs a license. You can use a licensed management company to bypass this, if your sponsor is not licensed.
- Private health care insurance is compulsory; however, EU residents can use the European Health Insurance Card (EHIC) for medical treatment. Minimum health care insurance coverage varies across the regions .
- Cost of living tends to be expensive and in some areas, ethnic minorities are prejudiced against.

3. **Germany:**

- Although most Germans can understand some English, you would enjoy your stay more whilst in Germany if you spoke a little German.
- Upon arrival, you are required to register your address at the Einwohnermeldeamt and then at the Immigration/Alien's office.
- There is a large and established expatriate community in most major German cities.
- You will need a tax code to work in Germany. Request a Lohnsteuerkarte (wage tax card) from the tax office.
- Germany observes a 183-day, residency tax rule. To avoid paying German taxes, do not exceed this limit.
- You can use an E101 for social services; however, you will still be required to maintain NI payments back in the UK, to be entitled to this.
- If you decide to become a resident alien in Germany, you will be entitled to pay the German income tax, health insurance, unemployment and retirement plans.
- Contractors will be required to hold appropriate labour leasing licenses. Depending on your set-up, you or

someone else (such as your sponsor), can hold these licenses.

4. **Belgium:**

- Brussels is the hotbed of contracting in Belgium, with most international companies adopting English as their spoken language. French and Dutch is also advantageous to know.
- The average working week is 40 hours.
- Has some of the highest taxes in Europe.
- You can work there for 183 days without paying tax to the Belgian tax authorities; however, as soon as you exceed this time period, all your earned income in the country will come under Belgian tax laws. This is one place where you should avoid accepting extensions.
- Belgium treats Ltd. companies with one employer, or Ltd. companies where the employers are related, as Belgian based. In this case, the 183-day rule will not apply. Therefore, to work in Belgium make sure your limited company is comprised of other, unrelated staff.
- You can consider using a Belgian Ltd company. This offers many tax-deductible benefits such as car cost, consultant fees, health insurance and pensions.
- You can also set-up a company to retain profits until it is dissolved, whereby these profits are redeemed. Consult a tax specialist concerning how to use this method effectively. For short contracts, this option is not so viable as it involves a fair amount of paperwork, management and bureaucracy for a what will be a measly retention at the end.
- Avoid freelancing in Belgium. Their tax laws will treat you as an employee of the sponsor, leaving you exposed to the full brunt of the high Belgian taxes.
- Many management companies offer solutions for contractors in Belgium. However, make sure the liability

lies with them and not you. Normally, this route greatly reduces the benefits of contracting in Belgium, due to the PAYE taxes and management charges involved.

5. The Netherlands:

- The hot areas for IT contracting is currently Randstad and the Haag.
- You need a tax identification number (SOFI number). If you are already an EU citizen, you simply need your passport to attain one.
- A 183-day, tax-free stay is not available here for contractors, as local payroll responsibilities apply. To protect themselves from this, employers may insist on withholding your local payroll taxes.
- The first 30% of your income will be tax-free. This is to cover all your expenses.
- Home ownership entitles you to tax relief on the interest payments.
- Buying a bicycle allows you €500 tax break. Other tax loopholes exist, however, you will need to look harder and work with a specialist to make use of these.
- Rates are generally lower than the UK but the average working week is shorter (35 hours).
- Partial residency or full residency status is available. Partial residents' employment income derived in The Netherlands attract taxes, whilst non-employment income does not. Full residency status entitles you to the same benefits and tax treatment as the local Dutch residents.
- Private health care insurance is compulsory; however, EU residents can have their sponsors apply for an E101 certificate that entitles them to use the European Health Insurance Card (EHIC) for medical treatment.

6. U.A.E.:

- Earnings rates are lower than in the UK, but attract no tax and, when working through a sponsor, car (or car and driver), accommodations and meals, as well as flights can be part of the package.
- Dubai has Dubai Internet City – an IT hub.
- Buy private health insurance, although this can be very expensive.

7. **America:**

- Contractors need a working visa.
- Working visas or (H1B Visas) are only available through your sponsoring employer. The application must be from a sponsor, and for a role requiring someone with four years of college education or more. Furthermore, you can only have a H1B for up to six years. Issued initially for up to three years, H1Bs are renewable or extendable only once—for a further three years maximum (only).
- You will need health care insurance to live in the U.S.A. The best option is to purchase insurance through your sponsor, as it will be a tenth of the price of buying personal health insurance on your own.
- As soon as you arrive in America, obtain a social security card from a tax office. Almost every institution you will deal with, requires this card.
- Open a bank savings and checking account, then apply for a credit card to start establishing your credit history. You will need this to buy a car or home, if using a loan.
- Apply for a driver's license.
- File your annual income tax to acquire the relevant paperwork to apply for a green card, and to avoid the huge penalties and interest on any unpaid taxes.
- United States' contract rates are lower than the UK; furthermore, the U.S. contracting market has been in a slump since 2002, with little signs of a recovery in sight.

- The U.S. also has higher taxes due to its layered tax system. U.S. residents have to pay federal, city and local taxes that could amount to 49% of your income, in some cases.
- For a better understanding of the tax implications of the U.S., consult an American tax specialist. A proper treatment of this topic is beyond the scope of this book.
- If you are contracting through your foreign Ltd. company in the U.S.A., your company is still required to withhold U.S. taxes and forward your payment to the IRS. Failure to do this will result in charges, and incur interest charges as well.
- The U.S. tax system and laws affect resident aliens' world income, and they have complex rules for determining residency, making it easy to get caught if you are out of compliance with U.S. laws, rules and regulations.
- For short stays in America, it is possible to claim many tax deductions, however, consult a well versed tax specialist in this area, for specific details.

8. **Australia:**

- Sydney is the main base for IT contracting.
- Rates are much lower than in the UK and the contractor/permie divide in rates, is less wide than in the UK.
- You will need a working holiday visa. Under this, you are only entitled to twelve months stay in Australia and in that time, you can only work for one employer for a maximum of three months. Furthermore, you can only apply for the visa if you are under 30 years old, but above 18 years, have no kids, have income sufficient to sustain you during your stay, have no plans to undertake full time education and you have never previously held a working holiday visa before.

- If you have a sponsor, you can apply for a temporary resident visa. This is valid for four years.
- Australia taxes its residents on their world income. Non-residents are taxed only on Australian incomes.
- Your tax is deducted at source, at or above the 29% rate, if you have obtained a Tax File Number (TFN) and have completed a Tax File Number Declaration for your sponsor.
- You will be taxed 48.5% or higher, at source if you have no TFN.
- Your social security benefits are carried to Australia from the UK, although you still have to maintain payments in the UK. After fifty-two weeks in Australia, your social security payments cease in the UK and switch to Australia.
- Australian tax treatment and double taxation treaties with the UK can be complex. It is advisable that you seek a professional tax consultant in this matter.

Allaying outsourcing fears

In the run-up to 2000, many feared that outsourcing companies based in Ireland, India, Pakistan, Philippines and other Asian countries, would grow to make contracting obsolete in Europe – especially in the UK. Although many companies outsourced their service desks and call centres abroad, many have returned, as they encountered unforeseen problems. Language, corruption and poor service were some of the reasons many companies returned their call centres back to the UK and Ireland.

Many more companies however, did not return and even today, many are turning eastward for call centre relocation. This is still primarily price driven. The UK contracting market has comfortably absorbed the loss in 1st line support and the contractors skilled in this have either turned to other industries, continued to contract in the available call centres still in the UK, or moved into 2nd line support, desk side support and PC support.

An exodus of eastern developers has descended on the UK and other countries in Europe, raising the standards and competition in these areas. Today, the contracting market in the UK has a large, ethnic and foreign contractor population.

There are many IT professionals from India and Pakistan, Singapore, China, Australia, South Africa, New Zealand, West Africa and the West Indies and North America. In the higher ranks however, non-ethnic contractors still outnumber ethnic foreigners and ethnic non-whites.

The contracting market in the UK is well established. It does not show any signs of declining, or being crushed by foreign competition. Even as the Philippines[18], Dubai[19], Mauritius[20] and other countries expand their IT capabilities, the UK contracting market – if anything – is also growing and expanding. There has never been a better time to join the ranks of IT contracting in the UK, as there is now.

Web site usage

The use of a Web site to promote your services and to list and display your CV can be a great idea if executed properly. It need not be a complex Web site, a single page or a few pages will suffice to highlight all you need to present yourself effectively.

The following are a few points to keep in mind when using a Web site to promote your IT contracting services:

---

[18] The Philippines plans to overtake India as a major call centre provider to the world in the next five years. It is currently more popular with American companies than Indian companies.

[19] Dubai continues to expand Dubai Internet City. It currently houses Microsoft, Oracle, HP, IBM, Compaq, Dell, Siemens, Canon, Logica, Sony Ericsson and Cisco, to name just a few.

[20] Mauritius aims to raise its status as an ICT hub within the next five years.

- Do not include a hyperlinked e-mail address. Use an image instead. This is to stop crawlers and robots that are trawling for e-mail addresses to harvest yours.
- Do not include your personal home address on the site. Everyone, including identity thieves, scammers, crooks and con artists, uses the Internet. Do not give them information to use against you.
- Do not include print quality images of your certificates. If you are using images of your certificates, make sure the images are small and of an unsuitable resolution to be copied.
- Because the whole world can see your site, make sure the details provided are accurate.
- Do not display details of referees on the site. Agencies and Web opportunists could use the details to hound your referees.
- Make sure your site contains adequate disclaimers and usage policies. It is highly unlikely someone viewing the site will sue you; however, make sure you have covered your back against any damages that could result from the use of the content on your site.
- Make sure you have a copyright notice. A simple statement such as, "Copyright © 2007, Joe Bloggs. All rights reserved.", will normally suffice in most cases.
- Make sure you have a means for visitors to contact you. A contact link to a 'contact us' form will suffice. Make sure you have name, e-mail address and comment sections on the form. Telephone number, fax number, mobile number, company name, "Where did you hear about this site?", and address can be optional fields.
- If you are using JavaScript, flash or any other Web technology that would require the visitor to install an extra tool before they view the site, make sure you also offer a plain HTML version of your site. Some of your visitors may not be able to view your site otherwise.

- If you offer a forum or a blog on your site, make sure the contents are in line with your professional IT contracting image. Monitor forums for profanity, pornography and any other unsavoury posts.

You can promote your Web site using META tags and other SEO tools. For details on how to optimise your Web site for maximum visibility, see my other books on these subjects: *META TAGS - Optimising Your Website for Internet Search Engines* and, *Search Engine Optimization (SEO) How to Optimize Your Web Site for Internet Search Engines.*

A Web site is not usually necessary to have for IT contracting, unless you are a programmer, Web designer or other creative-medium contractor. In this case, a Web site may allow you to display your previous projects. This could include Web sites you have designed, programs you have coded and other designs and creations better showcased through the Web.

Today, almost everyone uses the Internet either directly (or indirectly through other peoples' help). The pervasiveness of this incredible medium has shaped and changed our society and this generation.

Agencies

In an ideal world, your next contract would be sourced directly with the client you will be contracted to. However, we do not live in an ideal world, and recruitment agencies serve the needs of clients who do not have the time and/or resources to find, draft and sign contracts, and manage the payment systems required for IT contractors.

Similarly, IT contractors may not have the time, contacts or resources to approach multiple clients, find out their requirements and match themselves with the relevant contracts. Therefore, IT contractors sometimes must turn to recruitment agencies that specialise in these tasks.

Whilst most of the time working with recruitment agents and their agencies will be straight forward, there may be times when the interaction and transaction will not be so smooth. Sometimes problems can stem from the contractor (you), the client or the agency.

We have already seen what problems a contractor may come across, and the rest of this book will cover many more of these possible issues. We have also discussed some of the problems contractors can face with clients (e.g., delayed payment, renewals, rate negotiation and rate changes, contract renewal and termination). In this section we will tackle the types of problems that can stem from using an unscrupulous agent or agency.

I don't want you to think that every agent and agency in the IT contracting business is a crook, a liar or a cheat. That would be untrue. However, the industry, job pressures and reward plans of most recruitment agencies are geared toward results – at almost any cost.

We will discuss why these circumstances have led many recruitment agents to take the crooked path of dishonesty and deceit. The following is a list of the tactics employed by some of these recruitment agents:

- Build their database of candidates.
- Acquire new clients or live roles.
- Sabotage other agents and agencies.
- Interfere with a contractors chances of acquiring a role.
- Undercut rates.
- Undermine renewals.
- Use unfair and restrictive contracts.
- Intentionally submit unqualified applicants for unsuitable roles.

- Make false claims.
- Avoid making, or delay making payments.
- Require candidates to subscribe to their supplementary packages, such as umbrella schemes, indemnity insurance, etc.

CV acquisition

A large part of every recruitment agency is having a large list of potential staff or contractors to place with clients. Every recruitment agency has (or should have) a department that specialises in acquiring CVs and vetting the candidates for suitability of employment placement.

This is not a problem, although it is a challenge for recruitment agencies. Some tackle the goal in an ethical way and some are more "flexible". The flexible agents and agencies may use some or all of the following methods to build their list:

1. **Bogus job ads online** – by placing non-existent roles on recruitment notice boards and job sites, unscrupulous agencies hope to attract new CVs from candidates applying for these roles.
2. **False job ads via email** – this is similar to the previous method, however in this method the agencies add spamming (sending unsolicited emails) to their crimes. By spamming IT professionals with enticing job roles, they hope to build their CV databases.
3. **System update requiring your CV update** – The recruitment agency industry has a very quick staff turnover rate. Some of the agents that leave an agency may steal part (or all) of the agencies' staff database in order to assist the agent in starting up an agency of their own, or keep in contact with their old candidates. You may find that new agencies you have never

heard about, suddenly email or contact you asking for your availability and an up-to-date CV. This is really not a problem for the contractor, as it simply means one more agency is working to source you work, however, it does highlight an unscrupulous act which should be a warning for later dealings with that agency.

Phishing for clients

If you are new to IT contracting, be prepared to receive calls from agents phishing for details of active roles and new clients. There are two main phishing methods employed. Examples of their tactics are as follows:

1. Where are you working now and for whom do you report?

    When an agency calls, the telephone conversation will normally go something like this:

    "Hello John,
    Yeah, I am just calling to ask if you are available because we have some roles that might be suitable for you.
    Tell me where are you working now?
    Oh yeah, I know them, I have some contractors placed with them. Who are you reporting to there, let me see if it's the same guy I deal with.
    Is it Joe Bloggs?
    No?
    Who are you working for then?
    How is that role going, do they look like they will be needing more staff soon?
    Okay John, where were you working before that, who were you working for there?
    Who did you deal with in HR...?"

You may be starting to get the gist of this type of call. It seems harmless, however, it may turn nasty down the line. The agent could call your manager or HR and harass them, making it difficult for you to get a decent reference from them.

2. Asking for your references.

With this method, the agent will pretend to have a role you would be suitable for. However, before he can put you forward to the client, he will insist on two or more references from your previous contract roles. If you fall for this ruse, you will only discover it after he either never gets back to you, or he calls you to say the role has been filled by someone else.

Looking busy

Sometimes a recruitment agency's business plan rewards agents even if they are not selling. This could be in the form of a good basic pay, before a performance bonus is added. Other companies reward their agents for booked appointments and meetings. When this is the case, some unscrupulous agents will schedule meetings with clients and candidates just to look busy.

The two main methods employed are as follows:

1. Asking you to come to the recruitment agency office for an interview with a consultant, before your CV is passed to the client.
2. Taking you and/or the client out for a meal, drinks or other forms of entertainment. We cover this point in more detail in the next section.

In the case of the unplaced candidate meetings, this is often an excuse to acquire reference contact details as well as waste an hour of the candidates time. In all the time I have been contracting, I have never secured a role after any pre-interview meeting. In fact, in every case, the promised interview with the client never materialised.

Whilst this could be just a coincidence, it highlights the fact that these meetings, before you are put forward to the client meetings, are not necessary preceding an interview. In fact, my policy now is that if the agent wants to see me, they can meet me at the client's site, just before the interview.

The client and the placed candidate meetings are often an excuse for unscrupulous recruitment agents to get out of the office, get a free meal and/or drinks at the expense of their agency. I have even heard of other meetings at unsavoury establishments, obviously arranged for the sole entertainment of the agent. In one case, a female contractor was taken to a gentlemen's club for drinks by an unscrupulous agent.

If you decide to entertain these invitations, read the next section (Agency hospitality considerations), on how to maintain your professionalism at these meetings.

Don't get me wrong, not all meetings with recruitment agents are a waste of time. Legitimate agents also schedule these meetings, however, in their case they will be actively building relationships and seeking new business with the clients, and checking on the progress of their placed candidates. Similarly, some agencies legitimately do require to see all candidates before placing them with a client. They may be contractually bound by this.

However, be aware of the unscrupulous practices and do not waste too much of your job hunting time with these meetings, especially if the agents have previously shown you signs of having no integrity.

Sabotage

The recruitment business can be very competitive and sometimes downright cutthroat. You may get involved with some of these battles during your career as an IT contractor. Therefore, be aware of how these wars can work against you. The following highlights several of the major dangers:

1. Inter-agency wars – this can occur where rival agencies or agents attempt to steal a client (or placement opportunity), from a competing company. Agents will use some of the following methods to achieve this end:

    *   Discourage you from rival agencies by highlighting negatives about them. The agent might tell you horror stories about the rival agency's accounting system, pay cycles, reputation, track record, financial stability, etc.
    *   Put you off from rival contract roles by highlighting (or inventing) bad things about the client or role. An example is when an unscrupulous agent tells you that a client is a bad employer, client's business or future is uncertain or not secure, the site is too far to commute, the pay rate is too low for you, the length of the contract is too short and will not roll, etc. They will always follow this with how the role they have to offer is better in every way for you.

    Unscrupulous agents will also try to undermine your position with a client by offering them a competing candidate, through one of the following:

- Undercutting a rival agency's candidate by offering a cheaper contractor.
- Opportunity scuttling – telling the client that a contractor is unsuitable for the role, compared to another candidate.

The best way to avoid being embroiled in these agency/agent wars is never to divulge where your CV has been forwarded to, or with whom you have been recently interviewed by. Some of the information that unscrupulous agencies attempt to gather through phishing, may be used against you in these wars.

Misrepresentation

In an ideal world your recruitment agent would always have your interest at heart. He/she would constantly be keeping an eye out for your next availability date, and seamlessly connecting you with the next role when your current role comes to an end. The reality is often far from this ideal.

In all the contracts I have undertaken, I have seldom ever secured my next role through the same recruitment agency. In fact, it often seems that as soon as they place you with a client, recruitment agents forget about you. You will find the following treatment is prevalent among the more unscrupulous recruitment agents:

1. The passive agent – this agent does as little as possible for their commission. They may advertise roles, however, once you answer the job adverts, they seem to be very passive about pushing your case. Similarly, once they eventually place you in a contract role, they do not actively

negotiate extensions, nor pursue improvements to your rate during contract renewal.

2. Dropping you for a higher rate contractor – some agents lose interest in their lower rate candidates, preferring to spend more of their time on higher rate candidates.

3. Dropping you for a lower rate contractor – in competitive markets, some agents will avoid contractors asking for higher rates of pay in favour of those prepared to take the lowest rates possible. Cheap candidates often produce inferior results, and require more training than higher paid, experienced contractors. Whilst cheaper contractors can improve an agents chances of placing candidates with clients, it also is one of the fastest ways an agent can lose a client.

Encouraging CV doctoring

Some recruitment agents will go to any lengths to get their unsuitable candidates looking more suitable for a role. Some of the more unscrupulous agents will encourage contractors to do some of the following:

1. Change the job titles of your previous roles to better fit a requirement.

2. Change the job descriptions on your CV to better match a requirement.

These are the acts of unscrupulous agencies and agents. If you are asked to doctor your CV to better suit a particular role, note the name of the agent and the agency, avoid using them in the future, and definitely avoid giving them any contact details from your previous, current or future placements.

Technical tests

Whilst most technical tests for contract roles are conducted at the client's site during the interview process, you will occasionally come across technical tests offered by the recruitment agency. This is especially true for roles recruiting for a lot of people, as in a rollout or similar project. These tests are arranged by the client to scrutinize the staff being recruited. However, in an attempt to get more of their candidates in, some unscrupulous recruitment agents will employ some of the following tactics:

1. Give the technical test to candidates to finish in their own time.
2. Give candidates hints to the answers.
3. Give candidates a list of "possible" questions that might turn up in the test.
4. Give candidates multiple chances to get the right answers.
5. Doctor the technical test results presented for their candidates.

I have personally experienced all the above and know of many other contractors who similarly have been offered these shortcuts (and unfair assistance in technical tests. In the face of it, you may be wondering what is wrong with getting a little help. The answer to this will be apparent when you find yourself in a role with others whose skills are far inferior to yours, but who are also commanding the same rate as you get. In the end, these low skilled, inexperienced contractors give IT professionals a bad name, reputation and force all our rates unfairly lower. Avoid agents that practice this type of cheating.

Contract

As an IT contractor, you are bound by what is declared and specified in your contract. Make sure you read your contract carefully. Unscrupulous agencies use this document to manipulate contractors in many ways. The following are some of the tricks they employ:

1. Changing the original terms without notification – this can occur after you attend the interview and secure the role. The terms you may have originally (verbally) agreed to with the agent, may not be the same specified in the contract offered.

2. Changing length of role from original agreement – unscrupulous agents will often lie about the length of a role, so as to entice you into taking it. However, once you receive the contract, you may find that the length specified on it may be shorter (or longer) than you were led to believe.

3. Changing notice period – often recruitment agencies set out their contracts in a manner so as to secure their position with the client, but leave you unprotected. One such technique is to offer no notice period or an extremely short one from the client to you. However, no notice period will be allowed from you to the client. Thus, you cannot leave until the contract ends but the client can terminate upon short notice. These terms are mostly used by agencies to tie contractors down. You will find that the agency/client contract is more fairly worded, allowing the same notice period on both sides.

4. Changing payment period – a weekly payment run verbally agreed upon, may turn into a monthly payment cycle on your contract.

5. Changing overtime rate – time and half or double time for hours and weekends verbally agreed, may turn out to be different on the contract.

6. Changing travel requirement – a verbally agreed paid travel, accommodation and/or other expenses may turn out to be unpaid on the contract.

7. Not specifying expenses, calculations and inclusions – not specifying expense rates on the contract is another way unscrupulous agencies will try to avoid being bound to compensate you.

8. Switching the agency's name on the contract – unscrupulous agencies who are outsourced, subcontracted through other agencies, or simply source staff for outsourcing firms, may try to verbally hide this from you. They will normally do this because it highlights the fact that your rate is even lower than normal due to the multiple agents involved, each taking their commission from your contracting rate. They cannot omit this information from the contract, however, as it is a legal and binding document.

The key point to remember concerning your contract is to check it very carefully for all the details, as listed above. Do not sign any contract until all the discrepancies are corrected to your satisfaction.

Selling your details

Some agencies act as brokers of your CV and/or personal details, to other third parties. Whilst this may be unethical or even illegal in some cases, it is a practice that still continues among unscrupulous agents and agencies. Be aware that every time you send out your details to an agency, you are exposing yourself to one or more of the following:

1. Distribution or sale of your CV to third parties.
2. Sale of your email address to spammers.
3. Sale of your CV and address details to market researchers.
4. Sale of your address for junk mailers and direct mailing.
5. CV sale and distribution for new recruitment Web site..
6. CV and/or contact details sale for new recruitment agency database building.

Be careful to whom you send your personal details. Make sure you have read their privacy document and agree to their terms and conditions of use and distribution of your personal details.

Commissions

Agencies charge commissions for their work. They sometimes also offer commissions to people for helping them find and place new candidates. The average agency rate is between 20% and 25% of the contractor's gross rate, including VAT. Some agencies charge as low as 10% whilst some others may charge as high as 40%.

As a contractor, you will never see this figure, it is subtracted before the you receive your pay. Agencies can vary this commission rate wildly at times, however, you should always ask (in writing) how much the agency rate is for your contract, as some unscrupulous agencies will try the following tricks:

1. Charge a high agency rate and pay a low contractor rate – some dishonest agencies do not operate with a fixed rate for all contractors. They operate a variable rate dependent upon how low they can source a contractor.

2. The myth of the inflexible agency commission – most agencies would like you to think that their commission rates are inflexible. This is not true. All commission rates are flexible under the right circumstances. If the agency wants to secure a new client bad enough, they may even go as far as charging no commission at all, believing that the placement would be the first of many. Similarly, most agencies will accept a small drop in commission, if it means not doing so, would lose them the role to a rival.

3. Avoiding paying finder's fees – agents earn their bonuses and commissions from finding candidates to fill client requirements. They are obliged to share this commission if they alone were not responsible for the headhunt. Of course, all agents will try to avoid paying this commission wherever possible, therefore, they will offer to buy you a drink or simply thank you for helping. Do not settle for this. Always pre-agree the share of the commission, before you offer to help place a candidate. Remember, you are also running a business, and this commission is a revenue source.

Harassment

Because you will hardly ever see your recruitment agent, you may never experience the following problems, however, be aware that these problems do occur and guard against them as best as you can. Remember, keep your relationship with your agent professional and business – based. Female contractors should be especially mindful of devious tactics by some agents. Be careful of socialising with your agent, unless it is for business purposes only. It may also be advised to have a third party (your colleague or a representative of the client), present when meeting after-hours. Whenever possible, only meet in day time or public places and depart the meeting sober to remain safe.

The following are some of the issues I hope you never have to deal with concerning your recruitment agent:

1. Sexual – an agent may take a shine to you and do one or more of the following:
    a) Abuse your contact details.
    b) Use sexual innuendos when speaking to you.
    c) Annoyingly flirt with you.
    d) Make physical contact with you.
    e) Attempt to get you intoxicated.

    Report all cases of unprofessional behaviour to the proper authorities concerning sexual abuse by a recruitment agent. Either report the incident to his/her superiors or, if the matter is more serious, report it to the police. However, you are a professional and deserve to be treated with respect. Therefore, never feel that you must tolerate unwelcome advances, and be quick to let the agent know that his or her behaviour is unprofessional and thus, unacceptable.

2. Abuse of privacy – You may also be harassed by an agent via any of the following:

    a) Email
    b) Messaging/chat
    c) Phone
    d) Meetings

    Some agencies, can be a bit "heavy". I have even had one threaten me because I refused to accept a contract after attending an interview. One agent called a friend of mine eighteen times in 2 hours, and sent her numerous emails as well as used her email address to sign her up to spam sites to generate a stream of junk mail, (which still fills her email account today).

If you are experiencing these types of problems from an agent, first, ask (or demand), that the agent stop the harassment. Second, block them whenever possible from communicating with you, and cease communicating with them. If that fails, report them to their superiors or if the harassment is more serious, file a report with the police and retain any documentation you may have, to support your case against the offender.

Agency hospitality considerations

Some agencies offer hospitality lunches, evenings out or restaurant meals. Whenever these events do not make you lose contracting income, and if you have the time to attend them, you should. Thoroughly enjoy yourself without losing your professional edge. Remember that even the recruitment agent is monitoring your professionalism at all times. If you are out of control after a few drinks, he will be cautious about sending you to his most important client.

If your manager and other staff from the organisation are also invited, be even more careful. You are no longer there to enjoy yourself. You are there to sell yourself. Make sure you leave the event with your professionalism and integrity intact.

Normally, these events degenerate into drunkenness. It is better for you depart early, than stay until the last minute and be part of the show.

Before this, you may find these events great for networking, meeting the recruitment agency representatives and networking with other contractors, and your manager's superiors. Keep your ears open, you may hear of an opportunity you can exploit to your businesses advantage at a later time.

Keep it professional; avoid any activity that degrades your professionalism or integrity. If the group starts talking about going to an adult club, or some other sordid venue, excuse yourself from the excursion and say your farewells. It is hard to maintain your professionalism after you share such an experience with anyone.

Technical Considerations

As you work in IT, you will be required to follow certain standards and procedures. This will relate to industrial standards, knowledge sharing, documentation and handovers. It is important you understand what these standards and professional practices are, and what they are attempting to achieve in order to adhere to them correctly. In doing so, you will more likely increase your value as an IT contractor.

Documentation

The myth that you lock in your value to a client by hoarding knowledge is misguided. Firstly, a client will only tolerate your selfish habit as long as it does not cost the organisation money. As soon as the costs of your actions become apparent to the right managers and executives, you will find your role quickly ending with the organisation.

Most large organisations recognize and monitor their IT risks. It is dangerous for one person to hold all the knowledge concerning a key IT component of an organisation. An organisation will not leave itself exposed like this for long. Eventually they will take action to eliminate the risk. This may end your contract, if you were the guilty party.

Conversely, the myth that you are helping to end your contract by documenting your work to assist other people to understand what you do and how to do it, is also misguided. Organisations seldom terminate people who are taking action to help them become more efficient, save money and be more profitable.

Documenting helps you in several ways. These are as follows:

- Helps you analyze how you do things and how systems and processes work.
- Helps you to quickly refer to notes, saving you time in getting information on processes and information.
- Helps you to train and show new people how to do things.
- Assists you during renewal time, by showing the client that you have the foresight, professionalism, discipline and motivation to document your work to assist the team.
- Helps you to argue your case for a rate increase.
- Helps management to acquire new ways of monitoring resultant work – this will likely lead to an expansion of your role, therefore, further securing your role and renewal.

For the client, documentation helps them to:

- Standardize their processes, thereby minimizing or eliminating errors.
- Train new staff more quickly.
- Save time, and thereby save money.
- Quickly identify where processes are inefficient.
- Allows for easier delegation of tasks and processes.
- Improves management's visibility of process bottlenecks and arrears needing more resources and /or training.

When you document your work, you not only cover your back, minimize your errors, speed your work, and assist yourself in training others; you also help the client see more of your value to the organisation.

ISO 9001 and other standards

International Organisation for Standardization (ISO) is an international standards creation body. The ISO 9001:2000 is their current quality management systems standard. ISO 9001:2008 will replace it next year. However, the new standard promises not to be much different from ISO 9001:2000. The ISO 9001 are a set of standards that set out:

- A set of procedures that cover all key processes in an organisation.
- Monitoring processes that ensure they are adhered to and implemented.
- A means of record keeping of key processes, procedures and activities.
- A method of checking output for defects, and correcting or taking appropriate corrective action when necessary.
- A means of regularly reviewing individual processes, and the quality of the system itself for effectiveness.
- A way of facilitating continual improvement.

The earlier versions of ISO 9001 were paper intensive and produced mountains of documentation and records. ISO 9001:2000 allowed software and computer systems to replace many process documents. As computer systems, software programs and Web based smart forms facilitate the ISO 9001:2000 standards, it is necessary to learn more about ISO 9001, and how IT relates to it.

Refer to http://www.iso.org for more details about ISO 9001:2000.

We shall briefly look at some basic requirements of the standard.

- Documentation of business procedures – the formal documentation of all business critical processes, and the businesses process itself.

- Software based or paper based documentation record of key processes in the business.
- Document control – version revision and authorization procedures must exist on all documents – whether paper or software.
- System and processes review and monitoring through software based reviews, or meetings to ensure continued effectiveness and adherence to the standards.
- Record keeping – software is used to provide security, monitoring, time and date stamp, author details, storage, backup and offsite storage of backup media. Normally to reduce costs, the backup tapes are cycled.
- Implementation of process and software and systems upgrades, version updates, security patches and controlled process refinement.

The ISO 9001 standard allows organisations to control their documents, limit their risk of losing knowledge on key business processes, as well as focus on the business process itself. It allows an organisation to create clear guidelines on how processes should be undertaken, and introduces many ways that computer and software systems can assist in achieving and maintaining these standards.

Knowledge sharing

During the many contracts you will most likely undertake in your IT career, you will acquire a wealth of knowledge. How you share this knowledge will determine how high you will rise in an organisation. It is said that, "a rising tide raises all ships." I firmly believe in the wisdom of this saying. By offering others a hand up, you create many hands that can push you higher, however, by withholding your help and knowledge, others will also withhold theirs and you may be offered less assistance to advance.

Help your clients to become more effective, efficient and profitable and they will in turn help your company be more profitable. Withhold your full help from your clients and they in turn will do the same to you. You may find that your contract ends where a renewal and rate increase should have been.

If you are a developer, do not write bad code simply to inspire your employer to retain you to fix or maintain it. Similarly, if you are a project manager, do not hide behind reports and meetings, avoiding the real issues and results in favour of delay tactics and blame pointing.

Seek to empower others with knowledge. This frees you to concentrate on more pressing issues, as well as allowing someone else to undertake the task. Do not be so busy stopping others from moving ahead that you yourself stand still. Free yourself from your current position by empowering others to undertake you current burdens, allowing you to soar higher.

Handing over

You should always seek to hand over properly, before you leave a long-term role. It is unethical and unprofessional to leave a mess behind you upon your exit from a contract. Make sure your replacement or managers understand exactly what you were doing, what was completed and what remains to be finished, what issues are outstanding and who or what you are still waiting to hear back from.

Forward or give access to, all your work-related e-mail and postal communications to your replacement or manager. Clean your work area of non-business related materials, paperwork, personal effects and rubbish. If it complies with the company policy, set your e-mails to 'out of office', and forward or leave a message on your phone advising of your absence. Include details of your replacement for the new contact.

Finally, depart as you arrived; professionally. Avoid ruining your reputation and professionalism at the last minute by acting unprofessional at your farewell party. Remember, you are in a business and the people all around you are potential future customers. Return all security passes, phones, pagers, laptops, remote access secure ID cards, etc., and make sure that your timesheets and invoices to the agency or HR are up to date and correctly submitted before you leave the site.

Chapter 5
Investing for Financial Freedom

- Enterprise Investment Scheme (EIS)
- Individual Savings Accounts (ISAs)
- Venture Capital Trusts (VCTs)
- Corporate Venturing Scheme (CVS)
- Child Trust Funds (CTFs)
- Government & Corporate Bonds
- Index-Linked National Savings Certificates
- National Savings Children's Bonus Bonds
- Premium Bonds
- Fixed Interest National Savings Certificates
- Friendly Society Plans
- En Primeur Wine
- Property

Investing for Financial Freedom

The key to successfully amassing enough wealth to comfortably retire from contracting lies in effective financial planning. If you spend as much as you earn, you will never be free from your employment. However, saving is simply not enough, investing is the key. You have to make your money earn you the money to live on.

Many contractors love what they do; however, you have to be realistic – you can't contract into the grave. The time will eventually come when you are invited to interviews and dismissed, simply because you do not have a single non-grey hair on your head. Ageism laws have improved greatly however, the reality still stands that organisations prefer to hire younger staff.

Planning for your inevitable retirement is therefore wise and sensible. This starts with saving a sizable fraction of your income in a secure investment – preferably a tax free vehicle.

We have already looked at private pensions and life insurance policies. The former is essential for all IT contractors, whilst the latter is essential for all IT contractors who are concerned about the well-being of beneficiaries in the event of death.

Consult an independent financial advisor and purchase adequate life and health insurance coverage. Similarly, purchase a private pension and contribute as close to the maximum as you are allowed.

Next, turn to other tax-free vehicles such as those discussed next.

After exhausting these tax exempt vehicles, you can then turn to property, funds, stocks and shares, metal (e.g., gold and silver, etc.), precious stones (coloured diamonds, etc.), fine wine, collectables and offshore investments. Please see *The Ultimate Guide to Total Financial Freedom (Volumes 1, 2, 3,*

4, and 5) for more information on all these investment vehicles, and more.

Let us now take a quick look at the tax-exempt investment options available in the UK. The following is a list of what we will cover next:

- Enterprise Investment Scheme (EIS).
- Individual savings accounts (ISAs).
- Venture Capital Trusts (VCTs).
- Corporate Venturing Scheme (CVS).
- Child Trust Funds (CTF).
- Government & corporate bonds.
- Index-Linked National Savings Certificates.
- Fixed Interest National Savings Certificates.
- National Savings Children's Bonus Bonds.
- Premium Bonds.
- Friendly Society Plans.
- En Primeur Wine.

Tax laws change and other countries have different vehicles, please consult an independent financial advisor for more local and current information.

Enterprise Investment Scheme (EIS)

First introduced in 1994, the Enterprise Investment Scheme (EIS) was introduced to encourage individuals to invest. This was intended to help alleviate the problems faced by certain companies, in raising equity finance.

Your reward for risking your investment in these small, higher-risk trading companies, is income tax relief for new equity investments by external investors and business angels in qualifying, unquoted companies and capital gains tax exemption on disposal of shares.

This investment vehicle came with its own limitations and rules, however; investors who own more than 30% of the companies' shares were exempt from the tax savings. Later, in April 1998, capital gains tax reinvestment relief was merged with EIS to create a new, unified scheme allowing individuals (and some trustees) to defer the capital gains tax arising on their chargeable gains. They achieved this by investing the gain in qualifying companies[21].

Furthermore, investors can receive 20% tax relief on investments under £400,000 in any tax year. Relief is available only for new investments into new, ordinary shares in qualifying companies. All profits qualify for exemption from capital gains tax. Investors must hold on to these shares for at least 3 years to obtain income tax relief in full. If the company is wound up for a genuine commercial reason, this rule can be overlooked.

If you became a paid director on or after the date you purchased your shares in a qualifying company, you could qualify for income tax relief on your investment – if you were previously unconnected with the company, or involved in its trade. Furthermore, (as previously mentioned), you must not

---

[21] Qualifying EIS companies must be unquoted at the time the shares are issued to investors – and trade through at least a three-year period afterwards – and the money raised by the issue of shares must be employed in a qualifying business activity as follows: trades and research and development, intended to lead to a qualifying trade.

The following activities do not qualify as trade: dealing in land or shares; money lending, insurance and other financial activities; dealing in goods, other than ordinary wholesale and retail trades; leasing or letting assets on hire, except certain ship-chartering activities; and receiving royalties or licence fees (other than those attributable, broadly, to intangible assets created by the company), farming and market gardening, forestry, property development and operating or managing hotels, guesthouses, nursing or residential care homes.

Participation is limited to companies with gross assets of no more than £7 million immediately before raising funds under the scheme, and no more than £8 million immediately afterwards.

own more than 30% of the company in order to enjoy the tax break.

Additional information can be found at the following Web pages; www.hmrc.gov.uk/eis/eis-index.htm, or upon request from your local tax office. Potential investor inquiries and companies seeking scheme approval should contact the Small Companies Enterprise Centre in Cardiff on 029 2032 7400 or e-mail enterprise.centre@hmrc.gsi.gov.uk.

Individual Savings Accounts (ISAs)

ISAs were first introduced in 1999 and replaced TESSAs[22] and PEPs[23]. The ISA is a tax friendly investment wrapper that can be used to wrap cash, stocks and shares. A life insurance component was originally included; however, from April 2005 onwards, the life insurance component was merged with the stocks and shares component. The following are the main features of ISAs:

1. The annual subscription limit is £7,000, of which no more than £3,000 can go into cash and the remaining £4000 into stocks and shares.
2. The account is completely free of income and capital gains tax.
3. There is no statutory lock-in or minimum subscription.
4. The account is guaranteed to run tax free until 2010.
5. Everyone has the same opportunity to subscribe to the new savings account, irrespective of the value of their previous PEP and TESSA holdings.
6. The capital from maturing TESSAs can be transferred into the cash component of an ISA.

---

[22] Tax-Exempt Special Savings Account, a type of bank account in the United Kingdom.
[23] The Personal Equity Plan was a form of tax-privileged investment account in the UK.

7. Neither the annual subscriptions to TESSAs nor any maturing capital transferred to an ISA, will count against the annual subscription limit for the new ISA account.

Maxi ISAs incorporate both components, whilst Mini ISAs include only one component. Therefore, you can subscribe to two Mini ISAs in any tax year but not to both a Maxi ISA and a Mini ISA in the same tax period. Furthermore, you are only allowed a single ISA manager for Maxi ISAs, whilst with mini ISAs you can select different ISA managers for each component.

Stake Holder ISAs were introduced from April 2005, and replaced the CAT standard[24]. This laid down a set of voluntary standards designed to help investors find ISAs, which offer fair charges, easy access and decent terms. Please visit http://www.hmrc.gov.uk/stats/isa/menu.htm for more (and current) information.

Venture Capital Trusts (VCTs)

The Venture Capital Trust (VCT) scheme was introduced in 1995 to increase the supply of finance to small, unquoted higher-risk trading companies. It was designed to encourage individuals to invest in these companies indirectly through VCTs.

VCTs are companies that invest in small trading companies listed on the Stock Exchange. They are similar to investment trusts. VCTs must be listed on the Stock Exchange and can invest up to £1 million per year in each qualifying company in their portfolio. They are exempt from corporation tax on any capital gains arising on disposal of their investments. Therefore, by investing in a VCT, you too, avoid paying taxes on your investment.

---

[24] CAT stands for Individual Savings Accounts (ISAs) which have reasonable Charges, easy Access and fair Terms.

VCTs are restricted to investing at least 70% of their holdings into 'qualifying holdings'[25]. Each VCT has up to three years to meet this criterion.

You can invest up to £200,000 into a VCT. All investments into VCTs are entitled to claim 30% income tax relief, as long as these investments are held for 3 years or more. Similarly, no income tax is payable on VCT dividends. Reinvested dividends or profits from your VCT will attract capital gains tax; however, no capital gains tax is payable when you sell your ordinary shares holding in VCTs.

For information on Venture Capital Trusts, visit http://www.hmrc.gov.uk/guidance/vct.htm.

Furthermore, information on levels of investment in VCTs, and which VCTs are currently raising funds, please see http://taxshelter.systematicmarketing.com or contact them via phone at 0044 (0800) 339 999.

Corporate Venturing Scheme (CVS)

The Corporate Venturing Scheme (CVS), in essence are the corporate versions of VCTs. CVSs were introduced after public consultation and took effect from 1 April 2000. It encourages companies to invest in small, higher-risk trading companies, just as the EIS scheme is intended for individuals. CVS investments get corporation tax relief and can defer capital gains on profits and dividends invested in 'qualifying companies'.

To qualify for investment via CVS, a company must be unquoted at the time the shares are issued to investors and throughout a period of at least three years afterwards, the

---

[25] Qualifying Holdings consists of newly issued shares or securities – these can include loans of at least five years – in companies similar to those that would qualify for the Enterprise Investment Scheme (EIS).

company must exist for the purpose of a qualifying trade, and must not be under the control of any other company. Furthermore, the money raised by the issuance of shares, must be used in a qualifying business activity within strict time limits.

Qualifying business activities comprise not only trades but also research and development, which are intended to lead to a qualifying trade (the same as is required for EIS). Investment is limited to companies with gross assets up to £7 million immediately before raising funds under the scheme, and up to £8 million immediately afterwards.

Corporation tax relief is charged at 20% on CVS investments; however, to qualify, the investment must be in new, ordinary shares in qualifying companies and held for at least 3 years. Exemptions to this rule only apply if the company invested in is wound up before the 3 years deadline.

Similarly, there is no limit on the amount invested. You can also defer tax on the gains by investing in a qualifying company, as long as some corporation tax relief has also been obtained.

Visit http://www.hmrc.gov.uk/guidance/cvs.htm for more details. Potential investors and companies seeking scheme approval can contact the Small Companies Enterprise Centre on 0044 (029) 2032 7400 or via mail at:

Small Company Enterprise Centre
Centre for Research and Intelligence (CRI)
Ty Glas
Llanishen
Cardiff CF14 5ZG
United Kingdom

Child Trust Funds (CTFs)

All UK born and resident children[26] who are entitled to Child Benefit will receive £250 from the HMRC into a Child Trust Fund savings account. An additional payment of £250 is made for children in low income families. A further payment is made by the government upon the child reaching seven years old.

The fund matures when the child turns eighteen years of age. Until then, the funds in the CTF are inaccessible. After eighteen years of age, the child can withdraw the tax-free funds for any purpose.

The fund is opened via a voucher from the government. However, if parents do not claim the voucher within a year of issue, the HMRC will automatically open an account on behalf of the child by selecting a CTF provider from a rotating list. The following is a list of the key features of the CTF:

- Only your child may withdraw the funds from the CTF when he/she turns 18.
- All funds and profits made by the CTF are tax exempt.
- HMRC issues a £250 voucher to help start each child's CTF account (children in families receiving Child Tax Credit (CTC), with a household income not greater than the CTC threshold of £14,495 for 2007/'08 will receive an extra payment).

---

[26] Qualification is as follows:
- Your child was born on or after 1 September 2002.
- Your child lives in the UK.
- You receive Child Benefit for your child.
- Your child is not subject to immigration control.
- Children of Crown Servants (those working on behalf of the British Government and Armed Forces posted overseas) are treated as being in the UK.

- Additional investments up to a maximum of £1,200 each year can be saved in the account by parents, family or friends.
- Investments are one-way until the child turns eighteen, only then can withdrawals be made, and only by the child for any purpose he/she may choose.
- Investment decisions concerning how CTF funds are invested can be made by the child after they turn sixteen.
- At the age of seven, HMRC will make a direct payment of £250 into the CTF, with children in lower income families receiving an additional £250.
- Parents can choose the type of CTF account they want for their child.
- Account types and providers are changeable within the life of the CTF.
- Your child's CTF and contributions into it, will not affect any benefits or tax credits you receive.

There are three main types of Child Trust Fund (CTF) accounts:
- Savings – offers a fixed or variable interest rate (low risk, unlimited management charges).
- Shares – offers a rate of return equal to the securities invested in; (can go up as well as down – medium risk with unlimited management charges).
- Stakeholder – invests in qualifying companies; (higher risk, although spreads the risk by investing in a portfolio of companies – limited management charges to no more than 1.5% per annum).

You could also elect to have your CTF only invest in what is called 'ethical[27]', or even Sharia law[28] compliant investments.

---

[27] Investments observing ethical standards such as fair trade standards, not trading in arms, tobacco, alcohol or forced/child labour.

For more information on CTFs, visit the official Web site at http://www.childtrustfund.gov.uk or call 0845 302 1470 (if calling from within the UK), or 00 44 1355 359002 (if calling from abroad), or 0845 302 1489 (for Welsh speakers between 8:30 AM and 5:00 PM, Monday thru Friday). You can also write to:

Child Trust Fund Office
Waterview Park
Mandarin Way
Washington
NE38 8QG

Government & Corporate Bonds

Bonds are 'I owe yous' (IOUs) or loans to companies, local authorities or the government. They usually pay a fixed rate of interest each year and aim to pay back the capital at the end of a stated period. Corporate and government bonds are traded on the stock market, so their value can rise, as well as fall. Derivatives of these bonds are also traded, allowing buyers, speculators and bond sellers to trade bond futures.

There are six main categories of bonds. These are as follows:

1. Government bonds – UK government bonds are called 'gilt-edged' bonds, whilst other countries call theirs 'treasury bonds'. They are sometimes regarded as the safest bond investments, because the government of the country insures them. They also attract no capital gains taxes.
2. Supranational bonds – These are bonds issued by large multinational institutions, such as the European Investment

---

[28] Based on Islamic values – no pornography, alcohol, tobacco or gambling related investments.

Bank (EIB) and the World Bank. As such, they are regarded as the safest bond investments and normally have high credit ratings.

3. Corporate bonds – A corporate bond is issued by a company and is usually the riskiest type of bond investment. This is because companies are more susceptible to economic problems, mismanagement and competition than governments or large multinational institutions. However, corporate bonds can also be the most profitable, fixed-income investment. They generally reward investors well for the extra risk. Usually, the lower the company's credit rating is, the higher its bond interest rate will be.

4. Zero coupon bonds – These do not pay periodic interest like normal bonds. They allow investors to avoid paying income tax before maturity of the bond. However, when sold, they attract capital gains taxes.

5. Index-linked bonds – The rate of inflation is linked to the periodic interest (coupon) and capital redemption of this type of bond. When interest rates are high, it is wiser to purchase this type of bond so that you can lock in the high interest rate in the bond coupon.

6. Convertible bonds – companies who also offer other products that the bond can be exchanged for, normally issue these. In some cases, it is exchangeable for the companies' other products.

Normally, the longer the investment term is, the higher the interest rate associated. As bond prices move with changing interest rates, it is best to wait until times of higher interest rates, to buy bonds. Selling bonds on the secondary market at low interest rate periods, especially when the equity markets are underperforming, is likely to see the greatest profits. You can always re-enter the market during high interest rate and low equity market performance periods.

You can invest in gilts or bonds within an ISA and even within your private pension. There are rules associated with holding gilts or bonds in your ISA. In the case of gilts – they have to mature after five years from the date they were purchased and placed within the ISA.

Government bonds are perhaps the safest bonds to buy. However, not all governments are in the same secure position as the UK, America, Australia, Japan, or the EU member countries.

Standard & Poor's, Moody's and Fitch are private rating companies that rate bonds in terms of the issuer's financial strength, or their ability to pay a bond's principal and interest in a timely fashion. As an example, Standard and Poor's uses the following rating system:

- AAA and AA: High credit-quality investment grade.
- AA and BBB: Medium credit-quality investment grade.
- BB, B, CCC, CC, C: Low credit-quality (non-investment grade), or "junk bonds".
- D: Bonds in default for non-payment of principal and/or interest.

Whilst there are specialist fund managers and investors who hand pick and trade junk bonds, I wouldn't advise you to do so. They usually promise very high interest rates; however they also often default on payments. Knowing which junk bond is most likely not to default on payment of principle and/or interest, is often guesswork. If you must invest in bonds, stick to the safer, high credit-quality investment grade bonds.

Bonds, like stocks, are also traded in the secondary markets at exchanges and thus their values rise and fall daily due to long-term interest rate speculation. You can save money by buying bonds from the secondary market; however, if you do not understand this process you are better to purchase your gilts/bonds, as they are released by the government in the primary market or through a fund.

You can purchase gilts/bonds via gilt funds or bond funds. These funds; however, do not offer a maturity date, as they buy and sell bonds of different maturity dates, in the aim to make money from this trade. Therefore, when you choose to liquidate, you may not get as much as you might have if you had liquidated on the maturity date of the individual bonds in the fund.

To buy bonds yourself, you must use a stockbroker. For gilts, you can use the Bank of England Brokerage Service. Tel: (01452) 398080. For more information on funds that invest in gilts and bonds, visit www.trustfund.com.

Index-Linked National Savings Certificates

Another tax-free investment vehicle worth considering, especially during periods of rising interest rates, is the Index-Linked National Savings Certificates. Anyone seven years or older can buy one. The minimum purchase price is £100 and the maximum per issue is £15,000.

Because they are linked to the Bank of England's interest rate, the interest earned from them will always stay ahead of inflation, as measured by the Retail Prices Index (RPI). Furthermore, all interest from these certificates is free from UK income and capital gains tax.

Unfortunately, because inflation is constantly fluctuating, the maturity value of Index-Linked National Savings Certificates cannot be pre-calculated. However, you can be sure that the maturity value will have more buying power.

Visit www.nsandi.com/products/ilsc/rates.jsp for a listing of the current interest rates.

National Savings Children's Bonus Bonds

This is a debt product. In essence it is a loan to the government on behalf of your children (or child). The units cost a minimum of £25 and a maximum of £3000, and can be invested for anyone under sixteen years of age, and by anyone over the age of sixteen. Units can be purchased for five-year terms until the child's twenty-first birthday.

The interest rate is guaranteed during the five-year term and a bonus is guaranteed at the end. The current interest is 5.10% and currently issue (issue 24) earns a bonus of £2.22 per unit. The bonds are free from income and capital gains tax on the interest and bonuses. If you sell within the first year, you forfeit interest on your child's bonds. Terms and conditions apply and you should check these before buying them. See the following Web site for further details: (www.nsandi.com/products/cbb/termsandconditions.jsp).

Premium Bonds

Premium Bonds are a lottery style investment with monthly draws, and tax-free cash prizes. The prizes range from a £1,000,000 jackpot, and has over a million other prizes ranging from:

- £50
- £100
- £500
- £1,000
- £5,000
- £10,000
- £25,000
- £50,000
- £100,000

The bonds can be purchased in £100 units up to £30,000, and the more units you own, the higher your chances of winning the big prizes.

Everyone over the age of sixteen can buy this type of investment, and parents and grandparents can also buy Premium Bonds for children under the age of sixteen. There is no maturity date and the bonds can be held for as long as you want.

Because this type of investment only pays interest through the prize draws, there are no guarantees on interest growth. However, the reality is, that the longer you are invested in Premium Bonds the more likely you will be of winning prizes that add up to a respectable tax-free return.

Currently, the tax rate used to determine the monthly profit sharing through the prize draw is 4% per annum. The chance of winning per £1 is 21,000 to 1.

You can cash in your Premium Bonds at any time without penalty. Remember also, that inflation will gradually reduce the buying power of your capital over time.

Fixed Interest National Savings Certificates

Fixed Interest Savings Certificates are lump sum investments that earn guaranteed rates of interest over set periods of time – normally two or five years. Like the Index-Linked National Savings Certificates, they can be purchased for or by anyone aged seven or over. They also guarantee a fixed interest rate (currently 3.95% — equivalent gross rate of 4.94% basic rate, 6.58% higher rate) for the two-year product, and 3.85% (equivalent gross rate of 4.81% basic rate, 6.42% higher rate) for the five-year product.

Unlike the Index-Linked National Savings Certificates, the Fixed Interest National Savings Certificates value at maturity, can be accurately calculated beforehand. It is wise to only invest in this product during high interest rate periods – preferably just before interest rate cuts begin.

Correctly anticipating interest rate changes accurately is not so easy, however, the market normally knows when the economy is heading for recession, and a rate cut is expected. A rate cut, after many multiple rate hikes, is often a good signal to buy this product.

Again, Fixed Interest National Savings Certificates are free of UK income and capital gains tax. The minimum you can invest is the price of a certificate; currently £100 with a maximum per issue of £15,000.

Friendly Society Plans

Friendly societies are mutual organisations that provide socially beneficial, financial services. They played a bigger part in society before the modern day government and large institutional products for investments and insurance appeared on the market.

They are also afforded special tax treatment by the government on most of their products, and generally have a different philosophy towards your money, than the conventional insurance companies or financial institutions.

Friendly Societies offer the following products:

- **Investments** – Tax exempt savings, endowments, unit trusts, ISAs, bonds, child savings, funeral expenses and the new Child Trust Funds.
- **Medical Insurance** – Medical cash, sickness, permanent health/income protection, private medical, critical illness.
- **Life Insurance** – Term and/or whole-of-life assurance.
- **Pensions** – Personal pensions.
- **Annuities** – Compulsory purchase annuities, impaired life annuities, purchased life annuities.

- **Other Products** – Discretionary benefits, social and benevolent activities, general insurance and other services via subsidiary companies.

See Appendix 1 on page 428 for a list of friendly societies. Not all Friendly Societies offer all these products; however, you can find these products offered across the range of Friendly Societies in Appendix 1. Contact the organisations from the list for more information on what they offer.

En Primeur Wine

In the UK, investing in bonded fine wines can be one of the best long-term investments you can make. Bonded wines are wines that have not yet had the duty and VAT paid on them. Furthermore, they must be stored in a HMRC approved, bonded warehouse to remain in this tax-free state.

As an En Primeur investor, you must not take the wines out of bonded storage. The bonded wines can be sold directly from the warehouse; avoiding ever paying the duty, VAT, capital gains tax or income tax on the profits. This will save you a fortune, allowing you to have all the advantages of the capital gain tax free. The only stipulation is that you do not trade the wines as a business.

Wine investment has a long history – almost 250 years. Over this period, the French Bordeaux red wines have dominated the investment grade wine market, with annual profits of 25% on the best vintages, not being uncommon.

Buying wine on bond allows you to enter the market at one of the cheapest entry points. This is often before the wine is bottled or shipped. The profits you will earn – buying fine wine this way – are far greater than in buying wine retail. Similarly, as mentioned before, you will avoid income and capital gains taxes as well as VAT (17.5%) and duty; which, in the UK is levied at £1.25 per 75 cl (11.5% abv). Therefore, for a twelve bottle case of wine, the duty could be up to £15. Wine duties are levied as follows:

Wine and made-wine:
- 1.2% abv to 4% abv = £1.66 per 75cl
- 4% abv to 5.5% abv = £1.25 per 75cl
- 15% abv to 22% abv = £0.38 per 75cl
Still wine and made-wine:
- 5.5% abv to 15% abv = £0.53 per 75cl

There are no minimum or maximum investment amounts, however, there are a few unavoidable charges you need to consider. Namely: insurance, transportation and storage. You need to insure your wines before moving them and also whilst they sit in storage. You can cancel this insurance after you liquidate the investment (pardon the pun).

Insurance and storage fees vary. Expect to pay anything from under £10 a year to up to £50 a year, per twelve bottle case of 75cl bottles. There are a few wholesalers and retailers who own and offer storage facilities and insurance services. Before using their storage facilities, check to make sure your name will be on the cases, and not just the third-party company's name. This will help you to avoid problems later on.

It is best to arrange your own storage account with one of the large storage companies, such as Octavian (www.octavian.co.uk). Octavian storage includes insurance for each case. Their world class storage facilities across the country, offer controlled lighting, humidity, temperature, no vibration, case maintenance and insured transportation. They also produce regular case audits detailing the condition of your stored wines.

The En Primeur vintages are released around the second quarter of the year. To select the wines to invest in, wait for the wine tasting results. There are several tasting notes and ratings sources you can refer to. Try Jancis Robinson, Robert

Parker and Berry Bros. & Rudd; (www.jancisrobinson.com, www.erobertparker.com, and www.bbr.com).

Berry Bros. & Rudd rates wines out of a scale of 20 – only buy wines rated as 18 ½ or better, out of 20. Similarly, Robert Parker rates his wines out of 100, again aim for 94 or better out of 100. Once you have a short list of the latest En Primeur wines, you can contact a distributor, wholesaler or wine agent to source you the En Primeur from the Bordeaux chateaus. See http://www.wine-searcher.com/merchants.lml for a list of merchants who supply wines, worldwide.

Wine Funds

You can also invest in a wine investment fund. These normally charge a management fee of around 1.5% to 2.5% to cover trading transportation, storage and insurance, as well as the management of the account. They also allow you to set-up regular payments to purchase more units in the fund.

A performance fee, (generally 15% to over 25%) is also charged by most fund managers. A minimum, being normally £5,000 to £25,000, and a maximum investment amount, may apply. See http://www.wineinvestmentfund.com and http://www.wamllp.com/funds.aspx for examples of how these investments could work for you.

Cellar Plans

If wine funds are too expensive for your pallet, you could try a cellar plan. These plans are wine portfolios managed by wine investment companies and wine merchants. Wine cellar plans generally charge less than 2% for management, and no performance fee; however, they tend to charge you over the market price for the wines in your portfolio, as well as charging high fees for storage, transportation and insurance.

See Berry Bros. and Rudd's Cellar Plan on their Web site (www.bbr.com/GB/about/cellar-plan) or Wine Investment (www.bbr.com/GB/about/investment.lml), or Premier Cru's Managed fine wine cellar (www.premiercru.com/index.html).

Property

As a contractor, buying a home to live in, or buying a home for investment purposes can be challenging; however, getting a mortgage as a contractor use to be even worse in the nineties. Today, contractors can secure the same mortgages as permies.

The key to getting a mortgage quickly, lays in retaining the services of a specialist contractors' mortgage advisor. These specialist advisors have a better understanding of contracting and the type of incomes a contractor commands. They will also have contacts in the industry who can streamline your application to sympathetic and understanding mortgage underwriters.

Today, many mortgage service providers and brokers offer a variety of mortgage options to the IT contractor. The following are some of the typical offers and packages available:

- Competitive mortgage schemes with High Street lenders.
- Quick mortgages, often within weeks of starting your first contract.
- Mortgages requiring no deposit and in some cases, allowing you to borrow up to 125% of the value of the property.
- A choice of mortgages such as, cheque-book mortgages, offsets, fixed and discounted schemes.
- Services that repair your bad credit history and allow you to still buy a home.
- Let-to-buy mortgages.

- Buy-to-let mortgages.
- Overseas mortgages.
- Commercial mortgages.

Fee versus commissions

The Financial Services Authority (FSA) rules in the UK, now require your independent financial advisor (IFA) to offer you the option of paying a fee, in place of them receiving a receiver's fee (0.5% to 2%). This fee is normally 0.6% of the loan secured. If you opt for the fee option, the broker or IFA is obliged to refund you any excess commissions they receive from lenders. Similarly, you should not feel pressured to buy insurance from your lender or through your IFA or broker.

Many lenders will work with an annualized contract rate, and lend you up to four times your income. This avoids the need for company accounts; something you may not have if you are new to contracting.

Avoid lenders who offer extended loyalty clauses and hefty associated fees. This is often the case when your deposit is less than ten percent of the purchase price of the property.

Furthermore, bear in mind that your home may be repossessed if you do not keep up repayments on your mortgage. You should also arrange for a term life insurance cover to protect your home, in case of your death. You can also arrange other insurances to cover the payment of your mortgage interest only, in case you become critically ill.

If you are looking for an IFA who specialises in IT contractor mortgages, conduct a search on Google for, "IT Contractor Mortgage IFA". Check the validity of the registered IFA's credentials, and search around for the best deal before signing on the dotted line.

Home Information Packs

Since 1 August 2007, the UK government introduced the Home Information Packs or (HIPs), a new requirement for all homeowners seeking to sell their homes. Initially, HIPs were only required for four bedroom homes. However, from 10 September 2007, the requirement was expanded to include three bedroom homes. This pattern is set to continue until HIPs are required by all property sales. Scotland is set to see the introduction of a new and different HIPs to Britain, Wales and Ireland.

Whilst HIPs are not very different from previous documents and information collected during the conveyance process involved in property purchases, it has one new addition which is set to change the dynamics of property price negotiations – the Energy Performance Certificate (EPC).

This certificate is issued after a Domestic Energy Assessor visits your property, collects data and produces your EPC. The EPC will not only tell how efficient the property is, it will make recommendations for improvements to the energy efficiency.

With this certificate, sellers can negotiate their house price, and buyers can likewise negotiate based on how good or bad the EPC report reflects the property's energy efficiency. The buyer can attempt to have the cost of correcting the energy inefficiency of the property discounted off the price of the property.

HIP's prices vary wildly from free to over £600, therefore, shop around for the best deal.

Conclusion

IT is involved in almost every aspect of our lives. The people who create, sell, manage and support IT are creating vast incomes and changing our lives each day. To enter into this market as an IT contractor can be similarly very rewarding; however, for too long, newbie contractors have been misguided, whilst seasoned, contractor veterans have looked on, dismayed, at the damage caused by the uninitiated newbie.

Throughout this book, I have attempted to give you all the information required to enter the contracting market successfully, build your business efficiently, and effectively grow your skills and income progressively.

I have highlighted the importance of integrity, professionalism and hard work in achieving ultimate success in this business. I must stress this again, if you do not want to contract with integrity, professionalism and a hard-work ethic, you will fail abysmally.

The contracting path is not a paved road; this path promises regular heartache at the end of each contract, anxiety when approaching each interview situation, and rapid learning curves in each, new challenging role. That is why the IT industry rewards contractors so highly for their courage, conviction, determination, valour, industriousness and nerve to break free from the permie pack.

Follow the advice and suggestions in this book, by treating your contracting business like the big business it can become. Maximize your efficiency and that of your business, by streamlining and trimming the waste from how you run your business. Cut back spending on non-business growth purchases. Learn to invest in your contracting business by investing into your education and skills training.

Define your path through IT contracting. Set clear goals and start working to achieve these goals ahead of schedule.

Reward your efforts as soon as you have achieved a goal. Do not rest on your laurels, however. Re-set your goals and continue to build your business to even greater heights.

Seek a qualified tax consultant, and together work out how you can legally lower your tax liabilities. Do not just ask for tax advice; be ready and willing to act on it, immediately.

Work on improving your CV's effectiveness and your interview skills. Set a goal to acquire every role for which you interview. Be clear and confident about this, and do not allow any doubt or disbelief to enter into your mind. Your success is greatly dependent on your belief in yourself. Therefore, give yourself the best chance for success; learn to believe in yourself and be confident in your abilities.

The UK market is very healthy for contracting right now, however, other markets can also be lucrative. Before you move to contract in another jurisdiction, acquire all the facts. Take time to investigate thoroughly and visit the country. Talk to other contractors successfully working there; speak to agencies, management companies, accountants and corporate sponsors, and make an informed decision.

If you treat contracting as a business, there is no telling where it will take you. However, if you treat it simply as a job, it will return an average "job" income to you. Therefore, think big, work hard and let this amazing business opportunity allow you to soar.

Appendices

- List of Friendly Societies
- Investments Risk Tables (courtesy of HRMC)
- IT Certification

Appendix 1

List of Friendly Societies

The Children's Mutual
Brockbourne House
77 Mount Ephraim
Tunbridge Wells
Kent
TN4 8GN

Shepherds Friendly Society Limited
Shepherds House
Stockport Road
Cheadle
Cheshire
SK8 2AA

National Deposit Friendly Society Limited
4 Worcester Road
Clifton
Bristol
BS8 3JL

Scottish Friendly Assurance Society Limited
16 Blythswood Square
Glasgow
Scotland
G2 4HJ

Family Investments
17 West Street
Brighton
East Sussex
BN1 2RL

Wiltshire Friendly Society Limited
7 Market Street
Trowbridge
Wiltshire
BA14 8HB

Nottingham Friendly Society
29 Bridgford Road
West Bridgford
Nottingham
NG2 6AU

Compass Friendly Society Limited
Old Bank House--High Street
Odiham
Hampshire
RG29 1LF

Foresters Friendly Society
Foresters House
29/33 Shirley Road
Southampton
SO15 3EW

The Red Rose Friendly Society Limited
Parkgates
52a Preston New Road
Blackburn
BB2 6AH

Royal Standard Friendly Society
43 Replingham Road
London
SW18 5LT

New Tab Friendly Society
34 York Street
Twickenham
Middlesex
TW1 3LJ

Pioneer Friendly Society Limited
County Gate, County Way
Trowbridge
Wiltshire
BA14 7FJ

Rational Shelley Friendly Society Limited
Rational House
64 Bridge Street
Manchester
M3 3DT

Kensington Friendly Collecting Society Limited
1-3 Kengsington Road
Middlesborough
Teeside
TS5 6AL

Coventry Assurance Society
26 Queens Road
Coventry
West Midlands
CV1 3EG

POIS Assurance Limited
Cover House
Hazelwick Avenue
Three Bridges
Crawley
West Sussex
RH10 1PZ

Fire Service Friendly Society
42-44 Roseberry Avenue
London
EC1R 4RN

Friends Indeed Friendly Society Limited
PO Box 18005
London
EC3A 2DA

Anglo-Saxons Friendly Society
Anglo-Saxons Hall
2 Berkley Road
Gravesend
Kent
DA12 2EU

Railway Enginemen's Assurance Society Limited
727 Washwood Heath Road
Birmingham
B8 2LE

The Benenden Healthcare Society Limited
Holgate Park Drive
York
North Yorkshire
YO26 4GG

Rechabite Friendly Society Limited
School House
14 Byrom Street
Manchester
M3 4RB

LondonMidland&ScottishRailwayRunningDeptIn/Soc
c /o Brittish Rail
Room 4A
Crewe Station
Crewe
CW2 6HR

Merseyside Police Benefit Friendly Society
Merseyside Police HQ
Canning Place
Liverpool
L69 1JD

Cirencester Friendly Society Limited
5 Dyer Street
Cirencester
Gloucestershire
GL7 2PP

Manor House Friendly Society Limited
Stag House
Old London Road
Hertford
SG13 7LA

Strand Friendly Society
c/o Arthur Anderson
20 Old Bailey
London
EC4M 7AN

Dentists Provident Society Limited
9 Gayfere Street
Westminster
London
SW1P 3HN

Pension Annuity Friendly Society Limited
59/60 Mark Lane
London
EC3R 7ND

Druids Sheffield Friendly Society
Dove House
181 Brampton Road
Wath Upon Dearne
Rotherham
S63 6BE

Liverpool Victoria Friendly Society Limited
Victoria House
135 Poole Road
Bournemouth
Dorset
BH4 9BG

Grand Order of Israel & Shield of David F/Society
11 The Lindens
Prospect Hill
Waltham Forest
London
E17 3EJ

National Independent Order of Oddfellows F/Society
16 Ashley Drive
Swinton
Manchester
M27 0AX

Leek Assurance Collecting Society
4 Russell Street
Leek
Staffordshire
ST13 5JF

Sheffield Mutual Friendly Society
83 Wilkinson Street
Sheffield
S10 2GJ

Royal Liver Assurance
Royal Liver Building
Liverpool
L3 1HT

United Ancient Order of Druids Friendly Society
c/o Tyrrells
11 Cotham Road South
Bristol
BS6 5TZ

Order of the Sons of Temperance Friendly Society
176 Blackfriars Road
London
SE1 8ET

National Equalized Druids Friendly Society
40 Bronberrie Avenue
Horsforth
Leeds
LS18 5PN

British Benefits Friendly Society Limited
1 Trevor Street
Bedford
MK40 2AB

Transport Friendly Society Limited
9 Betterton Street
London
WC2H 9BP

Civil Service Healthcare Society Limited
Princess House
Horace Road
Kingston Upon Thames
Surrey
KT1 2SL

Original Holloway Friendly Society Limited
Holloway House
Eastgate Street
Gloucester
GL1 1PW

Homeowners Friendly Society Limited
Hornbeam Park Avenue
Harrogate
N Yorks
HG2 8XE

Bacon & Woodrow Friendly Society
Albert House South Esplanade
St Peter Port
Guernsey
Channel Islands
GY1 1AW

British Airways Benefit Fund
Vanguard House S492
PO Box 10 Vanguard Way
Hatton Cross--Hounslow
TW6 2JA

Tunstall Assurance Friendly Society Limited
Station Chambers
The Boulevard
Tunstall
Stoke On Trent
ST6 6DU

Communication Workers Friendly Society Limited
150 The Broadway
Wimbledon
London
SW19 1RX

Police Mutual Assurance Society Limited
Alexandra House
Queen Street
Lichfield
WS13 6QS

Hunt Servants Benefit Society
Parsloes Cottage
Bagendon
Cirencester
Gloucestershire
GL7 7DU

Carolgate Friendly Society
55 South Audley Street
Grosvenor Square
London
W1Y 5FA

The Oddfellows
Oddfellows House
40 Fountain Street
Manchester
M2 2AB

School Teachers Friendly Society
30 Mather Avenue
Liverpool
L18 5HS

Exeter Friendly Society Limited
Lakeside House
Emperor Way
Exeter
EX1 3FD

Bus Employees Friendly Society
1st Floor RDO House
Bancroft Road
Reigate
Surrey
RH2 7RP

Civil Servants Annuities Assurance Society
33 Birdhurst Rise
South Croydon
Surrey
CR2 7YH

Teachers Provident Society Limited
Deansleigh Road
Bournemouth
Dorset
BH7 7DT

Scottish Legal Life Assurance Society Limited
95 Bothwell Street
Glasgow
Scotland
G2 7HY

Universal Brotherhood of Speculative Mechanics F/S
22 Thrayle House
Stockwell Park Estate
Stockwell
London
SW9 0DE

The Dentists & General Mutual Benefit Soc Limited
St James Court   20 Calthorpe Road
Edgbaston
Birmingham
B15 1RP

United Kingdom Civil Service Benefit Society Limited
UK House--82 Heath Road
Twickenham
Middlesex
TW1 4BA

Appendix 2

Investments Risk Tables (courtesy of HRMC)

Low to Medium Risk

Investment	Tax Breaks	Investment Profile	Age limit (years)	Term (years)	Limits on Investment (£s)
Government & corporate bonds	Free of Capital Gains Tax (CGT) only	Fixed income and set value at maturity but variable value otherwise	None	N/A	No limits
Index-Linked National Savings Certificates	Free of income tax at all rates and CGT	Index-linking plus fixed interest rate	7 and over	3 or 5	100 to 10,000
Fixed Interest National Savings Certificates	Free of income tax at all rates and CGT	Fixed interest rate	7 and over	2 or 5	100 to 15,000
National Savings Children's Bonus Bonds	Free of income tax at all rates and CGT	Fixed interest rate for 5 years at a time plus guaranteed bonus	Aged 16 or over investing on behalf of somebody under 16	5	25 to 3,000
Premium Bonds	Prizes are free of income tax and CGT	Prize fund 3.2% pa. (Minimum prize £50, maximum £1 million)	over 16 can also be bought on behalf of under-16s by parents and grandparents.	N/A	100 to 30,000
Cash Mini ISA	Free of income tax at all rates	Variable interest rate	UK Residents16+	N/A	3,000

Medium to High Risk

Investment	Tax Breaks	Investment Profile	Age limit (years)	Term (years)	Limits on Investment (£s)
Friendly Society Plans	Free of income tax at all rates and CGT	Potential for capital growth from a wide range of funds	None	10	Up to £25 per month
Approved Pension Schemes	Tax relief on contributions. The fund is exempt from tax (no reclaim of UK Tax Credits). Partial tax-free lump sum on retirement from age 50	Potential for capital growth from a wide range of funds	All UK residents	Varies - Benefits can start at age 50	Varies
ISAs	Free of income tax at all rates and CGT	Potential for income and capital growth from a wide range of funds	UK residents age 18+	N/A	Varies up to 7,000
Qualifying Life Policies	Policy proceeds paid free of income tax and CGT (but may have an underlying tax)	Potential for capital growth from a wide range of funds	None	Usually 10 + years	Varies

441

High Risk

Investment	Tax Breaks	Investment Profile	Age limit (years)	Term (years)	Limits on Investment (£s)
Enterprise Investment Schemes	Income tax relief at 20% on share subscription Deferral of CGT from other assets, gains free of CGT whilst losses can usually be offset	Potential for income and capital growth from investment in a qualifying unquoted/AIM quoted trading company	None	3 years minimum for tax reliefs	£500 to £200,000 No limit
Venture Capital Trusts	Income tax relief at 40% on subscription for shares up to 5 April 2006, thereafter reducing to 20%, tax-free capital gains and dividends. No tax relief for capital losses.	Potential for income and capital growth from investment in a portfolio of unquoted/AIM quoted trading companies	18	3 years minimum for tax reliefs	Up to £200,000

Appendix 3

IT Certification

3COM

3M0-211	Certified Enterprise LAN Specialist
3M0-212	3Com Certified Enterprise LAN Specialist Final Exam v3.2
3M0-331	3Com WAN Specialist Final Exam v2.0
3M0-600	3Com Wireless Specialist Final Exam v1.0
3M0-700	Certified IP Telephony Specialist v2.5

Adobe

9A0-019	Adobe Photoshop 6.0 Product Proficiency
9A0-031	Adobe Photoshop 7.0 Product Proficiency Exam
9A0-035	Adobe Illustrator CS ACE Exam
9A0-036	Adobe PhotoShop CS ACE Exam
9A0-040	Adobe Premiere Pro
9A0-041	Adobe Acrobat 7.0 Professional Print Production ACE Exam
9A0-042	Prowith Adobe LiveCycle Designer ACE Exam
9A0-043	Adobe Illustrator CS 2 ACE Exam
9A0-044	Adobe Photoshop CS 2 ACE
9A0-045	Adobe InDesign CS 2 ACE Exam
9A0-046	Adobe GoLive CS2 ACE Exam
9A0-061	Adobe Premiere Pro 2.0 Professional ACE Exam
9A0-062	Adobe Encore DVD 2.0 ACE Exam
9A0-064	Adobe Flash Lite 2.0 Mobile Developer
9A0-310	Adobe Flex2 Developer Exam
9A0-311	Certified Macromedia Flash 8
9A0-602	Certified Macromedia Flash MX 2004 Developer
9A0-701	ColdFusion MX Developer Exam
9A0-702	ColdFusion MX 7 Developer
9A0-802	Certified Macromedia Dreamweaver MX 2004 Developer
9A0-803	Certified Dreamweaver8 Developer Exam

APC

PB0-200   NCPI Design

Apple

9L0-003   Apple Desktop Service Exam
9L0-004   Apple Desktop Service
9L0-005   Apple Desktop Service
9L0-060   MAC OS X 10.4 service and support
9L0-205   Apple Portable Service Exam
9L0-206   Apple Portable Service
9L0-207   Apple Portable Service Exam
9L0-400   Mac OS X Help Desk Essentials v10.3 Exam
9L0-401   Mac OS X Help Desk Essentials v10.4
9L0-504   ACTC Mac OS X and Mac OS X Server Essentials v10.2
9L0-505   Mac OS X Server Essentials v10.3 Exam
9L0-506   Apple Certified Technical Coordinator v10.3 Update Exam
9L0-507   Mac OS X Server Essentials v10.4
9L0-508   Apple Certified Technical Coordinator v10.4 Update
9L0-606   System Administration of Mac OS X Clients v10.3 Exam
9L0-607   System Administration using Mac OS X Server v10.3 Exam
9L0-609   Mac OS X Deployment
9L0-610   Xsan Administration v1.1
9L0-611   Directory Services Integration and Administration 10.4
9L0-612   Security Best Practices for Mac OS X v10.4
9L0-613   Podcast and Streamed Internet Media Administration Exam
9L0-614   Mac OS X Server Command and Line Install and Configuration v10.4
9L0-615   Network Account Management v10.1 Exam

BEA

0B0-101	BEA 8.1 Certified Developer: Build Solutions
0B0-102	BEA 8.1 Certified Developer: Portal Solutions
0B0-103	8.1 Certified Developer : Integration Solutions
0B0-104	Certified Administrator: System Administration
0B0-105	Certified Architect: Enterprise Architecture
0B0-108	BEA 9 Certified Administrator: System Administration Exam

BICSI

RCDD	Registered Communications Distribution Designer

CheckPoint

156-210	Check Point CCSA NG
156-215	Check Point Security Administration NGX (156-215.1)
156-310	Check Point CCSE NG
156-315	Check Point Security Administration NGX II (156-315.1)
156-510	VPN-1/FireWall-1 Management III NG
156-915	Accelerated CCSE NGX (156-915.1)

Cisco

350-001	Cisco Certified Internetworking Expert
350-018	CCIE Pre-Qualification Test for Security
350-020	CCIE SP Optical Qualification
350-022	CCIE® Written, Service Provider: DSL
350-023	CCIE® Written: WAN Switching
350-024	CCIE SP IP Telephony Qualification
350-026	CCIE SP Content Networking ENU
350-027	CCIE® Written: Metro Ethernet
350-029	CCIE SP Written Exam
350-030	CCIE Voice Written
350-040	Storage Networking
640-801	Cisco Certified Network Associate
640-802	Cisco Certified Network Associate
640-811	Interconnecting Cisco Networking Devices

640-821	Introduction to Cisco Networking Technologies (INTRO)
640-822	Interconnecting Cisco Networking Devices Part 1
640-861	Designing for Cisco Internetwork Solutions (DESGN)
640-863	Designing for Cisco Internetwork Solutions
642-052	Routing and Switching SE/FE Exam (RSS/FE)
642-053	Routing and Switching SE/FE Exam
642-054	Routing and Switching Solutions for Systems Engineers
642-055	Advanced Routing and Switching for Field Engineers
642-071	Cisco Unity Design and Networking
642-072	Cisco Unity Design and Networking
642-081	Business Ready Teleworker Solution Fundamentals (TELWRKR)
642-091	CRM Express Integration
642-103	Unified Communications for System Engineer
642-104	Unified Communication for System Engineers
642-142	CallManager Express Exam (CME)
642-143	IP Telephony Express Exam (IPTX)
642-144	IP Telephony Express
642-161	IP Contact Center Express Implementation (IPCCX)
642-162	IP Contact Center Express Implementation
642-176	Cisco SMB Engineer
642-291	Network Management
642-311	Cisco Optical SONET Exam (SONET)
642-321	Cisco Optical SDH Exam (SDH)
642-342	Content Networking Exam (CN)
642-351	Storage Networking Design Specialist (CSNDS)
642-352	Storage Networking Support Specialist
642-353	Cisco Storage Network Design
642-354	Cisco Storage Network Support Specialist
642-355	Cisco Storage Networking Design Specialist
642-356	ICisco Storage Networking Solutions Support Specialist
642-371	Foundation Express for Systems Engineers
642-372	Cisco Express Foundation for Systems Engineers

642-381	Foundation Express for Field Engineers
642-382	Cisco Express Foundation for Field Engineers
642-413	Enterprise Voice Over Data Design (EVODD)
642-414	Telephony Design Exam (IPTD)
642-424	IP Telephony Troubleshooting
642-425	IP Telephony Troubleshooting
642-426	Troubleshooting Cisco Unified Communications Systems (TUC)
642-432	Cisco Voice Over IP
642-443	IP Telephony Exam (CPIT)
642-444	IP Telephony Exam
642-445	Cisco IP Telephony for Release 5.0
642-452	Gateway Gatekeeper Exam
642-453	Gateway Gatekeeper
642-481	Cisco Rich Media Communications
642-501	Securing Cisco IOS Networks (SECUR)
642-502	Securing Networks with Cisco Routers and Switches
642-503	Securing Networks with Cisco Routers and Switches
642-511	Cisco Secure Virtual Private Networks (CSVPN)
642-513	Securing Hosts Using Cisco Security Agent
642-521	Secure PIX Firewall Exam (CSPFA)
642-522	Securing Networks with PIX and ASA
642-523	Securing Networks with PIX and ASA
642-531	Cisco Secure Intrusion Detection System (CSIDS)
642-532	Securing Networks Using Intrusion Prevention Systems
642-541	Cisco SAFE Implementation Exam (CSI)
642-542	Cisco SAFE Implementation
642-551	Securing Cisco Network Devices
642-552	Securing Cisco Network Devices
642-564	Security Solutions for Systems Engineers
642-565	Security Solutions for Systems Engineers
642-567	Advanced Security for Field Engineers
642-577	Wireless LAN for System Engineers (WLANSE)
642-582	Wireless LAN for Field Engineers Exam
642-586	Cisco Advanced Wireless LAN for System Engineers

642-587	Cisco Advanced Wireless LAN for Field Engineers
642-591	Implementing Cisco NAC Appliance (CANAC)
642-611	Implementing Cisco MPLS Exam (MPLS)
642-641	Quality of Service Exam (QoS)
642-642	Quality of Service (QOS)
642-651	Cisco Wide Area Applications Services Technical Training
642-652	Cisco Wide Area Application Services Technical Training (TRN-WAAS)
642-661	Configuring BGP on Cisco Routers (BGP)
642-691	BGP + MPLS Exam (BGP + MPLS)
642-801	Building Scalable Cisco Internetworks (BSCI)
642-811	Building Cisco Multilayer Switched Networks (BCMSN)
642-812	Building Converged Cisco Multilayer Switched Networks
642-821	Building Cisco Remote Access Networks (BCRAN)
642-825	Implementing Secure Converged Wide Area Networks
642-831	Cisco Internetwork Troubleshooting (CIT)
642-845	Optimizing Converged Cisco Networks
642-871	Designing Cisco Network Services Architecture
642-891	Composite Exam
642-892	Composite Exam
642-901	Building Scalable Cisco Internetworks
642-964	Cisco Data Center Networking Infrastructure Support
643-531	Cisco Secure Intrusion Detection Systems
644-101	Unified Communications for Systems Engineer (UCSE)
644-141	CallManager Express Exam (CME)
646-002	Advanced Routing and Switching for Account Managers
646-011	Storage Sales Specialist
646-056	Cisco Lifecycle Services Advanced Routing and Switching
646-057	Routing and Switching AM Exam

646-058	Cisco Lifecycle Services Advanced Routing and Switching
646-096	CRM Express for Account Managers
646-102	Wireless LAN for Account Managers Exam (WLANAM)
646-151	Cisco Sales Associate Exam
646-171	Cisco SMB Account Manager
646-202	Cisco Sales Expert Exam (CSE)
646-203	Cisco Sales Expert
646-222	IP Communications Express Account Manager
646-227	Cisco Lifecycle Services Advanced IP Communications
646-228	Cisco Lifecycle Services Advanced IP Communications
646-229	IP Communications Advanced Account Manager
646-301	VPN/Security
646-361	Foundation Express for Account Managers
646-362	Cisco Express Foundation for Account Managers
646-391	Cisco Lifecycle Services Express Exam
646-392	Cisco Lifecycle Services Express
646-401	Wireless LAN
646-411	Network Management AM & SE Exam
646-471	Content Networking Account Manager
646-521	Routing & Switching Exam (RSS)
646-561	Advanced Security for Account Managers
646-562	Advanced Security for Account Managers
646-573	Cisco Lifecycle Services Advanced Security
646-574	Cisco Lifecycle Services Advanced Security
646-588	Advanced Wireless LAN for Account Managers
646-589	Cisco Lifecycle Services Advanced Wireless
646-590	Cisco Lifecycle Services Advanced Wireless
646-653	Cisco Wide Area Application Services for Account Managers
646-967	Cisco Data Center Networking Sales
9E0-851	Customer Response Solution 3.0 Exam (CRS)
CCIE-LAB	CCIE LAB

Citrix

1Y0-222	Citrix MetaFrame Presentation Server with Feature Release 3
1Y0-223	Citrix MetaFrame Presentation Server 3.0: Enterprise Edition Administration
1Y0-251	MetaFrame Presentation Server 3.0: Management and Maintenance for the Enterprise
1Y0-252	MetaFrame® Presentation Server 3.0:Troubleshooting Enterprise Environment
1Y0-256	MetaFrame® Presentation Server 4.0: Administration
1Y0-258	Citrix Presentation Server 4.0:Support
1Y0-259	Citrix Presentation Server 4.5: Administration
1Y0-306	Citrix Access Gateway 4.2 with Advanced Access Control:Admin
1Y0-308	Citrix Access Gateway 4.5 Advanced Edition: Administration
1Y0-310	Citrix MetaFrame 1.0 or 1.1 Administration for UNIX Operating Systems
1Y0-326	Citrix Password Manager 4.0 Administration
1Y0-610	Citrix Core Technologies and Architectures
1Y0-611	Design, Integration and Methodology
1Y0-613	Citrix Access Suite 4.0:Analysis
1Y0-721	Citrix metaframe Secure Acess manager Administrator
1Y0-722	MetaFrame Secure Access Manager 2.2: Administration
1Y0-911	Citrix Resource Manager
1Y0-913	Citrix MetaFrame XP Presentation Server, Enterprise Ed, Feature Release 3: Administration
1Y0-921	Citrix Resource Manager
1Y0-962	Citrix Securing Application Deployment over the Web
1Y0-972	Citrix MetaFrame Password Manager Administration
1Y0-973	Citrix MetaFrame Password Manager 2.5: Administration
1Y0-991	Citrix MetaFrame XP Advanced Admin

1Y0-992   MetaFrame XP Presentation Server, Feature Release 3: Deployment and Support

CIW
1D0-410   CIW Foundations
1D0-420   CIW Site Designer
1D0-425   CIW E-Commerce Designer
1D0-430   CIW Application Developer
1D0-435   JavaScript Fundamentals exam
1D0-437   CIW Perl Fundamentals exam
1D0-441   CIW Database Specialist
1D0-442   CIW Enterprise Specialist
1D0-450   CIW Server Administrator
1D0-460   CIW Internetworking Professional
1D0-470   CIW Security Professional
1D0-510   CIW Certified Instructor
1D0-520   CIW v5 Site Designer
1D0-525   CIW E-Commerce Designer
1D0-532   CIW Web Developer
1D0-538   Object Oriented Analysis and Design (JCERT)

Comptia
220-301   A+ Hardware Technologies
220-302   A+ OS technologies
220-601   A+ Essentials
220-602   IT Technician
220-603   Remote Support Tech designation pathway
220-604   A+ Depot Technician
225-020   CDIA+
225-030   Certified Document Imaging Architech (CDIA+)
EK0-001   E-Biz+
HT0-101   HTI+ Residential Systems
HT0-102   Systems Infrastructure and Integration
IK0-002   I-Net+
N10-002   Network+
N10-003   Network+ (2005)
PK0-002   It Project+
RF0-001   Radio Frequency Identification
Sk0-002   Server+ (2005)

SY0-101	Security+
TK0-201	Certified Technical Trainer (CTT+)
XK0-002	Linux+

Computer Associates

270-132	Certified Unicenter Specialist Engineer
270-231	Certified Unicenter Specialist Administrator

CWNA

PW0-100	Certified Wireless Network Administrator (CWNA)
PW0-200	Wireless Security Professional
PW0-205	Wireless LAN Analysis

Dell

DC0-200	Certified Server Professional
DC0-261	Dell Storage Networking Professional Exam - version 2

ECCouncil

212-77	Linux Security
312-49	Computer Hacking Forensic Investigator
312-50	Ethical Hacker Certified
EC0-232	E-Commerce Architect
EC0-349	Computer Hacking Forensic Investigator
EC0-350	Ethical Hacking and Countermeasures

EMC

E20-040	EMC Technology Foundations
E20-050	EMC Technology Foundations - CLARiiON
E20-060	EMC Technology Foundations - Business Continuity
E20-070	Technology Foundations - SAN
E20-080	EMC Technology Foundations - NAS
E20-090	EMC Technology Foundations - Storage Management
E20-095	EMC Technology Foundations-CAS
E20-097	EMC Technology Foundations-Backup and Recovery

E20-320	EMC Assessment, Planning & Design Exam
E20-322	Technology Architect Solutions Design
E20-330	Business Continuity Implementation
E20-340	CLARiiON Solutions Implementation
E20-350	Network Storage - SAN Implementation
E20-360	Network Storage - NAS Implementation
E20-380	Storage Management Implementation
E20-510	Business Continuity Specialist Exam
E20-512	Business Continuity Specialist Exam for Storage Administrators
E20-520	CLARiiON Solutions Specialist
E20-522	CLARiiON Solutions Specialist for Storage Administrator
E20-530	Network Storage - SAN Specialist
E20-532	Networked Storage SAN Specialist Exam for Storage Administrators
E20-533	Network Storage - NS Specialist Exam
E20-535	Networked Storage - NS Implementation
E20-537	Network Storage - NAS for Storage Administrators
E20-540	Networked Storage - NAS Specialist Exam
E20-570	Networked Storage CAS Specialist Exam
E20-580	Storage Management Specialist
E20-582	Storage Management Specialist Exam For Storage Administrator
E20-590	Backup and Recovery Specialist Exam
E20-593	Backup & Recovery Implementation Exam
E20-597	Backup & Recovery Specialist Exam for Storage Administrators
E20-610	CLARiiON and UNIX Advanced
E20-611	CLARiiON Installation and Troubleshooting Specialist
E20-616	Symmetrix Installation and Troubleshooting Specialist
E20-651	Networked Storage-SAB Installation and Troubleshooting
E20-661	Networked Storage-NAS Installation and Troubleshooting
E20-670	Networked Storage-CAS Installation/Troubleshooting Specialization

E20-815	Business Continuity Expert Exam for Technology Architects
E20-820	CLARiiON Solutions Expert Exam for Technology Architects
E20-825	Networked Storage-SAN Expert Exam for Technology Architects
E20-840	Storage Management Expert Exam for Technology Architects
E20-845	Business Continuity Expert Exam for Implementation Engineers
E20-850	CLARiiON Implementation Engineer Expert
E20-855	Networked Storage-SAN Expert for Implementation Engineers
E20-860	EMC NAS Implementation Engineer Expert Exam
E20-870	Storage Management for Implementation Engineers
E22-106	EMC Legato Certified Availability Administrator (LCAA)
E22-128	EMC Legato Certified Networker 7.x Administrator (LCNA)
E22-141	EMC Legato Certified NetWorker 7.x Specialist (LCNS)
E22-181	EMC Legato Emailxtender Administrator Exam
E22-183	EMC Legato Certified EmailXtender and EmailXaminer Administrator (LCEXA)

Enterasys

2B0-011	ES Router Configuration
2B0-012	ES Switching Edition 4.0
2B0-015	ES Wireless
2B0-018	ES Dragon IDS
2B0-100	ESE Recertification
2B0-104	Enterasys Certified Internetworking Engineer(ECIE)
2B0-202	ES NetSight Atlas

Exam Express

| EE0-011 | ATG Certified Relationship Management Developer |
| EE0-021 | ATG Commerce Certification Exam |

EE0-071	Actuate Certified Professional Developer - Release 7
EE0-200	Certified LANDesk Engineer 8.5
EE0-411	Voice XML Application Developer Exam
EE0-425	Packeteer PacketShaper 6
EE0-501	F5 BIG-IP V4
EE0-502	BIG-IP Advanced
EE0-503	F5 3-DNS v4 Exam
EE0-505	F5 Fire Pass v5
EE0-511	F5 BIG-IP V9 Local traffic Management
EE0-512	F5 BIG-IP V9 Local Traffic Management Advanced

Exin
EX0-100	ITIL Foundation Certificate in IT Service Management

Extreme Networks
EW0-100	Extreme Networks Associate
EW0-200	Extreme Networks Associate
EW0-300	Extreme Networks Specialist

FILE MAKER
FM0-301	Filemaker 7 Developer Essentials
FM0-302	FileMaker8 Developer Essentials

Fortinet
925-201b	Principles of Network Security and FortiGate Configurations

Foundry
FN0-100	Foundry Networks CNE
FN0-103	Foundry Networks Certified Network Professional
FN0-125	Foundry Networks Certified Network Engineer (FNCNE)
FN0-202	FNC4-7E Foundry Networks Certified Layer 4-7 Engineer
FN0-240	Foundry Networks Certified Layer4-7 Professional
FN0-405	Foundry Networks Certifed Network Professional

FUJITSU

FD0-210	Implementing HP XP1024/128 Array Solution Fundamentals

Guidance Software

GD0-100	Certification Exam For ENCE North America
GD0-110	Certification Exam for EnCE Outside North America

HDI

HD0-100	Help Desk Analyst (HDA)
HD0-300	Help Desk Manager
HD0-400	HDI Qualified Customer Support Specialist
QQ0-100	Help Desk Analyst (HDA)
QQ0-200	HDI Qualified Help Desk Senior Analyst
QQ0-300	Help Desk Manager
QQ0-400	HDI Qualified Customer Support Specialist

Hitachi

HH0-110	Hitachi Data Systems Storage Foundations - Enterprise Exam
HH0-120	Hitachi Data Systems Storage Foundations - Modular Exam

HP

HP0-055	Implementing HP ProLiant Servers
HP0-064	HP BladeSystems C-Class Solutions 1
HP0-066	Advanced Lights-Out
HP0-081	OpenVMS System Administration
HP0-087	Planning and Designing HP Enterprise Solutions
HP0-091	HP-UX System Administration
HP0-092	HP-UX Advanced System Administration
HP0-093	HP-UX High Availability
HP0-094	HP-UX Networking and Security
HP0-176	Design & Implementation of HP SIM for ISS Solutions
HP0-205	Supporting the Enterprise Modular Library
HP0-207	ProCurve Adaptive Edge Fundamentals

HP0-216	Enterprise Systems Management
HP0-236	Supporting SAN Infrastructure & Solutions
HP0-238	Supporting the MSA1000 and SCSI JBODS
HP0-239	Supporting the Modular Array(MA) Storage Family
HP0-242	Supporting the ESL9000
HP0-244	Advanced Backup Troubleshooting & Tuning
HP0-255	Planning & Design of HP Integrity Mid-Range Server Solutions
HP0-264	Servicing HP Monochrome LaserJet Printers, High-End
HP0-265	Servicing HP Color LaserJet MFP Printers,High-End
HP0-276	OpenVMS Security Administration
HP0-277	OpenVMS Version 7.x to 8.2 Migration
HP0-302	Planning and Designing HP Superdome Server Solutions
HP0-310	HP OpenView Performance Insight (OVPI)
HP0-335	HP OpenView Operations (OVO) I 8.x UNIX
HP0-336	Identity Management
HP0-345	HP OpenView Operations (OVO) II8.x UNIX
HP0-380	Planning & Design of HP Integrity Entry-Level Server Solutions
HP0-382	Servicing HP Mid-Range Integrity Servers
HP0-390	Planning & Deployment of HP BladeSystem Solutions
HP0-402	Implementing HP Enterprise Virtual Array Solutions
HP0-409	OVIS/OVTA - OpenView Internet Services and OpenView Transaction Analyzer
HP0-417	Storage Essentials Fundamentals 5.0
HP0-427	Implementing & Supporting HP Storage Essentials v5.0
HP0-429	Installing & Supporting Standard HP SAN Environments
HP0-436	OpenVMS v7 Network Administration
HP0-438	Advanced SAN Architecture
HP0-450	OpenVMS v7 Advanced Administration. Performance, and Support

HP0-460	Implementing HP XP12000/10000 Solution Fundamentals
HP0-461	Supporting the Enterprise Virtual Array (EVA) Storage Family
HP0-490	HP BladeSystem p-Class Solutions I
HP0-500	HP ProLiant Server Maintenance
HP0-505	Planning and Designing HP Enterprise Solutions
HP0-512	Replication Solutions for the HP Storage Works EVA
HP0-517	HP Integrity Server Multi-OS Installation and Deployment
HP0-536	PC Workstations System Professional Test
HP0-606	Data Protector Basics for Windows
HP0-628	Implementing HSx80 Compaq Storage Solutions for UNIX
HP0-632	OpenView Network Node Manager I (7.X) Essentials
HP0-633	OpenView Network Node Manager II (7.X) - Customization
HP0-634	OpenView Network Node Manager III (7.X) Advanced
HP0-645	Implementing HP ProLiant Servers
HP0-648	ProCurve Adaptive Edge Fundamentals
HP0-655	Data Protector 5.5 Basics for Windows
HP0-656	Data Protector 5.5 Basics for UNIX
HP0-660	NonStop Kernel Basics (Level 1)
HP0-678	Implementing HP Enterprise Virtual Array Solutions
HP0-680	Implementing Enterprise Virtual Array
HP0-683	Implementing HP ProLiant Servers
HP0-697	HP ProLiant Systems Technologies
HP0-714	HP OpenView Storage Area Manager Fundamentals
HP0-719	HP OpenView Operations (7.x) Windows
HP0-725	Enterprise Integration and Management of HP ProLiant Servers
HP0-727	HP OpenView Operations (7.x) Windows
HP0-728	Replication Solutions for HP StorageWorks EVA
HP0-753	HP OpenView Service Desk 4.5

HP0-754	HP OpenView Operations I (7.x) UNIX
HP0-755	HP OpenView Operations II (7.x) UNIX
HP0-756	HP ProCurve Secure Mobility Solutions
HP0-757	HP ProCurve Security
HP0-758	HP ProCurve Mobility
HP0-759	HP ProCurve Combined Security and Mobility
HP0-760	NonStop Kernel Advanced (Level 2)
HP0-762	NonStop Kernel Platform Support
HP0-771	Designing & Implementing HP Enterprise Backup Solutions
HP0-773	Installing & Supporting Standard HP SAN Environments
HP0-780	NonStop Structured Query Language (SQL)
HP0-785	Install, Maintain, Upgrade NonStop Hardware
HP0-790	HP ProCurve Routing Switch Essentials v5.21
HP0-791	HP ProCurve Convergence
HP0-794	Implementing Windows Server 2003 on HP ProLiant Cluster Solutions
HP0-795	HP ProLiant Systems Management
HP0-797	Enterprise Integration and Management of HP ProLiant Servers
HP0-803	Implementing MSA Storage Solutions
HP0-815	Advanced SAN Architecture
HP0-841	Designing and Implementing HP SAN Solutions
HP0-891	Implementing HP XP1024/128 Array Solution Fundamentals
HP2-005	HP ProLiant Server Maintenance
HP2-056	HP ProCurve Sales Professional
HP2-061	HP ProLiant Server Maintenance

HUAWAI

GB0-180	Huawei Certified Network Engineer
GB0-280	Constructing Enterprise-level Routing Networks
GB0-320	Constructing Enterprise-level Switching Networks
GB0-360	Design Enterprise-level Networks

Hyperion

4H0-002	Hyperion Essbase 5 Certificaton
4H0-020	Hyperion Certified Solutions Architect - Hyperion System 9 Planning 4.1
4H0-028	Hyperion Certified Professional - System 9 Planning 4.1
4H0-110	Hyperion Essbase 6
4H0-200	Hyperion Enterprise 5 Certification
4H0-435	Hyperion Financial Management v3.51 exam
4H0-533	Hyperion Planning V.3.3.1
4H0-712	Hyperion Essbase 7x Certifcation Exam

IBM

000-041	Programming with IBM Enterprise PL/I
000-062	IBM System p5 Virtualization Technical Support AIX 5L V5.3
000-070	System x Sales V3
000-071	IBM xSeries Technical Principles V7
000-074	System x Windows 2000/2003 Installation and Performance Optimization V2
000-076	System x Sales V4
000-077	xSeries Technical High Performance Servers V2
000-078	eServer BladeCenter
000-093	IBM WebSphere Process Server V6.0, System Administration
000-094	Application Development with IBM WebSphere Integration Developer V6.0.1
000-142	XML 1.1 and Related Technologies
000-154	Web Developer
000-180	p5 and pSeries Enterprise Technical Support AIX 5L V5.3
000-190	AIX Basic Operations V5
000-191	IBM Certified Specialist - pSeries AIX System Administration
000-215	IBM WebSphere Commerce V5.6, Implementation
000-216	IBM WebSphere Commerce V6.0 Administration
000-217	WebSphere Commerce V6.0.Application Development

000-222	P5 and pSeries Administration and Support for AIX 5L V5.3
000-228	p5 and pSeries Technical Sales Support
000-229	IBM System p Solution Sales V5.3
000-232	pSeries Administration and Support for AIX 5L V5.2
000-233	AIX 5L Installation,Backup and System Recovery
000-234	AIX 5L Performance and Systems Tuning
000-235	AIX 5L Problem Determination
000-236	AIX 5L Communications
000-237	pSeries HACMP for AIX 5L
000-238	p5 and pSeries Technical Sales Support
000-239	p5 Solution Sales
000-252	WebSphere Application Server Network Deployment V6.0
000-255	Developing with IBM Rational Application Developer for WebSphere Software V6.0
000-256	Application Development with IBM Rational Application Developer for WebSphere Software
000-257	Enterprise Application Development with IBM Rational Application Developer V6.0
000-259	i5 iSeries Solution Sales V5R3
000-266	AS/400 RPG IV Programmer
000-267	AS/400 RPG IV Developer
000-268	eServer i5 iSeries RPG ILE Programmer
000-285	Certified Associate Developer Developing with IBM WebSphere Studio, V5.0
000-286	Application Development with IBM WebSphere Studio, V5.0
000-287	Enterprise Application Development with IBM WebSphere Studio,V5.0
000-288	Developing Web Services with WebSphere Studio Application Developer V5.1
000-293	WebSphere InterChange Server V4 and Toolset Deployment
000-294	WebSphere Business Integration Message Broker V5
000-296	IBM WebSphere MQ V5.3 Solution Design
000-297	WebSphere MQ V5.3 Solution Development

000-298	IBM WebSphere Business Integration Message Broker V5 System Administration
000-299	WebSphere Business Integration Message Broker V5, Solution Design
000-324	IBM eserver zseries technical. version 1
000-340	WebSphere Application Server V5.0, Basic Administration
000-341	WebSphere Application Server V5.0, Multiplatform Administration
000-347	Websphere Portal V5.0, Deployment And Administration
000-348	IBM WebSphere Portal V5, Application Development
000-351	i5 iSeries Single Systems Administrator V5R3
000-355	DB2 iSeries System Administration V5R2
000-356	iSeries System Command Operations V5R2
000-357	i5 iSeries Multiple Systems Administrator V5R3
000-365	i5 iSeries LPAR Technical Solutions V5R3
000-382	Open Systems Storage Solutions, Version 2
000-385	High End Tape Solutions, Version 3
000-386	High-End Disk Solutions, Version 3
000-387	IBM Open Systems Storage Solutions, Version 3
000-388	Storage Sales, Version 6
000-389	IBM TotalStorage Networking and Virtualization Architecture, Version 2
000-397	IBM WebSphere Portal V5.1, Deployment and Administration
000-399	IBM WebSphere Portal V5.1 Application Development
000-415	IBM WebSphere IIS DataStage Enterprise Edition v7.5
000-416	WebSphere IIS QualityStage v7.5
000-424	IBM zSeries Sales V1
000-425	System z Sales V2
000-426	System z Technical Support V2
000-442	Content Manager V8
000-443	DB2 Content Manager V8.3
000-444	IBM Content Management On Demand
000-484	Enterprise Connectivity with J2EE V1.3

000-486	Object-Oriented Analysis and Design with UML Test
000-512	DB2 UDB V7.1 Family Fundamentals
000-513	DB2 Administration for Windows, Linux & OS2
000-514	DB2 UDB V7.1 Family Application Development
000-516	DB/2 Administration for OS/390
000-594	IBM Tivoli Enterprise Console V3.9 Implementation
000-630	ClearCase for Windows
000-631	ClearCase for UNIX
000-632	ClearQuest
000-633	Object Oriented Analysis and Design - Part 1
000-634	Object Oriented Analysis and Design - Part 2
000-635	Fundamentals of Rational Rose
000-636	Requirements Management with Use Cases - Part 1
000-637	Requirements Management with Use Cases - Part 2
000-638	Rational RequisitePro
000-639	Rational Unified Process
000-640	Test Management
000-641	Robot
000-642	XDE Tester
000-643	UCM Essentials
000-645	XDE.NET
000-648	Rational Portfolio Manager
000-664	SOA Fundamentals
000-670	xSeries Sales V2
000-671	xSeries Technical Principles
000-677	xSeries Technical High Performance Servers
000-695	Fundamentals of Enterprise Solutions Using
000-700	DB2 UDB V8.1 Family Fundamentals
000-701	IBM DB2 UDB V8.1 for Linux, UNIX, and Windows Database Administration
000-702	UDB V8.1 for z/OS Database Administration
000-703	DB2 UDB V8.1 Family Application Development
000-704	UDB V8.1 for Linux, UNIX and Windows Advanced Database Administration
000-705	DB2 Business Intelligence Solutions V8
000-706	UDB V8.1 for Linux, UNIX, and Windows Database Administration Upgrade

000-710	U2 UniData Administrator
000-711	U2 UniData V6.1 for UNIX & Windows Administration
000-713	U2 Family Application Development
000-714	U2 UniVerse V10.1 for UNIX & Windows Administration
000-715	Alphablox
000-730	DB2 9 Family Fundamentals
000-731	DB2 9 DBA for Linux UNIX and Windows
000-733	DB2 9 Application Developer
000-740	IBM Storage Networking Solutions Version 1
000-741	IBM High-End Disk Solutions. Version 4
000-742	IBM Open Systems Storage Solutions Version 4
000-743	IBM Storage Sales, Version 7
000-745	Storage Networking Solutions Version 2
000-746	High-End Disk Solutions Version 5
000-747	Open Systems Storage Solutions Version 5
000-748	IBM Storage Sales Version 8
000-751	Retail Store Technical Solutions
000-771	IBM Tivoli Provisioning Manager with Orchestration V3.1 Implementation
000-773	IBM Tivoli Data Warehouse V1.2 Implementation
000-774	IBM Tivoli SAN Manager V1.3 Implementation
000-775	Applying Fundamentals of IBM Tivoli On Demand Automation
000-778	IBM Tivoli License Manager V2.1 Implementation
000-779	IBM Tivoli Workload Scheduler V8.2 Implementation
000-787	IBM Tivoli Business Sys MGR V3.1 Distributed Implementation
000-798	IBM Tivoli Monitoring For Transaction Perf V5.2 Implementation
000-799	Tivoli Storage Manager V5.3 Implementation
000-816	IBM Certified for On Demand Business Solution Sales
000-817	IBM Certified for On Demand Business - Solution Design V2
000-818	IBM Certified for On Demand Business-Solution Advisor V2

000-851	i5 Series Linux Solution Sales V5R3
000-852	i5 iSeries Windows Integration Solution Sales V5R3
000-853	i5 iSeries WebSphere Solution Sales V5R3
000-854	System i IT Simplification - Windows Linux and AIX 5L Solution Sales Version 1
000-855	i5 iSeries Domino Technical Solutions V5R3
000-856	eServer i5 iSeries Linux Technical Solutions V5R3
000-857	Windows Integration for iSeries Technical Solutions V5R3
000-858	i5 iSeries WebSphere Technical Solutions V5R3
000-859	iSeries Solution Sales (including eServer i5 & i5/OS V5R3)
000-866	i5 iSeries Technical Solutions Designer V5R3
000-867	i5 iSeries Technical Solutions Implementer V5R3
000-868	i5 iSeries Technical Solutions Designer V5R4
000-869	System i Technical Solutions€"Implementation (including i5/OS V5R4)
000-870	IBM Tivoli Configuration Manager V4.2.2 Implementation
000-872	IBM Tivoli Storage Manager V5.2 Implementation
000-873	IBM TotalStorage Productivity Center for Data V2.1 Implementation
000-875	IBM Tivoli Federated Identity Manager V6.0 Implementation
000-876	IBM Tivoli Access Manager for e-business V6.0 Implementation
000-877	IBM Tivoli Identity Manager V4.6 Implementation
000-881	IBM Tivoli Storage Manager V5 Administration
000-883	IBM Tivoli Composite Appl Mgr for WebSphere v6.0 Implement
000-884	IBM Tivoli Identity Manager Express V4.6 Specialist
000-888	IBM Tivoli Workload Scheduler V8.3 Implementation
000-890	IBM Tivoli Monitoring V6.1 Implementation
000-891	IBM Tivoli Federated Identity Manager V6.1
000-892	IBM Tivoli Netcool/xSM (ISM V2.4 and SSM V3.2) Implementation

000-900	IBM Tivoli TotalStorage Productivity Center V3.1
000-910	Managing and Optimizing Informix Dynamic Server Databases
000-915	System Administration for IBM Informix Dynamic Server V9
000-917	System Administration for IBM Informix Dynamic Server V10
000-990	IBM WebSphere Business Modeler Advanced V6.0 , Business Analysis and Design
000-993	WebSphere InterChange Server V4.3 and Toolset, Deployment
000-994	IBM WebSphere MQ V6.0 System Administration
000-996	IBM WebSphere MQ V6.0, Solution Design
000-997	IBM WebSphere Message Broker V6.0 Solution Development
000-998	WebSphere Message Broker V6.0 System Administration

IISFA

| II0-001 | Certified Information Forensics Investigator (CIFI) |

INTEL

| IL0-786 | Designing Flexible Wireless LAN Solutions |

Isaca

| CISA | Isaca CISA |

ISC

| CISSP | Certified Information Systems Security Professional (CISSP) |
| SSCP | System Security Certified Practitioner (SSCP) |

ISEB

| BH0-001 | IT Service Management Foundation |

ITIL V3

Foundation
Intermediate
Diploma

Advanced

ISM

630-005	C.P.M. Module 1: Purchasing Process
630-006	C.P.M. Module 2: Supply Environment
630-007	C.P.M. Module 3: Value Enhancement Strategies
630-008	C.P.M. Module 4: Management

Juniper

JN0-120	Networks Certified Internet Associate, E-series
JN0-130	Juniper Networks Certified Internet Specialist
JN0-201	Juniper Networks Certified Internet Associate
JN0-303	Juniper Networks Certified Internet Specialist
JN0-310	Juniper Networks Certified Internet Associate (JNCIA-WX)
JN0-320	Juniper Networks Certified Internet Associate
JN0-340	Juniper Networks Certified Internet Associate, J-series
JN0-520	Juniper Networks Certified Internet Associate, FWV
JN0-530	Juniper Networks Certified Internet Specialist
JN0-540	Juniper Networks - Intrusion Detection Protection
JN0-560	Certified Internet Associate
JN0-561	Juniper Networks Certified Internet Assoc(JNCIA-SSL)

Legato

LE0-406	Certified Availability Administrator

Lotus

190-273	Lotus Script in Notes for Developers
190-510	Domino R5 Designer Fundamentals
190-513	Using JavaScript in Domino R5 Applications
190-520	Maintaining Domino R5 Servers and Users
190-521	Implementing a Domino R5 Infrastructure
190-522	Deploying Domino R5 Applications
190-531	Administering Lotus QuickPlace 3
190-533	DOMINO.DOC SYSTEM ADMINISTRATION 3.0

190-602	Notes Domino 6 System Administration Update
190-610	ND6 Application Development Foundation Skills
190-611	Notes Domino 6 Application Development Intermediate Skill
190-612	Lotus Notes Domino 6 Developing Web Applications
190-620	Notes Domino 6 System Administration Operating Fundementals
190-621	Domino 6: Building the Infrastructure
190-622	Domino 6 Managing Servers and Users
190-623	Notes Domino 6 Configuring Domino Web Servers
190-701	IBM Lotus Notes Domino Application Development Update
190-702	IBM Lotus Notes Domino 7 System
190-710	IBM Lotus Notes Domino 7 App.Development Foundation Skills
190-711	IBM Lotus Notes Domino 7 App.Dev.Intermediate Skills
190-712	IBM Lotus Notes Domino 7 Developing Web Applications
190-720	IBM Lotus Notes Domino 7 SysAdmin Operating Fundamentals
190-721	IBM Lotus Notes Domino 7 Building the Infrastructure
190-722	IBM Lotus Notes Domino 7 Managing Servers and Users
190-737	Using LotusScript in IBM Lotus Domino 7
190-753	Using JavaScript in IBM Louts Domino 7 Applications
190-755	IBM Lotus Notes Domino 7 - Implement+Administering Security
190-821	Implementing and Administering IBM Workplace Collaboration Services 2.5
190-823	Implementing and Administering IBM Workplace Collaboration Services 2.5:Team Collaboration
190-827	Administering IBM Workplace Services Express 2.5
190-831	Developing Web Sites using IBM Workplace Web Content Management 2.5

| 190-833 | Creating App.Components Using IBM Workplace Designer 2.5 |

LPI

117-101	General Linux, Part 1
117-102	General Linux, Part 2
117-201	Linux Advanced Administration
117-202	Linux Networking Administration

McAfee

| 1T0-035 | Intranet Defense Specialist McAfee Certified |

McDATA

MD0-205	Certified Storage Network Designer
MD0-235	Certified Storage Network Implementer
MD0-251	McData Certified IP San Specialist

Microsoft

70-086	Implementing and Supporting Systems Management Server 2.0
70-089	Planning, Deploying, and Managing Microsoft Systems Management Server 2003
70-121	Designing and Providing Microsoft Volume License Solutions to Small and Medium Organisations
70-122	Designing and Providing Microsoft Volume License Solutions to Large Organisations
70-123	Planning, Implementing, and Maintaining a Software Asset Management (SAM) Program
70-210	Windows 2000 Pro
70-214	Implementing and Administering Security in a Microsoft Windows 2000 Network
70-215	Windows 2000 Server
70-216	Implementing and Administering a Microsoft Windows 2000 Network Infrastructure
70-217	Implementing and Administering a Microsoft Windows 2000 Directory Services Infrastructure
70-218	Managing a Microsoft Windows 2000 Network Environment

70-219	Designing a Microsoft Windows 2000 Directory Services Infrastructure
70-220	Designing Security for a Microsoft Windows 2000 Network
70-221	Designing a Microsoft Windows 2000 Network Infrastructure
70-222	Migrating from Microsoft Windows NT 4.0 to Microsoft Windows 2000
70-223	Configuring and Administering Microsoft Clustering Services by using Windows 2000 Advanced Server
70-224	Installing, Configuring and Administering Microsoft Exchange 2000
70-225	Designing and Deploying a Messaging Infrastructure with Microsoft Exchange 2000 Server
70-226	Designing Highly Available Web Solutions with Microsoft Windows 2000 Server Technologies
70-227	Installing, Configuring, and Administering Microsoft Internet Security and Acceleration (ISA) Server 2000, Enterprise Edition
70-228	Installing, Configuring and Administering Microsoft SQL Server 2000, Enterprise Edition
70-229	Designing and Implementing Databases with Microsoft SQL Server 2000, Enterprise Edition
70-230	Designing and Implementing Solutions with Microsoft BizTalk Server 2000
70-232	Implementing and Maintaining Highly Available Web Solutions with MS W2K Server Technologies
70-234	Microsoft Designing and Implementing Solutions with Microsoft Commerce 2000 Server
70-235	Developing Business Process and Integration Solutions Using BizTalk Server 2006
70-244	Supporting and Maintaining a Microsoft Windows NT Server 4.0 Network
70-270	Installing, Configuring, and Administering Microsoft Windows XP Professional
70-271	Supporting Users and Troubleshooting a MS Windows XP OS

70-272	Supporting Users and Troubleshooting Desktop Applications
70-281	Planning, Deploying, and Managing an Enterprise Project Management Solution
70-282	Designing, Deploying, and Managing a Network Solution for a Small- and Medium-Sized Business
70-284	Implementing and Managing Microsoft Exchange Server 2003
70-285	Designing a Microsoft Exchange Server 2003 Organisation
70-290	Managing and Maintaining a Microsoft Windows Server 2003 Environment
70-291	Implementing, Managing, and Maintaining a Microsoft Windows Server 2003 Network Infrastructure
70-292	Managing and Maintaining a Microsoft Windows Server 2003 Environment for a W2K MCSA
70-293	Planning and Maintaining a Microsoft Windows Server 2003 Network Infrastructure
70-294	Planning, Implementing, and Maintaining a Microsoft Windows Server 2003 AD Infrastructure
70-296	Planning, Implementing, and Maintaining a Microsoft Windows Server 2003 Environment for a W2K MCSE
70-297	Designing a Microsoft Windows Server 2003 Active Directory and Network Infrastructure
70-298	Designing Security for a MS Windows Server 2003 Network
70-299	Implementing and Administering Security in a Microsoft Windows Server 2003 Network
70-300	Analyzing Requirements and Defining Microsoft .NET Solution Architectures
70-301	Managing, Organizing, and Delivering IT Projects by Using Microsoft® Solutions Framework 3.0
70-305	Developing and Implementing Web Applications with Microsoft Visual Basic.NET
70-306	Developing and Implementing Windows-based Applications with Microsoft Visual Basic .NET

70-310	XML Web Services and Server Components with Visual Basic.NET
70-315	Developing and Implementing Web Applications with Microsoft Visual C# .NET
70-316	Developing and Implementing Windows-based Applications with Microsoft Visual C# .NET
70-320	XML Web Services and Server Components with C#.NET
70-330	Implementing Security for Applications with Microsoft Visual Basic .NET
70-340	Implementing Security for Applications with Microsoft Visual C# .NET
70-350	Implementing Microsoft Internet Security and Acceleration (ISA) Server 2004
70-431	Microsoft® SQL Server 2005 - Implementation and Maintenance
70-441	Designing Database Solutions by Using Microsoft® SQL Server„¢ 2005
70-442	Designing and Optimizing Data Access by Using Microsoft SQL Server 2005
70-443	Designing a Database Server Infrastructure by Using Microsoft® SQL Server„¢ 2005
70-444	Optimizing and Maintaining a Database Administration Solution by Using SQL Server 2005
70-447	UPGRADE: MCDBA Skills to MCITP Database Administrator by Using Microsoft SQL Server 2005
70-526	Microsoft .NET Framework 2.0 - Windows-Based Client Development
70-528	NET Framework 2.0-Web-based Client Development
70-529	Microsoft .NET Framework 2.0 - Distributed Application Development
70-536	Microsoft .NET Framework 2.0 Application Development Foundation
70-547	Designing and Developing Web-Based Applications by Using the Microsoft .NET Framework

70-548	Designing and Developing Windows-Based Applications by Using the Microsoft .NET Framework
70-549	Designing and Developing Enterprise Applications by Using the Microsoft .NET Framework
70-551	UPGRADE: MCAD Skills to MCPD Web Developer by Using the Microsoft .NET Framework
70-552	UPGRADE: MCAD Skills to MCPD Windows Developer by Using the Microsoft .NET Framework
70-553	UPGRADE: MCSD Microsoft .NET Skills to MCPD Enterprise Application Developer: Part 1
70-554	UPGRADE: MCSD Microsoft .NET Skills to MCPD Enterprise Application Developer: Part 2
70-620	Microsoft Windows Vista, Configuring
74-100	Microsoft Solutions Framework (MSF) Practitioner
74-131	Designing a Microsoft Office Enterprise Project Management (EPM) Solution
74-132	Designing Portal Solutions with MS SharePoint Products
10-184	US MS-03-010 Microsoft CRM Installation and Configuration v. 1.2
74-133	Customizing Portal Solutions with Microsoft SharePoint Products and Technologies
74-134	Pre-Installing MS Products using the OEM Pre-Install Kit
74-135	Developing E-Business Solutions Using MS BizTalk Server 2004
74-137	Developing Microsoft Office Solutions Using XML with Office Professional Edition 2003
74-138	Planning and Building a Messaging and Collaboration Environment using MS Office & MS Windows
74-139	Deploying Business Desktops with Microsoft Windows Server 2003 and Microsoft Office 2003
MB2-421	CRM 3.0 Installation & Configuration
MB2-422	CRM 3.0 Customization
MB2-423	CRM 3.0 Applications

MB3-207	Great Plains 8.0 Project Management & Accounting
MB3-209	Great Plains 8.0 Inventory & Order Processing
MB3-210	Great Plains 8.0 Report Writer
MB3-216	Great Plains 8.0 Financials
MB3-230	Great Plains 8.0 Human Resources Payroll(U.S)
MB3-408	Great Plains 9.0 Inventory & Order Processing
MB3-409	GP 9.0 Financials
MB3-412	GP 9.0 Installation & Configuration
MB3-430	Great Plains 9.0 Manufacturing Applications
MB3-451	Great Plains 9.0 Report Writer
MB5-294	FRx Report Design
MB6-202	Axapta 3.0 Programming
MB6-203	Axapta 3.0 Financials
MB6-204	Axapta 3.0 Trade & Logistics
MB6-205	Axapta 3.0 Production
MB6-206	Axapta 3.0 Installation & Configuration
MB7-221	Navision 4.0 C/SIDE Introduction
MB7-222	Navision 4.0 C/SIDE Solution Development
MB7-223	Navision 4.0 Warehouse Management
MB7-224	Navision 4.0 Manufacturing
MB7-225	Navision 4.0 Financials
MOS-A2K	MOUS 2000 Microsoft Access 2000 CORE
MOS-AXP	Access 2002 Core
MOS-E2E	Excel 2000 Expert
MOS-E2K	Microsoft Excel 2000 CORE
MOS-EXP	Microsoft Excel 2002 Core
MOS-O2K	Microsoft Outlook 2000
MOS-OXP	Microsoft Outlook 2002 Core
MOS-P2K	PowerPoint 2002 Core
MOS-W2E	MOUS 2000 Word 2000 Expert
MOS-W2K	Microsoft Word 2000 CORE
MOS-WXP	Word 2002 Core

Mile2

| MK0-201 | Certified Penetration Testing Specialist (CPTS) |
| ML0-220 | Certified Network Security Administrator |

M_o_R

Foundation
Practitioner

MSP

Foundation
Intermediate
Practictioner

Network Appliance

NS0-111	Network Appliance Storage Associate
NS0-121	Network Appliance Data ONTAP Advanced Exam 7G
NS0-130	Storage Professional Data Protection
NS0-131	Network Appliance Data Protection Exam 7G
NS0-141	Network Appliance High Availability Exam 7G
NS0-151	Network Appliance SAN Exam 7G
NS0-170	Network Appliance NetCache

Network-General

1T6-111	Troubleshooting and Management with Sniffer Distributed
1T6-303	TCP/IP Network Analysis and Troubleshooting
1T6-323	Microsoft Windows 2000 Network Analysis and Troubleshooting
1T6-510	Troubleshooting with Sniffer Portable/Sniffer Distributed
1T6-520	Application Performance Analysis and Troubleshooting
1T6-530	TCP/IP Network Analysis and Troubleshooting

Nokia

NO0-002	Nokia Security Administrator
NQ0-231	3G Radio Network Planning

Nortel

920-105	Symposium Call Center Server Installation & Maint.

920-110	Meridian SL-100 Maintenance
920-111	VoIP Communication Server(CS)2100
920-112	Media Processing Server(MPS)500-Technical Support
920-113	MPS 500 Installation and Maintenance
920-118	Symposium Call Center Server TAPI/Agent Inst/Maint.
920-119	Symposium Call Center TAPI/Agent
920-121	MPS Application Developer
920-124	Ethernet Switching
920-125	VoIP Succession BCM 3.0
920-127	VoIP Succession BCM 3.0
920-130	Symposium Express Call Center
920-131	Symposium Express Call Center Inst and Maint
920-133	BayStack Switching
920-136	Ethernet Switching Solutions
920-138	VoIP Succession 1000/1000M Rls. 3.0 Installation & Maintenance
920-139	VoIP Multimedia Communication Server (MCS) 5100 Rls. 3.0
920-140	VoIP Multimedia Communication Server (MCS) 5100 Rls. 3.0
920-141	Communication Server (CS) 1000 Release 4.0
920-146	Symposium Call Center Server 5.0
920-157	CallPilot 2.x/3.0
920-158	CallPilot 4.0 System Administrator
920-159	CallPilot 2.x/3.0
920-160	Communication Server (CS) Rls. 4.0 Hardware Installation & Maintenance
920-161	CallPilot Rls. 4.0
920-162	CallPilot 4.0 Installation & Maintenance (I&M)
920-163	Contact Center Manager RIs.6.0 Technical Support
920-164	Contact Center Manager RIs6.0 I & M
920-165	Contact Center Ris.6.0
920-166	Contact Center Multimedia Ris.6.0
920-167	Contact Center RIS.6.0 Application Developer
920-170	Symposium Call Center Server 5.0 Application Developer
920-172	Nortel Communication Control Toolkit Rls. 6.0

920-180	Real Time Networking
920-182	CallPilot Rls.5.0 Installation & Configuration
920-192	Business Communications Manager 50 Rls. 1.0
920-193	Business Communications Manager 50 (BCM50) Rls. 1.0
920-203	Passport 7000/15000
920-215	Passport 7000/15000
920-231	Contivity VNP Switch
920-232	Contivity VPN Switch Release 5.0
920-233	Nortel VPN Router (Contivity) Rls. 6.0
920-238	WLAN 2300 Rls. 4.1 Implementation & Management
920-241	Alteon
920-242	Contivity VPN Switch
920-245	Ethernet Switching
920-250	Passport 8600 Routing Switch
920-251	Alteon
920-252	Ethernet Routing Switch 8600
920-253	Nortel VPN Router (Contivity) Rls. 6.0
920-316	SCCS/Express/TAPI/Web Client/Agent
920-320	Meridian 1 Database
920-321	VoIP Succession 1000/1000M Rls. 3.0 DB Administrator
920-322	Succession 1000/1000M Rls. 3.0 for Technicians
920-324	Communication Server (CS) Rls. 4.0 Database Administrator
920-325	Communication Server (CS) Rls. 4.0 Software Installation & Maintenance
920-326	Symposium Contact Center Portfolio
920-440	Alteon Security
920-441	Contivity Security
920-442	Succession 1000/1000M Rls. 3.0
920-443	Succession 1000/1000M Rls. 3.0
920-447	Contact Center
920-448	Alteon Security
920-449	Contivity Security
920-450	ES NetSight Atlas
920-452	Communication Server 1000 Ris.4.0
920-453	CallPilot 2.x/3.0 Unified Messaging

920-460	Wireless LAN
920-461	Wireless LAN
920-462	Ethernet Switching
920-463	Ethernet Switching Design Expert
920-501	OPTera Metro 5000
920-569	OPTera Metro Solutions
920-803	Technology Standards and Protocol for IP Telephony Solutions
920-804	Technology Standards and Protocol for Converged Networks

Novell

50-632	Networking Technologies
50-634	NDS Design and Implimentation
50-650	Novell Internet Security Management with BorderManager 3.5: Enterprise Edition
50-653	Certified Novell Administrator 5.1
50-654	Novell NetWare 5.1 Advanced Administration
50-658	Service and Support
50-663	Integrating Novell eDirectory and Active Directory
50-664	Novell eDirectory Design and Implementation
50-665	GroupWise 6 Administration
50-676	Upgrade to NetWare 6
50-677	Foundations of Novell Networking: NetWare 6
50-681	NetWare 6 CNA Novell Network Management: NetWare 6
50-682	Advanced Novell Network Management
50-683	Desktop Management with ZEN works for Desktops 4
50-684	Novell eDirectory Tools and Diagnostics
50-686	Foundations of Novell Networking
50-688	Upgrading to NetWare 6.5
50-690	Novell Network Management; Netware 6.5
50-691	Advanced Novell Network Management: Netware 6.5
50-692	ZENWorks 6.5 Desktop Management
50-694	Novell ZENworks 7 Desktop Management Administration

50-695	Novell eDirectory Design and Implementation:eDirectory 8.8
50-888	Upgrading to Netware 6.5
50-890	Advanced Novell Network Management;Netware 6.5

OMG

UM0-100	Certified UML Professional Fundamental
UM0-200	OMG-Certified UML Professional Intermediate Exam
UM0-300	OMG-Certified UML Professional Advanded Exam

Oracle

1Z0-001	Introduction to Oracle: SQL and PL/SQL
1Z0-007	Introduction to Oracle9i: SQL
1Z0-020	Oracle8i: New Features for Administrators
1Z0-023	Architecture and Administration
1Z0-024	Performance Tuning
1Z0-025	Backup and Recovery
1Z0-026	Network Administration
1Z0-030	Oracle9i: New Features for Administrators
1Z0-031	Oracle9i:Database Fundamentals I
1Z0-032	Oracle9i:Database Fundamentals II
1Z0-033	Oracle9i:Performance Tunning
1Z0-035	Oracle 7.3 & 8 to Oracle9i DBA OCP Upgrade
1Z0-036	Managing Oracle 9i on Linux
1Z0-040	Oracle Database 10g: New Features for Administrators
1Z0-041	Oracle Database 10g: DBA Assessment
1Z0-042	Oracle Database 10g: Administration I
1Z0-043	Oracle Database 10g: Administration II
1Z0-045	Oracle Database 10g: New Features for Oracle8i OCPs
1Z0-101	Develop PL/SQL Program Units
1Z0-131	Oracle9i, Build Internet Applications I
1Z0-132	Oracle9i, Build Internet Applications II
1Z0-140	Oracle9i Forms Developer: New Features
1Z0-141	Oracle9i Forms Developer: Build Internet Applications

1Z0-147	Oracle 9i: Program with PL/SQL
1Z0-200	Oracle 11i E-Business Essentials
1Z0-301	Oracle9iAS: Basic Administrations
1Z0-311	Oracle Application Server 10g: Administration I

PMI

PMI-001	Project Management Professional

PRINCE 2

Foundation
Practictioner

Polycom

1K0-001	Certified Videoconferencing Engineer

RedHat

RH202	Redhat Certified Technician on Redhat Enterprise Linux 4 (Labs)
RH302	Red Hat Certified Engineer on Redhat Enterprise Linux

SAIR

3X0-101	Linux Installation and Configuration (Level 1)
3X0-102	Linux System Administration (Level 1)
3X0-103	Linux Networking (Level 1)
3X0-104	Linux Security, Privacy & Ethics (Level 1)
3X0-201	Core Concepts and Practices (Level 2)
3X0-202	Apache Webserver
3X0-203	Samba Resource Sharing
3X0-204	Sendmail Mail Systems

SAS Institute

A00-201	SAS Base Programming
A00-202	Advanced programming
A00-203	Sas Warehouse Development Specialist Concepts
A00-204	SAS Warehouse Architect Concepts
A00-205	SAS Webaf Server-Side Application Development
A00-206	SAS Warehouse Technology
A00-211	SAS Base Programming for SAS (r) 9

SAP
Associate (various roles)
Professional (various roles)
Master (various roles)

SCP

SC0-402	Network Defense and Countermeasures (NDC)
SC0-411	Hardening the Infrastructure (HTI)
SC0-501	Enterprise Security Implementation (ESI)
SC0-502	Security Certified Program (SCP)

See-Beyond

SQ0-101	e*Gate 4.5 Associate Developer

SNIA

S10-100	Storage Network Foundations
S10-200	Storage Networking Management/Administration
S10-300	SNIA Architect - Assessment, Planning & Design

Sun

310-011	Solaris 8 System Administration I
310-012	Solaris 8 System Administration II
310-014	Solaris 9 Sun Certified System Administrator Part I
310-015	Solaris 9 Sun Certified System Administrator Part II
310-016	Sun Certified System Administrator for Solaris 9, Upgrade
310-019	Sun Certified Associate for the Java Platform, Standard Edition
310-025	Sun Java Certified Programmer
310-035	Sun Certified Programmer for Java 2 Platform 1.4
310-043	Sun Certified Network Administrator for the Solaris 8 Operating Environment
310-044	Sun Certified Network Administrator For Solaris 9
310-051	Sun Certified Enterprise Architect for J2EE Technology
310-055	Sun Certified Programmer for the Java 2 Platform, Standard Edition 5.0

310-056	Sun Certified Programmer for the Java 2 Platform, Standard Edition 5.0
310-081	Sun Certified Web Component Developer for the Java 2 Platform, Enterprise Edition 1.4
310-090	Sun Certified Business Component Developer for the Java 2 Platform, Enterprise Edition 1.3
310-100	Sun Certified Data Management Engineer
310-101	Certified Data Management Engineer with VERITAS Volume Manager
310-110	Certified Mobile Application Developer for the Java 2 Platform, Micro Edition
310-130	Sun Certified Storage Architect
310-151	Sun Certified Backup and Recovery Engineer
310-200	Sun Certified System Administrator for the Solaris 10 OS, Part I
310-202	Sun Certified System Administrator for the Solaris 10 OS, Part II
310-203	Sun Certified System Administrator for the Solaris 10 Operating System Upgrade Exam
310-220	Certified Developer for Java Web Services
310-301	Sun Certified Security Administrator
310-302	Certified Network Administrator for Solaris 10 OS
310-303	Sun Certified Security Administrator for the Solaris 10 OS
310-330	Sun Certified Systems Installer for Sun Cluster 3.X
310-615	EDS Certified Sun Fire 15K Server Administrator
310-875	Level 1 Field Engineer Examination
310-878	SUN Certified Field Engineer
310-879	SUN Certified System Support Engineer
310-880	Sun Certified Senior System Support Engineer

Sybase

510-015	Adaptive Server Administrator Professional (Version 12.0)
510-020	Sybase Adaptive Server Administrator (Version 12.5)
510-022	Sybase Certified ASE 12.5 Administrator Professional

510-050	Sybase Certified Replication Server Administrator Professional (Version 12.5)
510-306	PowerBuilder Developer
510-309	Powerbuilder 10.0 Professional Exam
510-410	Adaptive Server SQL Associate (Version 12.5.2)

Symantec
250-101	Small Business Security
250-501	Intrusion Protection Solutions
250-502	Firewall & Integrated Security Appliances Solutions
250-503	Security Management Solutions
250-504	Virus Protection & Integrated Client Security Solutions

Teradata
NR0-011	Basics V2R5
NR0-012	Teradata Physical Implementation V2R5
NR0-013	Teradata SQL v2r5
NR0-014	Teradata Administration V2R5
NR0-015	Teradata Design Architecture V2R5
NR0-016	Teradata Application Development V2R5
NR0-017	Teradata Masters Update V2R5

TIA
| CCNT | Convergent Network Technologies |
| TT0-101 | Convergence Technologies Professional |

TIBCO
TB0-103	Tibco Businessworks 5.x
TB0-104	TIBCO Enterprise Message Service 4
TB0-105	TIBCO Staffware Process Definer i10
TB0-106	TIBCO Rendezvous 7 Certification Exam
TB0-107	BusinessWorks 5 Certification

TruSecure
| TU0-001 | TruSecure ICSA Certified Security Associate |

Veritas

BE-100W	Backup Exec 10.0 Administration
DP-021W	Design of Data Protection Solutions for Windows using NetBackup 5.0
DP-022W	Data Protection Implementation for Windows using NetBackup 5.0
DP-023W	Data Protection Administration for Windows using NetBackup 5.0

VMWare

VCP-101V	Infrastructure with ESX Server and VirtualCenter
VCP-310	VMware Certified Professional on VI3

Other Works by the Author

You can find all these titles at *www.PracticalBooks.org.*

The Guide to IT Contracting
ISBN: ISBN: 1-9057-8904-1

Search Engine Optimization (SEO) How to Optimize Your Web Site for Internet Search Engines (Google, Yahoo!, MSN Live, AOL, Ask, AltaVista, FAST, GigaBlast, Snap, LookSmart and Others)
ISBN: 1-9057-8906-8

META TAGS: Optimising Your Website for Internet Search Engines (Google, Yahoo!, MSN, AltaVista, AOL, Alltheweb, Fast, GigaBlast, Netscape, Snap, WISEnut and Others)
ISBN: 1-9057-8998-X

Tax Avoidance: A practical guide for UK Residents
ISBN: 1-4116-2380-0

How to Destroy Your Debts
ISBN: 1-4116-2374-6

The Practical Guide to Total Financial Freedom: Volume 1
ISBN: 1-4116-2058-5

The Practical Guide to Total Financial Freedom: Volume 2
ISBN: 1-4116-2057-7

The Practical Guide to Total Financial Freedom: Volume 3
ISBN: 1-4116-2056-9

The Practical Guide to Total Financial Freedom: Volume 4
ISBN: 1-4116-2055-0

The Practical Guide to Total Financial Freedom: Volume 5
ISBN: 1-4116-2054-2

Planning and Goal Setting For Personal Success
ISBN: 1-4116-3774-7

The Guide to IT Contracting

Living the Ultimate Truth, 2nd Edition
ISBN: 1-4116-2375-4

Developing Personal Integrity, 2nd Edition
ISBN: 1-4116-2376-2

The Guide to Real Estate Investing
ISBN: 1-4116-2383-5

Making Money with Funds
ISBN: 1-4116-2671-0

How to make a fortune with Options Trading
ISBN: 1-4116-2378-9

How to make a fortune on the Stock Markets
ISBN: 1-4116-2379-7

Attitude
ISBN: 1-4116-2382-7

How to Win at Online Roulette
ISBN: 1-4116-2570-6

The Ultimate Guide to Offshore Tax Havens
ISBN: 1-4116-2384-3

How to win at Greyhound betting
ISBN: 1-4116-2377-0

Sixty Original Song Lyrics
ISBN: 1-4116-2059-3

Investing in En Primeur Wine
ISBN: 1-4116-2867-5

Eight Steps to Success
ISBN: 1-4116-2738-5

Taking Action
ISBN: 1-4116-2735-0

Ultimate Online Roulette System: Advanced Winning Techniques for the Tax Conscious Casino Gambling Investor
ISBN: 1-4116-4374-7

Naughty Madge Goes To A Farm
ISBN: 978-1-905789-97-9

Notes

ABOUT THE AUTHOR

Samuel Blankson has authored over twenty books, *Search Engine Optimization (SEO), How to Destroy Your Debts, Living the Ultimate Truth, Developing Personal Integrity, The Practical Guide to Total Financial Freedom* volumes 1, 2, 3, 4 and 5, and *Attitude* are some of these works. He has also authored children's books, fiction novels and a range of calendars. He has written over 100 songs, sixty of which are featured in *Sixty Original Song Lyrics*. Samuel Blankson's books can be found at ***www.practicalbooks.org***.

Lightning Source UK Ltd.
Milton Keynes UK
UKOW05f1058231013

219605UK00001B/19/P